THE OXFORD HISTORY OF PHILOSOPHY

The Lost Age of Reason

THE OXFORD HISTORY OF PHILOSOPHY

The American Pragmatists
Cheryl Misale

The Lost Age of Reason: Philosophy in Early Modern India 1450–1700
Jonardon Ganeri

Thinking the Impossible: French Philosophy since 1960
Gary Gutting

The Lost Age of Reason

Philosophy in Early Modern India 1450–1700

Jonardon Ganeri

OXFORD
UNIVERSITY PRESS

OXFORD
UNIVERSITY PRESS

Great Clarendon Street, Oxford, OX2 6DP,

Oxford University Press is a department of the University of Oxford.
It furthers the University's objective of excellence in research, scholarship,
and education by publishing worldwide. Oxford is a registered trade mark of
Oxford University Press in the UK and in certain other countries

First published 2011
First published in paperback 2014

Published in the United States of America by Oxford University Press
198 Madison Avenue, New York, NY 10016, United States of America

British Library Cataloguing in Publication Data
Data available

Library of Congress Cataloging in Publication Data
Data available

ISBN 978–0–19–921874–5 (Hbk)
ISBN 978–0–19–870150–7 (Pbk)

Acknowledgements

I would like to express my gratitude to Peter Momtchiloff for inviting me to contribute to this new series in the history of philosophy. The support of the Leverhulme Trust, in awarding me a Research Fellowship between 2007 and 2009, has been invaluable. I would like also to thank Prabal Kumar Sen, Nirmalya Chakraborty, Sheldon Pollock, Richard Sorabji, Stephen Phillips, Anantalal Thakur, Shashi Prabha Kumar and Christopher Minkowski, Albrecht Hanisch and the staff of the Nepal Research Centre, the production team, Jennifer Lunsford, Ann Grant and Carolyn McAndrew, as well as the very helpful readers for Oxford University Press. I am grateful too to Stephen Menn, Andrew Nicholson, Rosalind O'Hanlon, Peter Flügel, and Jay Garfield. I am especially endebted to Sajjad Rizvi for additional information about Islamic philosophy in India, and for other help with Islamic sources.

Contents

Chronology ix
Principal Philosophers Discussed xi
Map xiii

Introduction 1

Part I. India Expanding 11

1 The World and India: 1656 13
François Bernier and his paṇḍit 13
The public profile of the 'new reason' 16

2 Dārā Shukoh: A Spacious Islam 22
Migrating texts 22
Translating Sanskrit into Persian 23
A religious cosmopolitanism 24
Meeting of two oceans 26
Another affinity 28

3 The Cosmopolitan Vision of Yaśovijaya Gaṇi 31
Studying the 'new reason' in Vārāṇasī 32
Secular intellectual values 33
Reflections on the self 35
Yaśovijaya and Dārā Shukoh: a cosmopolitan ideal 36

4 Navadvīpa: A Place of Hindu-Muslim Confluence in Bengal 39
A Bengali sultanate independent of Delhi 40
The curious biography of a teacher 41
Raghunātha Śiromaṇi (c.1460–1540) 44
The final years of Navadvīpa 51

Part II. Text and Method 61

5 Contextualism in The Study of Indian Philosophical Literature 63
Quentin Skinner and performative speech-acts 63
Intertextual intervention 65
Prolepsis and anticipation 68
Cultural indexicals 70
Immersion and Indian intellectual practice 72

6 Philosophers outside Academies: Networks 74
The new reason and the court of Akbar 75
A less embedded network 79

A Navadvīpa-based network 81
Rivalry over Raghunātha 84
New developments in Navadvīpa 85

7 An Analysis of the New Reason's Literary Artefacts 89
Commentaries 91
Internal critiques of Vaiśeṣika metaphysics 95
Research monographs 96
Manuals for new students 98

8 Commentary and Creativity 102
Commentary as mediating a conversation with the past 102
Towards a typology of commentary 104
Commentary as weaving a text 107
The singly authored principles-and-gloss text 112

Part III. The Possibility of Inquiry 117

9 Inquiry: The History of a Crisis 119
Inquiry in the knowledge disciplines 119
Inquiry in early Nyāya 122
Ways of gaining knowledge 125
Śrīharṣa's 'refutations' 127

10 Challenge From the Ritualists 131
Scepticism and truth in the *Gemstone* 131
Two models of inquiry 135
An intrinsicist theory of error in action 139
Knowing naturalized 142

11 Interventions in a New Research Programme 145
Difficulties in Gaṅgeśa's theory 145
The Precious Jewel of Reason: a genealogical state-of-research review 147
Self-conscious modernities 149
The weight of evidence 153
A method for rightly conducting reason in the *Garland of Principles* 157

Part IV. The Real World 163

12 Realism in Question 165
The reach of Vaiśeṣika realism 165
Realism and reference 168
Grades of existence 170
Epistemic constraints on the concept of truth 172
'Whatever is, is knowable and nameable' 175
Realism and reduction 179

13 New Foundations in the Metaphysics of Mathematics 181
Mathematics and the philosophical theory of number 181

Counting and construction 182
Numbers as properties of objects 187
Indefinite pluralities 191
Raghunātha's non-reductive realism 194

14 Metaphysics in a Different Key 200
Raghunātha's challenge 200
Naturalism and reductionism in the *Essence of Reason* 201
Escaping the oscillation between eliminativism and non-reductivism 206
The *Garland of Categories*: naturalism and reduction 211
Mechanical philosophy in the *Garland of Categories*? 214

Part V. A New Language for Philosophy 221

15 The Technical Language Assessed 223
The importance of disambiguation 224
The syntax of the formal system 226
A semantics for the language 228
Reparsing ordinary language 230
The new language and the predicate calculus 232

16 Rival Logics of Domain Restriction 237
Analysis from Buddhist sources 238
The early modern theory: a unified account 240

Conclusion 244

Recommended Further Readings 252
Bibliography 254
Index 279

Chronology

Until eleventh century: Nyāya philosophy develops in dialogue with Buddhism. Udayana and Vallabha are the last important voices.

Twelfth century: **Śrīharṣa** writes a set of sceptical 'refutations'.

c.1325: **Gaṅgeśa** writes the *Gemstone for Truth*, and a renovated Nyāya takes root in his hometown of Mithilā.

1460–1540: **Raghunātha Śiromaṇi** invents the 'new reason' in Navadvīpa, a town in Bengal. His immediate followers develop and teach his ideas both in Navadvīpa and also in Vārāṇasī.

1486: Birth of **Caitanya** in Navadvīpa.

1493–1519: Reign of the liberal sultan **Ḥusayn Shāh** in Bengal. His ministers include Rūpa and Sanātana Gosvāmi, exponents of Caitanya's Vaiṣṇavism.

1556: **Akbar** assumes the Mughal throne; the empire spreads throughout northern India. His ministers include the Hindus Mansingh and Ṭoḍarmal, both of whom encourage 'new reason' philosophers.

1582: Debate between **Vidyānivāsa,** a 'new reason' thinker, and Nārāyaṇa Bhaṭṭa at Ṭoḍarmal's house.

1597: Abū-l-Fażl writes the *Ā'īn-i-Akbarī*, a synopsis of life at the time of Akbar. Several 'new reason' philosophers are mentioned.

1605: Death of Akbar. He is followed by Jahāngīr r. 1605–27, Shāh Jahāṇ r. 1628–58 and Aurangzeb r. 1658–1707.

1613: **Roberto Nobili** writes the *Informatio*, containing a description of the new 'natural philosophy'.

1615: **Dārā Shukoh**, eldest son of Shāh Jahāṇ, born 20 March.

1620: **Francis Bacon** publishes the *Novum Organum*.

1621: **Sébastien Basso** publishes the *Natural Philosophy Directed Against Aristotle*.

1634: **Viśvanātha**, son of Vidyānivāsa, writes a commentary on the *Nyāya-sūtra*.

1637: **René Descartes** publishes the *Discourse and Essays*.

1638: **Kavīndra Sarasvatī** petitions Shāh Jahāṇ to repeal a tax on Hindu pilgrims.

1650: Death of Descartes.

1655: Death of **Pierre Gassendi**. His protégé **François Bernier** is with him.

1656: Dārā Shukoh assembles a team of Vārāṇasī scholars to translate the Upaniṣads into Persian. Bernier arrives in India, and works as physician to Shāh Jahāṇ and Dārā Shukoh.

1657: Leading Vārāṇasī intellectuals publicly meet and sign a letter of judgement.

1659: Dārā Shukoh is sentenced for heresy and executed, after a conflict with Aurangzeb. The key 'new reason' philosopher **Jayarāma**, an acquaintance of Kavīndra, finishes the *Garland of Categories.* He writes the *Garland of Principles about Reason* around this time too. **Raghudeva**, another 'new reason' philosopher, is doing similar work too and moving in the same circles in Vārāṇasī.

1658–61: **Dāniṣmand Khān**, an accultured nobleman who opposes the execution of Dārā, takes on Kavīndra, Bernier and others when they lose their patron. They exchange ideas, Bernier translating Gassendi and Descartes into Persian, Kavīndra bringing Vārāṇasī thinkers and Bernier into discussion.

1660: Foundation of the Royal Society in London.

1670: Bernier, back in France, publishes his *Travels in the Mogul Empire.* Henry Oldenburg, the first secretary of the Royal Society, will arrange for their English publication; John Dryden bases his 1675 play *Aureng-zebe* on them.

1677: Death of **Spinoza**. The *Ethics* is published.

1678: Bernier publishes his *Abrégé* of Gassendi's philosophy.

1688: Death of **Yaśovijaya Gaṇi**, a brilliant Jaina philosopher who responds to the 'new reason' and perhaps also to Dārā's project.

1690: **John Locke** publishes his *Essay Concerning Human Understanding*. He seems to have read Bernier's *Abrégé.*

1690s: Several 'new reason' thinkers are active in Vārāṇasī: **Mahādeva** writes the *Precious Jewel of Reason,* and **Mādhavadeva** the *Essence of Reason.*

1707: Death of Aurangzeb.

1757: The Battle of Plassey.

1765: East India Company obtains taxation rights over Bengal.

1769–70: Great Famine, caused by punitive taxation and grain stockpiling.

1776: Britain, defeated in the American war for independence, turns its attention to India, Warren Hasting drawing on a 'plan for the administration of justice'.

Principal Philosophers Discussed

I. Key individuals

Raghunātha Śiromaṇi (c.1460–1540), the inventor of the 'new reason' philosophy. Raghunātha lived in the dynamic multi-cultural town of Navadvīpa in Bengal. His *Inquiry into the True Nature of Things* shaped discussion in metaphysics throughout the sixteenth and seventeenth centuries, while his commentaries on older thinkers, called *Light-Rays*, bristle with new ideas and an innovative spirit which inspired later philosophers.

Vidyānivāsa (c.1500–90) an early 'new reason' philosopher. He and his sons, also philosophers, benefited with patronage from the Mughal court of Akbar and became well-established figures in Vārāṇasī.

Dārā Shukoh (1615–59), eldest son of Shāh Jahāṇ and heir apparent to the Mughal throne. Dārā sought a rapprochement of Hinduism with Islam, and sponsored a large translation project of Sanskrit texts into Persian. The project gave his brother Aurangzeb an excuse to have him tried for heresy. He was executed in 1659.

Kavīndra Sarasvatī (c.1600–75), a Sanskrit scholar and poet in Vārāṇasī, who received the patronage of Shāh Jahāṇ and Dārā Shukoh, and mediated a conversation between Sanskrit philosophers and the Mughal court. He negotiated with Shāh Jahāṇ the repeal of a poll-tax on Hindu pilgrims, and was in turn feted by Vārāṇasī intellectuals.

François Bernier (1625–88), French philosopher and physician, the protégé of Pierre Gassendi. Bernier came to India in 1656 and worked for Shāh Jahāṇ and Dārā Shukoh. After Dārā's trial, he spent the years from 1658 to 1661 with Kavīndra and other Sanskrit intellectuals in Vārāṇasī. He returned to Paris in 1667 and published first his travel memoir and then an *Abrégé* of Gassendi's work.

Jayarāma Nyāyapañcānana (mid seventeenth century), a leading 'new reason' philosopher in Vārāṇasī. Jayarāma knew Kavīndra and may have been in the Kavīndra–Bernier circle. He wrote an important work on the new metaphysics in 1659, *The Garland of Categories*, and a companion work on public reasoning, *The Garland of Principles about Reason*.

Yaśovijaya Gaṇi (1624–88), the most important Jaina intellectual of the seventeenth century. Yaśovijaya studied the 'new reason' in Vārāṇasī in the years before Dārā's project, and adapted it to suit a liberal syncretic philosophy.

Raghudeva Bhaṭṭācārya (mid–late seventeenth century) was a pupil of Harirāma in Navadvīpa but lived in Vārāṇasī and signed the 1657 'letter of judgement'. A prolific writer, his *Survey of What is Essential about Substance* is an important work on the theory of material objects.

Mahādeva Puṇatāmakara (late seventeenth century), originally from the south but living in Vārāṇasī. He is the author of the *Precious Jewel of Reason*, the most systematic 'new reason' work in epistemology, as well as the important *Examination into Selfhood as a Natural Kind.*

Veṇīdatta Vāgīśa Bhaṭṭa (late seventeenth century), author of a work in the spirit of Raghunātha, the *Embellishment of the Categories*, advocating a new five-category ontology.

II. 'New reason' philosophers located

	Mithilā	Navadvīpa	Vārāṇasī
1300s	Gaṅgeśa Upādhyāya		
	Vardhamāna		
1400s	Yajñapati		
	Jayadeva (Pakṣadhara)		
	Śaṃkara Miśra		
1500s		Raghunātha Śiromaṇi	
		Vidyānivāsa	
		Jānakīnātha	
		Kṛṣṇadāsa	
1600s		Rāmabhadra Sārvabhauma	
		Bhavānanda	Viśvanātha
		Dinakara	
		Jagadīśa	Rudra
		Śrī Rāma	Govinda Śarman
		Rāmarudra	
		Harirāma	Annambhaṭṭa
		Mathurānātha	Jayarāma
		Gadādhara	Laugākṣī
			Raghudeva
			Mahādeva
			Mādhavadeva
			Veṇīdatta
1700	Gokulanātha		

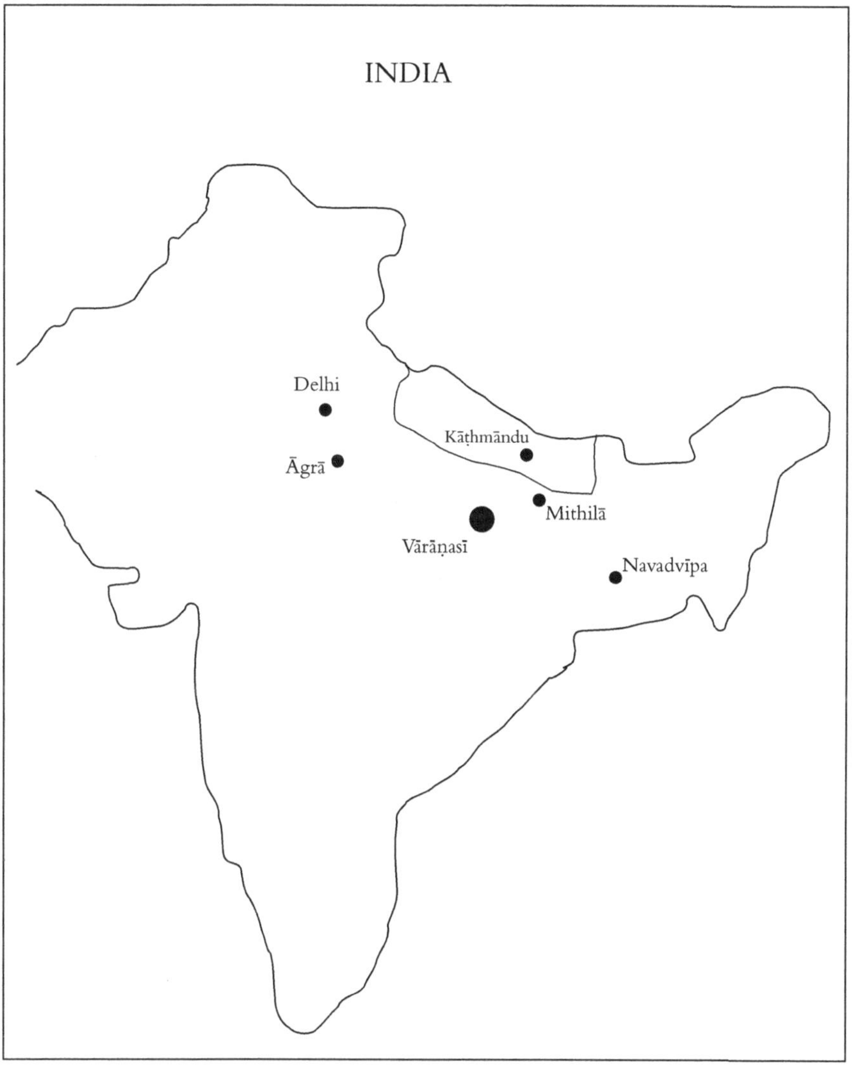
INDIA
Delhi
Āgrā
Kāṭhmāndu
Mithilā
Vārāṇasī
Navadvīpa

Introduction

The arrival of modernity at a certain point in the history of philosophy seemingly admits of two non-compossible explanations. One model presents modernity as involving a thorough rejection of the ancient—its texts, its thinkers, its methods—as starting afresh and from the beginning. This was how the two figures who are emblematic of the 'new philosophy' in Europe, Francis Bacon (1561–1626) and René Descartes (1596–1650), chose to present themselves.[1] A second model locates modernity not in a rejection of the past but in a profound reorientation with respect to it. The ancient texts are now not thought of as authorities to which one must defer, but regarded as the source of insight in the company of which one pursues the quest for truth. This new attitude towards the texts does not imply abandonment but a transformation in their place within inquiry, a change in conception of one's duties towards the past.

The first model has dominated the standard history of philosophy, which speaks of a revolution in philosophy in the early seventeenth century, one in which the Aristotelianism of the schools—with its obscure terminology, doctrine of forms and final causes, and schoolmen who 'loved Aristotle more than the truth' (Mercer 1993: 34)—is cast aside in favour of a new mechanical conception of natural explanation. Recently, however, this familiar account has begun to unravel. John Cottingham says, for example, that 'any picture of Descartes as a lone innovator setting out on a new quest for certainty cannot survive serious scrutiny' (Cottingham 1993: 150), while Dan Garber, pointing out that Descartes' correspondents did not find his project seriously in conflict with their own progressive Aristotelian ambitions, speaks of 'the revolution that did not happen in 1637' (Garber 1988). One of those correspondents, Libert Froimont, saw in Descartes' account of himself in the *Discourse* the renewal of a very ancient spirit:

[1] Bacon: 'There was but one course left, therefore,—to try the whole thing anew upon a better plan, and to commence a total reconstruction of sciences, arts and all human knowledge, raised upon the proper foundations.' (*Instauratio magma, Preface*; 1857–74, vol. 4: 8). Descartes: 'As soon as I was old enough to emerge from the control of my teachers, I entirely abandoned the study of letters . . . For it seemed to me that much more truth could be found in the reasonings which a man makes concerning matters that concern him than in those which some scholar makes in his study.' (*Discourse*, AT vi. 9; 1984: 115).

I seem to see a Pythagoras or a Democritus, a voluntary exile from his homeland who has traveled to the Egyptians, to the Brahmans, and around the entire globe, to investigate the nature of things and the nature of the universe.[2]

New work has revealed a complexity in Descartes' relationship with late scholasticism, including a tension between the self-presentation of the *Discourse* and views expressed in his letters (Ariew 1999; Secada 2000). In another vein, Julian Martin has described Francis Bacon's self-depiction as 'a studied pose', adding that 'when Bacon painted himself and his natural philosophy as modern and novel, he was moved to do so by local concerns and ambitions' (Martin 1993: 74).

There can be no doubt but that the new philosophers in seventeenth-century Europe were profoundly innovative, but the standard historiography simultaneously distorts two aspects of their relationship with the ancient. First, it misrepresents the dynamism and openness of progressive peripateticism. Many late scholastics, it is now becoming evident, were highly original in interpreting Aristotle and in fact saw no incompatibility between a recast Aristotelianism and the new philosophy (Schmitt 1983; Mercer 1993). Grievances against scholasticism gained succour from the stale academic practices in the universities, which opposed innovation without contributing anything new and treated scholastic philosophy as a monolithic never-changing whole. In a new intellectual climate there arose a new genre of very original interpretations of the philosophy of Aristotle—in the work, for example, of Jean-Baptiste du Hamel, Jean-Baptiste Morin, Erhard Weigel and Kenelm Digby. Weigel is typical in being willing to reinterpret basic Aristotelian notions in order to establish a reconciliation with the doctrines of the moderns, arguing for example that prime matter is fundamentally extension. In the judgement of Christia Mercer, 'early modern Aristotelianism not only shows impressive vitality and resilience, it also contributes to the intellectual debates at the centre of the philosophical revolutions of the period. It was a major force in early modern thought and one that has gone unexamined for too long' (Mercer 1993: 61).

The standard picture, furthermore, radically simplifies the complex ways in which the moderns drew upon the ancients. In the work of Leibniz, Spinoza, Basso and Gassendi, what one finds is a firm conviction that there is truth in the ancient philosophers, truth which might well stand in need of radical rejuvenation and reconfiguration, but truth which provides a gateway to new philosophy and is not a road-block to it. Leibniz described himself as seeking a 'reformed philosophy', one which put the mechanical philosophy on sound ancient foundations. That this is not simply to 'looke upon Nature, but with Aristotle's Spectacles'[3] is clear from the philosophical project of Pierre Gassendi. Gassendi uses recently retrieved Epicurean ideas in the development of a new atomism and empiricism. His Epicurean treatise, the *Syntagma Philosophicum*, is not exegesis but a creative recovery of the ancient materials

[2] Froimont 1637, quoted in Garber 1988: 476.

[3] John Donne, *Sermons*, vii. 260.

so as to inform a modern project (Lolordo 2007; Wilson 2008). Spinoza's engagement with ancient Stoicism has also, recently, begun to be more thoroughly explored and acknowledged (e.g. Kristeller 1984). Susan James' assessment is that 'much of the substance and structure of the *Ethics*—its central doctrines and the connections between them—constitute a reworking of Stoicism' (James 1993: 291). The fact is that the early modern philosophers had a far more subtle and interesting understanding of the relationship between their new work and the past than the standard model can accommodate. It is simply not the case that these early modern philosophers were merely residually scholastic; rather, a revival and retrieval of the ancient and a transformation of it into the modern was at the heart of their philosophical method. And that is not so different from those progressive Aristotelians who, says Leibniz, 'draw from the springs of Aristotle and the ancients rather than from the cisterns of the Scholastics' (1956: 124).[4]

When we come to look at early modern India it is especially important that we do so with eyes not blurred by the standard historiography of the battle between ancients and moderns in Europe. I am aware of no Indian thinker from the period who makes the sort of audacious self-proclamation that one finds in Bacon or Descartes, a sweeping dismissal of the ancient tradition and of everything associated with it. And yet a modernity there certainly was, one which had its equivalents of Leibniz, Spinoza, Basso, and Gassendi on the one hand, and Morin, Sennert, and Weigel on the other. I believe that in the sixteenth and seventeenth centuries a remarkable project began to take shape in the Sanskritic philosophical world. It is not just that the philosophers are willing to describe themselves as 'new', though that is indeed a striking feature of the period. Yet others before them had done the same, and the question is in what this self-attributed newness consists and what the self-affirmation means.[5] Was it only a newness in the ways that the ideas of the ancient authorities are described, a newness of style but not of substance? In asking this question, I have in mind Sheldon Pollock's well-known assessment of the new intellectuals of the seventeenth century, that their work displays a 'paradoxical combination of something very new in style subserving something very old in substance' (2001a: 407). That was certainly how a *pre-modern*, Jayanta, at the end of the first millennium, conceived of his own originality:

[4] P. F. Strawson therefore speaks of a 'vainglorious delusion' implicit in the studied pose: 'Many philosophers in the past—among them some of the greatest—have seen themselves as starting afresh, as setting out on a new path which they conceive to be the only sure one; and thus as freeing themselves, and us, from fundamental mistakes or misconceptions which have hitherto impeded the discovery of the true way. It is unlikely that any of us, in the second half of the twentieth century, will be buoyed up by any such glad, confident assurance—or, if you prefer, will be the victim of any such vainglorious delusion' (Strawson 1998: 20).

[5] Cf. Ariew 1999: ix: 'To understand what set Descartes apart both from the Scholastics and from other innovators, one has to grasp the reasons behind the various opinions; but, beyond that, one also has to understand the intellectual milieu in which these reasons played a role, to see what tactical measures could have been used to advance one's views or persuade others of them.'

How can we discover a new truth? So one should consider our novelty only in the rephrasing of words.[6]

This characteristically pre-modern attitude of deference to the past changes fundamentally in the work of Raghunātha Śiromaṇi (c.1460–1540). Raghunātha belongs to a tradition of philosophical speculation known as Nyāya, a term more or less synonymous with the appeal to reason and evidence-based critical inquiry—rather than scriptural exegesis—as the proper method of philosophy.[7] Raghunātha concludes his most innovative work, the *Inquiry into the True Nature of Things,* with a call to philosophers to think for themselves about the arguments:

> The demonstration of these matters which I have carefully explained is contrary to the conclusions reached by all the other disciplines. These matters spoken of should not be cast aside without reflection just because they are contrary to accepted opinion; scholars should consider them carefully. Bowing to those who know the truth concerning matters of all the sciences, bowing to people like you [the reader], I pray you consider my sayings with sympathy. This method, though less honoured, has been employed by wise men of the past; namely that one ask other people of learning to consider one's own words.
>
> (*Inquiry* 1915: 79, 1–80, 3; trans. Potter 1957: 89–90)

The new attitude was summarized at the time by Abū-l-Fażl, in a work—the *Ā'īn-i-Akbarī*—which relates the intellectual climate during the reign of the Mughal emperor Akbar. Abū-l-Fażl describes the philosophers as those who 'look upon testimony as something filled with the dust of suspicion and handle nothing but proof'.[8] In the writings of those philosophers who follow Raghunātha from about the middle of the sixteenth century until the end of the seventeenth there is a fundamental metamorphosis in epistemology, metaphysics, semantics, and philosophical methodology. The works of these philosophers—some of whom lived in Raghunātha's home-town of Navadvīpa in Bengal, others in the newly invigorated city of Vārāṇasī—are full of phrases that are indicative of a new attitude, phrases like 'this should be considered further', 'this needs to be reflected on', 'this is the right general direction to go in'.

[6] kuto vā nūtanaṃ vastu vayam utprekṣitum kṣamāḥ | vacovinyāsavaicitryamātram atra vicāryatām || (Jayanta 1936: 5, v. 8). Though certainly exaggerated, Jayanta's disclaimer is still less than that of the influential eighth-century Buddhist writer Śāntideva: 'Nothing new will be said here; nor have I any skill in composition. Therefore I do not imagine that I can benefit others. I have done this [simply] to improve my own mind' (na hi kiṃcitapūrvam atra vācyaṃ na ca saṃgrathanakauśalaṃ mamāsti | ata eva ne me parārthacintā svamano vāsayituṃ kṛtaṃ mayedam || (*Guide to the Path leading to Enlightenment* 1.2).

[7] Ganeri 2001a: 7–41. The term 'nyāya' has several meanings. It denotes a school of philosophy committed to the use of evidence-based methods of inquiry, including observation, inference, and testimony in so far as it is grounded in verifiable trustworthiness. The term also signifies a particular five-step pattern of demonstrative reasoning. In a rather different sense, 'nyāya' refers to a set of heuristic principles to guide practical reason (they are collected in Jacob 1900–4; Apte 1957). It is in this third sense that the term is used by Amartya Sen in his recent study of justice (Sen 2009).

[8] [1597] 1873: 537 (cited in D. C. Bhattacharya 1937). Abū-l-Fażl does not mention Raghunātha in the list of philosophers he provides to accompany this description, Raghunātha presumably already dead when Akbar came to the throne; but he does name someone with close ties to Raghunātha, Vidyānivāsa, and he also mentions Raghunātha's best-known student (see chapter 6).

Openness to inquiry into the problems themselves, a turn towards the facts, is what drives the new work, not merely a new exegesis of the ancient texts, along with a sense that they are engaged in a radical and ongoing project. The spirit which Raghunātha sought to provoke is clearly on display in a passage which asks about the meaning of historical and fictional terms:

How does it come about that, from hearing the word 'Daśaratha', people now, who never saw Daśaratha [the father of the legendary king Rāma] come to know of him? Likewise how, from the words [for fictional entities like] 'hobgoblin', do others come to know of them? I leave this for attentive scholars to meditate upon. I shall not expand further here.

(*Inquiry* 1915: 60,4–61,4; trans. Potter 1957: 76)

A second group of philosophers, again influenced by Raghunātha, aim to use his work in a profound reinterpretation of ancient metaphysics. In so far as their approach is that, when freshly interpreted and reconceptualized, there is no incompatibility between the ancient and the modern, these Vārāṇasī metaphysicians partly resemble the 'progressive' Aristotelians of early modern Europe. In the first instance, it is not to the most ancient thinkers that they return but to a pair of already innovative philosophers from the more immediate past, Udayana (eleventh century) and Gaṅgeśa Upādhyāya (fourteenth century). What stands in between, and takes the place of conservative Aristotelian scholasticism, is the work of a third group of philosophers who grew up in Gaṅgeśa's home town of Mithilā. One dimension of modernity in early modern Indian philosophy has the form of a reappropriation of Udayana and Gaṅgeśa from the Mithilā scholastics.

Other branches of scholarship, including linguistics (vyākaraṇa), philosophical theology (advaita, dvaita and viśiṣṭādvaita vedānta), ritual exegesis (mīmāṃsā), and jurisprudence (dharmaśāstra), encountered early modernity in ways that do not always agree that of the 'new reason', the later Navya Nyāya. Particularly worthy of notice are the Kerala mathematical astronomers, whose sensational work is increasingly being appreciated.[9] In view of the difficulty of the materials and the enormity of the work that remains to be done, I cannot hope to do justice here to every aspect of a hugely complex story. What I do hope is that a study focusing in as much detail as possible on a single aspect of South Asian early modernity will illustrate the nature of the period. Many important early modern Sanskrit intellectuals will not get a mention in this book at all, others in scant and insufficient detail. Nor will I be able to treat in anything like adequate thoroughness the relationship between the 'new reason' philosophers and their affiliates

[9] Nīlakaṇṭha (1444–1545) and Jyeṣṭhadeva (c. 1530) are exemplary figures. Jyeṣṭhadeva's Malayalam *Rationales in Mathematical Astronomy*, for example, contains results, using methods closely analogous to the infinitesimal calculus, for computing the equation of centre and latitudinal motion of Mercury and Venus, derivations in spherical astronomy, and proofs of the infinite series for π, the arc-tangent and the sine functions. See Sarma *et al.* 2008; Narasimha 2009. Raju 2007 presents the case for thinking that Keralan mathematics was transmitted to early modern Europe.

in other disciplines, not to mention their personal religious commitments and the many other factors that go into a complete intellectual profile.

The existence of this modernity, I have emphasized, can be seen only when we free ourselves from the idea that modernity involves a complete rejection of the ancient sources. Our philosophers still, for example, write commentaries, and still use concepts and categories that might, if looked at from a distance, seem archaic. What must be recognized is that the mere activity of writing a commentary, though now strongly associated with conservative scholasticism, does not by itself tell one very much about the author's attitude towards the text being commented on. The fundamental role of a commentary was to mediate a conversation between the past and the present. It therefore offers *us* a route into the question that lies at the heart of *our* study of early modernity in the sixteenth and seventeenth centuries: the question of *their* sense of *their* duties towards, or separation from, the ancient philosophical world. There are different sorts of commentary, and a fundamental distinction is between those whose ambition is to clarify or systematize the 'truths' already in the ancient treatise, and those which are using the treatise in the process of a creative pursuit of an inquiry into the truth itself. Early modernity expresses itself as a distinctive way of reading the past, and in our period this also finds a voice in a new genre of commentary, the commentary which digs up the deep or hidden meaning (*gūḍhārtha*) in an ancient text. A mistaken understanding of the ambitions of commentary has also led to a tendency to read new developments back into the original works, with the result that the originality of the later thinkers tends to disappear from view.

Other works structure themselves as auto-commentarial glosses on groups of tersely stated principles (*sūtras*; *kārikās*), in a style familiar to historians of early modern European philosophy through texts like Spinoza's *Ethics* and Descartes' *Principles*. Raghunātha is, nevertheless, also striking in his new promotion of the genre of philosophical treatise in which a problem is discussed directly; his *Inquiry into the True Nature of Things* is just such a work. In general, however, the discursive style in the works of the early modern Indian philosophers—mostly devoid of boastful self-assertion—can make it easy to overlook the originality of their ambitions.

Whereas in Europe the emergence of the new philosophy was inextricably interwoven with the emergence of natural science, in India this was not so. The failure to appreciate that the two developments are nevertheless distinct is another important reason why there has not been a proper diagnosis of early modernity in the philosophy. Generally speaking, what we can say is that early modern forms of philosophical inquiry in India are governed by data drawn from logical form and linguistic practice rather than the microscopic and distal observation of natural phenomena. Philosophy in early modern India made the discipline rest instead on the sort of linguistic turn that characterized, much later, the origins of analytical philosophy in European thought. Bearing this point in mind, it is no surprise that profound affinities should have been discovered between early modern theory in India and twentieth century analytical philosophy (Matilal 1985b, 1986; Ganeri 1999b, 2001a).

A very influential 'theory and method' for the history of philosophy has recently been developed by Quentin Skinner, the core idea of which is that one understands a thinker to the extent that one can fill in the context in which they write in sufficient detail to know what 'illocutionary intervention' their text makes in that context (Skinner 2002). Skinner's method is a very productive one, although I have found that his concept of context needs to be expanded to include what I will call 'intertextual' contexts of intervention. I have therefore taken great care to reconstruct in as much detail as I can the various contexts, social, political, intellectual, and intertextual, in which Raghunātha and his 'new reason' philosophers lived and worked. In the first instance it is within a community of peers that the philosopher seeks to make an intervention, against a background constituted by the history of their intellectual field. I have prefaced my examinations of the new epistemology and the new metaphysics with detailed reconstructions of the history so that the *contrast* between the new and the old, or the lack of it, is evident. It is also of enormous significance that this should be a period of strong Persianate influence and Islamicate power. The problem is to square this fact with another: that one finds very few direct traces, if any, of Islamic or Arabic ideas in the work of the Sanskrit philosophers of the time. It is not at all similar to the situation in astronomy, for example, where the confrontation between ancient Hindu cosmological models and the new Arabic sciences is a topic of heated debate. In philosophy, the causality, if it exists at all, is much more indirect. The Persianate context nevertheless created incentives that had not existed before. One fact to note is that the brightest and best Sanskrit intellectuals were actively encouraged, for instance by Akbar's great minister the Hindu Ṭoḍarmal, to learn Persian and join Mughal imperial office. Those who preferred instead to remain within the intellectual world of Sanskrit faced a very clear challenge to demonstrate the relevance and vitality of that world.[10] They did this by drawing on its resources without burying themselves within its folds. If in Europe power lay with the Aristotelians in the university departments, in India it was located in the Islamicate administration. By not becoming a part of it, the new philosophers were, one could say, in a state of internal exile. Modernity was the alternative to irrelevance. Another possibility is that rather than writing directly about Islamic thought they wrote instead about constructed surrogates within the Sanskrit milieu, reconstructions of Advaita Vedānta perhaps especially so. In any case what is clear is that the sheer presence of alternative modalities of thought presented motivations and opportunities that had not existed before.

The context of these new philosophers is therefore quite different from an earlier phase of renewal within the tradition. When Gaṅgeśa writes in the fourteenth century, he is responding to a variety of pressures internal to the Sanskrit world, critiques that

[10] An example is Bhārat Candra Raī, a prominent scholar in the court of Kṛṣṇacandra. According to an early report, 'his fondness for Sanskrit studies displeased his relations, who thought that an acquaintance with Muhammadan literature was a better passport to wealth and distinction than the Vedas and Purāṇas.' (Quoted in Wilson 1877: 155–156.)

had been gathering force for some time. One critique came from the direction of a rival philosophical theory about the nature of inquiry, developed within a context of defence of the legitimacy and authority of Vedic knowledge, Mīmāṃsā. If the Vedas are authoritative, then there is no question about the truth of the beliefs we form from them and no further project of verification. Such an attitude towards inquiry is profoundly at odds with one which sees the truth as a matter of discovery and confirmation. The other came from a challenge to the pluralist metaphysics of commonsense. Advaita Vedānta seeks to undermine the principle that appearance is trustworthy, and in particular that there is a world populated by middle-sized objects and known to a plurality of distinct cognizers; all there is, for Advaita, is consciousness, containing the world within itself. These internal challenges will lead Gaṅgeśa to bring to the surface two principles that had been less strongly emphasized before: a firm opposition to deference (an authority is not to be trusted just because it is an authority, but only when its credentials are in place; it is then apt, fit to be believed, *āpta*); and a robust commitment to the individual as a unit of intellectual, moral, and emotional life (the particular self—*ātman*—as a locus of psychological properties).

The two sources of internal challenge come both from rival Hindu theory. Gaṅgeśa's context was, in this respect, again very different from that of *his* predecessors, for whom the dominant intellectual circumstance was one fashioned by an intense and long-enduring dialectic with Buddhism (Matilal 1986; Ganeri 2007). It is entirely possible that it was precisely because Nyāya philosophers had configured themselves so as to be able to offer a robust answer to the Buddhists that their philosophy was left vulnerable to challenge from rival theory closer to home, in the turf-war which became possible only after Buddhist philosophers were exiled.[11] Be that as it may, and in spite of the description of his theory as 'new', Gaṅgeśa continued to be a premodern thinker in this sense: he writes to defend the ancient philosophy from rival critique rather than to channel its resources in the project of a new inquiry into the truth as such. Gaṅgeśa could not, as Raghunātha was to do, simply reject several of the ancient metaphysical categories on the grounds that they no longer made any sense. Nor could he bring himself to acknowledge new sources of knowledge and methods of inquiry. For all its originality, and despite the fact that later thinkers look to his and Udayana's work as laying the foundations of the new Nyāya, neither Gaṅgeśa nor any of the philosophers who lived after him in Mithilā can be described as other than premodern. If we compare with the *via antiqua* and the *via moderna* in the Renaissance, where those who follow the path of 'the ancients sought solutions to contemporary problems in the works of classical antiquity... [while those who follow the path of] the moderns believed that contemporary thinkers had in some cases improved on the works of the classical writers' (Osler 1993: 131), then, in this terminology, Gaṅgeśa remains a *via antiqua* thinker while Raghunātha is the first to adopt the *via moderna*.

[11] One of the forms which that configuration took was an emphasis on a 'medicinal' or 'therapeutic' understanding of philosophy; see Ganeri 2007; Ganeri and Carlisle 2010.

The Mithilā philosophers create, indeed, a genre of commentarial writing on Gaṅgeśa that comes to function a little like the conservative scholastic writings on Aristotle, a road-block to progress. It was left to two new communities of philosophers, one based in Raghunātha's hometown of Navadvīpa and the other in the historical city of Vārāṇasī, to fashion a new modernity. Vārāṇasī had in the course of the sixteenth century become a great meeting place and point of aggregation for Sanskrit scholars from all over India.[12] I will look first at three intellectual stories that are centred in this city in the seventeenth century: the stories of a Muslim Sufi, a Jaina, and a group of Hindu 'new reason' thinkers. Philosophers in Raghunātha's town of Navadvīpa, a famously cosmopolitan place with a long and complex history of Muslim–Hindu interaction, take Raghunātha's achievement to lie in his having perceived a new methodology for philosophy, a kind of logico-philosophical linguistics. They are less worried about compatibilism with the ancient tradition, more interested in pursuing a quite new research programme for philosophy, though one which is happy to draw upon and rework resources from the past.

As Julian Martin reminds us, however, 'For Ramus, Galileo, Descartes, and for Bacon, "modernity" was a studied pose, and since studied poses involve self-conscious choices, explaining why [they] chose to adopt it requires close attention' (Martin 1993: 74). I will describe some of the significance which the new philosophical ideas had in the seventeenth century. In the chapters that follow, I will say much more about the intellectual climate of the times in Vārāṇasī and in Navadvīpa. I will describe how philosophy was embodied: the nature of its texts, the genres in which it took form, both commentaries on established works, and, increasingly, in the production of short free-standing treatises on particular topics. I will offer a revised Skinnerian methodology for studying the philosophical literature of the period. In later parts of the book, I will explore in detail the substantive philosophical issues which the early modern Indian thinkers grapple with and their motivations for doing so. To make sense of their discussion, I will have to spend quite a lot of time reconstructing the intellectual context, which for these thinkers primarily means the centuries-long philosophical tradition a transformation within which was their primary aim. The issues I have chosen are those which constitute the fundamental underpinnings of the new philosophy: an epistemology to explain the possibility of systematic inquiry in the face of serious challenges from other sectors of the Hindu intellectual world; a new realism to explain the possibility of an objective conception of the external world; and a new language in which to formulate philosophical theory with precision and clarity.

It is only by going deeply into the thinking of the new philosophers that we will be able to establish for certain that theirs was a newness of substance and not merely of style. I believe that in a very complex political and intellectual climate the early modern 'new reason' thinkers were developing philosophical ideas of great radicality and

[12] 'Vārāṇasī in the seventeenth century witnessed a confluence of more or less free intellectuals . . . of a sort it had almost certainly never seen before' (Pollock 2001b: 21).

originality, initiating a line of philosophical inquiry that did not so much run its course as was brought to a virtual stand-still, in the first instance by the collapse in stable Mughal power and patronage, and in the second by the disruption caused to established patterns for conducting and financing education by the British imposition of new fiscal arrangements and educational policies. Work in the 'new reason' continued into the nineteenth and twentieth centuries in an educational set-up now sharply bifurcated between low-prestige traditional networks and well-funded colonial colleges and universities.[13] What was lost from this 'lost age of reason' is the what-might-have-been had that bifurcation not taken place. Much more work is needed to recover a fuller understanding of the philosophical project, but I hope that I have done enough to make a case for further interest in this phenomenally rich episode in the history of philosophy, a period from which all those who are interested in the nature of modernity and its global origins have a great deal to learn.

[13] See Krishna 1997c; 2001.

PART I

India Expanding

1

The World and India: 1656

François Bernier and his paṇḍit

India in the seventeenth century, the century after Akbar, was in intellectual overdrive. Muslim, Jaina, and Hindu intellectuals produced work of tremendous vitality, and ideas circulated around South Asia, through the Persianate and Arabic worlds, and out to Europe and back. If ever there were a concrete embodiment of the open and spacious 'idea of India' to which Rabindranath Tagore would later give voice, it was here.[1] To get an impression of the times let us fix our gaze on a single year, the year 1656. In India, this was the year in which a long-running process of religious isomorphism, pioneered by Akbar's chronicler Abū-l-Fażl and orchestrated around Ibn al-ʿArabī's idea of 'unity in being' (*waḥdat al-wujūd*), reached fulfilment in Dārā Shukoh's grand project to translate fifty-two Upaniṣads into Persian, a project for the sake of which he assembled in Vārāṇasī (Benares; aka Kāśī) a large team of bilingual scholars. Dārā believed that he could establish that the differences between Hinduism and Islam were largely terminological, and even that the Upaniṣads can be read as a sort of commentary upon the Qur'ān. The fallout from this remarkable project of Dārā, Akbar's great-grandson and heir apparent to the Mughal throne, would reverberate throughout the period and long afterwards.

1656 would also be the year in which the French philosopher and physician François Bernier would leave behind him the France of *les libertins érudits* on a journey that would soon bring him to Mughal India. In Bernier's travel writings, we will find a fragment of testimony to the aftermath of Dārā Shukoh's translational project. Before embarking on his travels, Bernier had been the protégé of the early modern philosopher, scientist, and mathematician Pierre Gassendi (1592–1655). Indeed, it was Bernier who would eventually—on his return to France—devote himself to making Gassendi's work available to French and British audiences. Before doing so, however, he was to spend years as the court physician first of Dārā Shukoh and then of Aurangzeb. In a letter written from Shiraz in 1667, some ten years after the Vārāṇasī project, Bernier describes how he had come to know one of the paṇḍits whom Dārā Shukoh had used,

[1] '[C]annot India rise above her limitations and offer a great ideal to the world . . . ? I feel that the true India is an idea and not merely a geographical fact . . . The idea of India is *against* the intense consciousness of the separateness of one's own people from others.' Tagore 1921: 287–288; see Amartya Sen 2005 for further discussion.

someone fluent in both Sanskrit and Persian, how they had exchanged the latest medical and philosophical knowledge, and, fascinatingly, how he had translated work by Descartes and Gassendi into Persian for the paṇḍit's benefit:

Do not be surprised if without knowledge of Sanskrit I am going to tell you many things taken from books in that language; you will know that my Agha, Dāniṣmand Khān, paid for the presence of one of the most famous paṇḍits in India, who before had been pensioned by Dārā Shukoh, the oldest son of Shāh Jahāṇ, and that this paṇḍit, apart from attracting the most learned scientists to our circle, was at my side for over three years. When I became weary of explaining to my Agha the latest discoveries of William Harvey and Pequet in anatomy, and to reason with him on the philosophy of Gassendi and Descartes, which I translated into Persian (because that is what I did during five or six years) it was up to our paṇḍit to argue.[2]

It is of considerable interest to those who are interested in the global circulation of ideas to be told here that the work of Descartes, by this time the leading French philosopher and a key figure in the Early Enlightenment, was available to the Vārāṇasī paṇḍits already in the early 1660s, barely ten years after his death. If Bernier's testimony is reliable, the migration of ideas was already remarkably swift. As for the name of Bernier's paṇḍit, and the nature of his reaction to the work of Descartes or Gassendi, that is a story which Bernier neglected to tell. He has now provisionally been identified (Gode 1954a) as the very influential scholar–poet Kavīndra Sarasvatī, an important intermediary between the Sanskrit intelligentsia and the Mughal court, and someone who built up a great library.[3] The patron of Bernier during this period was the Persian nobleman Dāniṣmand Khān, who was the only person to oppose the capital sentence against Dārā (Smith 1923: 415, 425), and who afterwards offered Kavīndra and Bernier employment. His generosity and openness created the space for a remarkable exchange of French, Persian and Sanskrit philosophical ideas in the three years from 1658/9 to 1661/2. Kavīndra was on good terms with perhaps the most important of the 'new reason' philosophers in Vārāṇasī, Jayarāma Nyāyapañcānana, about whom I will have much more to say. It would be during this period that Jayarāma would write two very unusual and significant works, *The Garland of Principles about Reason*, and *The Garland of Categories*.

Bernier does include in his letter a fascinating account of the secret doctrine which Dārā thought he had rediscovered in the Upaniṣads, a doctrine Bernier describes as having been the source of a considerable degree of fuss:

[2] 'Letter to Monsieur Chapelain, Despatched from Chiras in Persia, the 4th October 1667,' in Bernier 1981; translated in Bernier 1934: 323–325; again in Rizvi 1989.

[3] H. Shastri 1912: 11; Gode 1945. Shastri tells us that 'he was a great collector of manuscripts. It is not known how many thousands of manuscripts he collected, but all the manuscripts of his library bear in large, bold, and beautiful Devanāgarī character his signature *sarva-vidyā-nidhāna-kavīndra-sarasvatī*. That signature is a guarantee for the correctness and accuracy of the manuscript. It is not known when and how the library was broken up, but the manuscripts of his library can now be procured in Benares, and they are preferred by all Paṇḍits to other manuscripts.' The importance of Kavīndra is independent of the correctness of Gode's identification.

In conclusion, I shall explain to you the Mysticism of a Great Sect which has latterly made great noise in Hindustan, inasmuch as certain paṇḍits or 'gentile doctors' had instilled it into the minds of Dārā and Sultan Sujah, the eldest sons of Shāh Jahāṇ.

(1934: 345)

The doctrine in question, that the world is rationally ordered according to principles derived from final causes, is one which Bernier finds in the work of the Greeks:

You are doubtless acquainted with the doctrine of many of the ancient philosophers concerning that great life-giving principle of the world, of which they argue that we and all living creatures are so many parts: if we carefully examine the writings of Plato and Aristotle, we shall probably discover that they inclined towards this opinion. This is the almost universal doctrine which is held by the sect of the Sūfis and the greater part of the learned men of Persia at the present day.

(1934: 345–346)

Bernier is explicit about the reason for his antipathy towards this doctrine: in the version defended by Robert Fludd, it had itself been refuted by his philosophical mentor Gassendi.[4] Bernier's presentation of the doctrine clearly bears traces of his association with the Hindu paṇḍits. He describes the idea in question as being that

God has not only produced life from his own substance, but also generally everything material or corporeal in the universe, and that this production is not formed simply after the manner of efficient causes, but as a spider which produces a web from its own navel, and withdraws it at pleasure. The Creation then, say these visionary doctors, is nothing more than an extraction or extension of the individual substance of God, of those filaments which He draws from his own bowels; and, in like manner, destruction is merely the recalling of that divine substance and filaments into Himself.

He concludes that this idea has led him to take as his motto the slogan that 'there is no doctrine too strange or too improbable for the soul of man to conceive'.[5]

The year 1656 was to be fateful in Europe too, for it was the year in which Spinoza received his *cherem* in Amsterdam, an excommunication from the Portuguese Jewish community as a result of an anticipation of the heretical views he would later systematize, the pantheistic or atheistic doctrine that 'God or Nature' is the only substance, the denial of miracles, of prophecy, and of scriptural revelation. The influential French early moderns Bayle and Malebranche soon came to perceive China to be a land inhabited by Spinozists, but it would fall to Anquetil Duperron, while introducing his Latin translation of Dārā Shukoh's Persian Upaniṣads, to declare

[4] Fludd drew on Neoplatonist resources in a search for hidden connections between a purely intelligible realm and the realm of sensation.

[5] Perhaps Bernier had in mind Part Two of Descartes' *Discourse*, where Descartes, reflecting on the philosophical value of his own travels, says, '[I]n my school days I discovered that nothing can be imagined which is too strange or incredible to have been said by some philosopher; and since then I have recognized through my travels that those with views quite contrary to ours are not on that account barbarians or savages' (AT vi. 16; 1984: 118–119).

that the Upaniṣads represent a creed of 'true Spinozism' (1801–2: 659; 665). This identification of Upaniṣadic theory with Spinozism would have important consequences for later European perceptions of India. Reconstruals of the Upaniṣads are the conduit through which a variety of interpretative movements have taken place.

It is perhaps worth stressing just how well connected Bernier was with the circles that fashioned the Early Enlightenment in Europe, the *libertins érudits* and the *nouveaux pyrrhoniens*, a group whose members had been inspired by the rediscovery of the work of Sextus Empiricus (Popkin 2003). Among Bernier's correspondents, for example, was the prominent new sceptic, François de La Mothe Le Vayer; and if John Dryden had already penned his play *Aureng-Zebe* in 1675, this was only because Bernier's *Travels* had by then been rendered into English by the first Secretary of the Royal Society, Henry Oldinburgh, Dryden having been elected to the Royal Society in 1662. Bernier's *Abrégé*, published in 1678, which highlights Gassendi's atomism, empiricism, and materialist aspects of his thought, was almost certainly read by Locke and is an important source of influence on early British empiricism. With Gassendi's work rendered into Persian even before it was properly available in French, and the monistic pantheism of the Upaniṣads and Dārā Shukoh already in France and England years before Spinoza's *Ethics* were published, what more dramatic evidence could there be of intellectual globalization in the 1660s.

No reader of David Hume (1711–76) will fail to identify the image of the spider with which Bernier concludes. Hume decries the Hindu belief that God is a spider, in section vii of his *Dialogues Concerning Natural Religion*, precisely in the course of a discussion of the notion that the world has a soul:

> The Brahmins assert, that the world arose from an infinite spider, who spun this whole complicated mass from his bowels, and annihilates afterwards the whole or any part of it, by absorbing it again, and resolving it into his own essence. Here is a species of cosmogony, which appears to us ridiculous; because a spider is a little contemptible animal, whose operations we are never likely to take for a model of the whole universe. But still here is a new species of analogy, even in our globe.
>
> (Hume 1990: 90)

Hume may well have read Bernier directly, or it is possible that he obtained the simile from Bernier's correspondent Pierre Bayle, whose *Historical and Critical Dictionary* was published in French in 1697, and includes information from ancient Greek sources about the Indian Brahmins as well as from the contemporary accounts of Jesuit missionaries. Although it was certainly rhetorically convenient and effective for Hume to ridicule the notion in its Indian formulation, his attack on the rationalistic explanation of the unity of the world brought the career of that widely admired idea decisively to an end.

The public profile of the 'new reason'

Curiously, the metaphor of the spider had already been used by Francis Bacon to depict the method of the rationalists, who 'like spiders, spin webs out of themselves'. On the other hand those whom he called the 'empirics' simply collect data, and are no better than ants. Bacon argued that the true method of philosophy lay in between, to gather material and then transform it.[6] The 'new reason' philosophers in India depict materialism (Cārvāka) much as Bacon does the empiricists, and monism (Advaita Vedānta) the way he does the rationalists, in order analogously to secure a middle ground for themselves. Navya Nyāya, the 'new reason', flourished in Vārāṇasī and especially in a town in Bengal called Navadvīpa, which later received the Latinized name Nuddea or Nadia. Our period was indeed one of extraordinary innovation and dynamism in the philosophical activity of these intellectuals. Training centres for the 'new reason' flourished, attracting students from all over the Indian continent and perhaps further afield. There are reports even of Tibetan Buddhist students travelling from Lhasa to acquire a training in the 'new reason',[7] and a possibility that at least one 'new reason' thinker went to Tibet.[8] The methods and techniques of this new school of inquiry were highly effective and much emulated throughout the world of Sanskrit scholarship. While the roots lay in work done by philosophers in Mithilā in the fourteenth and fifteenth centuries, the shift in the centre of gravity to Navadvīpa and Vārāṇasī signalled a moment of radical transformation and renewal, much of it focused on an engagement with the ideas of the brilliant Raghunātha Śiromaṇi, as articulated in his *Inquiry into the True Nature of Things* and other important work.[9] Raghunātha's followers distinguished themselves from the older Navya Nyāya, by which they meant the scholastic commentaries from Mithilā. They regarded themselves as the new within the new, the truly modern (*navīna*). To any of the Sanskrit scholars in the circle around Bernier, Gassendi's atomist theory of matter and empiricist epistemology would unquestionably have put them in mind of the metaphysics associated with the 'new reason', diametrically opposite to the speculative doctrine of 'unity of being'. It too retrieves and reconstitutes a much more ancient atomism, the ancient Vaiśeṣika atomism of Kaṇāda and Praśastapāda, fashioned afresh for the modern world.

Of European writers from the period, only Roberto Nobili, living in south India, managed to include a discussion of the 'new reason'. He wrote about what he described as the 'natural philosophy of the *Cintāmaṇi*' in his *Informatio*, an extremely rich and insightful book written in 1613 but left unpublished by Rome.[10] Had it been

[6] Francis Bacon, *Novum Organum* [1620], aphorism 95.

[7] Sankhyatirtha 1964: 21; Sinha 1993: 7.

[8] At least four Sanskrit paṇḍits were to live in Lhasa in the seventeenth century. The brothers Gokulanātha Miśra and Balabhadra assisted the fifth Dalai Lama in his project to translate Pāṇinian grammars from Sanskrit to Tibetan in 1658 to 1660, while Kṛṣṇabhaṭṭa worked with the Tibetan historiographer Tāranātha (1575–1634) early in the seventeenth century, and Kṛṣṇodaya helped with a translation of grammatical literature. See Tucci 1949: 74, 137; Verhagen 1994: 137–140. For a provisional identification of Gokulanātha Miśra with the Maithilī 'new reason' philosopher Gokulanātha Upādhyāya, see Ghosh 1970: 37–39.

[9] Ingalls 1951; Potter 1957; Pahi and Jain 1997. For a summary of all Raghunātha's work, see Potter and Bhattacharyya 1993: 521–590.

[10] *Ad patrem nostrum generalem informatio, de quibusdam moribus nationis Indicae.* Translated in Nobili 1972.

published Nobili's work might fundamentally have influenced European perceptions of Indian philosophy. It was based on information about the text of Gaṅgeśa in Mithilā in the fourteenth century, a book called the *Tattva-cintāmaṇi*, the *Gemstone [fulfilling one's desire] for Truth.*[11] Nobili was unaware of all that was taking place in Navadvīpa and Vārāṇasī, of the new movements that in part found expression through the production of revisionary commentaries on Gaṅgeśa's text. As chance would have it, 1656 is also the year of Nobili's death.

It seems possible, however, that one European may have had an acquaintance with these new movements. Heinrich Roth joined the Mughal court and spent several years studying Sanskrit in Agra, probably the years 1654–60 (Camps 1988: 9). Halbfass (1988: 42) comments that

> In the North, where the Mughals had control of India, another Jesuit missionary followed Nobili's example several decades after the latter first began his work in South India. Heinrich Roth (1620–1668) devoted himself with considerable energy, but more strongly developed philological interests, to the study of Sanskrit and the literature of India, including works of a philosophical nature. Yet his writings, which include the first European Sanskrit grammar as well as a copy of the *Vedānta-sāra* by Sadānanda, also remained unpublished and have only recently been rediscovered in hand-written form.

Roth's Sanskrit grammar has finally been published along with the two Sanskrit manuscripts in his possession and his own marginal comments (Roth 1988). The *Essence of Vedānta* (*Vedānta-sāra*) is one of these, as Halbfass rightly says, but the one Halbfass does not mention is a Vaiśeṣika work on the five elements. This work is called the *Light on the Five Elements* (*Pañca-tattva-prakāśa)*. It was composed in 1644, and the author's name is Veṇīdatta.[12] It must be said that the *Light* is a basic work and a rather peculiar philosophical text to select for intensive study, especially since the transcription Roth worked on is corrupt; but Roth will certainly have gained from it a rudimentary understanding of Vaiśeṣika atomic theory and the nature of material composition. In Agra, Roth received Johann Grueber and Albert d'Orville, who arrived there from Lhasa in 1662 having discovered a land route from Beijing. He accompanied Grueber back to Rome but returned to Agra two years later. Bernier knew of Roth, and actually used materials Roth had deposited in Shiraz during his return trip in composing his famous 'letter to Chapelain' in 1667. Roth died in Agra in 1668, and his pioneering work on Sanskrit grammar and Sanskrit philosophical texts disappeared for the next three centuries.

[11] See Potter and Bhattacharyya 1993; Phillips and Tatacharya 2004; Mohanty 1966.

[12] Contra Potter (P 1351), he is not the same person as an important seventeenth-century philosopher Veṇīdatta Vāgīśa Bhaṭṭa, as is clear from what the authors say about their respective lineages: this Veṇīdatta is the son of Jagajjīvana and grandson of Nīlakaṇṭha, seemingly originally from Kashmir (Camps 1988: 17), while Veṇīdatta Vāgīśa is the son of Bhaṭṭa Vīreśvara, grandson of Lakṣmaṇa, of a family living in Vārāṇasī originally from Gujarat (Thakur 2003: 361). The second Veṇīdatta wrote a brilliant work based on Raghunātha's *Inquiry*, and itself very innovative (Veṇīdatta 1930; see also Thakur 2003: 361–363). I will discuss his ideas in later chapters.

Some thirty years before any of this, again in Agra, Dārā Shukoh had sat next to his father the emperor Shāh Jahāṇ as they received a deputation by Kavīndra Sarasvatī (later seemingly to join Dārā's project and discuss philosophy with Bernier), who had gone to the Mughal court to argue that a tax on Hindu pilgrimage to Vārāṇasī and other pilgrimage sites be repealed.[13] Kavīndra was one of the most influential people in seventeenth century Vārāṇasī, not only an accomplished scholar poet but also a very wealthy patron of Hindu scholarship. Kavīndra engaged Dārā and Shāh Jahāṇ in philosophical conversation, and indeed, perhaps astutely, talked to them about the contents of Śaṅkara's Advaita Vedāntic masterpiece, the *Brahma-sūtra-bhāṣya*,[14] a work which affirms monistic ideas. When he returned to Vārāṇasī successful and triumphant, the speeches in his honour were led by, among others, the 'new reason' scholar Jayarāma Nyāyapañcānana,[15] a senior public intellectual of the period and someone whose work I will examine in detail later in this book. Jayarāma had impeccable credentials in the 'new reason'. He is the author of two unusual and important books, the two *Garlands*—about reasoning in public situations, and about metaphysics—the second of which was written in 1659. Jayarāma was a signatory to a historically important document, the 1657 Vārāṇasī 'letter of judgement' (*nirṇaya-patra*). This letter was drawn up after a great assembly in the pavilion of the Viśveśvara temple, convened in order to discuss the caste status of Devrukhe Brahmins, and it is a document of great help in fixing the identity of the leading thinkers of the period.[16] Jayarāma's association with Kavīndra makes it not at all improbable that when philosophers were brought together by Dāniṣmand Khān, Jayarāma would have been among the group.

Vārāṇasī 'new reason' was to play a large part in the intellectual formation of Yaśovijaya Gaṇi (1624–88), by far the most brilliant and productive Jaina intellectual of the seventeenth century.[17] The tolerant pluralism of the Jainas had attracted Akbar, as it was to appeal to Gandhi much later, but Yaśovijaya's story holds a particular

[13] Dārā's presence is recorded in the *Kavīndracandrodaya* (Sharma and Patkar 1939), v. 169: 'śāhi-dārā-śakohaḥ.' In v. 170 it is stated that at the meeting were present Kashmiris, Portuguese, Iraqis, Afghans, Arabs, Turks and Mughals.

[14] *Kavīndracandrodaya* v. 92 by Nīlakaṇṭha refers to the 'bhāṣya,' which Raghavan 1940: 161 identifies with that of Śaṅkara.

[15] *Kavīndracandrodaya,* vv. 41–44. He is followed by Mādhava Bhaṭṭa (v. 45) and then by Rāmadeva Bhaṭṭacārya (vv. 46–47), the son of Viśvanātha Nyāyapañcānana Bhaṭṭācārya, another important 'new reason' philosopher in Vārāṇasī.

[16] The seventy-seven signatories include the 'new reason' philosophers Govinda Śarman, Jayarāma Nyāyapañānana, Raghudeva Nyāyālaṃkāra, Mādhavadeva Bhaṭṭācārya and Mahādeva Bhaṭṭa. The letter is published in Pimputkar 1926: 78–81 and Gode 1943/4: 133–138, and has been discussed by Kaviraja 1961: 69, D. C. Bhattacharya 1945, Pollock 2001b: 21, and O' Hanlon 2010: 229–234 (with a translation). Pollock comments that the document 'can be adduced as evidence of the remarkable transregional representation and vital interaction of intellectuals in Vārāṇasī . . . it is hard not to believe that the city's incorporation into the Mughal Empire at the end of the sixteenth century, and the growth of pilgimage, especially on the part of Maharashtrians, that may have been facilitated by the establishment of the empire, did not have something to do with the efflorescence of the intellectual class and its cosmopolitan mixture as represented in the document.' It is indicative of a new regime that Aurangzeb had the Viśveśvara temple destroyed in 1669.

[17] Jainas in the seventeenth century recorded their engagements with the Mughal court in a substantial and little studied body of texts; see Truschke 2012.

interest because he provides a link between the two traditions of thinking I have been describing, the monist 'unity in being' of the Upaniṣads, Dārā Shukoh and Ibn al-ʿArabī on the one hand, and the metaphysical pluralism, empiricism, and atomism of new reasoners on the other. Yaśovijaya spent an extended apprenticeship studying the new reason in Vārāṇasī, his stay coming to an end shortly before Dārā's translational project began. Yaśovijaya afterwards sought to achieve a transformation of the new reason, using its own techniques and methods and from a perspective informed by Jaina inclusivism, explicitly critical on occasion of the mainstream 'new reason' thinkers themselves. He then switched to writing works about the nature of the individual self and its relation to larger cosmopolitan identities, frequently mentioning the Upaniṣads and the *Bhagavad-gītā*. Both Dārā and Yaśovijaya would appeal to the venerable metaphor of the ocean and its waves to explain the relationship between the multiplicity of individuals and participation in a single unity, which they sought to articulate in their common quest for an interdoctrinal rapprochement. In the later work of Yaśovijaya, there is, as I will show when I discuss his work more fully, the clear identification and promotion of a range of intellectual values, including impartiality and balance, associated nowadays with political liberalism.

It is clear that there was a good deal of movement between the two great sites of the new reason, Vārāṇasī and Navadvīpa. An especially versatile thinker of the period, Mahādeva Puṇatāṃakara, whose work I will also discuss later, tells us that he himself made a number of trips from Vārāṇasī to Navadvīpa in order to study with the new reason paṇḍits there, and many of the most important families of Bengali scholars had family members living in Vārāṇasī. Large collections of new reason texts were being built up too by royal and private libraries in Kathmandu, a little over 300 kilometers away from Vārāṇasī, as well as in other libraries in India, whose owners could gain considerable academic prestige through their possession of a strong library of new reason work. I will later identify three networks of philosophers, each able to trace its lineage back to one or another of the earliest interpreters of Raghunātha. They promoted the use of different teaching manuals within their respective network, and had different readings and assessments of Raghunātha.

Europeans were beginning to make the journey too. One person to make at least part of that journey was the Englishman John Marshall (1641–77). Marshall was a friend of the Cambridge Platonist Henry More, to whom indeed he entrusted his literary remains (Marshall 1927: 27). He found work with the East India Company and travelled between Hugli and Patna in the early 1670s. Having learnt Persian and Arabic, Marshall prepared English translations of two originally Sanskrit works, the *Sāma-veda* from Madhusūdana's Persian, and the *Bhāgavata-purāṇa*.[18] E. B. Cowell would later declare that if Marshall's researches had been published at the time 'they would have inaugurated an era in European knowledge of India being in advance of

[18] On Madhusūdana Sarasvatī (c. 1530–1620), an Advaita Vedāntin who trained in the 'new reason' and was connected to Akbar's court, see Chapter 6.

anything which appeared before 1800' (Venn 1910–13: 592). In Marshall's diaries we find him drawing attention to the existence of the story of The Flood in the Hindu scriptures, presumably as it is found in the *Bhāgavata-purāṇa* itself, this over a century before William Jones made comparative mythology into a science. Marshall knew of the Hindu conception of the world as a web-like divine emanation as also mentioned by Bernier. His descriptions are especially remarkable in being free of the condescending tone that would colour later European writing from India.

I will turn now to detailed studies of two exemplary early modern Indian thinkers, the Muslim Dārā Shukoh and the Jaina Yaśovijaya Gaṇi. According to Sajjad Rizvi, there are three important trends in Islamic Philosophy in India during our period: first, the project of Dārā, involving the translation from Sanskrit and other vernaculars into Persian; second, the *sūfī* school of Ibn 'Arabī, and in particular the work of Muḥibbullāh Ilāhābādī (d. 1651), a prolific author in Arabic and Persian and defender of Ibn 'Arabī's philosophical theology; and third, the debate between Avicennans and Illuminationsts (*ishrāqī*), with the important philosopher Maḥmūd Jawnpūrī in the first camp (see Rizvi 2011). Then I will try to reconstruct the social historical context of a third early modern voice, the Hindu philosopher Raghunātha Śiromaṇi. His is the inaugural voice of the early modernity I have chosen to explore, a modernity that is emblematic of many others in sixteenth and seventeenth century India.

2

Dārā Shukoh: A Spacious Islam

Migrating texts

Hospitality, says Immanuel Kant in *Towards Perpetual Peace*, is a cosmopolitan right, the right of a stranger 'not to be treated with hostility because he has arrived on the land of another'.[1] What might it mean to say that the stranger has a right to hospitality when the movement involved concerns ideas? Viewed from the other side, what does it take for a tradition to have the ability to show hospitality to an intellectual stranger, in the form, for example, of a migrating text?

In order to explore these questions, I will take up an example which is of particular interest for several reasons. In the seventeenth century, India was under the political control of the Mughal Empire. The Mughals had brought with them a rich Persianate culture, with strong ties to the wider Islamic world, a culture that perpetuated and preserved itself in the course of two centuries of rule in northern India. The migration I want to consider concerns the movement of a Hindu text *into* that tradition. It was in or around 1656 that the crown prince Dārā Shukoh, the eldest son of Shāh Jahāṇ and the great grandson of Akbar, began to assemble a team of paṇḍit translators to help him in his project of rendering into Persian three great Hindu texts: the Upaniṣads, the *Bhagavad-gītā*, and the *Yoga-vāsiṣṭha*.[2] This project would indeed prove to be one of historic importance, for European scholars had Persian but not Sanskrit, and it would be through Anquetil Duperron's translation of the Persian into Latin that the Upaniṣads would bear upon nineteenth-century European thought. This was the text that would be read by Schopenhauer, whose reading would in turn directly influence the early Wittgenstein; this was the text a copy of which was held by the poet William Blake, and which was studied by Schelling. That further migration is not, however, my present interest. What I would like to explore is the character of the hospitality Dārā Shukoh showed towards these Hindu texts in inviting them to enter the world of courtly Persianate Islamic learning.

[1] Academy Edition 8: 357–359; trans. Gregor 1996: 311–352; at 328–329.

[2] Kavīndra Sarasvatī was perhaps involved; in any case he acknowledges Dārā in the colophon to his *Kavīndra-kalpadruma*: tatvajñānadūrīkṛta mahāmohasamavagata-saptabhūmikāsamāroha-mahammada-dārā-śiko-kṛtā nārāyaṇotyaṣṭākṣaramantrapūrvakā namaskārāḥ santi || (Gode 1954a: 378, n.1); and again in his Hindi *Kavīndra-kalpalatā* (Gode 1954b: 440, n.1). Another person probably involved was Gosvāmī Nṛhasiṃhāśrama, with whom Dārā corresponded in Sanskrit, and who signed the 1657 letter of judgement (Gode 1954b: 440, 447–451).

The nature of this project was, it should immediately be acknowledged, quite different in character from another large-scale translation project involving Sanskrit texts—the Tibetan reception of Indian Buddhism. One reason for being hospitable is prudential: one might welcome the stranger because one has something to gain from them. This was certainly the motive for the Tibetan interest in Sanskrit Buddhist texts, which were regarded as repositories of great, much welcomed, and hitherto unavailable knowledge. No such thought motivated Dārā Shukoh, however. As a devout Muslim and an adept Sufi practitioner, he was already firm in his convictions. He had no expectation of learning something *fundamentally* new from the Upaniṣads and the other Hindu texts, nor indeed any real openness to the possibility of doing so. Dārā Shukoh's hospitality had its roots in a different idea altogether, that the stranger, if welcomed and understood, would turn out to be no stranger at all. Dārā Shukoh hoped to show that treating the Hindu as an alien and an Other was a fundamental mistake, that there existed between Hinduism and Islam a pre-existing affinity, even an identity. The cosmopolitan right to hospitality is, perhaps, the right to have one's common humanity affirmed. Dārā repeats the famous verse of the Sufi poet Sanā'ī, in the misquoted version Akbar's biographer Abū-l-Fażl had had engraved on a temple in Kashmir used by both Muslims and Hindus: 'Infidelity (*kufr*) and Islam (*īmām*) are both following your path, crying, "He alone, he has no partner!"' the two being, in his words, parallel locks of hair not covering the face of the Incomparable One (Dārā Shukoh 1929: 37; cf. Ernst 2003: 187 n. 54).

Translating Sanskrit into Persian

Carl Ernst has made the most thorough study of Persian translations from the Sanskrit to date. With regard to the translations made of metaphysical and mystical texts, he notes their unusual method of production:

> This type of translation typically mediated Vedāntic philosophical and mystical texts through a loose oral commentary provided by Indian paṇḍits; this was rephrased in the Sufi technical vocabulary, presenting the texts as a kind of gnosis (Persian *ma ʿrifat*), and frequently amplifying their contents by the insertion of Persian mystical verses.
>
> (Ernst 2003: 183)

Although possibly true of many of the translations produced, the laxity implied by this description of the process could not be held against the translation of the Upaniṣads prepared under the auspices of Dārā Shukoh. If one compares that translation with the original, one finds it to be remarkably accurate; indeed, even the Latin text is a fairly close rendering. It was Dārā Shukoh's avowed intention to make 'without any worldly motive, in a clear style, an exact and literal translation'; and to that end he also included in the translation a Sanskrit–Persian glossary. At the same time, it does display a 'rephrasing' of Indian philosophical terms and names of the Vedic Gods in terms of Sufi parallels. For example, Mahādeva becomes Isrāfīl, Viṣṇu becomes Mikā'īl, Brahman

Jibra'īl or Adam; and likewise *brahma-loka* is rendered *sidrat al-muntahā*, *om* as *ism-i aʿẓam* (Hasrat 1982: 259–260). There are indeed also interpolations into the translated text, but they derive from Śaṅkara's commentary, which has clearly been used as a guide in preparing the translation of those Upaniṣads upon which such commentary is available.

Of Dārā Shukoh's translation of the Upaniṣads, Ernst says

> What is most distinctive about Dārā Shukuh's approach to Indian texts is that he treats them as scripture, in the same category as the Psalms of David, the Gospel, and the Qur'ān. Sūfis such as Mīrzā Maẓhar Jān-Jānān (d. 1781) also made this theological concession, but typically with the stipulation that such ancient scriptures had been abrogated by the most recent revelation, the Qur'ān. Dārā Shukuh viewed the Upaniṣads as hermeneutically continuous with the Qur'ān, providing an extended exposition of the divine unity that was only briefly indicated in the Arabic scripture.
>
> (2003: 185–186)

It is not the case that the Upaniṣads provide access to new truths; rather they provide a more detailed description of truths already sketched but less than fully explained in the Qur'ān. How, though, can an imported text from an alien tradition be thought of as in this way 'hermeneutically continuous' with Islamic scripture? For the answer, we will turn first to Dārā Shukoh's own preface to his translation.[3]

A religious cosmopolitanism

Dārā Shukoh called his Persian translation of fifty-two Upaniṣads *Sirr-i Akbar*, 'The Great Secret'. What might that secret have been? In his remarkably informative 'Preface' Dārā reveals a great deal about his thinking. He was, first of all, thirsty for a resolution to a variety of 'subtle doubts' that had occurred to him in the course of his studies. And

> whereas the holy Qur'ān is mostly allegorical, and at the present day persons thoroughly conversant with the subtleties thereof are very rare, he [Dārā] became desirous of bringing in view all the heavenly books, for the very words of God itself are their own commentary; and what might be in one book compendious, in another might be found diffusive, and from the detail of one, the conciseness of the other might be comprehensible. He had therefore cast his eyes on the Book of Moses, the Gospels, the Psalms and other scriptures, but the explanation of monotheism (*tauhīd*) in them also was compendious and enigmatical, and from the slovenly translation which selfish persons had made, their purport was not intelligible.
>
> (trans. Hasrat 1982: 265)

Dārā Shukoh represents his quest as a kind of research work, looking to a variety of sources in order to find answers to his questions. Among any variety of sources, some will offer clearer and more comprehensible accounts of certain details than others; it is therefore only rational to consult all of them. The unspoken assumption, of course, is

[3] I will say more about Indian notions of commentary in Chapter 8, ideas which might have helped Dārā to think of the Upaniṣads as commentary on the Qur'ān.

that all religious texts have a common subject matter, whatever their varying stylistic merits or drawbacks might be. In the background, then, is what might be termed a religious cosmopolitanism, a belief that there is a common spiritual heritage to all humanity. This is a manifestation of the Sufi doctrine of *waḥdat al-wujūd* ('Unity of Being'), which, as Muzaffar Alam has shown, contributed to the shape of Hindu–Muslim relations in northern India throughout the sixteenth and seventeenth centuries, from Akbar to ʿAbd al-Raḥmān Chishtī (Alam 2004: 91–98).

Dārā Shukoh then goes on to make a second legitimizing argument for the hospitality he shows towards the Upaniṣads in translating them into Persian:

> Then every difficulty and every sublime topic which he had desired or thought and had looked for and not found, he obtained from these essences of the most ancient books, and without doubt or suspicion, these books are first of all heavenly books in point of time, and the source and fountain-head of the ocean of Unity, in conformity with the holy Qur'ān and even a commentary thereon.
>
> (Hasrat 1982: 267)

That the Upaniṣads supply answers to the problems he had encountered in his Sufi studies is proof enough that they are genuine sources of spiritual insight, and they might even be said to provide a commentary upon the Qur'ān in so far as they explicate its puzzlingly allegorical statements. To a modern-minded religious pluralist, such a statement might seem almost unintelligible, but within Dārā Shukoh's religious cosmopolitanism, it makes perfect sense. Just as there is one astronomy or chemistry, which different peoples at different times have found out different things about, so too there is one spiritual adventure to which all the world is party. Dārā Shukoh does not think of himself as bringing two distinct religious traditions into conversation or dialogue, but as drawing together different strands of a common resource. Seyyed Nasr rightly states that 'the translations of Dārā Shukoh do not at all indicate a syncretism or eclecticism' (1999: 141), the reason being that he does not acknowledge the *difference* that a syncretic mission presupposes.

Dārā's final legitimization of his project is, however, the most daring of all. He now claims that the Upaniṣads are actually mentioned in the Qur'ān, and designated as scriptural texts:

> And it becomes clearly manifest that this verse is literally applicable to these ancient books: 'Most surely it is an honoured Qur'ān; in a book that is protected. None shall touch it save the purified ones. A revelation by the Lord of the worlds (Qur'ān lvi 77–80).' It is evident to any person that this sentence is not applicable to the Psalms or the Book of Moses or to the Gospel, and by the word 'revelation' it is clear that it is not applicable to the Reserved Tablet; and whereas the Upanekhat, which are a secret to be concealed and are the essence of this book, and the verses of the holy Qur'ān are literally found therein, of a certainty, therefore, the hidden book is this most ancient book, and hereby things unknown became known and things incomprehensible became comprehensible to this *faqīr*.
>
> (Hasrat 1982: 267)

Dārā Shukoh concludes his 'Preface' with a final definitive statement of what I have been calling his religious cosmopolitanism. The words of God, of which the Upaniṣads are a part, are available to all who are free of prejudice and bias:

> Happy is he who having abandoned the prejudices of vile selfishness, sincerely and with the grace of God, renouncing all partiality, shall study and comprehend this translation entitled the *Sirr-i-Akbar*, knowing it to be a translation of the words of God, shall become imperishable, fearless, unsolicitous and eternally liberated.
>
> (Hasrat 1982: 267–268)

The final sentiment sounds as if it has been inspired by the Upaniṣads themselves, and perhaps we can hear just a slight influence of his Indian source on his own thinking, overt denials that any such thing is possible notwithstanding. For although Dārā Shukoh has gone to extreme lengths to argue that there is no spiritual wisdom in the Upaniṣads that is not already contained in the Qur'ān, if only allegorically, it would not be surprising if their distinctive rhetoric of immortal freedom and release were to have infused itself into Dārā's own spiritual vision.

Meeting of two oceans

The formal translation of the Upaniṣads followed an intensive preliminary study of their contents. Two years before, Dārā Shukoh finished the composition of his great comparative masterpiece, *The Meeting-Place of the Two Oceans* (*Majmaʿ al-baḥrayn*). This is the work we must turn to if we are to understand in more detail what the migration of the Upaniṣads into Persian signified for him. A translation into Sanskrit, possibly made by Dārā himself, is entitled *Samudra-sangama* (cf. Gode 1954b.) Divided into discussions of twenty-two metaphysical topics, this work too begins with a revealing 'Preface'. Dārā states that

> Now, thus sayeth this unafflicted, unsorrowing *fakīr*, Muhammad Dārā Shukoh, that, after knowing the truth of truths and ascertaining the secrets and subtleties of the true religion of the Sūfis and having been endowed with this great gift, he thirsted to know the tenets of the religion of the Indian monotheists; and, having had repeated intercourse and discussion with the doctors and perfect divines of this religion, who had attained the highest pitch of perfection in religious exercises, comprehension, intelligence and insight, he did not find any difference, except verbal, in the way in which they sought and comprehended Truth. Consequently, having collected the views of the two parties and having brought together the points—a knowledge of which is absolutely essential and useful for the seekers of Truth—he has compiled a tract and entitled it *Majmaʿal-baḥrayn* or 'The Meeting-Point of the Two Oceans', as it is a collection of the truth and wisdom of two Truth-knowing groups.
>
> (Trans. Mahfuz-ul-Haq 1929: 38)

The extraordinary idea that Sufi and Hindu thought differ only terminologically determines the structure of the whole work, which seeks to establish notational isomorphisms in the philosophical vocabulary of the two disciplines. It is perhaps obvious that the execution of such an ambition will demand its author to be selective, and with bodies of literature as large and varied as these, careful selection will certainly be possible. With respect to the Upaniṣads, we must remember that this is itself a diverse, complex and diachronic collection of texts. Apart from the so-called 'major' Upaniṣads, the ones upon which Śaṅkara would write extensive commentaries in his attempt to impose a monistic vision in the seventh century CE, there are a great number of 'minor' and 'sectarian' Upaniṣads, the latter specifically connected with the Śaiva, Vaiṣṇava and Śakta traditions. The fifty-two chosen for inclusion in Dārā Shukoh's translation is an eclectic mix of major and minor (with none, however, from the Śakta tradition). While the very earliest Upaniṣads are probably pre-Buddhist, many of the minor ones are much later, the bulk probably in existence by the fifth or sixth century CE, a few very much more recent. It is certainly possible, then, that even if the paṇḍits with whom Dārā Shukoh sat had not relied on Śaṅkara's monistic exegeses, there would have been plenty of material in the later 'minor' and 'sectarian' Upaniṣads for him to draw upon in his search for substantial doctrinal affinities, these later Upaniṣads displaying significantly theistic elements. It is hardly surprising that from such a mass of spiritual writing, Dārā should be able to find terminological groupings that looked more or less isomorphic with those aspects of Sufi doctrine to which he wanted to give prominence. His paṇḍit guides will naturally have introduced him to the later Upaniṣ ads, both because of the greater doctrinal affinity, and also because the Sanskrit of the later verse Upaniṣads is more likely to have been accessible to him than the more difficult prose of the earlier texts.

As a reasonably representative example of Dārā Shukoh's method of notational congruence, let us take the section dealing with the self or soul (*rūḥ*). Here it is in full:

> The soul is of two kinds: (i) the (normal) soul and (ii) the Soul of souls (*abū-l-arwāḥ*), which are called *ātmā* and *paramātmā*, respectively, in the phraseology of the Indian divines. When the 'pure self' (*dhāt-i baḥt*) becomes determinate and fettered, either in respect of purity or impurity, He is known as *rūḥ* (soul), or *ātmā*, in His elegant aspect and *jasad* (body), or *śarīr*, in His inelegant aspect.[4] And the self that was determined in Eternity Past is known as *rūḥ-i aʿẓam* (or, the supreme soul) and is said to possess uniform identity with the Omniscient Being. Now, the Soul in which all the souls are included is known as *paramātmā* or *abū-l-arwāḥ*. The inter-relation between water and its waves is the same as that between body and soul or as that between *śarīr* and *ātmā*. The combination of waves, in their complete aspect, may be likened to *abū-l-arwāḥ* or *paramātmā*; while water only is like the August Existence, or *śudh* or *chitan*.
>
> (1929: 44–45)

Here we find a terminological triad. In addition to the individual soul (*rūḥ*), and its body, there is another soul (*abū-l-arwāḥ*, the 'soul of souls') in which all the individual souls are 'included', and there is also a supreme soul (*rūḥ-i aʿẓam*) that is

[4] There is certainly an echo here of Spinoza's 'double-aspect' theory, that mind and body are different modes of a single substance.

the Omniscient Being and the August Existence. Neither the relationship between the individual souls and the soul of souls, nor that between the soul of souls and the supreme soul, is stated explicitly, other than to say that the first relationship is one of 'inclusion'. Rather, these two relationships are clarified with the help of a rather beautiful metaphor: the individual souls are like waves on the surface of the ocean; the soul of souls is the single pattern of waves that includes each of them; and the supreme soul is the mass of water upon which both the individual waves and the pattern supervene.

I cannot speak of the Sufi sources on which Dārā Shukoh will have drawn in presenting this structure. What, though, of his attempt to bring it into isomorphism with terms and concepts drawn from the Indian literature? The Persian *rūḥ* is mapped onto the Sanskrit *ātman*, and the Persian *abū-l-arwāḥ* onto the Sanskrit *paramātman*. Strangely, no mapping is provided for the third element of the triad, *rūḥ-i-a'zam*, the supreme soul, a lacuna which is indicative, perhaps, of a difficulty. First, the term *paramātman* ('highest self') is not in early Upaniṣadic discourse; it is of comparatively later use. Although one Upaniṣad says 'He brings together the self in the higher self' (*Brahma*. 3), the term is most often used as a synonym for *brahman*: 'He, it is said, is indeed *brahman*, the highest self' (*Haṃsa*. 1). Yet *brahman* is also that which is defined as existing (*sat*), thinking (*cit*), and bliss (*ānanda*), and is clearly, therefore, the August Existence or Omniscient Being to which Dārā Shukoh also refers (his *śudh* is *sad* or *sat*, his *chitan* is *cetana* or *cit*). The metaphorical identification of this supreme self with the ocean is indeed a venerable Upaniṣadic one, where it functions as an image of that into which the individual rivers flow and in so doing lose their identity and individuality (*Chāndogya* 6.10.1; *Muṇḍaka* 3.2.8; *Praśna* 6.5); or, in Śaṅkara, of the metaphysical unity that the individual waves are strictly non-different from (*Brahma-sūtra-bhāṣya* 2.1.13).

It is not immediately clear how the provision of terminological mappings is meant to be explanatory of Qur'ānic doctrine. The idea, probably, is that these mappings will provide the Muslim reader with a tool with which to assimilate the Hindu texts once translated. The reader will now be able to appropriate the text as speaking about his or her own concepts, saints, and doctrines. Just as the translated *Bhagavad-gītā* would be read as an exposition of the Sufi doctrine of *mir'āt al-ḥaqā'iq* ('All is He'; Alam 2004: 97), so too Dārā Shukoh's *Meeting-Place* would furnish the essential prerequisite for a Sufi reading of the translated Upaniṣads. It is perhaps not by chance that he published this book *before* setting the translation project into motion.

Another affinity

I would like to canvass, albeit briefly and tentatively, a further explanation for the 'hermeneutical continuity' (Ernst 2003: 186) Dārā Shukoh finds between his own Sufi beliefs and the philosophy of the Upaniṣads, and for the 'subterranean cultural bonds' (Alam 2004: 96) he and other Persian-speaking scholars were to explore throughout the period. The possibility I am interested in is that what Dārā has done, in effect, is to discover within Sufism the archaic remnants of another migration. For it is possible that the translation of the Upaniṣads into Persian in 1657 was not the first time that they journeyed on an easterly wind. Many scholars have noted interesting affinities between the philosophy of the Upaniṣads and the thought of Plotinus (204–270 CE), the founder of Neoplatonism. Born in Lycopolis, Egypt, he studied philosophy in Alexandria under the enigmatic Ammonius. Wanting to study Indian philosophy in more depth, he joined the military expedition of Emperor Gordian III to Persia in 243. When Gordian was assassinated by his troops, Plotinus instead made his way to Rome, where he remained until his death. We do not know how much Indian philosophy Plotinus was able to learn, either in Alexandria or later, but similarities and parallels between his Neoplatonic doctrine and ideas to be found in the Upaniṣads, especially the later ones, are certainly striking (Staal 1961; McEvilley 2002). The incorporation of Neoplatonic thought into Islam is often considered to be one of the decisive ingredients in the formation of Sufism. Just possibly, then, what Dārā Shukoh has managed to perceive are the fragmentary remains of this much older journey of Upaniṣadic ideas, ideas that no doubt bear many signs of transformation and modification, but which nevertheless contributed to the constitution of Dārā Shukoh's own religious world view. If, as there seems to be, there was in Dārā Shukoh's mind a hint of the thought that the Upaniṣads were the ur-text of both traditions, then how appropriate for him to name his comparative masterpiece after the place in Khartum where two tributaries of the Nile rejoin *majmaʿal-baḥrayn*, 'the meeting-place of the two waters': (Qur 'ān 16:60)

Let me consider the point with reference to the doctrines about soul we have just reviewed. *Ennead* 4.3 [27] 2 reads:

> Is it not then a part in the way that a scientific theorem is said to be a part of a particular science? The science is in no way diminished, and each division is a sort of expression and actualization. In such a case each part potentially contains the whole science, which is thereby nonetheless a whole. To apply this analogy to the soul as a whole and parts: the whole whose parts are of this kind would not be the soul of something, but soul pure and simple; so it would not be the soul of the universe, but that too will be one of the partial souls. Therefore all souls are parts of a single soul and are uniform.

There is here a tripartite distinction between ordinary souls, a 'soul of souls', and the 'soul of the universe'. Each scientific theorem is a 'part' of the scientific theory as a whole, and both presuppose the mathematical system which permits their derivation. This analogy is similar in function to the one used by Dārā Shukoh, of waves and the single pattern they form, and the body of water on which they both supervene.

Another distinctively Neoplatonic idea inherited by Dārā Shukoh is that of the ascent and descent of the soul. Once again, he seeks an isomorphism with the Indian theory:

> According to certain Sūfis, the worlds, through which all created beings must needs pass, are four in number: *nūsūt* (the human world), *malakūt* (the invisible world), *jabarūt* (the highest world) and

lāhūt (the divine world) . . . According to the Indian divines the *avashāt*, which term applies to these four worlds, consists of four, namely *jāgart*, *sapan*, *sakhūpat* and *turyā*. *Jāgart* is identical with *nūsūt*, which is the world of manifestation and wakefulness; *sapan*, which is identified with *malakūt*, is the world of souls and dreams; *sakhūpat* is identical with *jabarūt*, in which the traces of both the worlds disappear and the distinction between 'I' and 'thou' vanishes . . . ; *turyā* is identical with *lāhūt*, which is Pure Existence, encircling, including and covering all the worlds. If a person journeys from the *nāsrūt* to the *malakūt* and from *malakūt* to *jabarūt* and from this last to the *lāhūt*, this will be considered as a progress on his part. But if the Truth of Truths, whom the Indian monotheists call *avasan*, descends from the stage of *lāhūt* to that of *malahūt* and thence to *jabarūt*, His journey terminates in *māsūt*. And the fact that certain Sufis have described the stages of descent as four, while others as five, is a reference to this fact.

(1929: 45–47)

It is not difficult to identify the Upaniṣadic source for the doctrine Dārā Shukoh speaks about here; it is the Māṇḍūkya description of the constitution of the self.[5] A world made of ordinary experience, a world made of dreams, a world characterized by the absence of dreams or experience, and a world uncharacterizable in terms either of their presence or their absence—this elegant model of the mental spaces available for human habitation is brought into isomorphism with a Sufi account of four worlds the passage through which is a form of spiritual progress or descent. The ultimate source of Dārā Shukoh's account of the twofold journey is again Plotinus, who describes the soul's descent in 'emanation' from The One, through Noûs ('intellect'), to Psyche ('soul'), and down to the world of the senses, and back up in a process of 'contemplation' (*Ennead* 4.8, 1.6).

The Upaniṣadic texts were welcomed by Dārā Shukoh as a stranger might be, not as someone with knowledge of their own to offer, but as offering external comment on one's own endeavour. The stranger is a means by which we see ourselves more clearly. For Dārā, that is exactly how the importation of the Upaniṣads into Persianate Islam was justified: they enabled the Sufi seeker to find answers to his own questions. The migrating text performs an important service to the tradition that hosts it, but a service largely extrinsic to itself. Allowing itself to be so used is perhaps the way for the migrating text to retain its own secrets.

Dārā's project led him to be condemned for heresy and executed by Aurangzeb in 1659. I cannot help but concur with the assessment of P. K. Gode: 'Dārā died a Socratic death' (Gode 1954b: 446). His legacy remained though, not least in that he had used his patronage to create a space within which philosophers from distinct intellectual worlds came together and collaborated. Dāniṣmand Khān would attempt to do the same, albeit on an incomparably smaller scale, as would some of the Muslim and Hindu rulers of Bengal (as I will describe in Chapter 4).

[5] Māṇḍūkya 1–7.

3

The Cosmopolitan Vision of Yaśovijaya Gaṇi

The idea that there is no one unique way of describing, depicting, representing, or otherwise capturing in thought the shared space we inhabit is nowadays associated with the work of Nelson Goodman (1978). 'Made worlds'—versions, views, renderings—differ, he claims, from one another as a novel might differ from a painting, or a poem from a news report. If that is right, and if we nevertheless want to be able to speak of conflict and consistency *between* worlds, then our standards of comparison and measures of rightness must appeal to considerations other than merely correspondence with the truth. Goodman therefore says that

> So long as contrasting right versions not all reducible to one are countenanced, unity is to be sought not in an ambivalent or neutral something beneath these versions but in an overall organization embracing them.
>
> (Goodman 1978: 5)

The notion of a 'made world' performs much of the same conceptual work as is done by its counterpart in Jainism, the concept of a *naya*, a perspective, standpoint or attitude within which experience is ordered and statements are evaluated (Matilal 1998: 133). With the Jainas too, a prominent thought is that conflicting right views are to be brought together not by trying to show that there is, after all, some single truth underneath, of which the views are but different modes of presentation, but rather that there is a coordinating unity above, to which each view makes a proper but partial contribution.

This familiar distinction between top-down and bottom-up models of unity is one much in evidence in recent discourse about cosmopolitanism. In favour of a top-down approach, for example, it has been said that 'transdisciplinary knowledge, in the cosmopolitan cause, is more readily a translational process of culture's inbetweenness than a transcendent knowledge of what lies beyond difference, in some common pursuit of the universality of the human experience' (Bhabha *et al.* 2002: 6f.). The idea that different viewpoints are co-inhabitants in a single matrix, and to that extent susceptible to syncretism, is what distinguishes the cosmopolitan vision from pluralism, whose cardinal tenet is that the irreconcilable absence of consensus is itself something of political, social, or philosophical value.

In early modern India these thoughts assumed a political as well as philosophical importance. For much of the sixteenth and seventeenth centuries, as we saw in the last chapter, the Sufi doctrine of *waḥdat al-wujūd* guided a quest for a single spiritual vision underpinning all religions. I described there how Hindu texts were translated into Persian in the belief that, suitably decoded, they could be read as speaking about that divine unity which is the proper concern of the Islamic mystic. The thought that the texts of other religions are, in Carl Ernst's (2003: 186) phrase, 'hermeneutically continuous' with the Qur'ān, served as the guiding force in an extensive translational exercise patronized by the Persianate court from Akbar through to Dārā Shukoh. This project was certainly neither pluralist nor syncretic, but nevertheless recognized the existence of a common religious space available for joint occupation by a plurality of religions.

Studying the 'new reason' in Vārāṇasī

It is in the context of these political and philosophical movements that I would like to examine the work of one of Jainism's great intellectuals, Yaśovijaya Gaṇi. Born in Gujarat in 1624, he died there in 1688 after a long and varied career. The Gujarat of his day was home to a diverse trading population, including Arab, Persian, Tartar, Armenian, Dutch, French, and English mercantile communities (Desai 1910: 54). Roughly speaking, Yaśovijaya's intellectual biography can be seen as falling under three heads: an apprenticeship in Vārāṇasī studying the new reason, a period writing Jaina philosophical treatises adapting the techniques and methods of the new reason, and a time spent writing works exploring the nature of the individual self.

Yaśovijaya's extended stay at a Nyāya teaching centre in Vārāṇasī lasted perhaps twelve years (from around 1642 to about 1654); certainly, it was enough to provide him, according to his own testament, with a broad knowledge of the new reason and to earn him the respectable title Nyāya-viśārada, 'One who is skilled in reason' (Yaśovijaya 1966: 181). According to some accounts, he came to Vārāṇasī in the company of his teacher Nayavijaya, both having disguised themselves as brahmins in order to gain admission. Since, however, there are reports of Buddhists from Tibet travelling to India to study Nyāya, and since, after all, teaching was the chief livelihood of the Nyāya paṇḍit, the veracity of this story is open to doubt. As for the identity of the ṭol to which Yaśovijaya was enrolled, it has been conjectured that it was the one headed by Raghudeva Nyāyālaṃkāra, primarily on the basis of the fact that Yaśovijaya mentions him by name.[1] Raghudeva did live in Vārāṇasī and was a prominent public intellectual of the period. Yaśovijaya, however, is *openly* critical of the founding figure of the new reason, Raghunātha Śiromaṇi (1966: 75, 96). I think that his teacher might therefore have been another prominent Vārāṇasī Naiyāyika of the

[1] Vidyabhusana 1910: 468; Kaviraj 1965: 79; cf. Jain 2006: 134.

same period, Govinda Śarman, the son of Rudra Nyāya-vācaspati. Rudra, as I will show below, was *openly* critical of Raghunātha.

One of the decisive events in Yaśovijaya's change in intellectual focus and turn towards the philosophy of the self was his meeting with the poet Ānanda-ghanjī (Desai 1910: 22). Before this, however, Yaśovijaya had produced several of the finest works in Jaina epistemology, including the *Jaina Language of Reason* and the *Jaina Amassed Morsels of Reason*, utilizing the methods of the new reason in a reformulation of Jaina thought, and indeed he provided an extended critique of 'new reason' assumptions from an outsider's perspective. He would write a treatise on the problem of ownership (*svatva*), about which the 'new reason' thinkers worked extensively (and he refers there to another one of them, Rāmabhadra; see Kroll 2010). It is of particular interest to see how Yaśovijaya takes the Nyāya idea that a single object can have an emergent colour (*citra-rūpa*)—for example, the single colour of a pot whose parts are blue and red—and how he carefully distinguishes their explanation of the way a single reality can have apparently mutually excluding properties from the Jaina explanation in terms of non-onesidedness (*anekānta-vāda*) (Yaśovijaya 1966; cf. Krishna 2001: 283). Yaśovijaya's bold ambition is to achieve a transformation of the 'new reason' itself. The importance of these ideas was not to be lost in the later works which will be my concern shortly, works in which a variety of ethical themes are explored within a non-onesidedness framework, including the moral and intellectual virtues worthy of cultivation, the nature of spiritual exercises, the idea of a spiritual path and its analogy with a medicine for the soul, and the concept of that self for the benefit of which all these virtues and practices are developed.

Secular intellectual values

In one of his ethical works, the *Essence of Knowledge*, Yaśovijaya systematically describes thirty-two moral and intellectual virtues jointly constitutive of a virtuous character. Many would be equally familiar to a Buddhist, Muslim or Hindu, but two are distinctive: neutrality (*madhyasthatā*) and groundedness in all viewpoints (*sarva-nayāś-raya*). Neutrality is explained in terms of the dispassionate use of reason: a person who embodies this virtue follows wherever reason leads, rather than using reason only to defend prior opinions to which they have already been attracted (Yaśovijaya 1973: 16.2). Yaśovijaya stresses that neutrality is not an end in itself, but rather that it is a means to another end. We adopt a neutral attitude, he says, in the hope that this will lead to wellbeing (*hita*), just as someone who knows that one among a group of herbs is restorative but does not know which one it is, acts reasonably if they swallow the entire lot (1973: 16.8). As we can see from this example, philosophy is thought of as a medicine for the soul, the value of a doctrine to be judged by its effectiveness in curing the soul of its ailments (Ganeri and Carlisle 2010). That is why it can be reasonable to endorse several complementary philosophical views simultaneously, just as one can take a variety of complementary medicines.

Being 'grounded in all viewpoints' means giving to each viewpoint its proper weight within the total picture. The benefit that accrues from this is again linked to the use of reason, this time the ability to engage in reasonable public discourse. Someone who is so grounded can enter into a beneficial discussion about religion and ethics (*dharma*); otherwise the talk is just empty quarrelling (*śuṣkavāda-vivāda*) (1973: 32.5). For Yaśovijaya in the *Essence of Knowledge*, the final goal to which the cultivation of these and the other virtues leads is the soul's fulfilment, a fulfilment consisting in 'consciousness, bliss and truth' (*saccidānanda*) (1973: 1.1). The idea that assuming a neutral attitude towards all views is the way to fulfilment is partially reminiscent of Greek Pyhrronism, where it is argued that developing an attitude of indiscriminate refusal to assent to any view (*epoche*) is the means to achieve that tranquillity of mind (*ataraxia*) necessary for happiness (*eudaimonia*).

Paul Dundas (2004) has shown how, in the *Examination of Moral Duty*, Yaśovijaya uses the concept of neutrality as the basis for an irenic strategy towards other religions. Followers of other religious traditions can be considered as conforming to the true path if their attitude towards the doctrines of their own tradition is sufficiently non-dogmatic. Dundas worries, reasonably enough, that in spite of being inclusivist, such a position nevertheless does still assert the superiority of the Jaina path. Perhaps that is why, in the *Treatise on the Concealed Teaching about the Self*, Yaśovijaya advances another strategy. He now argues that the virtues to which Jainism gives particular prominence, namely impartiality, neutrality, and non-onesidedness, are in fact already present in the various non-Jaina disciplines, albeit in an only implicit form. For all the disciplines seek an 'overarching organisation' when it comes to sorting out and arranging their internal doctrinal claims. All therefore do embody the quintessential Jaina principles and virtues in their own theoretical practice, whether or not those principles and virtues receive any explicit mention in the official meta-theory.

Let me examine this idea in more detail. Yaśovijaya argues that no body of 'theory' (*śāstra*), whether Jaina or non-Jaina, is to be accepted merely on the basis of sectarian interest. Instead, the theory should be subject to testing, just as the purity of a sample of gold is determined by tests involving rubbing, cutting, and heating (1938: 1.17). In a body of theory, the relevant test is to see whether the various prescriptive and prohibitive statements pertaining to some one issue 'rub together', that is to say, whether they cohere with one another and pull in the same direction (1938: 1.18). For example, in Jainism the prescriptions concerning religious meditation and the prohibitions on the use of violence are coordinate and together pull in the direction of liberation (1938: 1.19). In practice, of course, no reasonably large and complex body of theory will meet this test, nor can coherence be manufactured simply by 'cutting out' some statements and keeping others. The only method for dealing with such apparent incoherences as inevitably do arise is the method of conditionalized assertion (*syādvāda*) and non-onesidedness (*ānekāntya*). To say that the soul is eternal is to depict human subjectivity in one way; to say that the soul is non-eternal is to depict it in another: both depictions, in their own way, gesture at something right about what it is to be a human subject.

Yaśovijaya then shows how each of the non-Jaina disciplines does incorporate the spirit, if not the letter, of the principle of non-onesidedness (1938: 1.45–52). Referring by name to Sāṃkhya, Vijñānavāda Buddhism, Vaiśeṣika, the three Mīmāṃsaka schools of Kumārila, Prabhākara and Murāri, and Advaita Vedānta, he concludes that 'conditionalised assertion' (*syādvāda*) is a doctrine of all the disciplines (1938: 1.51). The Vedāntins, for example, say that the soul is both bound and unbound, relativizing those statements to the conventional and the absolute in order to avoid contradiction. Likewise, Kumārila says that entities are both particular and universal, conditioning these claims upon aspects of experience.

Yaśovijaya concludes by bringing the discussion back to the cultivation of an attitude of neutrality. All the different disciplines of belief are equal in requiring of their practitioners that they adopt an attitude of balance and coordination; indeed this balance and neutrality is the very point of *śāstra*. True religious and moral discourse (*dharmavāda*) is based on this; the rest is just a sort of foolish hopping about (*bāliśa-valgana*) (1938: 1.71). It is worth emphasizing that Yaśovijaya by no means considers the doctrines of conditionalized assertion and non-onesidedness to lead to a laissez-faire relativism, for he explicitly here dismisses the Cārvāka as being too confused in their understanding of the topic of liberation even to be said to have a 'view' (1938: 1.52). Neutrality does not mean acceptance of every position whatever, but acceptance only of those which satisfy at least the minimal criteria of clarity and coherence needed in order legitimately to constitute a point of view.[2]

Reflections on the self

We have seen that Yaśovijaya first identifies certain moral and intellectual virtues as being quintessentially Jaina, and how he then argues that if non-Jaina disciplines understood the nature of their own practice more clearly, they would see that they too embed those virtues in their conception of the philosophical path. I have also noted that the embodiment of those virtues is thought of as a means to some further end. In a final step, Yaśovijaya argues that the equanimity which is the end of the Jaina path is consistent with the realization of that self consisting of truth, bliss, and consciousness, also spoken of in the Upaniṣads and the *Gītā*.

In the first chapter of the *Treatise on the Concealed Teachings*, Yaśovijaya identifies two perspectives on the self. From a strictly etymological perspective, it is the one who performs a variety of actions and activities, while from the perspective of ordinary linguistic practice it is the mind as endowed with virtuous qualities like friendliness (1938: 1.2–4). In the second chapter, however, Yaśovijaya describes the state of true

[2] There is, in fact, nothing confused about the Cārvāka view; what they do however is to deny a fundamental presupposition shared by the other disciplines, namely that there is life after death.

self-awareness in decidedly Upaniṣadic terms, a state which is beyond deep sleep, beyond conceptualization, and beyond linguistic representation, and he says that it is the duty of any good *śāstra* to point out the existence and possibility of such states of true self-awareness, for they cannot be discovered by reason or experience alone. How, then, should these two visions of the self be organized, the one consisting in pure bliss and undivided consciousness, the other of a multitude of individual agents? One might have expected Yaśovijaya to say that both have their proper place in a non-onesided attitude towards selfhood, but in fact he gives clear preferential weighting to the unitary conception of self (a conception which he also identifies, in the final chapter, with *samatā*, a state of pure equanimity). That comes out most clearly in still another of his works, the *Essence of the Self*, where he states unequivocally that the apparent multiplicity of selves is an illusion, likening it to the illusion of a multitude of moons caused by eye disease (1973: 18.13, 20). Having repeated once again that the self consists in truth, consciousness, and bliss, he quotes with approval *Bhagavad-gītā* 3.42: 'The senses are high, so they say. Higher than the senses is the mind; higher than the mind is thought; while higher than thought is He (the soul)' (1973: 18.39–40). This is the spiritual fullness which Yaśovijaya has told us is the outcome of the exercise of neutrality and groundedness in all viewpoints. Both the *Essence* and the *Treatise*, we can note, are sprinkled with references to the *Bhagavad-gītā* and the Upaniṣads.[3]

Yaśovijaya and Dārā Shukoh: a cosmopolitan ideal

With this synopsis of the development of Yaśovijaya's thought, let me return to the political context in which he lived, and in particular to the religious cosmopolitanism of Dārā Shukoh. It was in 1656, at just around the time when Yaśovijaya completed his studies in Vārāṇasī, that Dārā Shukoh himself assembled in Vārāṇasī a team of the most renowned Sanskrit paṇḍits to help him execute his plan of translating the Hindu scriptures, or at least those of them that were 'hermeneutically continuous' with the Qur'ān. As noted in the last chapter, he was to supervise the translation into Persian of fifty-two Upaniṣads, of the *Yoga-vāsiṣṭha* and of the *Bhagavad-gītā*, all of which, he believed could be read as speaking of the divine unity, if one mapped their terminology into that of Sufism in accordance with the notational isomorphisms he had already established, in a book entitled *The Meeting-Place of the Two Oceans* (*Majma'al-bahrayn*), the title indicative of a conception of Hinduism and Islam as coming together at a point of confluence. In the 'Preface' to his translation of the Upaniṣads, Dārā Shukoh tells us that

> As at this period the city of Benares, which is the centre of the sciences of this community, was in certain relations with this seeker of the Truth [sc. Dārā Sukoh], he assembled together the paṇḍits and sannyāsis who were the most learned of their time and proficient in the *Upanekhat*, he himself

[3] See Kansara 1976; Shastri 1991; Krishna 2001: 284.

being free from all materialistic motives, translated the essential parts of monotheism, which are the *Upanekhat*, i.e. the secrets to be concealed, and the end of purport of all the saints of God, in the year 1067 AH [1657 CE].

(Hasrat 1982: 266)

That Yaśovijaya would have had a keen interest in Dārā Shukoh's inclusivist project, had he known about it, is certain. And it seems hard to imagine that he could not have known about it given the high status of the project, which gave employment to a great number of the most celebrated Sanskrit intellectuals of the day, and given also its pivotal role in one of the most momentous events of the epoch, providing Aurangzeb with an excuse to brand Dārā Shukoh a heretic and arrange for his execution (having already imprisoned their ailing father, Shāh Jahaṇ), thereby usurping the Mughal throne. Yaśovijaya was eventually to return to Gujarat, but according to a curious detail in his biography, he went first to Agra, the location of the Mughal throne, and continued his work there for a few years (Jain 2006: 134). Whether true or not, and one cannot be entirely sure, the detail is indicative of the circulation of both people and ideas at this time between centres of Islamic and Hindu intellectual influence.

Yaśovijaya, I have suggested, sought a top-down account of the unity to which the various viewpoints are susceptible, a unity grounded in a shared appreciation of the intellectual virtues associated with the 'translational process of cultures' inbetweenness'. I have also suggested that he felt a considerable pull towards another account of unity, the bottom-up account represented by his interest in spiritual unity and Upaniṣadic imagery. This second move would have served to bring his thinking into line with the 'unity of being' ideology currently in vogue in the centres of political power. The tension in Yaśovijaya's conception of a supra-religious community of individuals is apparent in the way he invokes that celebrated metaphor of identity-and-difference, the metaphor of the ocean and its waves. Yaśovijaya says:

The divisions born from the [various] standpoints are merged in a great universal form, just as the huge waves generated by strong winds in the ocean.

(1938: 2.41)

That seems both to recapitulate the Vedāntic use of the image of waves not different from the body of water that is the ocean and yet retaining their separate identity (e.g. *Brahma-sūtra-bhāṣya* 2.1.13), but also to hint that it is the emergent pattern produced by their interaction in which the unity is to be found. The ability to see this picture comes, however, with the cultivation of the distinctively Jaina virtues of neutrality and impartiality, which for Yaśovijaya are the grounding cosmopolitan virtues in a multi-faith community.

Dārā Shukoh appeals to the very same metaphor, again giving it a distinctive twist. To quote the passage again:

The inter-relation between water and its waves is the same as that between body and soul or as that between *śarīra* and *ātmā*. The combination of waves, in their complete aspect, may be likened to *abul-arwāḥ* or *paramātmā*; while water only is like the August Existence, or *sudh* or *chitan*.

(Dārā Shukoh 1929: 44f.)

Here we have on display the two models of unity with which I began, the model represented by the single pattern created by the waves in interaction with each other, and the model signified by the body of water itself, to which all the waves belong. In Yaśovijaya's case, however, the unifying conception is more like that of a shattered mirror, in which each fragment reflects some part or aspect of the reflected object, a representation of which is to be built up by reconstructing all the partial images, whereas for Dārā it is as if multiple images of some one thing, some clearer and some indistinct, are reflected in the surfaces of parallel facing mirrors.

Where one might have expected the Jaina Yaśovijaya to espouse the top-down model, and the Sufi Dārā Shukoh the bottom-up one, what one finds instead is a desire in each thinker to offer some accommodation to both. And perhaps, indeed, a robust religious cosmopolitanism does require there to be space for both a unifying vision and a vision of unity. Yaśovijaya and Dārā Shukoh have something else in common too, an extraordinary willingness to draw upon other intellectual cultures in the interpretation of their own. For Dārā this was the motivation for engaging in the translation of the Upaniṣads, while in Yaśovijaya's case it is a prerequisite intellectual value for engaging in public reason. Their 'idea of India' is one Tagore would have recognized.

In the time of Dārā and Yaśovijaya, the 'new reason' philosophy was in the middle of its most creative and flourishing period, an extremely important and powerful presence on the intellectual landscape. One of its most significant voices—Jayarāma—was close to Kavīndra Sarasvatī, the paṇḍit in Dārā's team who probably became Bernier's philosophical discussant. Another—perhaps Govinda Śarman or else Raghudeva—taught Yaśovijaya in Vārāṇasī. All three were prominent and prolific public intellectuals, no doubt aware of intellectual movements in early modern Islamic and Jaina thought. I will now turn to a detailed analysis of the circumstances in which the 'new reason' came into being, the influences on its founder, and the causes of its decline. In a later chapter I will explore in more detail its connections with the Mughal court.

4

Navadvīpa: A Place of Hindu–Muslim Confluence in Bengal

Raghunātha Śiromaṇi is the first modern philosopher, his ideas single-handedly responsible for the emergence of the 'new reason' in the sixteenth and seventeenth centuries. He grew up and lived in the remarkable town of Navadvīpa, a town roughly a hundred kilometres north of modern day Kolkata. I would like first of all to tell the story of how this town came to be the intellectual focal point that it was in the early modern world—the fascinating story sheds important light on the origins of the 'new reason' philosophy. Many modern Indians continue to this day to celebrate Navadvīpa as the birthplace of the religious reformer Caitanya, who was Raghunātha's peer and, at least according to legend, the student of a common teacher. I will then examine Raghunātha's achievement, and identify reasons why he was able to follow a *via moderna* and reject the *via antiqua* of his predecessors, and what, for him, following that course consisted in. Finally, I will look at the reasons that lie behind the eighteenth century collapse of Navadvīpa as an important intellectual centre.

In the fifteenth, sixteenth, and seventeenth centuries, the town of Navadvīpa, which is also known by its Latinized name Nadia or Nuddea, was one of the great sites of scholarship in South Asia. Students from all over the subcontinent, indeed from Nepal and possibly even Tibet, were attracted to a strict programme of studies in the 'new reason' a vigorous intellectual community, and the eventual prospect of prestigious certification by title. The programme of studies was provided in ṭols run by a series of celebrated paṇḍits, whose more important works were frequently transcribed and swiftly distributed throughout India. What made this city into the place it was? The socio-political history of the region during the period is complex: periods of stability and patronage for brahminical learning are interspersed with times of social upheaval and political unrest. Considerable historical documentation relates to Navadvīpa in the period, in the form of Islamic histories of Bengal, biographies-cum-hagiographies of the Vaiṣṇava saint Caitanya, documentation internal to the scholarly community of Navadvīpa, chronicles of the Mughal court, and, for the final years, the records of the East India Company. Comparison of the historical evidence with the preserved manuscript corpus strongly affirms a correlation between state or royal patronage, political stability, and degree of philosophical activity. Adequate fiscal support emerges as a crucial determinant of healthy scholarship, patronage that came initially from a liberal Islamic–Bengali sultanate and later from the regional Hindu kingdoms. The collapse of traditional systems of education is a key factor in the eventual decline of Navadvīpa as a dynamic intellectual centre.

A Bengali sultanate independent of Delhi

Our earliest reference to Navadvīpa is in Minhāj-i-Sirāj's *Ṭabaqāt-i Nāṣirī* (c. 1260 CE). Its author claims to have spent a number of months in Navadvīpa, and relates the events surrounding the successful conquest of Bengal by Muḥammad Bakhtyār Khaljī.[1] The city had been established by the Bengali king Lakṣmaṇa-sena (r. 1179–1206) as but one of a series of capital cities for the Sena Kingdom.[2] Khaljī, although nominally under the command of Quṭb-ud-dīn Aybak, enjoyed considerable military autonomy, and successfully drove Lakṣmaṇa-sena from Navadvīpa in a raid on the city in 1206, ending the Sena dynasty and creating the conditions for an Islamic Bengal politically independent of the Northern Indian sultanate, eventually drawing Bengal into relationship with the *khalifah* of Baghdad and a wider Muslim world. Sufis began to come to Bengal under the Khalji dynasty, the first perhaps being Shaykh Jalāl-ud-dīn Tabrīzī (Karim 1985: 40, 123–128). Clerical scholars too were drawn to the province, including the *qāḍī* Rukn-ud-din Samarqandī, who translated the *Amṛta-kuṇda*, a work of tantric mysticism, from Sanskrit into Arabic and Persian under the title *Ḥauḍ al-ḥayāt*. The *Amṛta-kuṇda* is itself a composition of Bhojar Brahman, a Hindu who arrived in Bengal from Kāṃrūpa in order to converse with the Muslim religioso, his subsequent discussions with Samarqandī ending with his conversion to Islam (Tarafdar 1965: 16, 221; Yousuf Husain 1928). This curious synthesis of Yoga and Sufism established a long tradition of syncretic writing in Bengal, and is an early indication of Bengali Muslim receptiveness to Sanskrit scholarship.

Bengal would be independent from Delhi throughout much of the next three centuries, resisting pressure from the Mughal sultanate. Ilyās Shāh (r. 1342–1358) repelled Fīrūz Shāh Tughluq's attempts to invade Bengal in 1353–54, and his son again in 1359–60. In 1415, the Shāhi sultanate fell to an internal rebellion led by the Hindu chief Rājā Ganeśa, one of many Hindus employed as officers to the

[1] See Roy 1941 for a critical translation of the relevant passage, and also for the account of the raid in 'Iṣāmī's *Futūḥ-al-salāṭīn* (c. 1350). Both accounts imply that Khalji arrived in Navadvīpa with an army, but masqueraded as a trader in order to dupe Lakṣmaṇa-sena. The popular story that he took the city with only eighteen horsemen, and that Lakṣmaṇa-sena put up only token resistance, is based on a mistranslation of the critical passage. Roy also reports that Abū-l-Fażl, in the *Ā'īn-i Akbarī* (1597 CE), says that 'at the time of Lakṣmaṇa-sena, Nadiyā was the capital city of Bengal, when it abounded with wisdom, but now it is thinly inhabited, although it is still conspicuous for learning.' Khalji's troops were responsible for the infamous sacking of the Buddhist monastery and university at Nālandā in 1193.

[2] The Sena dynasty, had naturally sponsored śāstric scholarship. Even earlier Bengali philosophers include Gauḍapāda (c. seventh to eighth centuries), Śrīdhara Bhaṭṭa (fl. 991), and possibly also Śrīharṣa (c. 1075–1160), whose important critique of the epistemological principles and methods of inquiry of the old Nyāya was one of the factors leading to Gaṅgeśa's reformulation. On the question of Śrīharṣa's Bengali roots, see Nilkamal Bhattacharya 1924; Majumdār 1971: 358–361, 395–398; Jani 1996; Granoff 1978.

administration. Rājā Ganeśa faced, however, the opposition of the renowned Chishtī saint Nūr Quṭb-i ʿĀlam, who invited Ibrāhīm Sharqī to invade Bengal. In order to assuage the situation, Rājā Ganeśa agreed with Nūr Qut-i-Alam that his son Jadu convert to Islam and be instated on the throne (Karim 1985: 48–51). Jalāl-ud-dīn Muḥammad, as the Hindu prince Jadu was henceforth known, embraced his new faith, and sought to fend off the encroachment of Sharqi influence first by building diplomatic ties with Egypt and China, and second by assuming the title *khalīfatullāh*, a move designed to appeal to the *Sunnī* leadership in Bengal (Tarafdar 1965: 4).

A brief period of rule by the family of Rājā Ganeśa, during which Bengali has become an official court language (Easton 1992: 169, based on the reports of contemporary Chinese travellers to Bengal), ends in 1435 with the restoration of the Ilyās Shāhi dynasty. The restored Sultan Naṣīr-ud-dīn Maḥmūd Shāh continues to promote Bengali literature and employs Hindus in key positions. Patronage of Brahminical literature is evident during the reign of Rukn-ud-dīn Barbak Shāh (r. 1459–74; on his patronage, see Easton 1992: 172), who also introduces a great number of Ethiopian or habshi slaves for his army. The Ilyās Shāhi dynasty ends abruptly in 1486, when those same slaves murder the last of the Ilyās Shāhi monarchs, Jalāl-ud-dīn Fātiḥ Shāh (r. 1481–86), and usurp the throne, initiating a brief period of Abyssinian rule in Bengal that lasts until 1493. In that year, Sultan ʿAlāʾ-ud-dīn Ḥusayn Shāh (r. 1493–1519), minister to the last Abyssinian king Muẓaffar Shāh, assumes the throne, and thus begins a period of rule under which brahminical scholarship flourishes and Navadvīpa emerges as the great centre for Navya Nyāya studies on the Indian subcontinent—the end result of an extended process of symbiosis in which Bengalification of the Islamic ran hand-in-hand with Islamicization of Bengalis.

The curious biography of a teacher

The achievement of Husain Shāh's dynasty lies in its securing of the territorial borders of Bengal, its resolution of tension with the Delhi sultanate, and its creation of stable institutions of social and political organization. Ḥusayn Shāh's military campaigns include the annexation of much of Bihar, occupation of the important city-port of Chittagong, conquest of Kāṃrūpa, and failed attempts in Orissa and Tippera. The last ruler of the Sharqi dynasty, also named Ḥusayn Shāh, had already been thoroughly defeated by Sikandar Lodhi in 1494, and was forced to seek refuge under his namesake in Bengal, bringing with him an important literati. The defeat of an army sent by Sikander to conquer Bengal resulted in Ḥusayn Shāh's concluding a peace treaty with the Delhi sultanate, under the terms of which neither party should attack the other or give shelter to their mutual enemies. Domestically, the administration appears to have been unusually liberal and tolerant, Ḥusayn giving a range of important positions to Hindu officers in his government. Tarafdar (1965: 64) summarizes the evidence from Vaiṣṇava sources:

Rūpa was the *Sākar Mallik* [chief secretary of state] and Sanātana the *Dabīr-i khāṣṣ* [private secretary] to the sultan. Rām Chandra Khān enjoyed a small estate in south-west Bengal. Similar was the case with the Majumdār family to which Hiraṇya Dās and Govardhan Dās belonged. Jagāi and Mādhāi were the *kotwāls* of Navadvīpa. Gopinātha Vasu, his minister, Mukunda-dās, his private physician, Keshava Khān Chhatrī, the chief of his bodyguards and Anupa, in charge of the mint, were Hindus.

Ḥusayn's governor in Chittagong, Parāgal Khān, commissioned the adaptation of the *Mahābhārata* into Bengali, the first translator being Kavīndra Parameśvara, followed by the poet Śrīkara Nandī, who received patronage from Parāgal's son Chhuṭi. The considerable literature in vernacular Bengali written under the reign of Ḥusayn Shāh includes Vijaya Gupta's *Padma-purāṇa*, the *Manasā-vijaya* of Vipradāsa Piplai, and Caṇḍīdāsa's *Śrīkṛṣṇakīrtana* (Tarafdar 1965: 241–251; Eaton 1992: 172). It is from the Vaiṣṇava biographies of the saint Caitanya (1486–1533) that further information can be gathered about the reception of brahminical scholarship during the period of the Ḥusayn Shāhi dynasty.

Vāsudeva Sārvabhauma[3], Raghunātha's tutor, had by this time already begun to establish Navya Nyāya in Navadvīpa. Although not the only Bengali to train in Mithilā, it is he who returned from Mithilī to Bengal carrying with him knowledge of contemporary Maithilī scholarship sufficient to establish a new school. He is the son of Maheśvara Viśārada, a *rāḍhi* brahmin of Vidyānagara in Navadvīpa.[4] It has been suggested that Vāsudeva fled Navadvīpa for Puri during a purge on brahmins under the reign of Ḥusayn Shāh (see for example Ingalls 1951; G. Bhattacharya 1976: 81). The textual source for the suggestion is a passage in the *Caitanya-maṅgala* of Jayānanda:

> Vāsudeva Sārvabhauma, son of Viśārada, removed to Orissa, leaving Bengal. The king of Orissa was then the illustrious Pratāparudra, famous for his valour in war. He worshipped the great scholar of Navadvīpa, presenting him with a golden throne. The brother of [Vāsudeva] Sārvabauma was Vidyāvācaspati, who remained in Gauḍa [Bengal], and their father Viśārada proceeded to Vārāṇasī, where he settled.[5]

The difficulty in identifying the Bengali king responsible for the purge with Husain Shāh is simply that this event is also situated by the *Caitanya-maṅgala* as happening during a famine shortly before Caitanya's birth, i.e. in 1486. O'Connell (1983: 302) therefore presumes that the king in question is Jalāl-ud-dīn Fātiḥ Shāh, and that

[3] P 921. Fl. c.1440–1540 (Gopikamohan Bhattacharya 1976: 81 suggests c. 1430–1530, but this requires some adjustment, for Vāsudeva was still alive when Caitanya died in 1533, and indeed went to live in Vārāṇasī thereafter). I will highlight the names of important 'new reason' philosophers in bold. 'P' stands for the person's entry in Potter's *Bibliography of Indian Philosophies*.

[4] Kaviraja 1961: 50.

[5] viśārad suta sārvabhauma bhaṭṭācārya| svayam utkale gela chāḍī gauḍa rājya|| utkale pratāparudra dhanurmay rājā| ratnasiṃhāsane sārvabhaume kaila pūjā|| tār bhrātā vidyāvācaspati gauḍavāsī| viṣārad nivās karilā vārāṇasī|| *Caitanya-maṅgala* 2.4 passim (quoted in Kaviraja 1961: 53). Kaviraja notices how many of the remaining mss of this family are now held in Vārāṇasī, and speculates that Viśārada took his private library there on retirement.

Pratāparudra was at some point the king during Vāsudeva's stay in Orissa, but not at the very time he arrived.[6] The implication of the story, if at all reliable, is that Vāsudeva had returned from Mithilā to Navadvīpa some time considerably before 1486, this being the year in which he fled Navadvīpa for Puri, where he would eventually receive the patronage of Pratāparudra of the Gajapati dynasty of Orissa (r. 1497–1525).

Caitanya himself was born in Navadvīpa in 1486, and lived there, even setting up a small ṭol, until a religious experience in Gayā at the age of twenty-two led him to become a *saṃnyāsin* in the Advaita-Vedāntic order of Keśava Bhāratī. It appears from the biographies that he left Navadvīpa for Puri in 1510, the beginning of a long pilgrimage to the south and west. In Puri he met and impressed Vāsudeva, already well established there, who invited him to sit in on his lectures on Vedānta.[7] Caitanya returned to Puri after five years, and remained there until his death in 1533. He again met Vāsudeva, who indeed outlived him.[8]

Vāsudeva is said by the tradition to have had four brilliant students: Caitanya, Raghunātha Śiromaṇi, Raghunandana, and Kṛṣṇānanda. With the exception of Raghunātha, this tradition is very questionable.[9] The only instruction Vāsudeva is known to have given Caitanya were the lectures Caitanya attended during his brief first visit to Puri in 1510; certainly there is no reason to think that Vāsudeva ever taught the young Caitanya in Navadvīpa. As for Raghunandana (1520–70; see Derrett 1973b: 56, n.358), the father of the Bengal school of Hindu law, there is no evidence at all of his having studied with Vāsudeva. Vāsudeva certainly, however, did have an important influence on the later development of Navya Nyāya scholarship in Navadvīpa. He trained his son, Janeśvara Vāhinīpati Bhaṭṭācārya Mahāpātra.[10] Vāhinīpati probably grew up and lived in Orissa, for the title 'Mahāpātra' is not Bengali but Orissan. A second, more important, channel of influence runs through his younger brother, Viṣṇudāsa (or Ratnākara) **Vidyāvācaspati**.[11] Vidyāvācaspati, as we saw, is referred to in the *Caitanya-maṅgala* as staying behind when Vāsudeva leaves Navadvīpa, but also in

[6] Jayānanda's report is summarized in O'Connell (1983: 302) as follows: 'At that time a rumour was circulating that the Brahmans of Navadvīpa were expecting a Brahman from their town to take power as king of Gauṛ. The hostile Yavanas of Piralyā for a while had the cooperation of the king in persecution of the Brahmans of Navadvīpa for their alleged sedition. During the persecution some noted Brahman scholars [the list of names mentions Viśārada] left Navadvīpa, among them Sārvabhauma Bhaṭṭācārya, the logician who eventually became a devotee while serving as a court paṇḍit for Pratāpa Rudra in Orissa. The Sultan, sobered by the loss of such valuable personnel and terrified by a vision of the Goddess Kālī, halted the persecution, compensated the victims, and assisted Navadvīpa to become the thriving town it was during Caitanya's years of residence there.'

[7] *Caitanya-caritāmṛta* 2.6; see Dimock and Stewart 1999: 15, 402–422. His commentary on a work by Pratāparudra's chief paṇḍit, Lolla Lakṣmīdhara's *Advaitamakaranda*, must be dated after 1511/2, for it refers to Pratāparudra's conflict with Kṛṣṇarāya in Kārṇāṭa, a king who did not come to the throne until 1510 (see De 1942: 85).

[8] Vāsudeva is recorded in Kavikarṇapūra's *Caitanya-candrodaya* as saying at the death of Caitanya that he will go to Vārāṇasī.

[9] See e.g. D. C. Bhattacharya 1940: 69. The tradition is already repeated by Colebrooke in 1810, in his introduction to Raghunandana's *Dayabhāga*.

[10] NCat 8: 42; P 947.

[11] P 944; fl. 1510.

the *Caitanya-caritāmṛta* (2.1.140, 2.15.133–136, 2.16.204), where he is depicted as living nearby Vāsudeva in Puri. He is the father of Vidyānivāsa, someone whose importance to the development of the new philosophy I will describe in Chapter 6.

Another reason for Vāsudeva's influence was his position as the teacher of Sanātaṇa Gosvāmi, a minister to Ḥusayn Shāh and a convert to Sufism. As we have seen, Sanātaṇa and his brother Rūpa were known in Ḥusayn's court as Dabīr Khāsa ('private secretary') and Sākara Mālik ('secretary of state') (Easton 1992: 177). Along with their nephew Jīva, they were to become brilliant scholars and the companions of Caitanya, developing the philosophy of Vaiṣṇavism into a new doctrine of *acintyabhedābheda*. New religious cultures are another component in the emergence of early modernity in India. Dimock and Stewart (1999: 24–25) report that

> Rūpa and Sanātana, and their nephew Jīva, were brilliant men, learned in the *śāstras* and every conceivable category of learning from aesthetics to grammar. Jīva was perhaps the most brilliant of all, and he has more than twenty Sanskrit works, covering grammar, poetry, poetics, ritual, theology, and philosophy to his credit, including the monumental *Tattra-sandarbha*, which is the first full treatment of the theology of the Bengal school of Vaiṣṇavism. The social situation of these three men is somewhat in doubt. It seems that their family was originally a *brāhmaṇa* one from the Carnatic region of southern India, settled in Bengal. But Rūpa and Sanātana had worked for the Muslims, and as they had done so they had lost their *brāhmaṇa* status.

Rūpa and Sanātana, it would seem, were more liberal in their approach to inter-religious contact than at least some of their more orthodox Hindu brethren, the concept of brahminical 'purity' continuing to serve as a vehicle within Hindu society for social exclusion and intellectual restriction, rather to the cost of the intellectual richness of that tradition itself.

Vāsudeva was, then, an important figure in the establishment of Navadvīpa as a centre of Navya Nyāya scholarship, even if he himself lived for the most part in Puri. He was a bridge between śāstric learning and popular Vaiṣṇava devotionalism. He was capable of devotional poetry, contributing several verses to Rūpa Gosvāmi's collection, the *Padāvalī*, of which one (v. 99) indicates that he was knowledgeable in all six disciplines of brahminical philosophy. In his pupil Sanātaṇa there was a link with the Muslim court of Ḥusayn Shāh, and in his nephew Vidyānivāsa, as we will see in a later chapter, a connection with the Mughal court of Akbar.

Raghunātha Śiromaṇi (*c.* 1460–1540)

With regard to **Raghunātha Śiromaṇi,**[12] it is indeed probable that Vāsudeva received him into his school, for children joined typically as soon as they could read, and there is

[12] NCat 8:26, P 948; c.1460–c.1540. D. C. Bhattacharya 1952. Ingalls 1951 suggests 1475–1550; Vidyabhusana 1971 recommends 1477–1541. D. C. Bhattacharya reaches this dating on the following basis: (1) a dating of 1375/80–1455/60 for Śūlapāṇi, Raghunātha's maternal grandfather; (2) a reference in Jayānanda to Raghunātha as a contemporary of the sons of Viśārada, i.e. Vāsudeva, Vidyāvirinci, Vidyānanda,

an anecdote about Vāsudeva explaining the phonetics of the alphabet to a demandingly inquisitive Raghunātha (Ingalls 1951: 12). Raghunātha records Vāsudeva's view in one of his works.[13] Raghunātha may well have studied for some time in Mithilā, possibly under Jayadeva, with whom he disagreed strongly, before returning to Navadvīpa. Whether or not he was actually a student in Mithilā, he supposedly defeated Jayadeva in a famous debate, the date of which lies between 1480 and 1485.[14] Raghunātha displays a greater tolerance for another Mithilā scholar, Yajñapati. As well as his commentary on Gaṅgeśa's *Gemstone*, Raghunātha prepared brief but penetrating comments on works by Udayana, Vardhamāna and Vallabha, all called *Light-Ray (Dīdhiti)* on the text in question. Raghunātha would write three short treatises,[15] the *Treatise on Negation* (*Nañ-vāda*), the *Treatise on Finite Verbal Forms* (*Ākhyāta-vāda*), and the *Inquiry into the True Nature of Things* (*Padārtha-tattva-nirūpaṇa*).[16] His impact is due to the originality of the ideas he puts out in the course of his commentaries, to the new approach to the study of language that his two works in semantics herald, and to the daring metaphysical ideas of the *Inquiry*. More than that, it is due to the spirit his writings embody, with their emphasis on independent thinking. Raghunātha certainly thought of his conclusions as original to him, urging potential critics to consider well his arguments before condemning them.

Gaṅgeśa had written only on epistemology. Indeed, he had argued that all philosophy 'rests upon' (*adhīna*) the study of the ways of gaining knowledge. That is why he organized his only work into four chapters, one for each of the four ways of gaining knowledge acknowledged in classical Nyāya. Later thinkers would follow this organizational principle, although they were not afraid to abandon a discussion of the third method of gaining knowledge, analogy (*upamāna*) as a principle of learning the meaning of words, when their new work in the philosophy of language made it superfluous. Gaṅgeśa's exclusive attention to epistemology nevertheless left a vacuum in the study of metaphysics, and made space for creative thinkers to embrace the spirit of the new philosophy and turn their attention to a reconceptualization of ancient metaphysics. The last important pre-Gaṅgeśa metaphysical works to have been written were Udayana's *Row of Lightbeams* (*Kiraṇāvalī*) and Vallabha's *Līlāvatī*. Gaṅgeśa's son, Vardhamāna, wrote commentaries on a number of these works, and it was that corpus

and Vidyāvācaspati; (3) a ms. in Navadvīpa, on the front cover of which is a book-list dated 409 lakṣmaṇavāda = 1517 CE and including the title *Guṇaśiromaṇi*; (4) a difficulty even among the earliest commentators, Kṛṣṇadāsa and Rāmabhadra Sārvabhauma, in critically establishing the text of the *Dīdhiti*.

[13] Under the heading 'But some say...' (*kecittu*) in the logical definitions; D. C. Bhattacharya 1940: 63–64.

[14] For an early report of the tradition concerning the encounter between Raghunātha and Jayadeva, see Ward (1811; different versions in later editions). Ward also claims, however, that Raghunātha was studying under Vācaspatimiśra II (c. 1400–1450), which makes his testimony unreliable.

[15] He is not, however, responsible for a commentary, the *Bhūṣāmaṇi*, on Śrīharṣa's *Amassed Morsels of Refutation*. D. C. Bhattacharya 1952 speculatively identifies the writer as Raghunātha Vidyālaṃkāra, author of the *Dīdhiti-pratibimba*.

[16] Summaries of the entire corpus are found in Potter and Bhattacharyya 1993: 521–590; S. Bhattacharyya 2004: 485–510. Krishna 1997b takes a broader view, while a detailed study in Sanskrit is Pandeya 1983.

of metaphysical texts which formed the object of Raghunātha's attention. To describe Raghunātha's notes on these works as 'commentaries' is potentially misleading, however. What they are, very often, are very provocative and stimulating thoughts about what he is reading. One might think, by way of analogy, of the notes Wittgenstein used to make on whatever he was reading. Sometimes Raghunātha's notes are about issues which the text has, in his opinion, failed to mention at all. Raghunātha, we might say, is not *explaining* the text but *thinking with* it. It is this feature of his 'commentaries' which made them profoundly interesting to the philosophers who came after him, and who in many cases, no longer commented about the original texts but only about Raghunātha's notes.

To give just one example, when Gaṅgeśa says, at the beginning of the *Gemstone*, that the whole world (*'jagat'*) is steeped in suffering, and that philosophy is a method of alleviation, Raghunātha's note refers to the scope of 'the world' which he affirms includes everyone, women and untouchables included. Matilal says that the view that 'world' refers to *all* sufferers is 'clearly ascribable to Raghunātha...according to Raghunātha's cryptic statement, Gaṅgeśa was saying that "philosophy" or *ānvīkṣikī* is open to all, not restrictive to the male members of the three *varṇas*' (Matilal 2002: 367).[17]

As if in acknowledgement of the restrictions imposed by the inherited framework, Raghunātha wrote a separate treatise in metaphysics in which a complete rethinking of the traditional system is undertaken, the *Inquiry into the True Nature of Things*. The treatise does not dismiss the ancient metaphysics, or offer some wholly different metaphysics in its place, but rather thoroughly reworks it.[18] Raghunātha wants to make the old system consistent with a new metaphysical principle, and is not afraid to dismiss those parts of the ancient theory which seem, from the new perspective, to be anomalous. This text therefore embodies a fundamentally new attitude towards the ancient text. The new attitude is that there is a good underlying metaphysical insight, but that it has not been articulated with clarity and consistency in the ancient texts or their pre-modern interpreters, who include much that is irrelevant and leave out much of what is important. Raghunātha's leading idea is that the defence of realism in metaphysics requires one to be a non-reductivist, and his reform of the ancient theory is such as to remove from it intermingled reductivist elements.

Raghunātha begins the work in a highly provocative manner:

> Among entities, space and time are nothing but God, since there is no proof [that they are distinct from God]. For wherever particular effects arise, these arise simply from God by his being combined with particular causes.
>
> (1,3–3,1; trans. Potter 1957: 23)

[17] Another representative example are the remarks about meaning and reference Raghunātha makes in the course of commenting on Udayana's metaphysics. These remarks became the basis for a new theory of meaning in the work of Jagadīśa, Bhavānanda and Gadādhara; see Ganeri 1999b for details.

[18] In addition to the summaries mentioned above, see also the introduction in Pahi and Jain 1997.

This identification of space and time with God, or of God with space and time, is startling enough, the second sentence meaning that God as delimited by a specific time and place is the cause of any given happening, i.e. that effects are spatio-temporally located occurrences. Yet it is only further into the work that the truly challenging dimension of Raghunātha's position is made clear:

The universal, selfhood, insofar as it is the limitor of the inherence-causality of pleasure etc., is not in God.

(44,2–45,1; trans. Potter 1957: 55)

A self is that which bundles psychological properties, and so that in virtue of which a pleasure or pain felt by one person does not belong to someone else. The individual ownership of psychological properties is the reason we need a plurality of individual selves, falling under a common kind, rather than an amorphous *consciousness*, which Advaita Vedānta thinkers identify both with 'every' self (*ātman*) and with *brahman*. The 'inherence cause' of a property instantiation is the substratum in which the property inheres. Raghunātha says, however, that such considerations do not apply to God, who does not feel pleasure or pain, for example, and does not need discriminating from other individuals. In saying this, he is breaking with the ancients, who had argued that God must be a self because no other type of entity has psychological properties, and God has the property of thinking (*buddhi*) (Vātsyāyana 1997: 228, 6). This argument from elimination was not entirely free from difficulty, even for the ancients, because they took it that thinking, like all other psychological attributes, requires embodiment. One solution, albeit an *ad hoc* one, was to say that God's psychological attributes are different in kind from human mental properties, and in particular, that its 'thinking' is eternal (Uddyotakara 1997: 432–433). Such a view is not obviously at odds with the one we found in Dārā Shukoh, with its talk of individual souls, a 'higher soul', and a 'soul of souls'. But one can appreciate the force of Raghunātha's new claim if one thinks that, rather than persist with the argument from elimination, one instead admits that God does not belong to the same kind of thing as human selves. As we will see when we examine his realism in detail, this is in fact a standard move for him, one which I will argue is a form of non-reductivism. It is preferable to admit a new type of entity into one's ontology than to get into all of the ancient contortions that come with attempts to fit round pegs into square holes. Raghunātha begins several of his treatises, including the *Inquiry*, with a homage to the supreme self, which is of the nature of bliss and consciousness (*akhaṇḍānanda-bodhāya pūrṇāya paramātmane*). Superficially that sounds very much like Advaita Vedānta, but the crucial difference is that Raghunātha does not endorse the Vedāntic reduction of human selves to delimitations or reflections of the supreme one.[19] The whole topic of the

[19] Veṇīdatta worries, nevertheless, that a collapse is on the cards: '[Raghunātha's claim about God, space and time] will have the unintended consequence of not being able to admit either the multiplicity of individuals or the extendedness of the self, since a judgment that 'this is Caitra, this Maitra, this Devadatta' could also be based on God through artificial delimitations' (ahaṃ caitro 'yaṃ maitro 'asau devadatta ityādipratītīnām api tattadupādhibhedeneśvarād eva vailakṣaṇyasaṃbhave vibhujīvātmanām anaṅgīkārapra-

individuation of selves, and the question of whether selfhood was a natural kind also embracing God, developed as an important topic for some 'new reason' philosophers. Not all found themselves able to agree with Raghunātha, but all recognized that they needed to think afresh about the fundamental issues involved, rather than continue simply to follow the ancient tradition.[20]

The spirit in which Raghunātha writes the *Inquiry* is clearly seen from this passage, in which he wonders about how fictional and historical names get their reference:

> How does it come about that, from (hearing) the word 'Daśaratha', people now, who never saw Daśaratha [the father of the legendary king Rāma] come to know of him? Likewise how, from the words [for fictional entities like] 'hobgoblin' do others come to know of them? I leave this for attentive scholars to meditate upon. I shall not expand further here.
>
> (1915: 60,4–61,4; trans. Potter 1957: 76).

In saying that he will leave the matter for others to think about, the clear message is that it is the philosopher's responsibility to think about the issues and problems, in the course of a search for the truth, rather than merely revert to exegesis of texts or ancient tradition. Raghunātha puts a new set of intellectual values at the heart of philosophy, including lack of deference, independent mindedness, and above all a sort of playfulness which is absent in the scholastic tomes.

The modern nature of Raghunātha's question about reference is indicative of another major source of his influence. His composition of individual treatises examining the semantic role of two types of linguistic expression reveals a new approach to the study of language. Previously, Nyāya philosophers treated language in the context of a study of the sources of knowledge. So the question about language was: how does it function so as to enable the possibility of testimony (*śabda-pramāṇa*)? Language is one of the four ways of gaining knowledge, and it is in that context that Gaṅgeśa devotes a chapter to language in the *Gemstone*. It is significant then that Raghunātha feels the need to write these two treatises, which again fill in lacunae in the original. I think that Raghunātha perceives in Gaṅgeśa something that the Mithilā scholastics did not, namely that language can be used as a vehicle for philosophical investigation, separated from its epistemological moorings. In this new pursuit of a new philosophical method, based on a careful attention to logical form and the way words work, many later Nyāya thinkers follow Raghunātha's lead, and indeed this became one of the leading features of seventeenth-century philosophy in Navadvīpa and Vārāṇasī.

Raghunātha's innovativeness consists, in the first instance, in a radically new conception of one's duties, as a philosopher, to the past. The new spirit is nicely put by Veṇīdatta at the end of his *Embellishment of the Categories*. He says that it is acceptable

saṅgāt jīvabahutvānaṅgīkāraprasaṅgāc ca; Veṇīdatta 1930: 2). In other words, one could treat individuals as spatio-temporally delimited regions of God, just as one speaks of the space in the kitchen, the space in the lounge, the space in the hallway. See also Potter 1957: 24; Mishra 1966: 193.

[20] Mahādeva's *Examination of Selfhood as a Natural Kind* is the most sustained discussion. I hope to publish an edition and translation of this text in the future.

to modify (*ūh-*) the old scheme of metaphysical categories if it is done on the basis of a deliberation (*vicāra*) involving considerations of simplicity and complexity, even without there being a conflict with the ancient sources, and that Raghunātha's theory too could thus be modified. Indeed, if this were not the case, a scepticism which denies all the categories would be confirmed, for while one can agree to reject categories that do conflict with the ancient sources, the rejection of a category which does not must be a matter of careful thought.[21] The early modern philosopher enters into a conversation with the ancient texts, neither discarding them altogether nor allowing one's own reason to be subservient to them. Veṇīdatta refers to a type of reasoning, 'modification' as one of the key instruments in the new approach to the past.[22]

What underpins the new attention to language is the idea that philosophical linguistics can become a new *method* in philosophy. To illustrate the new method, let me draw an example from Raghunātha's study of negative constructions, his *Treatise on Negation*. He carefully distinguishes various sorts of logical work that the negative particle might perform, before turning to what some of the Mīmāṃsā ritualists say about prohibitions. They think that the sentences 'One should perform ϕ' and 'One should not perform ϕ' are contradictory, and in cases where the ritual texts mention both, the performer of the ritual has the 'option' (*vikalpa*) to suspend the prescriptive force of one or the other. Raghunātha points out that 'One should perform ϕ' means 'Performing ϕ is the means to one's desired outcome'. So then 'One should not perform ϕ' can mean 'Performing ϕ is not the means to one's desired outcome' but it can also mean 'Performing something not-ϕ is the means to one's desired outcome'. There is now no contradiction and so no need for the strange doctrine of optionally suspended injunctive force. The issue for philosophical linguistics hinges on whether a negative particle can attach to the verbal root rather than only to its suffix, and that is why this discipline can become part of a new method in philosophy.

By the end of the seventeenth century the method had gained considerably in sophistication. A second example will illustrate the development. In his *Essence of Reason*, Mādhavadeva considers afresh the problem we mentioned above, that if a self is, for some given pleasure or pain, the place where it inheres, then God is not a self. Mādhavadeva moves the problem up to the level of language, and asks us to think about what it means to say 'I am in pain' or 'I am in a state of pleasure'. The word 'I' gets its meaning fixed as referring to something which has the property of being a self. Once we have fixed the referent of 'I' we attribute it with the quality of pleasure or pain. So while it is certainly true that selfhood is what delimits the substratum of states

[21] yathāyathaṃ lāghavagauravābhāṃ śrutisūtrāvirodhena vicārya padārthā ūhanīvāḥ | asmākam iva gauḍaśiromaṇer apy ayam eva panthā ūhyaḥ | anyathā sarvapadārthāpalāpe vaitāṇḍikatvaṃ sidhyedi ti santoṣṭavyaṃ sudhībhiḥ | śrutisūtraviruddhānāṃ khaṇḍanaṃ svīkaromy aham | khaṇḍanaṃ tv aviruddhānāṃ padārthānāṃ mataṃ sama | | (Veṇīdatta 1930: 36).

[22] Veṇīdatta here finds a new application for a conception of reason as modification (*ūha*) that had already achieved considerable theoretical articulation, especially in the work of Mīmāṃsā ritualists who seek rationally to adapt the ancient ritual prescriptions to suit modern times. See Ganeri 2004.

of pleasure and pain, that remains the case even when the word 'I' refers to God. It doesn't matter that God doesn't feel pain or enjoy pleasure. All that means is that, if uttered by God, the sentence 'I am in pain' would be false.[23]

In the presentation of this argument, Mādhavadeva uses various elements of a technical apparatus. Where I said that the word 'I' gets its meaning fixed as referring to something which has the property of being a self, for example, he says that *referenthood as conditioned by the word 'I' is delimited by selfhood.* Selfhood is also, in the apparatus, what delimits substratum-causehood-to-pleasure. The point of the technical apparatus is that we can now see clearly that there are two distinct logical roles in play, which happen to be performed here by one and the same entity.

It is the early modern use of these highly artificial constructions which baffles and sometimes misleads. It might look like it is just the same old argument, the one we have already seen in Vātsyāyana, but reformulated in an elaborately adorned style. I hope that I have been able to show, however, that this is far from being the case. I will clarify how the apparatus of the early modern technical apparatus works in a later chapter (Chapter 15). To a first approximation, its sentences are equivalent to statements in a quantified language with dyadic relations including identity. The two sentences about the self are, to this approximation, equivalent to the claims that whatever is a causal substratum of pleasure is a self, and that anything referable to with 'I' is a self. These two sufficient conditions, it is now easy to see, are *compatible with* the further claim that God is a self which is not a substratum of pleasure. This method, then, serves the same function—albeit in a very different way—as the introduction of new methods into philosophy by early modern thinkers in Europe.

In the first part of this chapter I described in some detail the social historical context in which Raghunātha lived, and now I have also indicated, in still insufficient detail, what sort of philosopher he was. Is it possible to reach any conclusions about the type of 'illocutionary intervention' in Quentin Skinner's sense of the term (on which see Chapter 5), that Raghunātha took his work to be making? Clearly, he was fortunate in living in a highly accultured city at a time of relative calm and surrounded by many sources of intellectual inspiration. One text from the period concludes by saying that it was written in Navadvīpa in 1494, under the peaceful governance of Majlisavarvaka, a place full of learning and learned men.[24] Raghunātha, of course, would have been among them. On the basis of this document, D. C. Bhattacharya is—and in this he is,

[23] ātmatvajātimān ātmā | ātmatvaṃ tu sukha-samavāyikāraṇatāvacchedakatayā sidhyati | na ca sukha-samavāyikāraṇatāvacchedakatayā siddhasyātmatvasyeśvara-vṛttitve pramāṇābhāveneśvare 'vyāptir iti vācyam | ahaṃ sukhī ahaṃ duḥkhī ityādipratyakṣa-sukhādyāśraye prakāratayā bhāsamānāyā ātmatvajāteḥ pratyakṣa-siddhatayā tasyā evātma-śabda-śakyatāvacchedakatayā śrutāv ātma-śabdasya mukhyatayaivopapattyā ceśvare tatsiddhau tasyāḥ sukhādi-samavāyikāraṇatāvacchedakatvāt | na ceśvare sukhādyāpattiḥ | adṛṣṭāder abhāvāt nityasyetyāder aprayojakatvāt | (Mādhavadeva 1903–4: 55).

[24] Mahādevācārya Siṃhā's commentary on Bhāvabhūti's *Malatimādhava* (Sāhitya Pariṣat Patrikā, p. 245; D. C. Bhattacharya 1952 [35]).

regrettably, unique among Navya Nyāya historians—willing to allow the importance of benign Muslim governance:

The historical importance of this newly discovered information should not be overlooked. In the cultural history of Bengal, [Raghunātha] Śiromaṇi's victory over Mithilā and his writing the *Dīdhiti* are unique events, and it is indeed interesting information, according to the new evidence, that behind the writing of the *Dīdhiti* was the unhesitating inspiration of Muslim kingly power.

The claim that there was an 'unhesitating inspiration' might well be an exaggeration, but there is little doubt that during Raghunātha's lifetime Navadvīpa was a place of great scholarship and comparatively peaceful Muslim rule. This, though, does not in itself explain his originality, even if it is a *sine qua non*. One further consideration is Raghunātha's relationship with the scholastic community in Mithilā. Both he, and before him his teacher Vāsudeva, went, it seems, to study in Mithilā before returning to Navadvīpa. There seems to be a clear sense in which one of the things Raghunātha is trying to do is to retrieve Gaṅgeśa from them, to recover a thinker lost in the mires of a conservative scholasticism. Another consideration is Raghunātha's relationship with Vāsudeva, someone who taught the convert to Sufism, Sanātaṇa Gosvāmi, the private secretary of Husain Shāh, who left Navadvīpa for Orissa, and wrote and taught both Navya Nyāya and Vedānta, and was the uncle of the well-connected Vidyānivāsa, a man who would emerge as the head of an important stream of the 'new reason'. It would have worked to Raghunātha's advantage that he was not himself a member of that powerful family, not having to bear responsibility for the family's prestige and wealth. Being on the periphery, he was able to benefit from a close association without the burden. I highlighted a particular intellectual virtue in his work, namely its provocative playfulness, its lack of a certain sort of heaviness. I am suggesting that what made this possible is his location in the *penumbra* of scholarly power, neither too remote nor too close. A final consideration is his exposure to other very dynamic and engaging intellectual programmes in a culturally hybrid city under the administration of the liberal Husain Shāh. Even if one is not inclined towards syncretism or overt dialogue, the existence of alternative world-views as real lived possibilities exerts its own influence, and not stifled in the conservative environment of Mithilā, Raghunātha had options the Mithilā scholars did not have.

The final years of Navadvīpa

The thirty-year period immediately after Raghunātha was troubled, not good either for the production, or else for the preservation, of works in the 'new reason'. This was indeed a time of political uncertainty in Bengal, as the Ḥusayn Shāhi dynasty crumbled and Shēr Shāh Sūr captured Bengal, before eventually seizing the Delhi Sultanate from Humāyūn. Sher Shāh Sūr's reign lasts from 1540, and Humāyūn returns from exile in 1556, but only briefly; when he is killed in an accident, Akbar assumes the throne.

Bengal remains a region independent of Delhi until 1574, when Akbar succeeds in his campaign to defeat the young Sultan of Bengal, Dā'ūd Khān Karrānī. During those thirty years, there are signs of displacement of philosophical activity from Navadvīpa to Vārāṇasī.[25] From 1574, Bengal is subject to the Delhi Sultanate under Akbar (r. 1556–1605), Jahāngīr (r. 1605–27), and Shāh Jahāṇ (r. 1628–58). We move now into a fresh period of relative stability, the Mughals content for local principles of law to apply in different regions and sectarian principles of justice to govern different sections of the population. Patronage returns to the centres of brahminical scholarship, flowing from local Hindu kings who have obtained the non-transferable right to their territories in exchange for annual 'tributes' sent to Delhi.

The next hundred years will prove to be a golden period for the 'new reason', and would be at the heart of philosophical life throughout the seventeenth century. As well as hosting a lively philosophical culture, Navadvīpa would have an important role in the sustenance it gave to academic communities in Vārāṇasī. I will look in more detail at the development and flourishing of the 'new reason' in later chapters. Broadly speaking, there were three sorts of response to the challenge which Raghunātha's work presented. One response was to embrace its spirit, to extend the underlying methodology and push it into new areas. A second response was to argue for a compatibility between his seemingly new ideas and the tradition, appearance not withstanding. Some commentaries on the ancient texts had this as their ambition. Finally, a third response was to reject Raghunātha's views, but to acknowledge that he had challenged philosophers who wanted to defend the tradition to produce more careful and sophisticated explanations and arguments. No post-Raghunātha thinker could defend the seven-category ontology of pre-Raghunātha Vaiśeṣika without engaging with the topic of realism in a wholly new manner. As I will show, the later thinkers who did defend that ontology based their advocacy on a very sophisticated treatment of realism.

I want to finish this chapter by describing how this remarkable city of learning and cultural hybridity came to an emblematic end. Government land records reveal that in 1662 a son of the new philosopher Gadādhara received a land grant from the then Rājā of Navadvīpa, Rāghava Rāy. Aurangzeb (r. 1658–1707) had only recently usurped the Delhi throne; it was not until 1680 that he would attempt, without success, to extend the imposition of *jizya* (a tax on non-Muslims) to Bengal. The lineage of Navadvīpa

[25] Pragalbha Miśra [NCat 12:226; P 901; fl. 1470] is a Bengali who went to Mithilā and then to Vārāṇasī, where his school flourished until the end of the sixteenth century (D. C. Bhattacarya 1952 [38]; 249–259). Pragalbha wrote commentaries on Gaṅgeśa, Vardhamāna, Śrīharṣa and Vallabha. It appears that Raghunātha's ideas were introduced in Vārāṇasī early on, by Rudra Nyāyavācaspati certainly, and perhaps earlier by Rāmakṛṣṇa Bhaṭṭācārya Cakrabārti [P1024; fl. 1570 Potter], Raghunātha's pupil (cf. D. C. Bhattacharya 1952 [41]). Abū-l-Fażl *Āīn-i-Akbarī* names a Rāmakṛṣṇa, most likely Raghunātha's student (on this identification: D. C. Bhattacharya 1937: 34; Ingalls 1951: 16; incipit to IO ms. 2068). Another ms., IO 2069, is transcribed in 1603. This Rāmakṛṣṇa is not to be confused with another, later, Rāmakṛṣṇa, son of a pupil of Bhavānanda and great grandfather to the nineteenth-century Kṛṣṇakānta Vidyāvāgīśa (Ingalls 1951: 16, n. 67); they are conflated in Chakravarti 1915: 276–277, Kaviraja 1961: 75, and Potter P 1024. Rāmakṛṣṇa wrote on several of Raghunātha's works (Ingalls 1951: 16).

Rājās, upon whom the scholarly community was by now financially dependent, is complex and obscure, but much can be learned from an article entitled 'The Nadiyā Rāj', which appeared in the *Calcutta Review* for July 1870 (reprinted in Wilson 1877: 142–164). The article confirms Rāghava's generous patronage, inviting 'learned paṇḍits from Anga, Banga, Kāśi and Kānchi' to his palace in Reui (renamed Kṛṣṇanagar by his son), and his scrupulous care in sending tributes to Delhi. Rāghava, we are told, is the grandson of Durgadās, who secured the kingdom by a royal *firman* from Jahāngīr. Durgadās himself cooperates with the Mughal forces of occupation, assuming an office and acquiring the new title Majmuā-dār-Bhavānand. He is confirmed as the ruler of the small kingdom of Patkābarī, already bequeathed to him by his foster-father, and rules for twenty years. He cooperates again when Mansingh arrives to put down the rebellion of Pratāpāditya of Jessor, providing his army with food, lodging and aid. This support Mansingh eventually repays by presenting Majmuā-dār to the court of Jahāngīr, where Kāśinātha's kingdom is restored to him, and the title of Mahārāja conferred. Mansingh returned to Bengal in 1601 and again in 1605, on the accession of Jahāngīr. Majmuā-dār sought to divide his kingdom among his three sons, Śrī Kṛṣṇa, Gopāl, and Govind Rāma. Śrī Kṛṣṇa died of smallpox, and Rāghava, Gopāl's son, eventually inherited the kingdom, succeeded by Rudra Rāy and then by Rām Kṛṣṇa, a patron of Jayarāma Nyāyapañcānana (cf. Vidyabhusana 1971: 477). After his son Raghu Rāma, there would be a line of Candras: Kṛṣṇacandra (r. 1728–82), Śivacandra (r. 1782–88), Īśvaracandra (r. 1788–1802), Giriśacandra (1802–42), Srīśacandra, and Satiśacandra.

This succession of kings runs from the reign of Akbar and beyond the last years of Aurangzeb. Pressures from rival local kingdoms, from the native Bengali Muslim *qāḍī*, and from adjacent mughal *subahdars* notwithstanding, it is a period of considerable stability in Navadvīpa. The Rājās pay an annual tribute to Delhi, in return for which they are confirmed in their kingdoms, and run the affairs of state more or less as they please. The last quarter of the sixteenth century was unusual in several respects: most importantly, in the immediate aftermath of the Mughal conquest of Bengal, there is neither strong independent Muslim *ulema* nor an installed Hindu king. It is nevertheless in this period, under the governorship of Mansingh and Ṭoḍarmal, that philosophy in Navadvīpa began truly to flourish. The kings of this period were able successfully to juggle competing economic demands, to pay tribute to Delhi and to keep on good terms with the provincial mughal governor, while maintaining underneath them a healthy society. The ability of the Hindu kings to cooperate with the Mughal authorities was critical to their capacity to provide a buffer to the intellectual community.

A new governor comes to Bengal in 1696: 'Aẓīm-ush-shān, a grandson of Aurangzeb. The Mughal empire was already beginning to fracture, and the violent wars of succession that immediately follow Aurangzeb's death in 1707 would result in its dissolution. Bengal is, once again, something of a special case: between 1696 and 1728, it is protected from instability by the rigid economic control of first Azim-us-shan and then Murshid Qulī Khān. As govenor of Bengal and Bihar between 1696 and 1706, Azim amassed for himself a vast fortune (Richards 1993:26). Murshid Qulī Khān, formerly a brahmin servant, whose talents for finance were noticed by Aurangzeb, and who rose to become diwan of Bengal in 1707. Under Murshid's rigorous revenue collection, Bengal bankrolled the Mughal empire, between 1712 and 1727 sending an average of 10.5 million rupees per year to Delhi (Richards 1993: 277). Closer to the ground, the Hindu kings also suffered under the hostile administration of Ja'far Khān, who taxed and imprisoned first Rām Kṛṣṇa, then Raghu Rām. In spite of Bengal's relative political stability, in the period 1696–1728 the Rājās are unable to shield the scholarly community from an acquisitive regime.

If this period marks the beginnings of the decline of the 'new reason' in Bengal, in the mid-eighteenth century there would be a partial revival. Kṛṣṇa candra seems to have been remarkable. The account of his reign as depicted in 'The Nadiyā Rāj' is worth quoting at length:

One of the first acts of the Mahārāja Kṛṣṇa Candra Raī was the celebration of *yajñas* [ritual ceremonies], or festivals called *agnihotra* and *vājpeya*. He spent twenty lākhs of rupees in the ceremony. Learned paṇḍits from different parts of Bengal and from Benares came by invitation to assist in the performance of the *yajñas*.[26] They were rewarded with valuable presents, according to their respective ranks; and in return for the same, as well as for the recognition of the merits supposed to inhere in the performance of the *yajñas*, they conferred upon him the title of Agnihotrī Vājpeī Śrīmān Mahārāja Rājendra Kṛṣṇa Candra Raī.... He established in connection with the palace an asylum for the infirm and the aged poor, and also several *pāthsālās* and ṭols for the benefit of Sanskrit scholars.... In order to encourage the cultivation of Sanskrit learning, he fixed a monthly allowance of Rs. 200 as stipends to students who came from a distance to study in the ṭols of Nadiyā. This allowance was perpetuated by his grandson Īśvara Candra, who made arrangements with the Government for its punctual payment, and Rs. 100 are now paid every month from the collectorate of Nadiyā. The munificent patronage accorded by him to various branches of learning formed a leading glory of his administration, and still renders it famous. He not only made princely donations to distinguished paṇḍits, but gave *lākhirāj* or rent-free lands for the support of *catuṣpātīs*, with several lākhs of rent-free bighās to learned brāhmaṇs.... The custom of inviting and giving pecuniary presents to learned brāhmaṇs on occasions of *śrāddhas*, marriages, etc., received encouragement from him. Among the paṇḍits who flourished in his Court may be mentioned Śrīkānta, Kamalakānta, Balarāma, Śaṅkara, Devala, Madhusūdana.[27] The other literary personages that flourished under his patronage were Rām Prasād Sen, a Sanskrit scholar; Bhumeśvāra Vidyālaṇkāra, an eminent poet; Saran Tarkālaṇkāra, a Naiyāyika or logician; and Anukūla Vācaspati, a great astronomer. The Naiyāyika Kālidāsa Siddhānta was the presiding paṇḍit of his Court. Govind Rām Raī of Sugandhyā in Hūglī was the physician-in-

[26] Apparently Jagannātha Tarkapañcānana of Triveni, on whom see further below, alone was uninvited. Jagannātha, the story goes, nevertheless arrived at the *vājpeya* with his students, but refused the hospitality of the Rājā. When asked how it had gone, he replied that a *śabha* where Jagannātha was not invited was a grand meeting of paṇḍits indeed! (Sinha 1993: 222).

[27] The first four were 'the four top-ranking Naiyāyikas in Bengal' at the time, Śaṅkara Paṇḍita (1724–1817) reputed to have as many as eighty non-Bengali students in his ṭol (Sinha 1993: 20–21).

chief, and well versed in Caraka...Bhārat Candra Raī was one of the ornaments of the Court of Kṛṣṇa Candra...His fondness for Sanskrit studies displeased his relations, who thought that an acquaintance with Muhammadan literature was a better passport to wealth and distinction than the Vedas and Purāṇas. Smarting under their displeasure, he commenced a study of the Persian language, and made rapid progress in it...The Nadiyā Rāj has exercised an important influence on the literature and politics of Bengal. It contributed in no inconsiderable degree to the development of the Nyāya philosophy. Mahārājā Kṛṣṇa Candra Raī was the Mecaenas of his age, acting up to the dictum of Manu, that 'a gift to an ordinary brāhman is doubly meritorious, but one to a learned brāhman is ten thousand more so'.

(Wilson 1877: 155–156)

In a period of turmoil and encroaching political instability, Kṛṣṇa candra was able to sustain a remarkably healthy intellectual community in Navadvīpa.[28] A woman, Hatī Vidyālaṇkāra, joined the ranks of the new philosophers.[29] Between 1757 and 1772, there is a dyarchy of Sultanate and East India Company, and absence of consistent governance in the region. When, in 1765, the East India Company obtains the Diwani from the Mughal Emperor, the right in perpetuity to collect revenues in Bengal in return for an annual tribute of Rs. 2,600,000, a period of fiscal and agricultural misrule ensues (O'Malley 1925: 162–197), culminating in the famine of 1769–70, which brought disaster to the countryside of rural Bengal. Hunter (1897: 19):

In the cold weather of 1769 Bengal was visited by a famine whose ravages two generations failed to repair. English historians, treating of Indian history as a series of struggles about the Company's charter enlivened with startling military exploits, have naturally little to say regarding an occurrence which involved neither a battle nor a parliamentary debate. [James] Mill, with all his accuracy and minuteness, can spare barely five lines for the subject...but the disaster which from this distance floats as a faint speck on the horizon of our rule, stands out in the contemporary records in appalling proportions. It forms, indeed, the key to the history of Bengal during the succeeding forty years.

One-third of the population are calculated to have died by the end of May 1770, and the official estimate at the time was that a half of the farming and revenue paying populace would perish of hunger. Along with the collapse of the rural economy went the impoverishment of the noble families:

Before the commencement of 1771, one-third of a generation of peasants had been swept from the face of the earth and a whole generation of once rich families had been reduced to indigence....From the year 1770 the ruin of two-thirds of the old aristocracy of Lower Bengal dates. The Maharajah of Burdwan, whose province had been the first to cry out and the last to

[28] It is possible that Kṛṣṇa candra had a part to play in the British defeat of Sirāj-ud-dawla, in 1757, at the Battle of Plassey; curiously, we are also told that 'in 1758, the Nadiyā Rāj became a defaulter to the English Government, on which Mr. Like Scrafton proposed to send a trusty person to Nadiyā to collect the revenues for the Mahārāja, and to deprive him of all power in his District, allowing him Rs. 10,000 for his subsistence.'

[29] Sinha 1993: 33. Sinha says that 'not only did she teach in the ṭols, she also participated in debates in Nyāya-śāstra in the assemblage of paṇḍits.' She may have moved to Vārāṇasī on becoming a widow, and might have been the teacher of Gosvāmi Bhaṭṭācārya, who was born in around 1730.

which plenty returned, died miserably towards the end of the famine, leaving a treasury so empty that the heir had to melt down the family plate, and when this was exhausted to beg a loan from the Government, in order to perform his father's obsequies.... The Rajah of Nuddea, another powerful nobleman of the last century, emerged from the famine impoverished and in disgrace, very thankful, it would seem, to have the management of his estates taken out of his own hands and vested in his son.

The Company, whose revenue from the taxation of Bengal was in excess of £100,000 p.a., disbursed from its treasury a total of £6,000 in famine relief.[30] The famine was made worse by the stockpiling of grain by Company agents.[31] After the great famine of 1769, 'the history of rural Bengal becomes a narrative of severities for wringing a constantly increasing revenue out of a starved and depopulated province' (Hunter 1897: 309). Warren Hastings himself boasted, in his report to the Company in November 1772:

The effects of the dreadful Famine which visited these Provinces in the Year 1770, and raged during the whole course of that Year, have been regularly made known to you by our former advices...But its influence on the Revenue has been yet unnoticed, and even unfelt, but by those from whom it is collected; for, not withstanding the loss of at least one-third of the Inhabitants of the Province, and the consequent decrease of the Cultivation, the nett collections of the year 1771 exceeded those of 1768, as will appear from the Abstract of Accounts.[32]

It is not difficult to imagine the combined effects of severe famine and punitive taxation on the community of intellectuals in Navadvīpa. By 1811, Lord Minto is puzzling over the causes of the deterioration of native learning, and claiming the problem has something to do with the narrowness of the curriculum. The enduring myth that the Navya Nyāya philosophers of early modern India were concerned only with logical minutiae perhaps begins here. In 1829, the Board of Revenue queries the authority on which the Rs. 100 grant is being paid, and it is suspended. Students at Navadvīpa submit a letter of protest; in response, H. H. Wilson is sent to visit the ṭols. Following his report, the pension is reinstated with arrears.[33] He too condemns the restrictedness of the curriculum, and reports that there are now in total 500–600 students. When, in 1864, E. B. Cowell visits the ṭols in Navadvīpa he reports that there are fewer than 150 students and he recommends an expansion of the curriculum to incorporate elements of a Western education.

[30] In 1789, the revenue collected by the Company was £101,302 16s, and the expenditure was £5,400 (Hunter 1897, Appendix 1).

[31] O'Malley 1925: 192: 'It seems only too true that the servants of the Company and their agents bought up the previous season's rice and making a corner in it sold it at an enormous profit. Stavorinus, a Dutch admiral who visited Bengal at the time, states categorically that they raised the price of rice to such an extent that the people could not buy one-tenth of the quantity they required; and both Mr. Becher, the Resident at Murshidabad, and Muhammad Reza Khan accused the agents of the English not only of monopolizing grain but of compelling the poor peasants to sell the seed wanted for the next harvest.'

[32] Reprinted in Hunter 1897, Appendix A.

[33] Cowell 1867; the correspondence is published in Vidyabhusana 1971: 490–491.

Conclusion

There was still scholarship in Navadvīpa after 1772, but there is evidence too that scholars continued to migrate to Vārāṇasī (Mishra 1966: 441). There were new indications of vitality in Mithilā too. Gokulanātha Upādhyāya and Giridhara Upādhyāya, both from Maṅgaraunī, produced important work. Gokulanātha rejected the new movement of Raghunātha and his followers, and, with the collapse of Navadvīpa, sought to reinstate a much updated form of scholastic Navya Nyāya in Mithilā. Scholarship in Mithilā received an earlier lift when Akbar granted the Kingdom of Mithilā to the Nyāya paṇḍit Maheśa Ṭhakkura in 1557 (see Mishra 1966: 355–356). Gokulanātha himself, after an extended period at the court of Fateh Shāh in Garhwal (when perhaps he also visited Lhasa; see Chapter 1), returned to Mithilā in 1699, and served as the court Paṇḍit to Mahārāja Mādhava Siṇha from 1700 until 1739.

Patronage of Navadvīpa Naiyāyikas by members of the royal household would certainly continue, albeit on a much reduced scale. But perhaps the story of Rāmnāth 'the Wild' best sums up the new conditions.[34] Rāmnāth refused financial help from any quarter. He set up his ṭol in the forest outside Navadvīpa, and was very poor. The Rājā Śivacandra came to visit; entering the class, he asked if Rāmnāth needed any help. Rāmnāth replied that he was able perfectly to explain the logic of the *Gemstone*, and needed no help to do so; he invited the students to say if *they* needed help. The Rājā went to ask his wife instead, but she replied that she had a sari to wear, a metal pitcher, a mat to sleep on, and an iron bangle, and was, therefore, perfectly content and without need. On another occasion, the story goes, Rāmnāth defeated the legendary Jagannātha Tarkapañcānana in debate. The Rājā hosting the debate was impressed and offered Rāmnāth a tidy sum, which Rāmnāth immediately refused, explaining that money was to him no better than crow-shit.

The same Rājā Śivacandra would be requested by William Jones, in 1784, to find him a Navadvīpa paṇḍit with whom to study. Rāmalocana Kavibhūṣana, a *vaiśya*, was finally persuaded when no brahmin paṇḍit would agree to teach a *mleccha*, an 'outsider' (Sinha 1993: 28). We can but speculate on the direction events might have taken had the brahmins managed to be less closed and insular, and instead sought to persuade Jones of the beauty of the 'new reason' instead of *Śakuntalā*, his first translation might well have been of Śiromaṇi.

Was Navadvīpa only a bastion of brahminical insularity, turned inwards in an arrogant defiance of the Islamic world around it? Or was it able to flourish because of a religiously tolerant Islamic dynasty, which attached intrinsic value to learning and scholarship? The suggestion that abstract scholarship provided intellectual relief for the disenfranchized brahmin nobility fails to do justice to the remarkable vigour and boldness of the new philosophers' ideas, but reflects a common worry that the apparent

[34] See Rahri 1891: 94–99; Sinha 1993: 15–17.

absence of direct Islamic reference in their work is explicable only by way of a self-imposed cultural isolation. Tarafdar (1965: 194) suggests that:

> Now that the Muslim rule had come to stay, the Brahmins could hardly expect anything tangible in the field of politics. All that they could do was to put emphasis on their intellectual superiority by resorting to cultural pursuits. This seems to explain why the life of contemporary Navadvīpa was characterized by intense intellectual activities. Barren and abstruse branches of knowledge like logic, grammar and *smṛti* could now easily attract their attention... Thus Brahminism wanted to lead a self-centred existence within the walls of the ancient *dharmaśāstra* which it had raised around itself.

I have argued that just the contrary is the case: these thinkers were engaged in a very radical reconceptualization of the intellectual foundations of philosophy, precisely in response to the demands of the times, and with considerable support from and engagement with Muslims. The Vaiṣṇava poet Jayānanda reports that the brahmins in sixteenth-century Navadvīpa had adopted customs, mannerisms and dress-codes from the Muslims (*Caitanya-maṅgala* 1.14), suggesting a cultural liberalism in tandem with preservation of tradition. O'Connell concludes his study of Vaiṣṇava representations of Islam in the Caitanya biographies in a similar vein:

> At the level of personal religious faith Vaiṣṇavas of Bengal in the sixteenth century perceived individual Muslims in terms of respect and trust, not bitterness and fear.
>
> (1982: 310–311)

It is of course the case that traditions, and especially traditions of apprenticeship and training, must know how to preserve themselves and protect their boundaries, if they are to survive at all, and I will later describe how the system of ṭols worked and what sustained it. I have also tried to show, though, that the external robustness in pedagogical discipline existed in tandem with enormous intellectual vitality.

In conclusion, then, three significant periods for the history of philosophy in Navadvīpa can be discerned. The first is the dynasty of Husain Shāh, a remarkable Bengali sultanate largely isolated from northern India. The complex nature of the Ḥusayn Shāhi dynasty go some way to explain its predisposition towards patronage of the brahminical community of Navya Nyāya in Navadvīpa. A second distinct interval of systematic patronage is the period from Akbar's conquest of Bengal until the beginnings of the disintegration of the Mughal empire. Between these two, there is a period of political instability created by Sher Shāh's capture of Bengal and his eventually successful effort to take power from Humayun. A third period of stability and patronage in Navadvīpa begins in 1728 with the ascension of Kṛṣṇa candra, a wealthy Hindu Rājā whose endowment sustains a sizeable body of scholars at Navadvīpa until the great famine of 1770.

The Ḥusayn Shāhi sultanate witnesses the first flowering of Navya Nyāya in Bengal. The first great Bengali Navya Nyāya paṇḍit, Vāsudeva Sārvabhauma, having returned from studies in Mithilā (the older centre for Navya Nyāya), has already left again for

Puri. His brilliant pupil, Raghunātha Śiromaṇi is living in Navadvīpa. What he writes will lead, over the coming century, to the 'new reason' in Vārāṇasī and Navadvīpa. Also there is Vāsudeva's nephew, Vidyānivāsa, whose own sons were to become important voices of the new philosophy.

The second flourishing of 'new reason' scholarship occurs under the auspices of the mostly stable Mughal reign of Akbar, Jahāngīr and Shāh Jahāṇ. Akbar's reign, in particular, was remarkably liberal, and Bengal from 1580 was under the formal control of his Hindu chief minister, Ṭoḍarmal. The interest even of the later Mughal governance of Bengal is in the steady flow of revenue to Delhi, and brahminical scholarship is supported by a line of regional Hindu rājās and the well-to-do public (Raychaudhuri 1953: 146–147). This period shows a remarkable intensity of literary production, with the work of scholars circulating quickly throughout the subcontinent, strongly influencing correlative branches of śāstric learning. As the Mughal empire broke up and bankrupted itself in the course of fractious internal feuds of succession, a period during which the Mughal governor of Bengal was collecting more than ten million rupees per annum in revenue to send back to Delhi, the patronage of scholarship in Navadvīpa again dried up. It was briefly to be rekindled for a third time, under the reign of Kṛṣṇa candra, who made provision for students studying in Navadvīpa extended even to foreigners.

This final period of systematic patronage brought out a group of brahminical scholars, including most famously Jagannātha, who were later to secure for the paṇḍit a significant new role, cooperating with the British from 1772 in the development of an Anglo-Hindu legal system. Under the provision of Plan for the Administration of Justice, 15 August 1772, the East India Company under the presidency of Warren Hastings decreed that the civil courts should in a range of cases administer Islamic law to Muslims and the law of the 'Shaster' (*dharmaśāstra*) to Hindus. As Derrett (1973b: 9) says:

> Within this pattern of cultural extension there lies the hard fact that in securing the approbation of the British administrators in 1772 *śāstrīs* of Bengal vindicated for the *śāstra* what was virtually a new field for Hinduism at its most consciously normative: they used their rulers as a means whereby what had formerly been of suasive authority reappeared as positive law.

If this certainly involved an adaptation of the *dharmaśāstra*, it also served to guarantee the paṇḍit a continuing position of some importance in a new political regime. The point is illustrated by Jagannātha's *Vivāhabhaṅgārnava*, a work commissioned by William Jones under Lord Cornwallis. Jagannātha's brief was to prepare a digest of Hindu law in which all the important texts and their commentaries would be collated and conflicting interpretations explained. Jagannātha produced instead an adaptation of the old law that might apply to the new circumstances (Sinha 1993: 223–224). That was still another modernism, following again the model I outlined in my introduction to this book, coming later than those parallel modernisms in philosophy and devotional theology I have already described.

PART II

Text and Method

5

Contextualism in The Study of Indian Philosophical Literature

Quentin Skinner and performative speech-acts

When J. L. Austin introduced two 'shining new tools to crack the crib of reality' (Austin 1979: 241)—the theory of performative utterances and the doctrine of infelicities—he could not have imagined that he was also about to inaugurate a shining new cottage industry in the philosophy of the social sciences. But with its evident concern for the features to which 'all acts are heir which have the general character of ritual or ceremonial' (1962: 18–19), Austin's theory soon became indispensable in the analysis of ritual, linguistic, and every kind of social action.[1] Although Indianists such as Frits Staal (1990) and Bimal Matilal (1986: 88–89; 1999: 52–54) have made good use of the work of Austin, Searle, and other members of the 'ordinary language' school, it is Quentin Skinner who has attempted to turn Austin's insights into a general 'theory and method' for the study of intellectual cultures. The topic I want to raise in this chapter has to do with the application of Skinnerian techniques to the study of Sanskrit philosophical culture in early modern India. Skinner's methods, I will argue, do not completely suffice for the new context; but identification of the points at which they are insufficient will serve to clarify the distinctive contours of Indian intellectual history, and suggest appropriate methodological innovation.

According to Austin, we do more with words than merely describe or misdescribe facts: in producing utterances, we also perform illocutionary acts with perlocutionary effects. When I say, 'I will see you in the cafe at six' my utterance is a performance of the illocutionary act of making a promise, and its perlocutionary effect, perhaps, is that you go to the cafe at that time. To produce an utterance is therefore also, as Skinner puts it, to make an 'intervention'.[2] The cardinal assumptions of Skinner's historical method are, first, that it is possible to recover the illocutionary force of *past* linguistic acts (as also of linguistic acts in 'alien' societies and cultures), and, second, that the

[1] A good example is Tambiah 1979.

[2] Skinner 2002: 115. Skinner's articles on method in intellectual history are collected in his 2002, and all references will be to this edition. Concentrating exclusively on the theory of performatives, Skinner pays virtually no attention to its twin, the doctrine of infelicities. This omission has unfortunate consequences for his approach.

illocutionary force of a linguistic act is good evidence in figuring out what sort of thing the author of that act was up to, the nature of his or her 'intervention'. What was Cervantes up to when he wrote *Don Quixote*—was he representing the forlorn quest of an outmoded knight, satirizing the ideal of chivalry itself, or something else? Skinner says that we cannot hope to understand *Don Quixote*, let alone Cervantes, without addressing ourselves to this question, and that we cannot address ourselves to the question, a question about the intended illocutionary force of the novel, unless we can situate the act of writing it in a context, a context that will include information about Cervantes' life as well as the general social circumstances and political environment, not to mention the literary culture into which *Don Quixote* is inserted (Skinner 2002: 122–123). No amount of reading 'over and over' the text alone, Skinner says, will get us its illocutionary force.[3] The fundamental object of analysis for Skinner, therefore, is what I will call the 'text in context': a particular document or pronouncement situated in a biographical, social, political, and literary context rich enough to enable an inference to be drawn about the nature of the illocutionary intervention the document embodies. The recovery of such contexts permits Skinner to study the relationship between social and rhetorical change, and he has examined in particular the way that manipulations of the evaluative force of terms are used to foster transformations in social perceptions (Skinner 2002: 158–174).

There is a first reason why the intellectual historian of India can find it challenging to make use of a Skinnerian framework: it has very often seemed as if it is all text and no context. Consider the way Skinner begins a book on Machiavelli (Skinner 2000) a contemporary of Raghunātha. After a photograph of the building in which Machiavelli is known to have worked from 1498 to 1512, Skinner goes on to cite from the diary which Machiavelli's father kept between 1474 and 1487, giving information about Machiavelli's childhood and the books that were in the household; he refers to information from Paolo Giovio's *Maxims* about Machiavelli's early university education; he chronicles Machiavelli's first emissarial commission, to France in July 1500, and his second, to Imola on 3 October 1502; and so on. It is clear that when Skinner comes to ask after the illocutionary force of a passage in Machiavelli's *Il Principe*, he has a rich context on which to ground his conclusion that the work is intended as an attack on the humanist morality of earlier advice-books to princes. Detail of this sort is rarely conceivable with respect to intellectual literature in classical Sanskrit. We think we know that Jayanta wrote his *Nyāyamañjarī* while in prison, but there are doubts about the passage where he seems to claim this. We thought we knew that Śrīharṣa was from Bengal, but he could have been from Kashmir; he was honoured by king Govindracandra, or perhaps it was Jayacandra.[4] Matters are much better for the sixteenth- and seventeenth-century

[3] Skinner 2002: 143. This is Skinner's contextualist criticism of textualism: the recovery of context is *essential* to understanding the text.

[4] On the question of Śrīharṣa's Bengali roots, see Nilkamal Bhattacharya 1924; Majumdār 1971: 358–361, 395–398; Jani 1996; Granoff 1978.

philosophers I am discussing, and there is certainly more hope of reconstructing a rich context here than for any earlier epoch. We see, for example, their involvement in acts of public protest, in staged debates at religious ceremonies, as well as in running teaching centres. We will also be able to trace different lines of development and groups of scholarly affiliation, sources of patronage, spatial locations. I will be careful not to rely only on what the philosophers tell us about themselves in their texts, which Skinner too agrees is a limited source of contextual insight. After a careful study of the works of the seventeenth century Vārāṇasī philosopher Raghudeva Bhaṭṭācārya, Prajapati (2001: 66) sums up a general frustration, remarking that

> It is a fact that not a single work dealing with the history of Nyāya philosophy furnishes any information about his birth place and names of his parents. Moreover, his own works also frustrate us in getting any clue. It is therefore presumed that he was not interested in noting down his biographical details in his works.

It is a mistake to think that the relevant context should be reconstructed only by reading the author's works. Nevertheless, our current biographical knowledge about Raghudeva can be put in a single sentence: he was a pupil of Harirāma, is mentioned by Cirañjīva, had his work transcribed by Mahādeva, lived in Vārāṇasī, and signed the 1657 letter of judgement. Deep historical detail is not always any better available for early modern Europe, as the paucity of information about the important Sébastien Basso goes to show (Lüthey 1997).

In short, there is often simply no prospect that the level of detail about individual circumstance which Skinner claims to be required will be available. Skinner says that

> It may indeed be impossible to recover anything more than a small fraction of the things that Plato, say, was doing in *The Republic*. My point is only that the extent to which we can hope to understand *The Republic* depends in part on the extent to which we can recover them.
>
> (2002: 107)

I think that Skinner is led into such an extremely implausible position because he relies on an overly narrow and restricted conception of context, as I will now show.

Intertextual intervention

In India, certainly, poverty of information about physical and social context is twinned with a superabundance of textual materials, which provide an immensely rich literary context. Moreover, there is good evidence for the conjecture that the first context in which the Indian writers seek to make an 'intervention' was a literary/intellectual rather than a physical/socio-political context.[5] First, an important self-conception was that of affiliation to a *śāstra* or *tantra*, a disciplinary intellectual system. Such disciplines

[5] This is not to deny that cases of political intervention can be found; for instance in the interest of later 'new reason' philosophers in the question of property ownership (*svatva*).

were held to possess an extraordinary degree of diachronic continuity, conceived of more as organized structures than as living organisms, albeit structures the full contours and proportions of which had not yet been fully charted.[6] Second, intellectual innovation was sometimes presented as a matter of rediscovery, rather than invention, new discoveries about 'lost' grammatical rules explaining linguistic change much as new discoveries about 'lost Vedas' were held to explain moral and social change.[7] Third, individual linguistic 'interventions' (for example, the composition of a commentary) were shorn *by their own authors* of almost all significant autobiographical, social, or political context, a fact which suggests that such details would be a distraction from the intended illocutionary act. Indeed, if conspicuous silences are as much a part of the 'total speech act' as actual utterances, then conclusions from this singular omission are justified even on ordinary Skinnerian grounds. Some texts, indeed, are described as 'authorless' (*apauruṣeya*), an act of de-authorship that is itself a significant and telling speech-act.[8]

I suggest, then, that Skinner's methodology can be expanded to fit the specifics of Indian intellectual history if we study the interventions of individual authors in terms of their illocutionary force within what I will call 'intertextual' contexts. The first step will be to identify specifically intertextual kinds of illocutionary act. One area of study here is the subdivision of the genre of commentary, about which I will have much more to say in later chapters. Some commentaries are *elucidations* of difficult points, some are *completions* of gaps in the main text, others consist in *extraction* of the deep meaning, still others are *superimpositions* of a newer framework onto an older text, and so forth. I think we can reasonably say, for example, that as linguistic acts, Vardhamāna's commentaries on pre-Gaṅgeśa works were superimpositions of the structures of Gaṅgeśa's *Gemstone* onto the older texts, with the intention of demonstrating that the new system was fully consistent with the older tradition and so could claim to be an authentic restatement of it (and, indeed, this is the reason why Vardhamāna remains an essentially pre-modern thinker). But, to repeat Skinner's caution, this is not something one could discover by going 'over and over' Vardhamāna's work, because this is 'not a fact contained in the text'. It is an intertextual intervention, which can be appreciated only by considering the place of Vardhamāna's commentary in a literary and hermeneutical context.

A second area in which to discover intertextual speech-acts is in the nature and function of definitions. The search for extensionally adequate definitions occupied a position of canonical stature in Nyāya intellectual practice, but we may well ask what

[6] 'A *tantra* is a specification with respect to an assembly of matters connected with one another; this is also called a '*śāstra*' (tantram itaretarābhisaṃbaddhasyārtha-samūhasyopadeśaḥ śāstram; Vātsyāyana 1997: 27, 15); 'A *śāstra* is particular structured assembly of words, denoting such things as the ways of gaining knowledge' (śāstraṃ punaḥ pramāṇādivācakapadasamūho vyūhaviśiṣṭaḥ; Uddyotakara: 1997: 1, 11).

[7] Deshpande 1985: 122–149; Kahrs 1998: 187. See also the discussion by Śabara and Kumārila under *Mīmāṃsā-sūtra* 1.3.1–2.

[8] Compare Pollock 1989: 603–610.

the provision of a new definition signified as a linguistic act. First of all, definitions are offered only of contested concepts—it is precisely because the concept of *pratyakṣa* 'perception/sensation' was contested that Buddhists and Naiyāyikas alike sought new definitions of the term. The provision of a definition, therefore, is an act of attempted consolidation.[9]

Indeed, definitional acts can satisfy more straightforward Skinnerian requirements. Referring to Gaṅgeśa's statement, at the beginning of the *Gemstone*, that the whole *jagat* (world) is steeped in suffering, and that philosophy (*ānvīkṣikī*) provides the road to their release, Matilal says that the view that *jagat* refers to all sufferers, including women and *śūdras*, is

> ... clearly ascribable to Raghunātha ... [A]ccording to Raghunātha's cryptic statement, Gaṅgeśa was saying that 'philosophy' or *ānvīkṣikī* is open to all, not restrictive to the male members of the three *varṇas*. Unfortunately, such informal social critique often goes unnoticed by us today ... [but] it would be stupid to neglect the strong undercurrent of criticism of religious and social practices by the classical thinkers.
>
> (Matilal 2002: 367)

Whatever we are to make of this particular example, the point is that definitions can also be acts of social criticism.[10]

A second, possibly clearer, example is to be found in the provision by certain 'new reason' philosophers of definitions and detailed analyses of the concept of property (*svatva*).[11] This intervention into a contemporary jurisprudential debate is certainly amenable to analysis as an act of social and political significance. One of the Nyāya authors to write on ownership, Jayarāma Nyāyapañcānana, as we have already seen, was certainly a public figure, being a co-signatory to the judgement of the Vārāṇasī paṇḍits in 1657, as well as a recipient of the patronage of Rājā Rāmakṛṣṇa of Kṛṣṇapur and a contributor to the *Kavīndra-candrodaya*. Jayarāma was also of impeccable disciplinary lineage, a student of Rāmabhadra Sārvabhauma, who ran one of the most influential ṭols in Navadvīpa, and himself the teacher of Laugākṣi Bhāskara.

Skinner himself formulates a strong version of the thesis:

> It now seems to me, in short, that all attempts to legislate about the 'correct' use of normative terms must be regarded as equally ideological in character. Whenever such terms are employed, their application will always reflect a wish to impose a particular moral vision on the workings of the social world.
>
> (Skinner 2002: 182)

[9] Matilal hints at such a possibility, stating that '*lakṣaṇa* or "definition" is also used ambiguously to denote an act that the philosophers perform when they utter a definition-sentence. Arguably, *lakṣaṇa* in this sense may belong to the class of "illocutionary acts." ... In fact, some sort of a speech-act analysis of the act of definition, i.e. *lakṣaṇa*, may be fruitful.' (Matilal 1985: 176).

[10] Matilal's source is the late Navya Nyāya commentator Dharmarāja Rāmakṛṣṇa, who mentions Raghunātha as an 'opponent's view' (*pūrvapakṣa*). Matilal comments that 'Rāmakṛṣṇa, however, being an orthodox *vaidika*, readily rejected Raghunātha's view' (2002: 367).

[11] See for example Derrett 1956: 475–498; Kroll 2010.

That seems to me to overstate the case, and risks turning a moderate contextualism into an extreme form of social constructivism.[12]

Prolepsis and anticipation

I turn now to a third sort of case, where a text can be read as an act of intra-systemic intervention. When an Indian author situates himself as a writer within a *śāstra*, he locates himself in a scholarly practice that has both a history and a future. If, looking back into the past, our author observes that important works had received commentarial attention, he may well assume, by an elementary induction, that his own work, if it is of any merit, will be commented on by future writers in the tradition. That is to say, when the intellectual 'context' is a Sanskrit knowledge system, an entity conceived of by its participants as possessing enormous longevity, the possibility arises for *proleptic* speech interventions intentionally directed towards future audiences. One possibility is the deliberate use of what we might call 'open texture': knowing that my future commentator will be contending with hostile critics whose arguments I cannot anticipate, and knowing too that a commentator is (generally) a sympathetic interpreter, I insert a degree of plasticity into the text. In other words, it is my actual intention in writing the text that it be creatively interpreted by future commentators in response to critical circumstances whose existence but not exact nature I can anticipate. The idea of an intentionally proleptic illocutionary act is overlooked by Skinner, who concentrates instead on decrying what he calls the 'mythology of prolepsis':

> When considering what significance some particular text may be said to have for us, it is rather easy in the first place to describe the work and its alleged relevance in such a way that no place is left for the analysis of what its author may have intended or meant. The characteristic result of this confusion is a type of discussion that might be labelled the mythology of prolepsis, the type of mythology we are prone to generate when we are more interested in the retrospective significance of a given episode than in its meaning for the agent at the time. . . . The characteristic, in short, of the mythology of prolepsis is the conflation of the asymmetry between the significance an observer may justifiably claim to find in a given historical episode and the meaning of that episode itself.
>
> (Skinner 2002: 73)

What Skinner overlooks is that the 'meaning of the episode itself' is potentially proleptic, that an agent might be engaged in an activity of self-consciously addressing a future audience whose socio-political and intellectual context is unknown.[13]

[12] For a related distinction between 'strong' and 'weak' contextualism, see Fisher 2005: xxiii–xxv.

[13] Even Descartes claims to be writing with a future audience in mind: '[I]f my writings have any value, those who get them after my death can make the most appropriate use of them. But I was determined not to agree to their publication during my lifetime . . . it is also true that our concern ought to extend beyond the present . . .' (AT vi. 66; 1984: 145).

Skinner is similarly dismissive of the historian's use of the notion of 'anticipation'. He criticizes the 'mythology of doctrine', a presumption that there is some given set of doctrines held to be constitutive of a field, which then tempts the historian into trying to find out what each classical author had to say or failed to say about them (Skinner 2002: 59). But again, in the case of India, the 'mythology of doctrine' is a part of the intellectual reality that we are trying to study. How else can we explain the fact that a host of later writers, spanning two millennia and widely different socio-political contexts, should regard the very ancient *sūtras* not as historical documents but as current statements of philosophical knowledge? One good way to make sense of this absence of the *archaic*, of the idea of something becoming obsolete simply because it is old, is precisely by appeal to an idea of 'anticipation'; specifically that *they* took the developed doctrine and argument of the *śāstra* in question to have been already anticipated in its earliest writings. The illocutionary force of the textual interventions of later authors is made sense of by ascribing this belief to *them*.

John Newman's suggestion that healthy traditions tend to 'anticipate' themselves might provide a useful further extension of the idea:

> Since, when an idea is living, that is, influential and effective, it is sure to develop according to its own nature, and the tendencies, which are carried out on the long run, may under favourable circumstances show themselves early as well as late, and since logic is the same in all ages, instances of a development which is to come, though vague and isolated, may occur from the very first, though a lapse of time be necessary to bring them to perfection . . . and it is in no wise strange that here and there definite specimens of advanced teaching should very early occur, which in the historical course are not found till a late day.[14]

If the genuine development of a tradition consists, as Newman claims, in the 'perfection' of its underlying idea and its principles, and if the possibility of such a perfection has existed from the first, then we might well expect to find, albeit in an inchoate and undeveloped form, anticipations of such later developments in the earlier strata of the tradition.

For an example of both prolepsis and anticipation, consider *Vaiśeṣika-sūtra* 3.2.15 on the oneness of self:

> Self is one because there is no distinction in the production of pleasure, pain and cognition.

The very next *sūtra*, however, asserts that selves are many, and this indeed is the standard Vaiśeṣika doctrine. 3.2.15 therefore raises an obvious problem for later Vaiśeṣikas. Some take the *sūtra* to be the statement of an opposite view (a *pūrvapakṣa*), others that it refers to the divine or universal self. The post-Diṅnāga philosopher Vyomaśiva, however, is unique: he finds in the *sūtra* an anticipation and refutation of Vijñānavāda punctualism:

[14] Newman 1890: 195–196.

The *śākyas* think that the many cognitions (*vijñāna*) that exist in a single body constitute [each of them] a 'self'. In order to deny such an assertion, [it is said that] for each body there is one [self] not many.[15]

Now clearly the *sūtra* was not composed with the Vijñānavāda Buddhists consciously in mind; the claim is rather that early Vaiśeṣika articulates an underlying 'idea' that already contains resources sufficient to respond to the Buddhist challenge. *Vaiśeṣika-sūtra* 3.2.15 and 3.2.16 together give the text an 'open texture' and offer Vyomaśiva an important resource in a new intellectual climate.

Cultural indexicals

We have seen that Skinner's conception of context is both too rich and too poor to do justice to the Indian knowledge systems. Too rich, because the level of microscopic detail he claims to be necessary is simply not one to which we will always have access; too poor, because our objects of study are whole *śāstras* or *tantras*, and they create broader contexts of intellectual intervention than Skinner considers. Skinner's appeal to context is, I think, overly narrow in still another sense. His appeal is primarily evidential: context provides the historian with the best evidence for the kinds of illocutionary acts being performed. Philosophers of language, however, have given greater weight to another use of context, its role in reference-fixing. Indexical terms are terms whose reference varies according to determinate aspects of the context of use. They have also begun to take notice of the phenomenon of 'hidden indexicality' in which the reference of terms that do not have the surface grammar of an indexical nevertheless display sensitivity to contextual parameters. The buried indexicality of such terms remains hidden if the range of contexts of use is restricted within a single value of the relevant parameter. To take a simple example, consider the term 'the moon'. This is a hidden indexical, the relevant contextual parameter being the planet upon which the speaker is situated. Only with the possibility (actual or imaginary) that this parameter might vary does the buried indexicality of the expression become apparent or salient.

This phenomenon will be of interest to the historian of intellectual cultures, because it might well turn out to be the case that important terms (and the concepts they express) are indexicals of broad features of cultural context. If this is correct, then the study of diverse intellectual cultures assumes an importance unacknowledged by Skinner. Skinner himself, I should stress, is unusually sensitive to the importance of studying cultural diversity. His reason for attaching value to this domain of study is, first and foremost, that 'seeing things their way' encourages us to be less parochial about our inherited beliefs. Skinner's position is that the historical study of past cultures helps us to reassess the value we attach to our own, to become less provincial, more tolerant,

[15] tathā hy ekasmin śarīre 'nekaṃ vijñānam ātmeti śākyā manyante | tatpratiṣedhārthaṃ pratiśarīram eko nānekaḥ | (Vyomaśiva 1983, v. 1: 155, 9–11).

enlarged in our horizons. That is to say, it helps with the evaluative stance we assume towards 'our own way'. As I mentioned above, this is indeed the very attitude in which Dārā Shukoh approached the Sanskrit texts.

My argument is that the study of past cultures is relevant for another, perhaps more fundamental, reason. Our most basic normative expressions, the terms in which we express our deep values and standards of appraisal, turn out not to be proper names but cultural indexicals, and to understand the meaning of such indexical terms is to know how they map from cultural context to reference, rather than simply knowing their reference alone. Consider what Bernard Williams says about the virtue of sincerity. Sincerity has been held to be a value in many epochs and many cultures, but the way it gets to be valued varies according to circumstance. Although there is a basic shape to the notion of sincerity—saying only what one believes to be true—the 'reference' of the concept will vary with context. Thus, for Rousseau and the European Enlightenment, sincerity meant authenticity and confession, revealing the secrets of one's heart, while in the *Mahābhārata*, sincerity took thirteen forms, including impartiality, self-control, toleration and non-violence (*MBh.* 12.156.3–26). Williams says

> Everywhere, trustworthiness and its more particular applications such as that which concerns us, sincerity, have a broadly similar content—we know what we are talking about—and everywhere, it has to be related, psychologically, socially, and ethically, to some wider range of values. What those values are, however, varies from time to time and culture to culture, and the various versions cannot be discovered by general reflection . . . Sincerity has a history, and it is the deposit of this history that we encounter in thinking about the virtues of truth in our own life. This is why at a certain point philosophy needs to make way for history, or, as I prefer to say, to involve itself in it.
> (Williams 2002: 92–93)

Networks of local value make sense of sincere speaking as a practice worth engaging in. Attention to the way sincerity is understood in a variety of cultures is part of the way to understand the concept itself.

To clarify this point, it may be helpful to refer to a well-known account of indexicality. According to David Kaplan (1989), there are two ingredients in the meaning of an indexical, the 'content' and the 'character'. The content of an indexical is the object it refers to on any given occasion of its use (or, more generally, the contribution made to the truth-value of the statement in which the indexical occurs). The character of an indexical is a function from aspect of context to contents. For example, the character of 'I' is the function expressible as 'Any utterance of the word 'I' refers to the person who utters it'. Sincerity, we can now say, is a sort of cultural indexical, its content varying according to local systems of commendation that make sense of it as something of value, while its character (saying what you believe to be true) remains constant.[16]

[16] This is the way to avoid the pitfall of cultural relativism. For similar remarks with respect to the parameterization of objectivity, see Amartya Sen 1993.

Immersion and Indian intellectual practice

There is one further lesson to be drawn from these points about indexicality. The account implies that there are in fact *two* contexts to take into consideration whenever an indexical expression is used. Consider an utterance like 'Tomorrow, it will be sunny'. The character of the indexical 'tomorrow' tells us that it refers to the day after the day on which the utterance is made, and the truth or falsity of the utterance depends on how things stand on *that* day. So we must distinguish between the *context of utterance* and the *context of evaluation*, and notice that they might be, but do not have to be, identical. To put it loosely, some indexical utterances 'refer out' of their own contexts of use; they make assertions evaluable only with respect to some other context.

Such acts of 'referring out' of one context and into another carry types of illocutionary force unique to themselves, and it is a drawback of Skinner's presentation that, because he does not distinguish between evidential and reference-fixing appeals to context, he does not discuss *these* sorts of performative utterance. Skinner assumes, to put it crudely, that agents in other cultures and times must be talking about their own time and culture; 'seeing things their way' is seeing how they talk about their times.[17] This seems to me to omit from the discussion an important class of illocutionary act, which we might call 'indexical illocution'.

To give an example, consider how the Mādhyamika philosophers, especially Nāgārjuna and Candrakīrti, attempt to make sense of the entirety of the Buddhist canon. Given that many of the statements there attributed to the Buddha cannot be true by his own lights, and on the further assumption that the Buddha is not simply a liar, one explanation is that the Buddha's assertion indicates to the later philosopher its definitive (*nītārtha*) meaning, a meaning that is disguised by the non-definitive (*neyārtha*) meaning the Buddha didactically intends his specific audience to comprehend. That suggestion represents the Buddha as making a double intertextual intervention, first in the particular dialogical circumstance in which he is speaking, and second an act of 'referring out' to the future hermeneutical tradition or the Buddhist scholarly community. Indeed, the hermeneutican identifies the Buddha's definitive meaning by calculating what definitive meaning could explain the particular dialogical intervention.[18]

For what is, at first sight, a rather different sort of case, consider some of the studies of Indian intellectual culture produced by a modern interpreter; for the sake of argument, let us take a book entitled *Perception,* the classic work of Bimal Krishna Matilal. The context of utterance of this study is clearly the contemporary community of anglophone analytical philosophy. This is evident from a number of facts: the study

[17] '[T]he aim is to return the specific texts we study to the precise cultural contexts in which they were originally formed' (2002: 125).

[18] See Ruegg 1985: 309–325, Ganeri 2007: 110–115.

is written in English, it uses the jargon of that culture, it makes constant references to the leading participants of analytical philosophy, and is even dedicated to two of them, it is published by Oxford University Press, and so on. The context of evaluation, equally clearly, is the intellectual culture of classical India, for it is that culture with respect to which the truth or falsity of specific utterances are to be evaluated. I do not see why we should not try to analyse the illocutionary intervention made by the publication of *Perception*, just as Skinner does the publication of Cervantes' *Don Quixote*; but if we do so, it is clear that the performance essentially involves two contexts, not one. To put the point another way, we can understand Matilal's work as a 'commentary' on the Indian sources, one which mediates a conversation between them and a contemporary readership of anglophone philosophers. It is commentary that bridges two separations simultaneously, that between past and present, and that between East and West.

In the seventeenth century, 'new reason' philosophers were seeking new forms of accommodation between the ancient tradition and an emerging philosophical modernity. Jumping back across a rupture, while continuing to be indelibly marked by it, reconceptualizing the pre-rupture past in the categories of a post-rupture present—these are among the most characteristic hallmarks of early modern Indian intellectual practice. This is, I have argued, a deeply Indian hermeneutical stance. India was also able to draw upon these deep intellectual resources when confronted with the profoundest rupture of all, the colonization by Britain; and some of these same resources were to enable it not only to survive but to emerge in people like Gandhi, Tagore, and Matilal with a new modernity.

6

Philosophers Outside Academies: Networks

Some of the most powerful intellects of South Asia were working in Vārāṇasī and Navadvīpa in the sixteenth and seventeenth centuries. Among them were prominent contributors to the revitalized 'new reason' and it seems very probable that some would be among the 'learned scientists of our circle' who associated with François Bernier.[1] These philosophers were engaging in a profound and radical dialogue, with each other and with the tradition from which they had emerged. My aim in this chapter is to show how educational networks centred on individuals and their families provided the structures needed for the 'new reason' to flourish in Islamicate India, but I will also argue that their very nature, particularly the fiscal arrangements surrounding them, hampered as well as nurtured innovation. It is striking that several of the most original 'new reason' philosophers existed on the periphery of these structures, benefiting from them without being too closely implicated in their perpetuation.[2] Others were able to participate in broader networks, such as those I have already described as existing in Navadvīpa at the time of Raghunātha, or the type of informal umbrella of association created by a patron like Dāniṣmand Khān, which 'brought together a Frenchman of Paris, a Muslim of Persia and a Brahmin of Benares' (Gode 1954a: 376).

A ṭol or maṭh is a teaching arrangement whereby the student receives board, lodging, and instruction from the paṇḍit, generally without payment. The costs imposed by such an arrangement serve to reinforce the necessity of patronage. According to one later eyewitness report,

> The paṇḍit of a ṭol should properly not only instruct his pupils gratuitously, but he should also provide them with food, clothing and lodging during their stay under his teaching. He himself is to be remunerated indirectly by the invitations and presents which celebrity as a teacher would ensure his receiving at the religious ceremonies of the neighbouring zemindars.
>
> (Cowell 1867: 87–88)

[1] Jayarāma, for instance, who knew Kavīndra Sarasvatī, might well have been one of them. Bernier reports that he was introduced to 'the six most learned paṇḍits in the town' of Vārāṇasī (1934: 342).

[2] The story of Yaśovijaya provides another good illustration of this point.

It was a well-established practice among wealthy or royal families to organize public debates at their homes on important occasions (for example, the ritual honouring of one's dead relatives known as *śrāddha*), remunerating the participating paṇḍits according to their prestige and performance. The paṇḍit's profile as a public intellectual in circumstances of patronage secures to him an income in the absence of a fee-paying student body. It is said of Harirāma, for example, that 'he used to get the highest reward in all public assemblies, a distinction which has invariably been confined to the scholar occupying the foremost rank at Nadia for erudition and controversialist eloquence' (Kaviraja 1961: 63). The ṭols of Navadvīpa and the maṭhs of Vārāṇasī were the backbone of the intellectual communities throughout our period.

I will distinguish several 'streams', organized around different histories of pedagogical transmission, the use of different teaching manuals, having different sorts of relationship with political power, and making different sorts of accommodation of the ancient with the new. Each of these streams traces its origins to one of the first interpreters of Raghunātha, philosophers who were active around the time of Raghunātha's final years and death (c. 1540). There was a real contest as to how to give voice to his legacy.

The new reason and the court of Akbar

Raghunātha's teacher, Vāsudeva, belongs to a family of Navya Nyāya philosophers, whose members were to become a powerful presence in Navadvīpa and then Vārāṇasī. First and foremost is Vāsudeva's nephew and a broad contemporary of Raghunātha, **Vidyānivāsa** Bhaṭṭācārya.[3] The *Ā'īn-i Akbarī* of Abū-l-Fażl, written in 1597, includes an important list of names of prominent Muslim and Hindu scholars alive during the reign of Akbar. Among the 140 Muslim scholars listed, almost all were dead by 1597; so the list is of the figures of the northern Indian intellectual world who were in their prime in the years immediately after Raghunātha's death. The list is divided into five groups, of which in the fourth are the philosophers, those who, says Abū-l-Fażl, 'look upon testimony as something filled with the dust of suspicion and handle nothing but proof' (Blochmann 1873: 537). Fifteen Hindu and seven Islamic philosophers are mentioned.[4] Several are Mithilā Naiyāyikas, and five are Bengali. What is important is that Vidyānivāsa's name is on the list. D. C. Bhattacharya (1937: 35) states that Vidyānivāsa was 'the accepted leader of the Naiyāyikas of Bengal' in the mid-sixteenth century.[5]

[3] P 920; fl. 1540.

[4] The Hindu names are Nārāyaṇa, Madhu[sūdana] Bhaṭṭa, śrī Bhaṭṭa, Viśvanātha, Rāmakṛṣṇa, Balabhadra Miśra, Vāsudeva Miśra, Vāmana Bhaṭṭa, Vidyānivāsa, Gaurinātha, Gopīnātha, Kṛṣṇa Paṇḍita, Bhaṭṭācārya, Bhagīratha Bhaṭṭācārya and Kāśinātha Bhaṭṭācārya. The Islamic philosophers include Abdul Baqī, Mizra Muflis, Qasim Beg and Nuruddin Tarkhān.

[5] See further B. Upādhyāya 1983: 30; Shastrier 1939, v. 6: lxxxiii; NCat 1: 574a. He wrote teaching notes or *vivecana* on Gaṅgeśa (Potter and Bhattacharyya 1993: 374–375; cf. NCat 6: 271).

One of the most interesting reports we have about Vidyānivāsa is that he engaged with the famous Nārāyaṇa Bhaṭṭa[6] in a public debate at the house of Ṭoḍarmal, Akbar's finance minister between 1572 and 1589.[7] Haraprasad Shastri (1912: 9–10) summarizes the report of this debate:

At a *śrāddha* ceremony in Delhi in the house of Toḍar Mal, he [Nārāyaṇa Bhaṭṭa] worsted in disputation all the paṇḍits of Gauda [Bengal] and Mithilā with Vidyānivāsa at their head.[8] Toḍar Mal was a patron of Sanskrit literature, having caused excellent compilations in *smṛti, jyotisha, vaidyaka* and other *śāstras*. He was long the *Subahdar* of Bengal. It is not unnatural, therefore, that he should invited Bengal paṇḍits at a *śrāddha*. Vidyānivāsa was then the leading paṇḍit at Navadvīpa. He was a Banerji. His father Vidyāvācaspati is described as one whose feet were constantly rubbed by the crown jewels of Rājās.[9] Vidyānivāsa's sons were all well-known paṇḍits. His second son was the author of the *Bhāṣā-pariccheda*, a standard work of *Nyāya* all over India.[10] His third son was in high favour with Bhāva Siṃha, the son of Mān Siṃha of Amber.[11] Even Vidyānivāsa had to yield his palm to Bhaṭṭa Nārāyaṇa and the point of debate was one of vital importance to modern Brāhmanism. The ancient ṛṣis declare that at the performance of a *śrāddha*, live brāhmaṇs are to be fed with the cooked food offered by the manes [sic.]. Bengal holds that this is impossible in the Kāliyuga as there are no brāhmans worthy to feed. And so they feed symbolical brāhmans (brāhmans made of *kuśā*-grass). The southern people [Nārāyaṇa was from the south] hold that the injunctions of the *śrāddha* should be respected, and live brāhmans are to be fed.[12]

No date is given for the ceremony, but Akbar divided the empire into twelve *subahs* or provinces only in 1579, and Ṭoḍarmal was dispatched to Bengal in 1580, not returning to Delhi for at least two years. I surmise, then, that the event in question

[6] Nārāyaṇa Bhaṭṭa, a Mīmāṃsā scholar, belonged to one of four powerful families in Vārāṇasī: the Bhaṭṭas, the Śeṣas, the Dharmādhikāris and the Maunis (D. C. Bhattacharya 1937: 34; Shastri 1912; Benson 2001). The report is from a family history, the *Gādhivaṃśavarṇana,* written by his second son Śaṃkara Bhaṭṭa.

[7] Rājā Ṭoḍarmal (c. 1515–89) was the great general, finance minister, administrator and friend of Akbar. He reformed the system of revenue collection, inventing a new system; he encouraged Hindus to study Persian that they may prosper under the new administration, perhaps thereby contributing to the emergence of Urdu; and he commissioned between 1572 and 1589 the preparation of an encyclopaedic digest of Hindu learning, called the *Ṭoḍarānanda*. The patronage supported a team of paṇḍits, primarily in Vārāṇasī, but perhaps from other regions too. There is no strong evidence for the claim that the team was led by Nārāyaṇa Bhaṭṭa (cf. Vaidya 1948: xxv; Das 1979: 214–215), at whose behest Ṭoḍarmal would fund the reconstruction of the temple to Śrī Viśvanātha in 1585.

[8] Kaviraja 1961: 74, n. 35 states that Vidyānivāsa was the victor, while D. C. Bhattacharya 1937 says only that they debated.

[9] The source of this description is the final verse of a poem, the *Bhramaradūta*, by Vidyānivāsa's son Rudra; cf. Chakravarti 1915: 286, n. 2; Kaviraja 1961: 55.

[10] The attribution is now regarded as flawed; see below for details.

[11] Umesh Miśra 1966: 434 states that Rudra was the eldest son and Viśvanātha the youngest, MM Kaviraja 61: 156 that Viśvanātha was the eldest son and a younger son was Nārāyaṇa.

[12] The whereabouts of the manuscript Shastri consulted is unclear. Benson 2001, however, summarizes the contents of a manuscript of the text he has located in the Chandra Shum Shere collection in Oxford. In this text, Benson reports, the argument was said to be about the prohibition of meat (*pala*) at a *śrāddha* in the Kāli age. Benson asks: 'Could *pala*, which means meat or straw, have been taken by Shastri somehow to refer to straw brāhmaṇas?' (2001: 113). See also Vaidya 1948: xxvii–xxviii.

took place around 1583. Other evidence confirms that Vidyānivāsa was still alive at that time, although he would certainly have been a very old man.[13]

It appears from the report that the family of Vidyānivāsa enjoyed the patronage of the Kachvāhā house in Amber, Vidyānivāsa himself honoured by Mansingh, his son a favourite with Mansingh's son Bhāvasingh. This refers us to the Hindu–Muslim alliance between Akbar and the Rājput family of Amber, which began in 1562 with the marriage to Akbar of the daughter of Bharmal, an alliance that secured for Bharmal Mughal support against a rival, and for Akbar enduring Rājput loyalty. Along with his daughter, he gave to Akbar his brilliant nephew Mansingh, who would become one of Akbar's most trusted generals. The Rājput presence in Akbar's court would be of immense importance to Akbar's astonishingly liberal governance. Between 1563 and 1564, for example, Akbar forbade the enslavement of Hindu prisoners of war, remitted the tax on Hindu pilgrims, and abolished the *jizya* or poll-tax on Hindu families (Sarkar 1984: 39). Mansingh and Ṭoḍarmal secured Bengal for Akbar in 1580 from an independent *ulama* hostile to the Mughal throne, who were, indeed, to issue a *fatwā* against Akbar in protest against his religious unorthodoxy and interference in the internal affairs of the province (Shein 1963). Mansingh would be made Governor of Bihar in 1588, overseeing the eastern state for twenty years, and also Governor of Bengal between 1594 and 1605, a critical period for the emergence of the new philosophy. It ought not surprise us, then, if Mansingh and Ṭoḍarmal were to seek support from, and offer encouragement to, the brahminical scholars in Bengal.

Vidyānivāsa's sons relocated to Vārāṇasī. One is **Viśvanātha** Nyāyasiddhānta Pañcānana,[14] someone who would become well known for his commentary on the *Nyāya-sūtra,* written in 1634, in retirement in Vṛndāvana. He explains that he has written a terse and easy commentary on the *sūtras* with the help of the amassed words of Raghunātha.[15] This is a first indication of a concern to demonstrate compatibilism between Raghunātha and the ancients. He also wrote commentaries on Raghunātha's three treatises.[16] His son[17] is among those who celebrated Kavīndra's triumphant return from Agra to Vārāṇasī, having persuaded Shāh Jahāṇ, with Dārā Shukoh at his side, to repeal a pilgrimage tax on Hindus.

In a more unusual intellectual contribution, Viśvanātha wrote a refutation of Advaita Vedāntic monism, the *Proof of Distinction* (*Bheda-siddhi*), specifically directed against Madhusūdana Sarasvatī's *Proof of Non-dualism* (*Advaita-siddhi*). Madhusūdana (c. 1530–

[13] D. C. Bhattacharya 1937: 35 claims that his name is on a document from 1583 and was living still in 1588; Shastri 1939: 90 says that Vidyānivāsa employed his scribe Kavicandra to copy a text for him the *Kṛtyakalpataru* in 1581.

[14] P 1179.

[15] eṣā munipravaragautamasūtravṛttiḥ śrīviśvanāthakṛtinā sugamāplavarṇā śrīkṛṣṇacandra-caraṇāmbujacañcarīka-śrīmacchiromaṇivacaḥpracayair akāri (Viśvanātha 1922: 401). In the next line he identifies himself as the son of Vidyānivāsa Bhaṭṭācārya.

[16] On the *Inquiry* (IO 2097; c. 1650, the scribe's name is Mahādeva); on the *Treatise on Negation* and the *Treatise on Finite Verbal Forms,* see NCat 2:9.

[17] Rāmadeva Bhaṭṭācārya; see *Kavīndracandrodaya* vv. 46–47.

c. 1620), like Yaśovijaya afterwards, had himself been trained in the techniques and methods of the 'new reason'. Originally from Bengal, he studied Navya Nyāya in Navadvīpa before moving to Vārāṇasī; the identity of his teacher is unknown, but must presumably be either Vidyānivāsa himself or one of his contemporaries. Madhusūdana too is mentioned in Abū-l-Fażl list, and appears to have been acquainted with Akbar's court through Ṭoḍarmal, perhaps by helping him stage Hindu–Muslim debates.[18] He seems to have been a contemporary of Rūpa and Jīva Gosvāmi, although the relationship between his interpretation of Advaita Vedānta and Bengali Vaiṣṇavism is complex (Gupta 2006). That Viśvanātha should have made a particular effort to counter his work therefore affords an insight into the relationship between the early 'new reason' philosophers and a monistic Advaita Vedānta, certainly influential among those in the Mughal court with Sufi leanings.[19]

Viśvanātha's brother, **Rudra** Nyāyavācaspati,[20] was a prolific commentator (Mishra 1966: 432–433) and author of a poem, the *Bhāva-vilāsa*, in praise of Bhāvasingha (Chakravarti 1915: 286). From Rudra we learn that Raghunātha was aware of and responsive to the thought of Vidyānivāsa: Raghunātha refers to and rejects an idea for fixing a definition supplied by Vāsudeva, and Rudra says that the idea in question is his father's.[21] Rudra's son, **Govinda Śarman**,[22] signed the 1657 letter of judgement of Vārāṇasī scholars.

Vidyānivāsa is a figure of authority for the Bengal school of Navya Nyāya in the mid-sixteenth century. We cannot be exactly sure of his relationship with Raghunātha Śiromaṇi, who began to write towards the end of the fifteenth century and soon became the leading intellectual spirit of the Navadvīpa school—there is enough of an overlap for Raghunātha to be responding to his ideas and for his sons to be writing about Raghunātha. He is in any case the nephew of Vāsudeva, Raghunātha's tutor in Navadvīpa. If we want to conclude something about the 'intervention' that the work this family of philosophers made, we can make use of three clues. They are, first of all, closely associated with the centres of power, with the Rājput Mansingh and with Ṭoḍarmal, and through them, with the Mughal establishment. Second, they move from Navadvīpa to Vārāṇasī, from a relatively distal intellectual community to the great centre of brahminical intellectual life, and indeed become prominent participants within it. Finally, we have Viśvanātha's own declaration as to his motive for writing his commentary on the *Nyāya-sūtra*, that he did so with the help of all the words of Raghunātha so as to make the ancient work easy to understand. These facts lead me to conjecture that this first group of 'new reason' philosophers is fairly conservative,

[18] There is some evidence that he translated or arranged for the translation of the *Sāma Veda* into Persian, the Persian text on which John Marshall would later write; see Chapter 1.

[19] For further discussion, see Krishna 2004: 210–263; Minkowski 2011.

[20] P 1144. In the colophon of Bodleian ms. 618, Rudra identifies himself as the son of Vidyānivāsa.

[21] SBSL ms. 455, fol. 67/1; cf. ms. 467 (source: D. C. Bhattacharya 1952 [37]).

[22] NCat 6:203, 207; P1142. Fl. 1629, the composition date of his *Nyāyarahasya*. See also D. C. Bhattacharya 1945; 1952 [5, 28].

wanting to be near to sources of influence, and wanting to demonstrate that the new is perfectly compatible with the old. They seek to update but remain faithful to the past: for them the value of Raghunātha's modern thought is in the help it provides explaining and making salient the ancient tradition itself. Raghunātha was critical of Vidyānivāsa, and the family relocated to Vārāṇasī; perhaps there was also a wish to domesticate the new rather than promote it.

A less embedded network

I turn now to a second network of scholars, this one must be less well entrenched. I will mention four individuals. The first is **Kṛṣṇadāsa** Sārvabhauma.[23] Kṛṣṇadāsa is mentioned in a text written before 1553.[24] He lived in Navadvīpa and wrote commentaries on Raghunātha.[25] D. C. Bhattacharya has shown that he is the author of a famous manual in 'new reason' philosophy, the *Divisions of Language* and its auto-commentary, the *Pearl-necklace of Principles about Reason*, contradicting the traditional attribution of the work to Viśvanātha.[26] The attribution has been endorsed by many recent scholars,[27] and I too will take it that this manual is taught by our second group of 'new reason' thinkers.

One student, again relocating to Vārāṇasī, is **Bhavānanda** Siddhāntavāgīśa.[28] In his work, we find indications of an important trend in the new system, a strong interest in philosophical grammar and, in particular, the semantics of the Pāṇinian theory of thematic case roles (*kārakas*). Raghunātha began this trend with his works on negation and the logic of action statements. Bhavānanda would write commentaries on both of these works, as well as on the thematic roles, the ten classes of finite verbal forms, and on semantics in general.[29] Bhavānanda also wrote a long and a short commentary on the *Gemstone*, which he called *Illumination of the Hidden Meaning*.[30] The Navadvīpa philosophers I will speak about in the next section reject his commentaries; seemingly motivated by jealousy or competitiveness, they try to question their reliability.

[23] NCat 4:320, P 1027. Fl. 1575 (NCat).

[24] By the Jaina philosopher Guṇaratna; Parikh 2001: 10, 29–30.

[25] On the *Light-Ray* (IO ms. 1927, dated 1602; BHU, vol. 6, p. 222), and on the *Treatise on Negation* (Stein I.P. 226; Bikaner 1614).

[26] A number of old manuscripts say as much (an example not noticed by Bhattacharya is BHU, vol. 6, p. 244, ms. C5367). Furthermore, there is a manuscript of a commentary on the *Necklace*, copied in 1611, too early for the main text to be by Viśvanātha (the *Ullāsa*: BORI 1895–1902, ms. 301; 1925, p. 11). See D. C. Bhattacharya 1941b, 1948, 1952: 117–120.

[27] Mishra 1966: 422; Matilal 1977: 109; Thakur 2003: 339–340.

[28] P 1082; Mishra 1966: 427. Fl. 1600 (Potter). Bhavānanda is the grandfather of Rāmarudra Tarkavāgīśa, the author of a famous commentary on the *Pearl-necklace of Principles*. Another commentator on this manual, Dinakara Bhaṭṭa, had already written a commentary on Bhavānanda. There is clearly a strong affinity in the school of Bhavānanda for the *Pearl-necklace*, a fact that gives further credence to the suggestion that it is the work of that school's founder, Kṛṣṇadāsa.

[29] The *Kāraka-cakra*, the *Daśa-lakāra-vādārtha*, and the *Śabdārtha-sāra-mañjarī*.

[30] *Gūḍhārthaprakāśikā*, often referred to simply as the *Bhāvānandī*.

Raghudeva Nyāyālaṃkāra,[31] whom I mentioned in the last chapter, is said to be related to Bhavānanda. He lived in Vārāṇasī but had been a student in Navadvīpa.[32] He signed the letter of judgement in 1657 and is mentioned by Yaśovijaya. In addition to the standard fare of commentarial notes, Raghudeva wrote several rather unusual works, including a commentary directly upon the *Vaiśeṣika-sūtra*,[33] another on Śrīharṣa's 'refutation' of Nyāya, the *Amassed Morsels*, and a work on the philosophy of material bodies, the *Survey of What is Essential about Substance*. Like Bhavānanda, Raghudeva is willing to innovate both in choice of subject matters and in types of genre. His work too, however, was largely unwelcome in Navadvīpa.[34]

It would fall to **Mahādeva Punatāṃkara**,[35] a philosopher from southern India but living in Vārāṇasī, fully to appreciate the value of Bhavānanda's work. Mahādeva explains that he wrote his own commentaries 'to remove the so-called mistakes which have been pointed out in the work of Bhavānanda by the zealous Bengali paṇḍits'.[36] Mahādeva seems himself to have been an unusually broad-minded and serious scholar, willing to learn from any philosopher and making copies for himself of a great many texts:

> From an entry in one of his mss. it appears that Mahādeva once went to Nadia on tour, either in search of mss. or on invitation to attend some meeting of the paṇḍits. He was in touch with the scholars of Bengal whose learning he deeply appreciated.
>
> (Kaviraja 1961: 80)

He copied one of Raghudeva's works in 1682.[37] Mahādeva is the author of two important and original treatises. One, the *Precious Jewel of Reason (Nyāya-kaustubha),* is a very significant contribution to the new epistemology, and I will discuss it in some detail in a later chapter (Chapter 11). The other is a treatise on the problem of the individuation of the self, the *Examination of Selfhood as a Natural Kind* (*Ātmatva-jāti-vicāra*). This text was at the forefront of an important controversy about the nature of the self in the early modern period, again inspired by Raghunātha, about the distinction between human selves and God, as well as between one self and another. The new interest in the individual is another indicator of modernity.

There are two immediately striking facts about this second group of 'new reason' philosophers. The first is that they seem to be outcasts in one sense or another, ignored

[31] P 1228. Fl. 1660 (Potter). See also Prajapati 2001; 2008.

[32] With Harirāma; see *Survey of What is Essential about Substance* (Stein 2766, fol. 132). D. C. Bhattacharya suggests that another teacher is Cirañjīva (1952: 280; Mishra 1966: 444). Kaviraja 1961: 72 notes a reference to 'jagadīśa' at the end of his commentary on the *Treatise on Negation*, and says it 'seems to show that he read also with Jagadīśa. Or perhaps the word *jagadīśa* means God and nothing more.' Raghudeva seems, though, to have written a commentary on Jagadīśa's *Tarkāmṛta* (NCat 8: 135).

[33] *Vaiśeṣika-sūtra-vyākhyā* (ms. in Gokul Giri, Vārāṇasī; Potter).

[34] D. C. Bhattacharya 1945: 93.

[35] P 1288. Manuscripts copied by him date from 1670 to 1696 (Kaviraja).

[36] *Bhāvānandī-prakāśa*; cf. Mishra 1966: 429, Chakravarti 1915: 285, n.2.

[37] Ms. in Govt Sanskrit College Library Benares; cf. Kaviraja 1961: 73.

in Navadvīpa and not in with the Vārāṇasī establishment either, let alone the Mughal court. One of this group is a migrant from the south, and neither of the others has any obvious affiliation with any powerful family of scholars. The misattribution even of their manual, the *Pearl-necklace of Principles*, seems to be a further indication of their marginalized status. The second striking fact is the originality and daring of their work, which seems less concerned about domesticating Raghunātha than taking his innovating spirit forward into new areas. The 'hidden meaning' genre of commentary embodies a quite different attitude towards the ancient than the one voiced by Viśvanātha. It seeks to bring the past into the present, rather than reduce the present to the past. They are all, moreover, exceptionally productive, and much of their other work is innovative in content and style. If I were to hazard a speculation about the type of intervention that this body of work makes, it is that it attempts to be faithful to Raghunātha's spirit, and, in particular, to the new method which attaches great importance to the use of language as a tool in philosophy. I am tempted to go further, and conjecture that it is precisely because they are less constrained by the demands of a scholarly 'family business' that they are able to exercise a sort of intellectual independence not so evident in the first stream, linked as that is to prestige and status and position.[38]

A Navadvīpa-based network

My third group consists of what one might call the 'Navadvīpa establishment'. It begins again with one of Raghunātha's immediate followers, a philosopher called **Jānakīnātha** Bhaṭṭācārya Cūḍāmaṇi.[39] He was active in 1529, if it is true that there is a letter to him from Māheśa Ṭhakkura, a Mithilā philosopher who would become the Rājā of Mithilā in 1557.[40] He is the author of a second popular teaching manual, *The Panicle of Principles about Reason* (*Nyāya-siddhānta-mañjarī*). He precedes a quotation from Raghunātha with the words 'The new thinkers, however, [say that] . . .', implying an acknowledgement already of the innovativeness and importance of Raghunātha's ideas among his peers.[41] He wrote the *Analysis of the Nature of Philosophical Method* (*ānvīkṣikī-tattva-vivaraṇa*), in the form of a commentary on Chapter 5 of the *Nyāya-sūtra*.[42]

I will very briefly mention **Kaṇāda** Tarkavāgīśa, the somewhat obscure pupil of Jānakīnātha and/or contemporary of Raghunātha. He might have also studied with

[38] Another instance is **Veṇīdatta** (P 1351), who writes with much originality about Raghunātha's *Inquiry into the True Nature of Things*, but is again, as far as we know, something of an outsider.

[39] NCat 7:237, P975. Fl. 1540 (Potter); 1550 (NCat).

[40] H. Shastri 1912: 9 mistakenly identifies the recipient of the letter as Raghunātha Śiromaṇi. D. C. Bhattacharya 1952: [36]: 'Mr. Śāstrī wrote that a letter by Maheśa Ṭhakkura to "Tārkikacūḍāmaṇi" was found in a book called *Vaivasvata-siddhānta* in Navadvīpa which was written in 1529. It is a matter of great regret that the *Vaivasvata-siddhānta* or the valuable letter found there has been lost. This 'Tārkikacūḍāmaṇi' is undoubtedly Jānakīnātha Bhaṭṭācārya Tārkikacūḍāmaṇi, and he was a contemporary of Maheśa Ṭhakkura.' Ingalls 1951: 22 reaches the same conclusion.

[41] Chakravarti 1915: 274; Matilal 1977: 109; D. C. Bhattacharya 1952: 106–108; Gelblum 1960.

[42] P. K. Sen 2003.

Vāsudeva.[43] He wrote a work called *The Jewel of Language* (*Bhāṣā-ratna*), mentions Raghunātha, and distinguishes between the ancient and the modern philosophers.[44] Also obscure is Jānākīnātha's elder son, **Rāghava** Pañcānana Bhaṭṭācārya,[45] who wrote an intriguing work by the name *Awakening of the Truth about the Self* (*Ātmā-tattva-prabodha*).[46] He criticizes Raghunātha's analysis of the Buddhist concept of momentariness, saying that 'what the new thinkers say is not right' (navyoktam na yuktam; D. C. Bhattacharya 1952 [48], Mishra 1966: 421). Puzzlingly, he also says at the end of the work that 'He who would take the sentences of others and describe them as his own will roast in hell with the elders'.[47] That comment is very interesting because it indicates a new concern with authenticity, authorial originality, and correct attribution, virtues distinctively associated with modernity.

The younger son, **Rāmabhadra Sārvabhauma,**[48] establishes an extremely successful ṭol in Navadvīpa, one which would go on to produce a generation of the most important voices of the 'new reason' in Bengal. Yaśovijaya mentions him by name. His literary corpus includes commentaries on Raghunātha's treatises, on the first four chapters of the *Nyāya-sūtra*, on his father's *Panicle*, and several other works.[49] He adopts and greatly develops Raghunātha's technique of writing treatises on particular topics. His commentary on the *Nyāya-sūtra* is called 'rahasya' typically indicating an intention to uncover the hidden or deep meaning in the text. In contrast with the desire to find compatibility between the new and the ancient, this again reveals a more constructive intention, to engage the ancient text in a creative dialogue with the present. Rāmabhadra indeed begins his work with a 'boastful comment' (P. K. Sen 2003: lxxxviii), in which he ventures to be critical of the ancients.[50] Rāmabhadra is clearly an independently minded philosopher in the new mould, a *via moderna* thinker, frequently disagreeing both with the ancient tradition and with Raghunātha. For example, he rejects Raghunātha's claim that the role of the negative in the sentence 'One should

[43] See his commentary on the *Tattvacintāmaṇi* (Asiatic Society mss 785, 3504; cf. NCat 3: 126, 8: 21; see also Chakravarti 1915: 276, n. 2). According to D. C. Bhattacharya (1952 [51]), at fol. 15/2, Kaṇāda refers to Vācaspati Miśra II as a 'navya-naiyāyika.' The introductory verse acknowledges Sārvabhauma, and Bhattacharya therefore speculates that Kaṇāda began his studies with Vāsudeva, putting his birth at 1460/70 and his productive period at 1510–25.

[44] D. C. Bhattacharya 1952 [49]; Matilal 1977: 109. E.g. fol 3a of Asiatic Soc. 7889. Shastri says 'The author Kaṇāda is regarded by the paṇḍits of Bengal as an elder contemporary of Raghunātha Śiromaṇi. [They say that] it is Kaṇāda who induced Raghunātha to proceed to Mithilā to complete his education in Nyāya-śāstra. But this idea seems to be wrong, for Kaṇāda quotes Raghunātha' (1939: 282). Bhattacharya corrects Aufrecht's mistaken assertion that Kaṇāda wrote the *Āpa-śabda-khaṇḍana* (NCat 3: 126).

[45] P DU555, NCat 2.46.

[46] The manuscript is fragmented: one part is Baroda ms. 4179, another part is Stein ms. 2530. Rāghava might also have written on Raghunātha's treatise on verbs (IO ms. 2048).

[47] paravākyaṃ gṛhītvā tu svayam uktaṃ vadettu yaḥ akalpyam pacyate ghore narake pitṛbhiḥ saha . . . ; (quoted in D. C. Bhattacharya 1952 [47–48]).

[48] P 1113.

[49] P. K. Sen 2003: lxxiii–lxxxvi.

[50] bhāṣyādīnaṃ vacanaracanā kevalaṃ, prāyo yatra prakaraṇakathā prākṛtī bhāratīva | sūte tattvaṃ na hi tadubhayaṃ kintu mohaṃ prasūte, ko jānīyāj jagati matimānasya śāstrasya tattvam | | (Rāmabhadra 2003: 1, 9–12).

not eat *kalañja*' is such that it says that the non-eating of *kalañja* will lead to one's desired end, rendering the sentence as saying, instead, that the eating of *kalañja* will lead to something not desired—death or sin (Matilal 1968: 166). Likewise, he argues against several of the metaphysical positions Raghunātha adopts in the *Inquiry*.[51] Though he takes issue with Raghunātha, he is not a conservative scholastic by any means, and he is willing to argue for strikingly unorthodox views. Against the overwhelming consensus—ancient and modern—that the liberated self has no mental states at all, Rāmabhadra argues that it is in a state of permanent happiness.[52]

There is good evidence that his commentary on Udayana incorporates work by the pre-Raghunātha Mithilā philosopher Śaṃkara Miśra.[53] Gaṅgeśa's son, it is true, would often reproduce blocks of his father's work wholesale, but his intention could not have been to pass off such text as his own (who could he have hoped to fool?); rather, it was to superimpose the theoretical framework of the *Gemstone* upon more ancient Nyāya works. The significance of Rāmabhadra's appropriation is less clear.

Rāmabhadra's most important student is **Jayarāma** Nyāyapañcānana, someone who also migrates from Bengal to Vārāṇasī.[54] I have mentioned Jayarāma several times already, and will discuss his work in detail in later chapters of this book. He is a public figure: he signed the declaration of the Vārāṇasī paṇḍits in 1657; he received the patronage of Rājā Rāmakṛṣṇa of Kṛṣṇapur; he contributed prominently to the tributes to Kavīndra; he is mentioned in Bhīmasena Dīkṣita's *Alaṅkāra-sāra-sthiti*, written in 1655 during the rule of Ajitasiṃha in Jodhpur (Chakravarti 1915: 284). Developing the genre from Raghunātha and Rāmabhadra, Jayarāma wrote a large number of treatises on many topics, and his work on the ownership of property (*svatva*) represents an important development of a brief remark by Raghunātha. This treatise indicates a willingness to apply the techniques of the 'new reason' to contemporary problems of law; it is the earliest of at least four such works. In 1659 Jayarāma completed his magnum opus on metaphysics, the *Garland of Categories* (*Padārtha-mālā*). Janārdana Vyāsa and Laugākṣā Bhāskara, his students, will both write commentaries on the *Garland* and also on Jānakīnātha's *Panicle* (Potter 1210.1, 2; 1236.3, 4). Jayarāma wrote about Mammaṭa's work in poetics, the *Kāvya-prakāśa*; and in this Janārdana will follow, writing a commentary, the *Ślokadīpikā* (NCat 7: 153), on Mammaṭa under the patronage of Kavīndra himself. This further confirms the connection between Jayarāma and Bernier's 'paṇḍit'.

[51] Thus, he disagrees with Raghunātha about emergent colour-topes or *citra-rūpa* (P. K. Sen 2003: lxxv), and about the nature of the self (Pahi and Jain 1997: 12–13).

[52] *Mokṣavāda* (Poona ms. 460, fol. 20b–21b; quoted and discussed by P. K. Sen 2003: lxxv–lxxviii). Sen notes that his view about liberation resembles that of Advaita Vedānta, and suggests that he was the reason later Naiyāyikas went to some lengths to argue for the privative nature of *mokṣa*.

[53] Kaviraja 1961: 64, n. 16.

[54] NCat 7:188, P 1127. Fl. 1650. That he is a pupil of a Rāmabhadra is clear from the opening verse of his commentary on the *Light-Ray* (IO ms. 1900). M. D. Shastri's argument (Jayāyrama 1927–8: 17–19) that this is not Rāmabhadra Sārvabhauma but Rāmabhadra Siddhāntavāgīśa is disputed by D. C. Bhattacharya 1945, and the matter conclusively settled by Sen 2003: cxiii.

Jayarāma's *Garland of Principles (Nyāya-siddhānta-mālā)*, written after the *Garland of Categories*[55] and copied as early as 1676, is a remarkable work. It is primarily a commentary on selected sūtras from the *Nyāya-sūtra*, the selection being of the parts of the text dealing with the method of inquiry. A final section to the text (1927: 171–179), which gives an account of the main doctrines of various Indian philosophical systems, turns out to be almost identical to a part of Śaṅkara Miśra's *Vādavinoda* (1915: 53–58). Jayarāma concludes his text with a verse asserting authorship, and there is here no question of a simple miscollation of manuscripts (Mishra 1966: 440). It thus seems that both Rāmabhadra and Jayarāma have made use of Śaṅkara Miśra's material.

Mathurānātha Tarkavāgīśa[56] is famous for his many and voluminous commentaries, of which his commentary directly on Gaṅgeśa's *Gemstone* is regarded highly because of its exemplary clarity, whereas his commentary on Raghunātha is overshadowed by the better works of Jagadīśa and Gadādhara. While Raghunātha did not comment on every section of the *Gemstone*, and even when he did have a comment it was generally laconic, Mathurānātha set himself to explain and clarify the whole of the text. Mathurānātha is the son of Śrī Rāma, and another pupil of Rāmabhadra.[57] Daniel Ingalls records a parallel passage in the work of Mathurānātha and Jānakīnātha, one involving a particularly strained interpretation, and remarks that 'Mathurā's prejudice is easier to explain when we recognize that he is trained in a school that goes back to Jānakīnātha' (Ingalls 1951: 23). He cautiously surmises Mathurānātha's dates to be 1600–75 give or take 25 years.

Rivalry over Raghunātha

Can we draw any conclusions about this third group on the evidence assembled here? The first point is that they are strongly based in Navadvīpa, with only Jayarāma going to Vārāṇasī. In this group, as in the first, there is a concern with the very ancient, manifested in the collaborative commentary on the *Nyāya-sūtra*, but there is also a desire to be autonomous, to follow the *via moderna*. There is the rather strange way in which the work of Śaṃkara Miśra, a Mithilā philosopher from a previous century, is incorporated. And there is, in one of this group, an explicit concern with proper attribution. I have already described in some detail the unusual circumstances in Navadvīpa in the sixteenth and seventeenth centuries, with patronage from Muslim sultans and Hindu rājās, and an emergent Bengali Vaiṣṇavism. I think that one can say, at the very least, that these philosophers are committed to the continuation of Navadvīpa as a place famous for learning, able to attract students from far afield, a vital intellectual hub. It seems to be the case that in Navadvīpa educational techniques

[55] To which it refers: 1927: 4, 1; 7, 3.
[56] P 1188. Fl. 1650 (Potter).
[57] See P. K. Sen 2003: cxiv; D. C. Bhattacharya 1952: 128, 162.

were developed which encouraged innovativeness, with students being asked to write papers with their own original ideas, and learning how to do so by watching teachers debating with each other (Sankhyatirtha 1964: 19, 46; Sinha 1993: 6). Innovative teaching methods were perhaps one of the ways in which Navadvīpa distinguished itself from Vārāṇasī and other, more traditional, centres of scholarship.

It is also clear also that there is considerable rivalry between this group and the other two. Rivalry is exemplified clearly in their advocacy of different teaching manuals with similar names—the *Pearl-necklace of Principles about Reason* and the *Panicle of Principles about Reason*.[58] It is also evident in their hostile and competitive attitude towards Bhavānanda. One interesting form that the rivalry took concerns the establishment of the text of Raghunātha's work. The laconic and difficult style of the *Light-Ray* made it hard accurately to transcribe, and it seems that within an exceptionally short period of time real controversy about the correct reading was possible. There is clear evidence that Rāmabhadra and Kṛṣṇadāsa established the text differently, and these differences were propagated in their respective schools. An example occurs with respect to a paragraph in which Raghunātha analyses the logical fallacy known as 'unestablished' (*asiddha*). Jagadīśa (on whom see below) observes that there are variant readings of the text.[59] The reading he selects is approved by Jayarāma and identified as the one accepted by his teacher, Rāmabhadra.[60] The other reading is one Bhavānanda endorses.[61] Mathurānātha too notes the two readings.

New developments in Navadvīpa

In fact, **Jagadīśa** Tarkālaṃkāra[62] seems to have had a foot in both camps, perhaps sequentially.[63] That it was possible for him to do so is due, in part, to his apparently

[58] Other texts have a similar function. Shastri says of a work on the Navya Nyāya theory of joint causation: 'Every family of Naiyāyikas in Bengal has a *sāmagrī-vicāra* of its own' (Shastri 1939 on RASB 7820, 7821).

[59] ucyata ityanantaram asmatsampradāyasiddhaḥ pāṭho likhyate | (Jagadīśa 1908: 1184). For another instance where Jagadīśa disagrees with a textual emendation of the *Light-Ray* suggested by Bhavānanda, see K. Bhattacharya 2001: 22.

[60] gurucarana itthvaṃ pāṭhaṃ kalpayanti | (Jayarāma, *Hetvābhāsa-dīdhiti-ṭippaṇī*, Asiatic Soc. ms. 7627 (548), fol. 61v). Compare Jayarāma 1927: 107.

[61] In rare editorial footnotes, the editors of the *Jāgadīśī* and the *Gādādharī* quote the alternative reading and attribute it to Bhavānanda: 'atra ucyate ityārabhya vaktavyam ityantaṃ bhavānandādīnām anyathaiva dīdhitipāṭhaḥ sammataḥ iti pāṭhadvaividhyasya prasiddhatayā jagadīśena svābhipretapāṭham ullikhya vyākhyo kṛtā' (Jagadīśa 1908: 1184, fn.); 'ayam atra jāgadīśasampradāyiko dīdhitipāṭhaḥ, bhavānandādisammatas tu...' (Gadādhara 1927: 1853, fn.).

[62] NCat 7:126, P1133. Fl. 1600–20 (a ms. of *Tarkāmṛta*, Deccan College Cat. of 1881–82, no. 386, is dated 1631).

[63] That he was a student of Rāmabhadra is established by his statement in the *Maṇimayukhya* (Sans. Coll. Cat. III: 324, ms. no. 575, v. 2); that he is a student of Sārvabhauma, together with his reference in the *Illumination of Semantic Powers* (1980–85: 25) to the *Nyāya-rahasya* as a text written by his teacher (cf. Chakravarti 1915: 282, n. 1; Mishra 1966: 352; Sen 2003: cxii). The evidence for his apprenticeship with Bhavānanda is less sure: Mishra 1966: 351 refers to an oral tradition among Bengali paṇḍits.

having Maithilī and not Bengali roots.[64] Of all the commentaries on the *Light-Ray*, Jagadīśa's was swiftly endorsed as the best. Many sections of this work are found as individual tracts. If an apprenticeship under Rāmabhadra equipped him as a consummate commentator on the canon, his encounter with the new semantic methods being pioneered by Bhavānanda would bear another fruit, his *Illumination of Semantic Powers*, a brilliant inquiry into the nature of meaning.

Another voice of the 'new reason', and an exceptionally important one, is **Harirāma** Tarkavāgīśa Bhaṭṭācārya,[65] a brilliant, prolific and highly original thinker. He was the teacher of Raghudeva, but it is not wholly clear who his own teacher was.[66] As I noted earlier, he commanded great respect and high fees in open debate as the recognized head of the community of Naiyāyikas in his day. Spurning the commentary,[67] he instead wrote short treatises on a host of contemporary philosophical problems. Some works include the term 'new' in the very title: the *Nyāya-navya-mata-vicāra* and the *Navya-dharmitāvacchedakatā*. Many of the treatments deal with specific concepts in the theory of the process and forms of inference; some deal with the philosophy of mind, specifically the theory of cognitive content; others are works of metaphysics, especially the theory of causation.[68] He writes on philosophical grammar, on the gerundive affix (*ktvā*), the particle 'only' (*eva*) as well as the thematic case roles. In one work, he deals with the concept of liberation (*mukti*), Naiyāyikas since Raghunātha having argued over exactly which type of absence is involved in the 'absence of suffering' definitive of liberation.[69] Harirāma's unconventionality is striking.

Gadādhara Bhaṭṭācārya[70] is another of Harirāma's students.[71] He has no academic title, a fact explained in oral tradition as due to his inheriting Harirāma's ṭol before he had a chance to be examined. His commentary on the *Light-Ray* is exhaustive, and it acquired great popularity and was 'commented, criticized and defended by dozens of

[64] Mishra 1966: 351, who somewhat bizarrely lists him under the Mithilā school; cf. D. C. Bhattacharya 1952: 167.

[65] P 1168. Fl. 1640 (Potter). He is older than 1644, the transcription date of a manuscript (Chakravarti 1915: 288); and one of his students signed the 1657 letter of judgement.

[66] D. C. Bhattattacharya 1952: 3, 19 is willing to speculate that Harirāma belonged to the ṭol of Rāmabhadra because his student Gadādhara endorses this school's establishment of Raghunātha's text. If the speculation is correct, then the dates would point to his being a direct student of Rāmabhadra. P. K. Sen 2003: cxiv is, however, unconvinced.

[67] His perfunctory commentary on the *Gemstone* exists only in fragments, and is said to be 'a mere adaptation' of the original (Kaviraja 1961: 65). His only other commentary is on Śivāditya's *Saptapadārthī* (Kaviraja 1961: 68; no ms.). His treatise on Taraṇi Miśra's *Ratnakośa* (Potter 1168.22) is an independent tract, an extended refutation. Taraṇi Miśra [P 780; fl. 1300 Potter] is an important but forgotten pre-Gaṅgeśa Naiyāyika. He is quoted by Maṇikaṇṭha, Vācaspati Miśra II, Vardhamāna and Śaṃkara Miśra; his definition of an inferential fallacy (*hetvābhāsa*) is criticized at length by Jayarāma in the *Garland of Principles*. See also Gopikamohan Bhattacharya 1966.

[68] Birajmohan 1963: 1–23 has useful notes on several of Harirāma's treatises.

[69] Harirāma, Raghudeva, Gadādhara and Gokulanātha all wrote a *Treatise on Liberation*, the impetus coming from Rāmabhadra's controversial claim that it consists in something more than a mere absence. See Prajapati 2001: 81–82; 2008.

[70] NCat 5:295, P 1237. Fl. 1604–1709.

[71] Curiously, there does not appear to be any hard evidence, but neither has anyone doubted the claim.

writers, mostly non-Bengalis' (Chakravarti 1915: 289). This is one piece of evidence of a migration of the 'new reason' from the beginning of the eighteenth century, as Bengal began to afford a less hospitable environment. Although certainly a masterful commentator, Gadādhara's much greater celebrity derives from his composition of a great number of critical treatments of individual topics. The *Treatise on Semantic Powers*, a work in the philosophy of language, contains both a fully worked-out general semantics and a very detailed analysis of the semantics of a host of individual terms, including proper names and theoretical terms, anaphoric pronouns, and semantically difficult terms like the conjunctive 'sun and moon' (*puṣpavant*), and so on.[72] Some of his discussions reach a degree of analytical sophistication not seen in Europe until the late twentieth century (Ganeri 1999b). The *Vyutpattivāda* is another very important work of philosophical grammar, as is the *Viṣayatāvāda* on cognitive content. Gadādhara echoes Harirāma in choice of material: a great many of his essays are on topics in philosophical logic and philosophical grammar, and there are texts entitled *Navya-mata-vicāra*, *Navya-dharmitāvacchedaka-vādārtha* and *Navya-viṣayatā-vāḍa*, explicitly declaring themselves to be about the modern view. Gadādhara displays a keenness to apply the new methodology to a range of philosophical problems which overlap with religion and law, including marriage, liberation, the nature of obligation (*vidhi-svarūpa*), and heaven.[73]

This fourth group, probably part of the third, is in many ways the most innovative of all. Harirāma seems to be one of the most thoroughly and deliberately modern of all the philosophers to contribute to the 'new reason'. He seems to have recognized the most clearly that there is a new method, involving the analysis of semantic structure and cognitive content, and to have put this in the foreground of his work. He had virtually no interest in writing commentaries at all.

I began talking about the ṭols, ways of organizing learning around a teacher working at home. One of the results of our study is that there is a strong orientation towards the family in the lines of transmission, in some cases philosophy looking almost like a 'family business'. This method of organization had many strengths, and created the conditions for a sustainable intellectual activity over many generations. On the other hand, it was also in a sense a weakness, for it was inimicable to the development of other forms of knowledge organization and intellectual freedom. Academic virtuosity,

[72] The *Śaktivāda* received the attention of several important post-Gadādhara writers, including Jayarāma Tarkālaṃkāra [NCat 7: 188, P 1278; fl. 1700 NCat], Gadādhara's pupil (Kaviraja 1961: 73) and the son of a court paṇḍit; Kṛṣṇa Bhaṭṭa (Ārde) [NCat 4: 335, P 1268; 1750–1825 NCat], a southerner resident in Vārāṇasī; Kṛṣṇakānta Vidyāvāgīśa [NCat 4: 320, P 1476; fl. 1780 NCat], a contemporary of Mahārāja Giriśacandra. Sudarśanācārya Panjabi [P 1667; fl. 1901 Potter] would comment on the *Śaktivāda* too, and also write a work on the *Nyāyasūtra* entitled *Prasannapadā*, as well as a discussion of Rāmānuja's *Śrībhāṣya*. This latter discussion is evidence of an interest in Viśiṣtādvaita among 'new reason' scholars in Bengal. Gaṅgādhara Kaviratna wrote a commentary on the *kārikās* of Udayana's *Offering*, but interpreting them according to the doctrine of Rāmānuja (CSC 203, p. 170; CSC 750–752).

[73] Two unusual works, the *Devatātma-cetana-vāda*, and the *Viṣṇu-prīti-vāda*, deal with issues in the philosophy of religion.

if too closely allied to family prestige, which in turn brings with it financial reward by way of invitations to public debates and other forms of sponsorship, is thereby constrained, as I think our first group of philosophers demonstrates. There is a greater willingness to be innovative in the more marginalized second group, and in the Navadvīpa-based third and fourth groups. We find in these groups a clear conception of the *via moderna*, in a new willingness to criticize and depart from the ancients, in an emphasis on the individual, on authenticity and correct attribution. These networks of collaboration and contestation create a broad and very critical audience into which any new philosophical text makes an intervention.

I hope also through this survey to have begun the process of putting to an end an enduring but unwarranted myth in Indian philosophical historiography, that Raghunātha's unquestionable innovativeness left little or no trace on his successors, a view rehearsed by Ingalls and Halbfass. As Daya Krishna has effectively shown, however, histories of Indian philosophy which emphasize continuity have their own reasons for doing so, and

> A more adequate picture of the development of Indian philosophy . . . can better be told in terms of the disruption, deviation and innovations which are masked by their apparent disregard and neglect in the *sampradāyas* [ṭol-based schools] themselves. In a culture where a *sampradāya* boasts of its unchanging continuity from the times of its founder, it should be the task of the historian to search for, identify and reconstruct the influence of the radical innovators in the philosophical traditions of India. Perhaps, if we look at Raghunātha's successors in this light we may find that his innovations and departures were not as ineffective as many of the historians have assumed.
> (Krishna 1997b: 180)

Krishna has also emphasized that the ṭol-based system did continue into the eighteenth, nineteenth, and twentieth centuries, and this is true; but with the contraction in fiscal support the opportunity for there to be viable careers on the outskirts of the remaining ṭols diminished, the philosophers who continued naturally tending, like our first group, to have the preservation of the ṭol itself as their primary consideration. The pattern of radical innovation which requires a more penumbral location with respect to the ṭol—as exemplified by the second of our groups—was to become increasingly unsustainable.

7

An Analysis of the New Reason's Literary Artefacts

New genres of philosophical writing, as well as new developments of old genres, emerge in Vārāṇasī and Navadvīpa in the sixteenth and seventeenth centuries. I will here review the main trends, in the hope that doing so will throw still further light on the philosophical programme of the 'new reason' philosophers. Cutting-edge research is performed in the nit and grit of often very large commentaries on the canon, and more free-standing interjections make a stance on some particular topic of controversy. Other texts try to consolidate the new work, either in advanced textbook-type works or in manuals designed to train beginners. The overall contours of this body of philosophy reveals a dynamic and fluid research programme, strong in both research and teaching, one in which, moreover, new ways of writing are developed in order to promote new styles of thinking. I will look in detail at the nature of philosophical commentary in the next chapter, and at several particularly unusual and interesting works in subsequent ones; what I want to do now is to get a sense of the state of the discipline from a survey of its literary artefacts.

Derrett's generic classification of śāstric literature into five groups is a useful initial schema of division. Class A is the simple commentary:

> Some time before the seventh century the simple commentary had arrived. Words had become obsolete or ambiguous. Ellipses needed to be filled. Flexibility had to be found in a text incapable of being repealed ... The commentator adopted a modest tone, frankly admitting that any of several incompatible interpretations might be correct, and sometimes he said that further (unspecified) explanations were needed.
>
> (Derrett 1973a: 48)

Class B is the digest, compositions in verse and prose purporting to be a distillation of doctrine. Derrett stresses the role of such texts in pedagogical instruction:

> Didactic presentation of discordant, co-authoritative sources, these works would be required by any aspiring teacher, and to repeat the gist of any one would be part of the exercises demanded of any candidate for a qualification in the *śāstra*.
>
> (Derrett 1973a: 50)

In class C falls the work of any controversialist who writes a treatise on some point of theory. In the treatise, arguments for and against a thesis are rehearsed with fullness and concision. Derrett's observation on the style of argumentation is important, for it reveals the treatise as aspiring to the ideals of harmony and balance that characterize debate and the deliberative use of reason:

> [T]he opposing view is stated first, with a sign that it is disapproved, or even without this. The reasons and citations behind that view are bracketed carefully with it. The denial and refutation follows, bearing its own reasons and citations. Expected objections to the argument or any article of it are stated and refuted as the exposition progresses.
>
> (Derrett 1973: 51)

A fourth literary form is the 'scissors-and-paste' compilation, amalgamations, typically very bulky, of quotations from previous works. Such works were popular in the Dharmaśāstra, the reason being that compilations of the law were largely the product of royal commission, the work of administrator–scholars. Belonging to class E is a new genre of digest, which, besides being a comprehensive survey of doctrine, aspires fully to report and rehearse the argumentation with respect to conflicting views.

The 'scissors-and-paste' compilation does not seem to be exemplified in early modern philosophy; this genre is more specifically related to the juridical functions of the law-books. The commentary, independent treatise and comprehensive survey or manual, however, are not only exemplified but enriched and developed by the writers on Navya Nyāya. Raghunātha's commentary, *The Light-Ray* (*Dīdhiti*), on Gaṅgeśa's *Gemstone*, itself became a focal point for considerable subcommentarial literary endeavour. The *Dīdhiti* introduces into the genre of commentary elements of other philosophical styles, specifically the survey and the treatise. Raghunātha not only purports to explain Gaṅgeśa's text, but relates and adjudicates the conflicts among an earlier generation of commentators, particularly Yajñapati and Jayadeva, and as well inserts discussions of philosophical topics not specifically dealt with in the commented-upon text. An example is the *Explanation of What it is to be a Limitor* (*Avacchedakatva-nirukti*), inserted between chapters, in which Raghunātha supplies a treatise-like treatment of an important logical concept. The 'insertion' (*kroḍapatra*; *pātrikā*) would evolve into a philosophical genre in its own right, the short, topical treatment gradually acquiring favour as a vehicle for advancing philosophical discussion. Raghunātha experiments too with the genre of treatise, his *Treatise on Negation* and *Treatise on Finite Verbal Forms* being prime examples. The independent treatise is a style which Harirāma and Gadādhara would make uniquely their own; and it proved an appropriate vehicle in the separation of philosophical inquiry from exegetical analysis. If a *vāda* is a treatise about a topic or concept on which the earlier literature was agnostic or indifferent, Raghunātha's *Inquiry into the True Nature of Things* marks an important innovation in genre, for in this text the purpose is not to explain or develop the canon, but revise and re-evaluate it. In this text, Raghunātha pioneers the genre we might call 'critical treatise' in which deference to the letter of the canon is abandoned in favour of critical assessment, revision, and, where possible, reconstruction.

It is worth noting here that Abū-l-Fażl, in the *Ā'īn-i-Akbarī* (1597 CE), reports a classification of Sanskrit literary–philosophical genres as understood by writers in his day. He distinguishes twelve forms—(1) *sūtra* 'a short technical sentence', (2) *bhāṣya* 'commentary on a somewhat difficult *sūtra*', (3) *vārttika* 'a critical annotation on the two', (4) *ṭīkā* 'commentary (properly of the original or of another commentary) on no. 3', (5) *nibandha* 'an explanation of technical rules', (6) *vṛtti* 'a brief elucidation of some complicated subjects in the first mentioned', (7) *nirukta* 'etymological interpretation of a word'..., (8) *prakaraṇa* 'a section treating of one or two topics', (9) *āhnika* 'a short task sufficing for a diurnal lesson', (10) *pariśiṣṭa* 'a supplement to a technical work', (11) *paddhati* 'a manual of the texts relating to each of the six sciences in prescribed order', (12) *saṃgraha* 'an epitome of the sciences' (Blochmann and Jarrett, vol. 3, 1894: 149–150). I will have more to say about the first five items on this list, in particular, in the next chapter.

Commentaries

The richness and complexity in the genre of commentary in Indian philosophical literature is one of its hallmarks and its strengths. A commentary, as I will explain more fully in the next chapter, mediated a conversation between the past and the present. The commentary therefore offers *us* a route into the question that lies at the heart of *our* study of early modernity in the sixteenth and seventeenth centuries, the question of *their* sense of *their* duties towards, or separation from, the ancient philosophical world. The first step is to determine just what it was, about their philosophical past, which attracted their attention.

First of all, we find in the early modern period a new interest in writing commentaries about the most ancient of all the philosophical treatises that lie in the philosophical past of the 'new reason' philosophers, namely the *Nyāya-sūtra* and the *Vaiśeṣika-sūtra*. Analysis of the sūtra as a genre itself calls for a certain theoretical machinery, and I will postpone putting that in place until the next chapter. It is certainly interesting and important that the early moderns should assume a new interest in producing commentaries on the ancient ur-text of the system, the *Nyāya-sūtra*. Prabal Sen (2003) has the most thorough study of the phenomenon to date, exploring it in detail and with sophistication. The fifth book of the *Nyāya-sūtra* is a treatment of the terms and categories of debate, and is textually somewhat independent of the preceding four chapters.[1] Udayana had already set a precedent for treating it as a separate object of attention, and Jānakīnātha, as we have seen, does the same, as does Annambhaṭṭa. Rāmabhadra supplements this with a fresh commentary on the first four books, thereby providing for his ṭol a complete analysis from their theoretical standpoint. Jayarāma writes the *Garland of Principles* on selected portions of the *Nyāya-sūtra* relevant to methods of inquiry. Viśvanātha wrote a popular commentary on the whole, often drawing upon Rāmabhadra's and occasionally disagreeing with it (Sen 2003: cv–cx). Both Gaurīkānta and Mahādeva Bhaṭṭa are said to have written,[2] and the practice was continued even into the nineteenth century by Kṛṣṇakānta and Sudarśanācārya.

[1] Two good studies are Matilal 1998 and Todeschini 2010.

[2] Mahādeva Bhaṭṭa's *Mitabhāṣiṇi* (SB 185) covers the first four chapters (Kaviraja 1961: 76).

Commentarial interest in the ancient ur-text of the Vaiśeṣika system is far less pronounced. While the Maithilī scholar Śaṃkara Miśra wrote his well-known *Upaskāra*, the only philosophers in the post-Raghunātha 'new reason' known to have attempted something like a commentary is Raghudeva.[3]

It seems then that it is really Rāmabhadra, along with his father, who is responsible for this reappraisal of the very ancient. The practice is subsequently copied by philosophers in his network. Rāmabhadra does not ignore the great number of interpretations that stand between the ancient past and himself; indeed, he makes frequent reference to many of them (Sen 2003: lxxxvii–lxci). What is unmistakable is that these interpretations are not regarded as unchallengeable 'authorities' and Rāmabhadra feels every entitlement to use his own judgement and philosophical instinct. Just what does entitle him to disagree with Vātsyāyana, for example, which he does on at least two occasions? How can he reach back across fifteen hundred years in this way? We might ask exactly the same question, of course, of Gassendi or Spinoza. The answer must be that it is the 'new reason' and the new perspective which it affords, along with its claim to be exploring the facts themselves, which makes this possible. Rāmabhadra is not looking at the world through Gautama's glasses; he is looking at Gautama with all the philosophical clarity that the new vision affords. This is the fundamental shift in the conception of one's duties towards the past which is the key characteristic of early modernity. Why then, we might wonder, is he not willing to disagree with Gautama too? The answer has to do with the very nature of a sūtra text, its textual plasticity making outright disagreement otiose. I will try to show how that can be in the next chapter.

These commentaries on the most ancient texts, although fascinating in their own right and for the insights they afford into the nature of early modernity in India, must be counted as a curiosity. The real focus of interest is elsewhere. The most fundamental stratum of their philosophical past that the early modern writers appeal to is a millennium later, when Gaṅgeśa engages in the renovation of philosophy. Gaṅgeśa himself wrote no commentaries; his only work is the *Gemstone*. His son, Vardhamāna, did, however, and what drew his attention were the two philosophers from a century or two before, Udayana and Vallabha. For the philosophers of our period, it is this stratum which is of real interest, comprising the work of Udayana, Vallabha, Gaṅgeśa, and Vardhamāna's Gaṅgeśa-inspired reading the first two.

One principal reason for returning to Udayana and Vallabha is that it brings metaphysics back into the frame, and indeed effects the well-known merger of two systems that had previously been distinct: Vaiśeṣika and Nyāya. Two of our authors write commentaries on Udayana's *Row of Lightbeams* (*Kiraṇāvalī*), itself a commentary on the metaphysics of an earlier writer, Praśastapāda. Rāmabhadra comments on the chapter about qualities, and Mādhavadeva will subcomment. Raghunātha himself

[3] *Vaiśeṣika-sūtra-vyākhyā* (ms. in Gokul Giri, Vārāṇasī; Potter).

made comments on two chapters of Vardhamāna's commentary, the ones on substances and on qualities, but not on Udayana directly. He also made notes on both Vallabha's *Līlāvatī* and Vardhamāna's commentary on it. After that it was Raghunātha's work which attracted attention, rather than any of the earlier texts in themselves. His student Rāmakṛṣṇa commented on Raghunātha's texts, as did Guṇānanda, Jagadīśa and Rudra. The one exception is the indefatigable Mathurānātha, who managed to write commentaries on all four—Udayana, Vallabha, Vardhamāna, and Raghunātha.

Udayana is also responsible for two other works that our early modern thinkers find extremely interesting. One is his *Discrimination of the Truth about the Self (Ātmatattvaviveka)*. Raghunātha chose to comment on this important critique of Buddhist philosophy, perhaps primarily because it contains valuable meta-philosophical reflection on the Nyāya theory itself. Śrī Rāma and Mathurānātha follow suit, while Guṇānanda and Gadādhara write about Raghunātha's exposition. The other text is Udayana's defence of theism in a group of verses, *An Offering of Flowers* (*Kusumāñjali*), to which he supplied his own surrounding commentary. It is curious that the verses attracted a lot of interest, but not the commentary. Raghunātha and his contemporary Haridāsa, both students of Vāsudeva, write about them, as do Guṇānanda, Rāmabhadra and Rudra. Rāmabhadra's commentary was especially popular, and even seems to have become part of the standard curriculum in Navadvīpa.[4] Jayarāma, Gadādhara and Raghudeva would all write commentaries. All these authors preferred the verses themselves even over Raghunātha's commentary—a pattern the exact reverse of which we found to be true of Udayana's metaphysical work. Another commentary on the verses is the joint work of Śaṅkara Miśra and Rāmabhadra (Kaviraja 1961: 64, n. 16; Mishra 1966). This commentary goes by the name *Āmoda* in Mithilā and *Rāmabhadrī* in Navadvīpa. The opening verse points to Śaṅkara Miśra as the author (Kaviraja 1961: 41), and one manuscript clearly states that the first part is written by him and the second part by Rāmabhadra. This is another instance of Rāmabhadra's use of Śaṃkara Miśra's material.

I suspect that much of the interest in Udayana's theistic verses is pedagogically motivated: this was a useful text to have in the curriculum. On the other hand, what drives the interest in the metaphysical work seems to be, not so much Udayana's text itself, but rather Raghunātha's comments on it. Raghunātha, in the habit of making extremely interesting and provocative, but very elliptical, remarks on whatever text he was reading, gave the philosophers of the 'new reason' a treasure-trove of philosophical insight. A good analogy might be with the notes Wittgenstein made while reading, notes which have stimulated and challenged a generation of thinkers in the last fifty years. The aim is not so much to explain what Wittgenstein really had in mind, but to think through the consequences of the new perspective which the comments bring to view. I think that is exactly how Raghunātha's taciturn commentarial interjections

[4] P. K. Sen 2003: lxxxvi; D. C. Bhattacharya 1952: 123, 193.

functioned in the century after him. That is why, among other things, these later philosophers were less interested in going back to the texts themselves. Mathurānātha has, clearly, an agenda of his own. Indeed, he told us what it is—to fill in whatever Raghunātha had missed so as to provide a complete commentary on each of the texts. He is a system-builder.

Finally, there is a vast body of commentarial literature on Gaṅgeśa's *Gemstone*, on an old and heavily criticized reading of it, Jayadeva's *Light* (*Āloka*), and on Raghunātha's new reading, the *Light-Ray* (*Dīdhiti*). Known commentaries on the *Gemstone* include those of Viśārada, Vāsudeva, Raghunātha, Jānakīnātha, Kaṇāda, Haridāsa, Vidyāvināsa, Bhavānanda, Guṇānanda, Rāmabhadra, Jagadīśa, Rudra, Mathurānātha, Raghudeva, Gadādhara, Jagannātha, Hanumad Bhaṭṭa, Kṛṣṇakānta, and Mukunda Bhaṭṭa.[5] There is considerable imbalance in the coverage of these commentaries; many are only on the second chapter of the book, the book about inferential reasoning. Matters are also confused because individual sections of Gaṅgeśa's text are treated as separate works in their own right, and spawn their own commentarial trees. One reason for the great number of commentaries is that certain sections of the 'inference' chapter came to form part of the standard curriculum in the ṭols, and every teacher therefore produced teaching notes on them, or tried to display their virtuosity over other teachers with flashy interpretations. The number of commentaries on the Maithilī scholar Jayadeva, whose interpretation is firmly rejected by Raghunātha (having defeated him in a famous debate in around 1480), seems to suggest that it was used as a foil. Most recent scholarship on the 'new reason' has also focused on the curricular 'definition of pervasion' literature,[6] a fact which is regrettable because it gives a quite distorted impression of the whole period and its importance. It became easy for any critic who wanted to diminish the significance of the 'new reason' to caricature it as obsessed with the minutia of obscure logical conundrums. Our philosophers cut their teeth here, and won or lost their reputation in exhibition displays of cleverness (something that can still be seen in Tibetan monasteries today); but none of this is, fundamentally, what the 'new reason' represents.

What is the meaning of our philosophers' return to Gaṅgeśa? The answer is not difficult to find. After Gaṅgeśa, a whole industry grew up in Mithilā, and a great body of commentaries on Gaṅgeśa were written. Raghunātha was from Navadvīpa, and went to Mithilā to study before returning there. He will have seen the Mithilā philosophers as an embodiment of a very conservative form of scholasticism, the sort that would, in Europe, give Aristotelianism a bad reputation. And just as progressive Aristotelians wanted to return to Aristotle, so Raghunātha and his new school return to Gaṅgeśa. There will be many disagreements among them, and much debate and

[5] The following later authors, at least, wrote commentaries on Raghunātha: Bhavānanda, Mathurānātha, Jagadīśa, Gadādhara, Jayarāma, Kāśīnātha, Nīlakaṇṭha, Nṛsiṅha Maheśvara, Rudrabhaṭṭa. On Jayadeva, the list is similar.

[6] Ingalls 1951; Wada 1990, 2007; K. Bhattacharya 1977–2005; G. Bhattacharya 1968–69, 1984.

controversy, but all of it based on the principle that there is something valuable in Gaṅgeśa's renovation, something to which the Mithilā scholastics had not remained true. What they find in Gaṅgeśa's text is the beginnings of a new way of doing philosophy, one which proceeds through the close logical analysis of language. Indeed, Raghunātha's two treatises on the negative particle and on finite verbal forms seem to fill lacunae in Gaṅgeśa's work. He was the first to read Gaṅgeśa in this new way.

Internal critiques of Vaiśeṣika metaphysics

Quite different from the Udayana and Gaṅgeśa commentaries is a body of work in metaphysics that takes its leave from Raghunātha's *Inquiry*. Largely it is produced by Vārāṇasī-based thinkers, many of whom, including Viśvanātha, Rudra, Jayarāma, and Raghudeva, would comment directly on the *Inquiry*. It is true that Rāmabhadra and Govinda Śarman too commented on the text, but in Navadvīpa it is Raghunātha's works on logic and philosophical grammar that attract the greater interest. Indeed, we can see the broad lines of the intellectual split between Vārāṇasī and Navadvīpa during this period as one that is determined by the transformation of metaphysics, in Vārāṇasī, and in the construction of a new philosophical method in problems of epistemology and logic, in Navadvīpa. Several Vārāṇasī philosophers also write works that are responsive to the *Inquiry* without being commentaries on it. One of the most original is the *Embellishment of the Categories* (*Padārtha-maṇḍana*) by Veṇīdatta, a work which closely follows the topics and ordering of the *Inquiry* but with considerable philosophical prowess. Veṇīdatta, for example, offers a solution to the problem of historical and fictional names, which Raghunātha had thrown as a puzzle to his contemporaries (1930: 30–31). Another metaphysical work responsive to the *Inquiry* is Jayarāma's *Garland of Categories*, which his students, Laugākṣi Bhāskara and Janārdana Vyāsa, again subcomment on, as they also do on his poetics and on the *Panicle*. Another important work in the same class is Mādhavadeva's large *Essence of [theories about] Reason* (*Nyāya-sāra*). At almost the same time, Raghudeva composes his *Survey of the Essence [of theories about] Substance* (*Dravya-sāra-saṃgraha*). Two grammarians, Kauṇḍa Bhaṭṭa and Nāgeśa Bhaṭṭa, both turn their hand to metaphysics, writing simpler works named *Lamp [shining on] the Categories* (*Padārtha-dīpikā*).

Some authors write treatises which tackle just one issue raised in the *Inquiry*. Very significant among these is a text on the nature of the self by Mahādeva Puṇatāṃakara, the *Examination of Selfhood as a Natural Kind* (*Ātmatva-jāti-vicāra*). This concerns a point of fundamental disagreement between the 'new reason' philosophers, who affirm that there are a plurality of distinct individuals, and thinkers, such as Advaita Vedāntins, who deny that there are. Another topic is the question of the ownership of property. Jayarāma's text, the *Examination of Ownership* (*Svatva-nirūpaṇa*), is one of several to have been written, Gadādhara and Gokulanātha also working on a problem which, yet again, has its roots in the *Inquiry*.

The existence of this genre of little-known work proves that Raghunātha's *Inquiry* was taken very seriously in the seventeenth century, in spite of the fact that it very radically alters, while remaining reliant upon, the traditional metaphysics of the *Vaiśeṣika-sūtra* and Praśastapāda's expansion. It is not revolutionary in the sense of casting aside the entire Vaiśeṣika account in favour of a quite different one, but rather it reworks the basic ideas in line with a new underlying principle. The new principle, as I will show in a later chapter, is an anti-reductionist realism. Much of the ancient metaphysics could be squared with this principle; and much could not be. Raghunātha, in trying to make constructive metaphysics rest on a clear philosophical foundation, has no choice but to engage in a reworking of the ancient categories. His attitude towards ancient philosophy, then, seems to be that there is a good underlying metaphysical insight, but that it has not been articulated with clarity and consistency in the ancient texts or their pre-modern interpreters. One form that the response to Raghunātha takes is to offer a different foundational principle, which, it is claimed can salvage more of the ancient theory. As I will demonstrate later, for many of the Vārāṇasī metaphysicians, that principle is a 'sophisticated' reductive realism. In either case, the point I want to stress is that there has been a fundamental shift in attitude towards the ancient: no longer one of deference, the new attitude is to enter into conversation with, to learn from, ancient sources, but not be beholden to them. This is precisely the attitude, I have claimed, which we find in many of the early modern philosophers in Europe too. It is the distinctive trait of early modernity.

Research monographs

The habit of writing pamphlets on particular topics began with Raghunātha in two short treatises about philosophical linguistics. Bhavānanda did the same, and the technique was greatly expanded by Harirāma, as well as his students Gadādhara[7] and Radhudeva, not to mention Jayarāma. Prahlada Char has studied the genre in considerable detail. He observes (2001: 130) that

> It is fairly clear that by the latter half of the seventeenth century, the attention of Nyāya thinkers had shifted to considerations other than those which related to the notion of truth [*pramātva*]. In fact, an analysis of the *vāda-granthas* which began to be produced during this period...shows that most of them were concerned with issues of epistemology, language and meaning.

A slightly different practice also developed, of writing 'insertions' called *kroḍapatra*, which are short monologues on some topic or issue, inserted into the body of a larger text. Prahlada Char is again one of the few people to have looked at these texts. He remarks (2004: 355–356) that

[7] Many of Gadādhara's treatises are collected in Gadādhara 1933–40.

The very title '*kroḍapatra*' suggests the purpose and scope of the small treatises that are called *kroḍapatras*. '*Kroḍa*' means *madhya* or middle. The term '*patra*' which in common parlance means a letter, also means an article, analytical in nature. Thus, a *kroḍapatra* is an article or a collection of articles with a critical perspective that aims at discussing a point which occurs in the middle of a topic being discussed in the original text. Another explanation given to the term is that *kroḍapatra* is a paper kept in between the pages... Generally the authors of the *kroḍapatras* commence their discussion on a point which the original writer has stated as final.

The genre proved resilient, and a nineteenth-century philosopher Kālī Śaṃkara Siddhāntavāgīśa was particularly prolific.[8]

I have already mentioned that Raghunātha wrote two short autonomous treatises, one on the negative particle 'not' (*nañ*), and one on the meaning of finite verbal forms (whose technical name in Pāṇinian grammar is *ākhyāta*). These two works were discussed very extensively, especially in Navadvīpa, and treatments of other difficult or philosophically interesting parts of grammar were also perpared. These included especially the notion of a *kāraka*, which is something like thematic case role, the meaning of the scope-restricting particle *eva* 'only', the meaning of verbal classes (*lakāra*), the concept of a nominal compound or *samāsa*, and the meaning of the absolutive (*-ktvā*).

Many early modern philosophers would write a commentary on Raghunātha's treatises about negation and finite verbal forms, including Rāmakṛṣṇa, Rāghava, Kṛṣṇadāsa, Bhavānanda, Rāmabhadra, Viśvanātha, Rudra, Mathurānātha, Jayarāma, Gadādhara, and Raghudeva. Later on, Jagannātha of Trivenī, Rāmnāth 'the wild', and Rāmacandra would continue the tradition. Few if any subcommentaries on these texts seem to have been written, a fact which supports my earlier conjecture that their primary function is pedagogical; but no proper comparative study of them has yet been undertaken.[9]

Viśvanātha and Rudra deal with the problem of case roles in separate treatises, following the lead provided by Bhavānanda. Rāmarūdra writes a commentary on Bhavānanda's work, as does the nineteenth-century author Bhāvadeva. However, the ṭol of Rāmabhadra also took an interest in the issue, and three seventeenth-century authors, Harirāma, Jayarāma, and Gadādhara, all discuss it, as does Jagadīśa in his *Illumination of The Power of Words*. The 'new reason's interest in thematic case relations is explicable in terms of their concern with the deep logical form of sentences (Matilal 1991; Ganeri 1999b).

Recognition of the logical significance of the particle *eva* 'only' goes back to the Buddhist logician Diṅnāga, and to his famous commentator Dharmakīrti, both of whom used the particle to disambiguate the clauses of their logical theory (*trairūpya*). New reason thinkers, for whom an interest in the expression of quantification was

[8] See Sastri 1968; Prahlada Char 2001: 147–151, 188–209.

[9] The commentaries on the *Treatise on Verbal Forms* have been very well edited in Bakre 1931 (Mathurānātha, Jayarāma, Rudra, Rāmakṛṣṇa, Rāmacandra), Sen 1979 (Rāmabhadra), and Tatacharya 1972 (Raghudeva); but on the *Treatise on Negation* only those of Raghudeva (Tatacharya 1972) and Gadādhara (Lokanatha 1899) have been edited to date.

natural, construct a theory for the semantics of *eva* importantly distinct from that of the Buddhists. The sentence 'Pārtha alone is an archer' means, to a first approximation, that no one other than Pārtha is an archer; but one question is whether this *asserts* or merely *implicates* that Pārtha himself is an archer. Bhavānanda again seems to have been the first to provide an independent discussion, followed by Mathurānātha, Harirāma and Gadādhara. Laugākṣī and Mādhavadeva also treat the topic, the term having already been analysed in some detail by Jayarāma in his *Garland of Principles*. Needless to say, the origins of the whole discussion are due to Raghunātha, who remarks on the term in the course of his commentary on Vallabha. This is a good example of the point I made about Raghunātha's commentaries, that they essentially function as extremely thought-provoking asides. In any case, the whole discussion of *eva* among these philosophers is highly instructive of the new logical–semantical methodology for philosophy they were developing, and for this reason I have included a more detailed exploration later in this book.

There are treatises on the compounding (*samāsa*) of nouns. An important issue in the construction of a compositional semantics and in any case a rich and distinctive feature of Sanskrit, the topic of compounds was treated by Rāmabhadra, Govinda, and Jayarāma in independent tracts, and by others in composite works. It is sometimes unclear whether a tract is actually part of a larger work, lost or unfinished. There are treatises too about verbal groups (*lakāra*). Once again, it is Bhavānanda who first writes on this topic separately, with Gadādhara following suit. There is work on the absolutive (*ktvā*). The problem here is that in a sentence with two verbs, there are issues about temporal ordering. The only known treatise independently discussing this is by Harirāma (Stein 2556, CSC 807; acc. no. 560). There are treatises on the notion of a limitor (*avacchedaka*). This is an important concept in 'new reason' logic, and again it is Raghunātha who first writes about it, in an insertion into his commentary on Gaṅgeśa. It is in this same text that he formulates his new theory about the nature of mathematical entities, which I will examine in detail in a later chapter. Bhavānanda, Jagadīśa, Mathurānātha, Gadādhara, Mahādeva, and Gokulanātha all write tracts in which they develop the theory of limitors and associated concepts. There are treatises on notion of truth and knowledge (*prāmāṇya*). Here, Harirāma's *Treatise on Truth* (*Prāmāṇyavāda*) is a significant and well-known work. Many other short treatises are written in the seventeenth century, on a variety of topics, certainly including many details of the epistemology of inference.[10]

Manuals for new students

A fair number of teaching manuals in the new theory were written in the sixteenth century. The very fact that a need for them was felt is indicative of the increasing

[10] A useful list of such treatises is in Krishna 2001: 372–373.

importance of popular dissemination, and a new demand for training. They are designed to present the broad outlines of the theory in relatively easy language, and do not have a rich dialectical structure, rarely presenting many of the arguments for and against a position. Jānakīnātha's *Panicle of Principles about Reason* (*Nyāya-siddhānta-mañjarī*) received commentary from his son Rāmabhadra, and then from two pupils of Rāmabhadra's student Jayarāma, Laugākṣi Bhāskara and Janārdana Vyāsa, all living in Vārāṇasī.[11] Laugākṣī wrote his own manual too, the *Moonlight of Reason* (*Tarka-kaumudī*). More popular, however, was Kṛṣṇadāsa's work, with a title which echoes Jānakīnātha's, the *Pearl-necklace of Principles about Reason* (*Nyāya-siddhānta-muktāvalī*). It is an auto-commentary on a set of verses called the *Necklace of Verses* (*Kārikāvalī*), also known by the title *Divisions of Language* (*Bhāṣā-pariccheda*). It attracted a whole series of nested commentaries, most familiarly those by two Bengalis living in Vārāṇasī, Dinakara and Rāmarudra. A comparative study of the respective seventeenth-century commentaries on these two manuals would be of considerable social historical interest. Another manual, the *Survey of [what can be known through] Reason* (*Tarka-saṃgraha*) with auto-commentary, was written by Annambhaṭṭa in the seventeenth century, a south Indian who spent time in Vārāṇasī and taught the work of Gadādhara to his students (Thakur 2003: 351–352). This manual became very popular and has been used by teachers of the 'new reason' ever since. Annambhaṭṭa says explicitly that his intention was to write a book that would be of help to beginners in the field.[12] The grammarian Kauṇḍabhaṭṭa somewhat surprisingly turned his hand to writing an introduction similar to Annambhaṭṭa's, the *Lamp on the Categories* (*Padārtha-dīpikā*), and indeed he too says that he did so 'in order to bring light to the minds of beginners'.[13] On the other hand, a teaching manual is by nature rather conservative and simplistic, and too great a focus on these manuals, which lack rich argumentative depth or daring innovation, has been a limiting factor in the study of early modern philosophy, and possibly the cause of a certain impression among historians that the period lacks vitality (cf. Frauwallner 1994a: 45).

In the early modern period, it is not uncommon for a commentator to write both a long and a short commentary on the same text, the shorter work being often an 'epitome' of the long one.[14] Mahādeva writes a shorter version of his longer *Illumination of Bhavānanda's Commentary* (*Bhāvānandī–prakāśa*), called the *Aid to the Bhāvānandī* (*Bhāvānandī-sarvopakāriṇī*). Kauṇḍa bhaṭṭa writes a distillation of his *Ornament of Grammarian Philosophy* (*Vaiyākaraṇa-bhūṣaṇa*) on Bhaṭṭoji Dīkṣita's *Emergence of Grammatical Thought* (*Vaiyākaraṇa-matonmajjana*), called the *Essence of the Ornament* (*Vaiyākaraṇa-bhūṣaṇa-sāra*). Another grammarian, Nāgeśa, wrote a long and a short version of his

[11] Jādavācārya, the student of one of Raghunātha's, might also have commented on this treatise, as might Śrīkṛṣṇa Sārvabhauma.

[12] 'I wrote the *Survey of Reason* in order to improve the understanding of beginners' (bālānāṃ sukhabodhāya kriyate tarkasaṃgrahaḥ | (1918: 1, 2).

[13] bālabuddhi-prakāśārthaṃ padārthānāṃ pradīpikā | (Kauṇḍabhaṭṭa 1900: 51).

[14] OED, sv. *epitome*: 'A brief statement of the chief points in a literary work; an abridgement, abstract.'

commentary on Bhaṭṭoji Dīkṣita's *Precious Jewel of Principles* (*Siddhānta-kaumudī*), the *Long and the Short Divine Crest of Language* (*Bṛhat-śabdenduśekhara* and *Laghu-śabdenduśekhara*). He likewise prepared a long and short version of his work on grammatical philosophy, the *Long* and the *Short Basket of Principles* (*Bṛhat-mañjūṣā* and *Laghu-siddhānta-mañjūṣā*), and developed the genre a step further by writing an extremely short version of the same, the *Extremely Short Basket* (*Parama-laghu-siddhānta-mañjūṣā*). This was no doubt very helpful for the progressive education of students in grammar.

This survey of the literature clearly attests to the existence of an active and ongoing research programme. The 'cutting edge' here is the intensive work being done within the detailed commentaries, properly accessible only to those at the very forefront of the field, and in the research monographs, equally difficult for non-specialists to appreciate. The commentaries, especially on the difficult sections of the *Gemstone*, were a crucible for innovation, a forum for the generation of new theoretical ideas. My survey raises a question about Sheldon Pollock's view of the new intellectuals of the seventeenth century, that their work displays a 'paradoxical combination of something very new in style subserving something very old in substance' (2001a: 407). According to Pollock,

> The 'new logicians' or 'new grammarians' demonstrated discursive innovations that were substantial—the terminology, style, and modes of analysis underwent a radical transformation across these and other disciplines—though their conceptual breaks remain to be clearly spelled out, and at first view seem for the most part modest or subtle or questions of detail rather than structure.
>
> (2001a: 405)

What we have now seen is that there was indeed a structural transformation in, first of all, the attitude towards the past, and, secondly, the emergence of a new methodology for philosophy. Pollock may have been misled by the production during the period of manuals, which gained very wide circulation but which are misleading in the impression they give of the fluidity and dynamism of the field.[15] On the face of it, at least, there seems to be nothing modest in the 'new reason' philosophers' ambitions in the foundations of metaphysics, in the possibility of inquiry, and in language as a new tool for transforming philosophy. The breadth of the agenda can be seen when we look upon the corpus of literary artefacts in the round.

Let me highlight here four works of particular interest in establishing the philosophical contours of the 'new reason'. Mādhavadeva writes a kind of advanced textbook, the *Essence of Reason*, a work which must be distinguished sharply from the manuals for beginners. It is a treatise that presents a unified picture of the research programme as it appears from the cutting edge. Mahādeva writes a sort of 'state of the art' review, *The*

[15] Pollock might also have been influenced by the work of Erich Frauwallner. Frauwallner studied the 'new reason' between 1962 and 1967, and his writings from that period display a clear bias in favour of Gaṅgeśa, with a corresponding desire to downgrade the later contributions; he is condescending even about Raghunātha, whose laconic style clearly irritates him (see Chapter 13 below).

Precious Jewel of Reason, in which the full complexity of the range of different positions and theories is brought together in a single framework. It is a kind of stocktaking, needed to get a sense of perspective in an active ongoing research programme. Jayarāma's *Garland of Principles about Reason* is a guide to conducting inquiry, one which assumes the form of a selective commentary on the ancient sources. His *Garland of the Categories* is perhaps the most thorough 'new reason' work on metaphysics. I will attend, in later chapters, to these four works as a principal way to explore the philosophical content of the 'new reason' programme, and so to form a clearer picture of where its 'conceptual breaks', if indeed any there were, might occur.

8

Commentary and Creativity

Commentary as mediating a conversation with the past

In early modern India the genre of commentary continues to be a very important form of philosophical writing. There are commentarial assimilations of the older tradition, and there are rival commentaries on the core texts of the new movement, texts such as Gaṅgeśa's *Gemstone* and the *Light-Ray* of Raghunātha. Commentaries were also written as teaching aids, being either teacher's notes or student exercises. I have surveyed these genres of commentarial writing in the last chapter. It is essential, if we are to understand the philosophy of the period, to have an understanding of what it meant to write a commentary, and how philosophy is done in a commentarial medium. One principal function of commentary is to mediate a conversation between a contemporary readership and an ancient text, and for that reason commentaries give historians a very useful tool to examine how early modern philosophers conceived of their duties to the past. An extremely influential genre of commentary is one which takes the aphoristic assertions of the ancient *sūtra*-compilations and weaves them into a unified, coherent text. A very important development occurs when authors begin to invent their own 'aphorisms' which are now more like axioms or principles, and write a narrative gloss around them. This genre is one which is very familiar to historians of early modern philosophy in Europe, through works like Descartes' *Principles* and Spinoza's *Ethics*.

It has been said that an interpretation of a literary work is prized to the extent that it shows the work in question to possess those qualities which, in the opinion of the times, distinguish literature from other forms of writing (Fish 1980: 351). Adapting this suggestion, we might say that a commentary on a philosophical treatise succeeds to the extent that it demonstrates that the treatise is rich in the features which, for the community of readers to whom the commentary is directed, are held to be characteristic of good philosophy. A successful philosophical commentary helps its target audience to *read philosophically* the text being commented upon, and as such it mediates between the text and a given readership. A commentary is an 'intervention' in the sense of the previous chapters: it brings the past to the present. Potentially, the features which can be used in this way to mark out a text as being a valuable work of philosophy might include coherence and completeness in the description of a point of view, sound argument in favour of the view described, engagement with alternative views, demonstration of the utility of the view in question, and so on. At later times or in different cultural communities, new audiences can examine a commentary as a window through which to see what the practice of philosophical reading meant at the time when the commentary was written.

Formally, two aspects of philosophical commentary in Sanskrit are especially noteworthy. First, the base texts are generally extremely compact. Indeed, compactness is seen as a commendable property in the foundational texts of all types of technical writing. So a characteristic function of one genre of philosophical commentary is to *decompress* the text being commented on. Second, commentary writing is heavily nested; that is to say, there are in general multiple commentaries on any given text, commentaries on those commentaries, commentaries on the subcommentaries, and so on. This nesting gives rise to another characteristic function of philosophical commentary, which is to *adjudicate* between rival commentary at a lower level. These two aspects lead to a distinctive, canonical pattern in the older commentarial literature:

0. *sūtra*. An aggregation of short formula-like assertions.
1. *bhāṣya*. A commentary on a *sūtra* whose function is to unpack and weave together the elliptical assertions.
2. *vārttika*. A subcommentary on a *bhāṣya*, defending its particular construction of the *sūtra* over alternatives, making revisions and adjustments as necessary.
3. *nibandha*, and other higher-level commentarial works, which continue the process of revision and adjustment until a state of reflective equilibrium is reached.

The importance accorded to such a commentarial activity reveals that one of the most prized qualities of a philosophical work resides in its ability to enable the reader to understand patterns of inter-relatedness within a complex set of ideas. Typically this is achieved in a two-step process in which the *sūtras* are first marked up as belonging to small thematically unified groupings (*prakaraṇa*), and then contiguous groupings are made to stand in causal, evidential, or explanatory relationships with one other (*saṅgati*), a process governed by the commentator's overall aim, which typically combines a systematic ambition to *display* the text as having a certain content (*abhidheya*) with a pedagogical goal to *guide* the audience's reading in such a way that their understanding improves (*prayojana*). This commentarial pattern is creatively appropriated and adapted in a variety of ways. So powerful is the basic style that it is not uncommon for a writer to construct a single text imitating and playing with the formal structure. In such compositions, the *sūtra*-like skeleton are called *kārikā*.[1]

[1] And also sometimes *vārttika*, in what is a second sense of that term: for example, the grammatical *vārttikas* of Kātyāyana, or Dharmakīrti's *Pramāṇa-vārttika*. Kumārila's *Śloka-vārttika* is both a free commentary on Śabara's *bhāṣya* on the *Mīmāṃsā-sūtra* and a collection of *vārttikas* in the *śloka* verse-form.

Towards a typology of commentary

First of all, every commentary engages to a lesser or greater extent in the basic activity of explaining individual expressions, thereby aiming to clarify the syntax of the text and to supply paraphrases of its lexical items, phrases, and sentences. This is how the generic term *vyākhyāna* 'commenting' is understood in Jhalakīkar's synopsis of early modern Nyāya thought, the *Nyāyakośa*:

Stating the meaning [of the root text], using different words which have the same meaning [as those in the root text], with the aim of preventing confused opinion (*apratipatti*), contradictory opinion (*vipratipatti*), or contrary opinion (*anyathāpratipatti*). For example, in Nyāya, the *Light-Ray* and the *Māthurānāthī* [of Mathurānātha] are commentaries on the *Gemstone*. In Vedānta, the *Nyāyasudhā* is a commentary on an exegetical work (the *Anuvyākhyāna* of Madhva) which explains the meaning of the *Brahma-sūtra*.

This has been said: 'Commenting has five characteristic features: 1. word-division, 2. stating the meaning of the words, 3. analysis of grammatical compounds, 4. construing the sentences, 5. solving problems (*ākṣepeṣu samādhāna*)'. A divergent reading [of the above statement] has it that there are considered to be six aspects of commenting, with solutions (*samādhāna*) and problems (*ākṣepa*) kept distinct. In every commentary, however, the 'root' (*bīja*) should be thought of as [preventing] confused, contradictory, and contrary opinions.[2]

A commentary which confines itself solely to performing this role will call itself a *vṛtti* or *vivṛti* or *vivaraṇa*.[3] In a more technical sense, a *vivaraṇa* is a kind of grammatical–semantic analysis, combining structural paraphrase and lexical substitution. The canonical form of such a paraphrase is into a qualificand–qualifier structure, in which the principal qualificand is either the nominal subject or the finite verb. For example, one can paraphrase 'Hari sees a bird' (*śarīr vihagaṃ paśyati*) as either 'Hari is qualified by an effort generating the activity of seeing which has a bird as object' (*vihaga-karmaka-darśanānukūla-kṛti-mān hariḥ*) or as 'The operation generating the activity of seeing which has a bird as its object is qualified by Hari as its doer' (*vihaga-karmaka-darśanā-nukūla-vyāpāro hari-kartṛkaḥ*).[4] If an obscure word occurs in the original, it might be replaced in the paraphrase with a more familiar equivalent. It goes without saying that both in the provision of lexical alternatives and in the decomposition of compounds there is frequently room for considerable exegetical licence. What is interesting to note is that, even at this minimal level, commentary is given the evaluative task of considering alternative possibilities and steering the reader away from mistaken, confused, and contradictory construals.

A commentary whose function is only to elucidate obscure or otherwise tricky words in the text is called a *ṭīkā*. One source defines a *ṭīkā* as 'an explanation of difficult

[2] *NK* sv. vyākhyānam. For further analysis of this passage, see Prabal K. Sen 2003 vol. I: xlviii–xlix; Tubb and Boose 2007: 3–5.

[3] See the entries for these terms in the *Śabda-kalpa-druma* 2006.

[4] This nice example is in Matilal 1985: 411–412. For a more detailed discussion of *vivaraṇa*: Cardona 1975: 259–281.

words [in the root text]'.[5] We might compare this with the *Oxford English Dictionary* definition of the English *gloss*: 'A word inserted between the lines or in the margin as an explanatory equivalent of a foreign or otherwise difficult word in the text; hence applied to a similar explanatory rendering of a word given in a glossary or dictionary. Also, in a wider sense, a comment, explanation, interpretation'. When the text being thus elucidated is itself a commentary, the elucidation will often be called a *ṭippaṇa* or *ṭippaṇī*.[6]

A highly distinctive and fundamental style of philosophical commentary in the Sanskrit literature is known as *bhāṣya*. I will say much more about it in the next section. It represents an 'elaboration' or 'development' of an aggregation of brief statements called *sūtras*, a reading—or literally, a 'speaking'—of them. While *bhāṣya* represents the extraction and elaboration of philosophical systematicity from the *sūtras*, *vārttika* stands for a critical engagement with the ideas so elaborated, including processes of defence, revision, and adjudication. One source says that it is 'a reflection on ideas expressed, not expressed, and badly or wrongly expressed'.[7] There is a role for such commentary when competing elaborations exist on a single set of *sūtras*, and when ideas from 'outside' need to be evaluated. It is thus a critical analysis of earlier commentaries, with two aims: (1) to achieve reflective equilibrium in the system, and (2) to defend the system against competitor systems. Uddyotakara, for example, begins his *Nyāya-vārttika* by saying that his aim is to remove the errors of certain 'poor reasoners'.[8] Who were they? First, Diṅnāga and other Buddhists who were challenging the philosophical doctrines and methods of the Nyāya system, and, second, rival interpreters of the *Nyāya-sūtra*. Uddyotakara's adjustments were radical enough for there to come to be two Nyāya camps, the Followers of the Commentator (*vyākhyātāraḥ;* Vātsyāyana), and the Followers of the Teacher (*ācāryāḥ;* Uddyotakara).[9] Each philosophical system, school or subschool develops through subcommentary towards a stable state, a process driven by dialectic between rival readings and rival systems. A general term for commentarial work of this sort is *nibandha*.[10] Dissatisfaction with the achieved stable

[5] viṣama-pada-vyākhyāyām (*Śabdārtha-cintāmaṇi* 1992, vol. 2: 1031). The term *ṭīkā*, again like *gloss*, is also used in a more general sense, as a synonym then of *vṛtti* or *vivaraṇa* (*Śabdārtha-cintāmaṇi*; sv. ṭīkā. *Śabda-kalpa-druma*, sv. ṭīkā).

[6] Cf. Apte, sv. ṭippaṇa: 'a gloss on a gloss'.

[7] uktānuktaduruktānāṃ cintā yatra tu kriyate | taṃ granthaṃ vārttikaṃ prāhuṃ vārttikajñāḥ manīṣiṇaḥ | | (*Śabdakalpadruma*, sv. vārttika, citing Hemacandra).

[8] yadakṣapādaḥ pravaro munīnāṃ śamāya śāstraṃ jagato jagāda | kutārtikājñānanivṛttihetuḥ kariṣyate tasya mayā nibandhaḥ | | (Uddyotakara 1997: 1, 1–2).

[9] Jayanta Bhaṭṭa 1982, vol. 1: 105–106. For a detailed and informative discussion, see P. K. Sen 2003: xxxiv–xli. In Tibetan exegetical literature the distinction between *bhāṣya* and *ṭīkā* is preserved, though not systematically, in the terms *'grel ba* and *'grel bshad*: see Dreyfus 2005: 285; Gomez 1987: 532.

[10] For comparison, consider the sequence of texts on grammar: sūtra = Pāṇini's *sūtras*, the *Aṣṭādhyāyī;* vārttika = Kātyāyana's vārttikas; bhāṣya = Patañjali's *Mahā-bhāṣya*; ṭīkā = Bhartṛhari's *Mahā-bhāṣya-ṭīkā*; nibandha = Kaiyaṭa's *Mahā-bhāṣya-pradīpa*. While the vārttikas are supplementary grammatical rules, perhaps reflecting developments in Sanskrit usage, 'the *Mahābhāṣya* analyses each rule into its components, adding items necessary for the understanding of the rule, giving examples and counter-examples illustrating how the rule operates and discussing the need for the *vārttikas* to bring out the full significance of Pāṇini's sūtra or to

state means going back to the *sūtras* and starting afresh. This is achieved either through a new commentary directly on the *sūtras* (as with, for example, the various early modern commentaries on the *Nyāya-sūtra*), or by writing a new text inspired by them.

Some commentators set out to uncover a hidden or deep meaning (*gūḍhārtha*) in the base text, often in opposition to earlier or more established interpretations. These commentaries might be thought of as allegorizations. Nīlakaṇṭha Caturdhara's famous commentary on the *Mahābhārata* has elicited mixed reactions among Indologists, who have frequently criticized it because of its lack of historical accuracy and apparent infidelity to original authorial intention. Muir said that '[i]t is scarcely necessary to remark that the narrator of the legend himself appears to have had no such idea of making it the vehicle of any Vedāntic allegory such as is here propounded', while Bopp speaks of 'scholiasts, who uncritically interpret everything in the biases of their sect and time, and who treat language and myths in an arbitrary fashion'.[11] We no longer imagine that the function of such commentary is to recover the author's intentions or provide historical analysis, but rather to mediate in a conversation between the text and a given community of contemporary readers.[12] This remains the case even if a commentator prefers to describe their work simply as 'making clear' what is going on in the text. Thus, among various terms used to indicate when the purpose of a commentary is the extraction of a deep or hidden meaning in the text, we find *tātparya* (or *tātparya-ṭīkā*) in the sense of a gloss revealing the true intended meaning of the author; *sphuṭārtha*, if the meaning is to be made bright and clear; *bhāva*, presenting the drift, gist, substance of the text; and *viveka*, the meaning discriminated, made distinct. Indeed, the 'hidden meaning' commentary has a distinctive role in early modernity, an attempt to retrieve from the past a new meaning adapted to the present times. In the work of such a commentator, the relationship to the ancient is one which is, as I explained in the Introduction, characteristically modern. It can be seen across the spectrum of disciplines in the early modern period: in philosophy with Bhavānanda, Jayarāma, and Raghudeva, in

account for usages apparently not covered by the rule or against the rule... Patañjali often presents arguments to support or reject several views, leaving it difficult to know his 'finally accepted view' (*siddhānta*).... The *Ṭīkā* is not a regular word-for-word commentary on the *Mahābhāṣya*. It contains observations and comments on select words and points raised by them... The *Pradīpa* is an elaborate and complete commentary on the *Mahābhāṣya*, elucidating the meanings of words and expressions in that work and discussing the different views held by scholars in the interpretation of particular passages... the importance of the *Pradīpa* in elucidating the views of Patañjali and Bhartṛhari is considerable.' Coward and Raja 1990: 115, 173, 204.

[11] See Minkowski 2005. Minkowski points out that the commentator Nīlakaṇṭha was perfectly 'aware that he was doing something unprecedented, both in his content and his approach' (2005: 237). In a different spirit, Pierre Hadot has observed how important what he calls 'creative mistakes' in exegesis have been to the development of philosophy (Hadot 1995).

[12] Cutler 1992 compares the brahminicizing commentary of Parimēlaḷakar with twentieth-century Dravidian interpretations of the Tamil classic *Tirukhuṟaḷ*.

theology with Nīlakaṇṭha, Vijayīndra, and Madhūsudana, in aesthetics, law, poetics, and grammar.[13]

There are still other genres of philosophical commentary. A *vivecana*, as Mishra (1966: 450) informs us, is a series of lecture notes:

> There were some scholars who, for some reason or other, could not produce any work, but were great teachers. They used their own notes on different topics almost every day which later on came to be known . . . as *vivecana* (Nyāya) or *khaḍarā* (Vaiyākaraṇa).

An example of this genre is Vidyānivāsa's *vivecana* on the *Gemstone*. When clarification is foremost, especially when there are divergent earlier readings and interpretations, a range of terms is available, including *pradīpa, prakāśa, prakāśikā, uddyotana, dīpa,* and *āloka*. Poetic terms such as *taraṅginī* (wave), *darpaṇa* (mirror), *candrikā* (moonlight), *amṛta* (immortal), are used with subtle gradations of commentarial intent. A *subodhinī* is a companion, an aid to understanding the primary text; while a *parīkṣā* or *vicāra* is an investigation, an examination.

Commentary as weaving a text

Udayana states that a technical treatise or *śāstra*, in any discipline, should aspire to clarity, compactness, and completeness.[14] A compilation of *sūtras*[15] maximizes compactness and completeness at the expense of clarity. A *bhāṣya* is complete and clear, but not compact. A 'section' or *prakaraṇa* of *sūtras* is clear and compact, but not complete. The *sūtras* achieve compactness by (1) making sequence significant, (2) letting one item stand for or range over many, and (3) using grammar and lexicon artificially. The background model is always Pāṇini's grammar for the Sanskrit language, the *Aṣṭādhyāyī*, which exploits a range of brevity-enabling devices to compose what has often been described as the tersest and yet most complete grammar of any language. In philosophy, collections of philosophical *sūtras* aspire to achieve in metaphysics, epistemology, or philosophy of mind what the *sūtras* of Pāṇini had accomplished for the Sanskrit language. Comparisons could be drawn with the philosophical application of Euclid's 'geometrical method' in such works as Spinoza's *Ethics*, and also with Wittgenstein's *Tractatus Logico-Philosophicus*. A compilation of *sūtras* aims at an ideal of maximal semantic content with minimal physical text.

[13] Madhusūdana Sarasvatī, for example, calls his commentary on the *Bhagavadgītā* the *Gūḍhārtha-dīpikā* because, as he says in the opening verse, he intends it to cast light on the deeper meaning. Similarly, as Prahlada Char 2001: 142 notes, 'Bachcha Jha names all his commentaries *Gūḍhārtha-tattvāloka* implying thereby that he is bringing to light hidden meanings involved in earlier discussions on the subject that had not been clearly formulated.'

[14] vaiśadyaṃ laghutā kṛtsnatā ca prakarsaḥ praśabdena dyotyate | sūtre vaiśadyābhāvāt bhāṣyasyātivistaratvāt prakaraṇādīnāñ caikadeśatvāt | (Udayana 1989: 34).

[15] Note that the term 'sūtra' is used to refer both to the individual statements and to a compilation of them.

The type of commentary known as *bhāṣya* binds the *sūtras* into a unified conceptual web (*tantra*; lit. 'warp'), and so into a text with coherence and continuity. Vātsyāyana says that 'a tantra is a system (*śāstra*) consisting in the statement of a collection of inter-related ideas'.[16] It has been defined in the tradition as

An amplification or expansion (*prapañcaka*) of what is said in the *sūtras*.[17]

Another traditional author tells us that it is a commentary

where the meaning of a *sūtras* is specified in terms that closely follow the *sūtras*, and its own terminology is also specified.[18]

It regards the root text as having a meaning that is not encrypted but only very compressed. Perhaps indeed it would be appropriate to think of a collection of *sūtras* as like a compressed archive file in need of 'decompression' with the caveat that the decompressed reading is not uniquely determined (just as different web browsers render the same html file in different ways). Given what we have said about the devices employed in a *sūtra* to achieve compactness, a number of prima facie constraints on *bhāṣya* follow. First, since the sequence in which the *sūtras* are arranged itself can be the vehicle for carrying information, a commentary should not re-order the *sūtras* without good reason. A typical *bhāṣya* extracts a great deal of content from the existing arrangement of the *sūtras* (see below). This echoes the fact that in Pāṇini's grammar, words and contexts carry over from one *sūtras* to the next within a specified range, thereby avoiding repetition and redundancy. If a commentary engages in wholesale rearrangement of the material in the *sūtras*, then its entitlement to the status of *bhāṣya* is compromised. Such is the case with Praśastapāda's *Padārtha-dharma-saṃgraha*, a text whose entitlement to its alternative title *Praśastapāda-bhāṣya* is tendentious: perhaps it is better regarded as an autonomous treatise. Second, a *bhāṣya* should fix the scope of general terms and other abbreviating expressions; in particular the range of the often-used particle *ādi* 'and so on'. Third, a *bhāṣya* should make decisions about what is colloquial and what artificial in the original text, if a term has been introduced by that text on the model of the technical terms in Pāṇini, or is in some way used with a sense specific to the text. For it is clearly the case that a technical treatise can achieve greater compactness through the judicious use of stipulation. In recognition of the importance

[16] tantram itaretarābhisaṃbaddhasya arthasamūhasya upadeśaḥ śāstram | (1997: 27,15).

[17] sūtroktārtha-prapañcakam | (*Śabda-kalpa-druma* 2006: 509, citing Hemacandra).

[18] sūtrārtho varṇyate yatra padaiḥ sūtrānusāribhiḥ | svapadāni ca varṇyante bhāṣyaṃ bhāṣyavido viduḥ || (*Śabda-kalpa-druma*, sv. bhāṣya, citing Bharata). The preceding two verses specify the ideal character of a *sūtra* text: svalpākṣaram asandigdhaṃ sāravadviśvato mukham | astobhamanavadyañca sūtraṃ sūtravido viduḥ || laghuni sūcitārthāni svalpākṣarapadāni ca | sarvataḥ sārabhūtāni sūtrāṇyāhur manīṣiṇaḥ ||. These verses 'maintain that a sūtra should contain only a few words, which are themselves formed out of only a few letters, they should indicated their meaning in such a way that there should be no doubt about their import, they should be free from defects (like containing unnecessary words), and they should also contain what is important or essential' (Prabal K. Sen 2003: xlviii).

of this function, Śabara begins his *bhāṣya* on the *Mīmāṃsā-sūtra* by setting out what his own policy is going to be:

The words of the *sūtras* are, wherever possible, to be taken in those senses only which are given to them in ordinary usage and speech: no special sense is to be attributed to them by means of the assumption of ellipses or of special technical significations. In this way, Vedic passages only are explained by the *sūtras*; while otherwise (i.e. if meanings other than the generally accepted ones were to be sought for the words of the *sūtras*) the task would become a doubly onerous one, as comprising in the first place the explanation of Vedic texts and, in the second place, the explanation of the meaning of the *sūtras*.[19]

Śabara cites economy of effort as his reason for assuming this literalist policy, but includes the caveat 'wherever possible'. In other words, a decision to accord a word a special sense must always be motivated, and the default position is to take words in their ordinary sense. Śabara does not tell us, however, whether this 'ordinary sense' refers to linguistic practice at the time when the commented on text was composed, or the linguistic practice at the time when his commentary is being read.[20]

It has been remarked that '[w]hen one takes a broad view . . . of traditional Indian literatures, one finds that texts created through a process of binding independent verses make up a major portion of the literary canon'.[21] The *bhāṣya* genre of commentary is paradigmatic of this approach to literary production, being a way to create a coherent text by stitching the *sūtras* together. It achieves this in three principal ways. *First*, identify a leading theme as the subject-matter (*abhidheya*) of the root text, identify something as the principal purpose (*prayojana*) of the text, and identify the relation (*saṃbandha*) between them. It is normal practice for a commentator to make such identifications in their prefacive remarks.[22] Gadādhara, in his comments on the first sentence of the *Gemstone*, which itself explains the declaration at *Nyāya-sūtra* 1.1.1 that philosophical knowledge leads to the highest good, shows in detail why the reader

[19] loke yeṣv artheṣu prasiddhāni padāni, tāni sati saṃbhave tadarthāny eva sūtreṣv ity avagantavyam | na adhyāhārādibhir eṣāṃ parikalpanīyo 'rthaḥ paribhāṣitavyo vā | evaṃ hi vedavākyāny eva ebhir vyākhyāyante | itarathā vedavākyāni vyākhyeyāni svapadārthāś ca vyākhyeyāḥ | tad yatnagauravaṃ prasajyeta | (Śabara on *Mīmāṃsā-sūtra* 1.1.1; trans. Thibaut 1910: 22).

[20] This is another sort of example of the role of double contexts which I discussed in Chapter 5.

[21] Cutler 1992: 560. Christopher Minkowski has pointed out an extreme example of such creative re-weaving in a genre invented by Nīlakaṇṭha called *mantra-rahasya-prakāśa*, in which Nīlakaṇṭha 'assembled verses selected from the *Ṛgveda* and commented on them in such a way that, regardless of their meaning in their Ṛgvedic context, they were found to disclose the narrative of the *Rāmāyaṇa* in one case, of the *Bhāgavatapurāṇa* in another, of the *Kāśīkhaṇḍa* in a third, and of the *Brahmasūtra* in a fourth' (Minkowski 2005: 234).

[22] For example, Śrīdhara explains the first verse in Praśastapāda's text: '. . . leading to the best of results, an anthology about the categories of things has been composed' (*padārtha-dharma-saṃgrahaḥ pravakṣyate mahodayaḥ*), as identifying the purpose of the work and the connection with its topic, explaining that a student will not be motivated to read, nor a reader motivated by their reading to engage in action, unless they understand these things, since all action must be motivated (Śrīdhara 1984: 6). See also Kumārila 1926: 1, 12–18, who adds that it is better for authors themselves to state the purpose of their text and not leave it to the commentator to do so!

must understand the connection between the subject-matter of a text and its purpose, as well as the two individually. *Second*, impose a structure on the list of the *sūtras*. This is done by ordering the collection of *sūtras* into thematically coherent and interconnected groups, each of which is called a 'section'. There are rules governing the internal structure of a section, and rules about the relationships between sections. In this way, what was a mere list becomes a richly articulated *web* of associated ideas and arguments. Many of the rules are such as to render the text essentially dialectical in structure, as we will see below. *Third*, contextualize interpretations of individual *sūtras* within the framework of a text that now has thematic unity and formal structure, in such a way as to establish coherence of meaning across the text. For an example of this, one might consider how Vātsyāyana achieves a consistency between *Nyāya-sūtra* 1.1.10 and 3.1.1, interpreting them in such a way that they both refer to an argument for the self based on facts of recognition and re-identification rather than on the idea that mental qualities must have a substratum.[23]

A block of *sūtra* text resembles a raw data file. Here, for instance, is a randomly selected part of the *Vaiśeṣika-sūtra*:

... kāraṇasāmānye dravyakarmaṇāṃ karmākāraṇam uktam | 1.1.29 | kāraṇābhāvāt kāryābhāvaḥ | 1.2.1 | na tu kāryābhavāt kāraṇābhāvaḥ | 1.2.2 | sāmānyaṃ viśeṣa iti buddhyapekṣam | 1.2.3 | bhāvaḥ sāmānyam eva | 1.2.4 | dravyatvaṃ guṇatvaṃ karmatvaṃ ca sāmānyāni viśeṣāś ca | 1.2.5 | anyatrāntyebhyo viśeṣebhyaṣ | 1.2.6 | sad iti yato dravyaguṇakarmasu | 1.2.7 | dravyaguṇakarmabhyo 'rthāntaraṃ sattā | 1.2.8 | ekadravyavattvān na dravyam | 1.2.9 | ....

In this block of text the supplied numbers are already indicative of structure, resembling the metadata that accompanies a computer file. With these numbers, the following tree-like structure is imposed on the text: (1) the list of *sūtras* is divided into *adhyāyas* or chapters; (2) each chapter is divided into two *āhnikas* (half-chapters) or four *pādas* (quarter-chapters); (3) each half- or quarter-chapter is made of several *prakaraṇas* or sections.[24]

A 'section' has a canonical inner structure, ideally including representatives of the following types of *sūtra*:

(1) A statement of the topic of the section (*viṣaya*).
(2) A statement of a doubt or question (*saṃśaya*).
(3) The view of an opponent, with reasons (*pūrvapakṣa*).
(4) The decided view, with reasons (*siddhānta*).
(5) The purpose served by the discussion in that section (*prayojana*).

[23] See here the discussion of *Brahma-sūtra* commentaries in Clooney 1991. Clooney has contributed immeasurably to our understanding of the relation between commentary and theology: see also his 1996 and 1990.

[24] Strictly, therefore, one needs four numbers not three, so that, for example, 2.1.3.7 would refer to adhyāya 2, āhnika 1, prakaraṇa/adhikaraṇa 3, sūtra 7. Usually, however, *sūtras* are numbered continuously within an āhnika.

A section is, therefore, a unit of dialogical argument, establishing a position with respect to some disputed issue in the face of a provisional opponent. It is important to stress that the text itself does not generally mark its own *sūtras* according to these types, and that the classification is largely the work of the weaving commentary. The text itself, in particular, will rarely mark a *sūtra* as its own position or that of an opponent. The fluidity in these processes of labelling and classifying lend plasticity, and leave room for later commentators to re-mould the text in response to changing circumstances, the emergence of new dialectical opponents or new domains of 'cultural values'. In an earlier chapter, I described these processes in terms of notions of prolepsis and anticipation. Consider again, for example, the three *sūtras* from the *Vaiśeṣika-sūtra*, which I use as an example there:

3.2.15 Self is one, since there is no difference in the production of pleasure, pain and cognition. 3.2.16 Self is manifold because of circumstance. 3.2.17 Also from the authority of the śāstra.[25]

One commentator (Śrīdhara) reads these *sūtras* as representing first an Advaitin opponent who thinks that there is just one self, *brahman*, and then the decided view, that there is a plurality of individual selves. But another commentator (Vyomaśiva) supplies a quite different interpretation, that the first view is the correct view that within a single body there is just one self, and the second view that of a Buddhist opponent who thinks that there is a continuous stream of momentary selves. In both cases, the interpretation is speaking to the concerns of a readership contemporaneous with the commentator. Here again there is a conversation in which the text is an instrument in a philosophical practice. It misses the point to ask if the commentary is 'faithful' to the author's original intentions, or is 'reliable' historically. In fact, there is a sliding scale with formal commentary at one end and autonomous treatise at the other; somewhere in between fall texts such as Jayanta's *Panicle of Reason*, a work which, as Esther Solomon has put it, 'used the Nyāya *sūtras* as pegs to hang on the detailed discussions of various problems of philosophy' (Solomon 1986: 565).

Having identified segments of text carrying internal dialogical unity, a commentary interrelates them. According to the standard theory (developed at length by the early modern authors), one of six types of inter-relation (*saṅgati*) should hold between consecutive sections within a chapter:

prasaṅga—corollary
upodghāta—prerequisite
hetutva—causal dependence
avasara—removal of an obstacle to further inquiry
nirvāhakaikya—the adjacent sections have a common end
kāryaikya—adjacent sections are joint causal factors of a common effect.[26]

[25] Trans. Thakur 2003: 65 (slightly modified).

[26] *NK*, sv. saṅgati; *Śabdakalpadruma*, sv. saṅgati (2006, vol. 5: 217); Veezhinathan 2006: 793–798. Vedāntic exegesis of the *Brahma-sūtra* finds that it needs to appeal, additionally, to 'chapter' (*adhyāya*-),

For example, a section in the *Nyāya-sūtra* in which a tripartite division of inference is described (2.1.37–38) is immediately followed by a section on the 'three times' past, present, and future (2.1.39–43). A commentator might wish to see such textual contiguity as indicative of a logical, explanatory or evidential relationship between the topics in the two sections. B. K. Matilal has argued that 'the discussion of the problem of three time-stages is related to the discussion of the examination of inference by *upodghāta saṅgati* or *prasaṅga saṅgati*' from which one can deduce that the tripartite division of inference has a temporal basis (Matilal 1985: 38). According to the *bhāṣya,* the sections of the first āhnika of the second adhyāya are as follows: (1) doubt; (2) sources of knowledge in general; (3) perception; (4) whole and part; (5) inference; (6) time; (7) comparison. A commentator might argue that the relationship between the section on perception and the section on whole and part is one of 'corrollary' (*prasaṅga*), and the relation between the section on wholes and parts and the section on inference one of 'removing an obstacle' (*avasara*), and be led to philosophically important ideas about the perception of whole objects and the role of inference in perception.[27] So a section creates a group of *sūtras* with a dialectical unity, and a chapter creates an explanatorily interconnected group of sections. The end result is a text with thematic coherence and formal continuity, modulating the representation of the world provided by the core *sūtra* text.

The singly authored principles-and-gloss text

It has been observed that 'a striking feature of the Sanskrit tradition is the frequency with which works that may as well have been independent treatises are cast into the external form of a commentary on an earlier text. In this way many treatises of great originality have been made to depend, at least nominally, on earlier works that they leave far behind' (Tubb and Boose 2007: 2). In fact, one can go further, for many treatises are composed in a 'text and commentary' form from the beginning, with a single author exploiting the expressive and hermeneutical richness of commentary to generate textuality and structure in their composition. The terms *kārikā* and *vārttika* are used instead of 'sūtra' when an author composes an original work mimicking the sūtra-bhāṣya genre. For example, Udayana's *Offering of Flowers* consists in a core set of *kārikās,* bound together with his own gloss. Other philosophers have felt free to write their own commentaries on these *kārikās*; there is even a late commentary on them from a Vedāntic rather than a Nyāya perspective.[28] A different example is Īśvarakṛṣṇa's

'objection' (*ākṣepa-*), 'analogy' (*udāharaṇa-*), and 'counter-analogy' (*pratyudāharaṇa-*) as modalities of *saṅgati.* There are important variations in the way different exegetical disciplines perceive structure in their respective *sūtra*-texts, only partly deriving from exigencies dictated by the texts themselves.

[27] As indeed Matilal has done; see his 1986: 266–275.

[28] Gaṅgādhara Kaviratna's commentary on the *kārikās,* which interprets them according to the doctrine of Viśiṣṭādvaita (CSC 203, p. 170; CSC 750–752).

Sāṃkhya-kārikā, a *sūtra*-like composition upon which Gauḍapāda's *Sāṃkhya-kārikā-bhāṣya* provides commentary. While the term 'sūtra' refers both to the individual affirmations and to the entire collection, the terms *saṃgraha, kośa, kārikāvalī* and *samuccaya* are used for collections of *kārikās*. The composers of such compilations will sometimes explain that the ideas and teachings about the topic in question are scattered throughout larger bodies of textual material, and so in need of orderly collation. A notable example of the *kārikā* genre from the sixteenth century is Kṣṇadāsa's *Kārikāvalī*, also known as the *Bhāṣā-pariccheda*, which as Matilal (1977: 110) says, 'consists of 166 memorable stanzas–not all of them of [the author's making]–which were known by heart by thousands of paṇḍits. The author supplied this manual with a commentary, the *Siddhānta-muktāvalī [Pearl-necklace of Principles]*'.

There can be a considerable degree of morphousness in the boundary between text and commentary, it being not always clear what belongs to the main text and what to the commentary. When the text is itself a commentary, but only a patchy or terse one, one finds what I will call 'the combined commentary', part commentary on the original (e.g. on those portions which the patchy commentary has ignored) and part commentary on the commentary. This is to be seen in some of the commentaries on the terse and patchy notes of Raghunātha. Thus, as Ingalls (1951: 25) observes, 'Mathurānātha frequently commented not only on the *mūla* or basic text, but on other scholars' commentaries on these texts as well'.

Buddhist philosophers play with the basic genre and adapt it to their own purposes.[29] First of all, they call the original dialogues of the Buddha 'sūtra', or 'sutta' in Pali. Early Sinhalese commentaries on the three 'baskets' (the Sutta, Vinaya, and Abhidhamma) were used as the basis of the great fifth-century Pali commentaries of Buddhaghosa.[30] Both Diṅnāga and Dharmakīrti write texts in the form of collections of verses accompanied with commentaries of their own composition: Diṅnāga's *Pramāṇa-samuccaya*, with his own *vṛtti*; Dharmakīrti's *Pramāṇa-vārttika*, with his *svopajñavṛtti*. Of particular interest is the *Abhidharma-kośa* of Vasubandhu, again a collection of verses and one on which Vasubandhu provides a commentary, which he actually calls a *bhāṣya*, the *Abhidharmakośa-bhāṣya*. According to one story,

> Vasubandhu supported himself by lecturing on Buddhism before the general public. At the close of each day's lecture, he composed a verse which summed up his exposition for the day. These constitute the *Abhidharma-kośa*.[31]

[29] Alsdorf 1977, Dundas 1996 and Jyväsjärvi 2010 document corresponding innovations from the Jainas.

[30] Bhikkhu Ñāṇamoli says that 'the system found in the Commentaries [of Buddhaghosa] has moved on (perhaps slightly diverged) from the strict Abhidhamma-Pitaka standpoint. The Suttas offered descriptions of discovery; the Abhidhamma map-making; but emphasis now is not on discovery, or even on mapping, so much as on consolidating, filling in and explaining. The material is worked over for consistency' (Buddhaghosa 1991: xlii). We know that Buddhaghosa came to Sri Lanka from India, where he had studied the Sanskrit philosophical śāstra, and he seems to have brought to bear his knowledge of Sanskrit commentarial theory.

[31] Anacker 1988: 16–17, referring to a story of Paramārtha.

If this story is to be believed, then we have a case in which the 'commentary' is written first, followed by the text being 'commented' on! According to another opinion, equally intriguing, Vasubandhu wrote the *kārikās* from one philosophical perspective, and the *bhāṣya* from another, having in the meantime switched allegiance from one Buddhist school to another. Another Buddhist philosopher, Saṃghabhadra, is led to write a rival commentary on the same *kārikās* in order to 'correct' Vasubandhu's own misleading commentary. Indeed, like several other authors, he wrote both a longer commentary, the *Nyāyānusāra*, and a shorter, abbreviated commentary, the *Abhidharma-samaya-pradīpikā*. In the introduction to the shorter commentary, he explains his intentions:

> By means of extensive explanations that conform to correct principle, I will counter the accepted positions of other schools and manifest the fundamental meaning. When the Sūtra master's statements conform to reasoned argument and scriptural authority, I will reproduce them as they are and not attempt to refute them. [However,] if they contradict the basic purport of the Abhidharma or the *sūtras* in any way, I am determined to scrutinize them further and vow to purge them. The treatise I have already composed is entitled 'Conformance to Correct Principle' (*Nyāyānusāra*); it is to be studied by those who delight in meticulous analysis . . . In contrast to the Sūtra master's erroneous explanations, I will present the correct interpretation and will manifest the true and extraordinary meaning of the accepted doctrines of our school'.
>
> (Trans. Collett Cox 1995: 55–56)

Saṃghabhadra accepts Vasubandhu's core text, the compilation of *kārikās*, but equips them with an entirely different commentarial gloss from that of Vasubandhu himself (the 'Sūtra master'). In effect, he creates a rival *bhāṣya* from the core text. If behind a work such as Vasubandhu's lies an anxiety that the truth of Buddhism will be buried in a welter of textual overproduction, Saṃghabhadra's worry is rather that it will be obscured by mistaken interpretation. This case is also a rather dramatic example of the point that the author has no special authority over the commentator in reading meaning from the text.

The commentary is a fundamental paradigm in Sanskrit philosophical literature. One basic reason for the discursive richness of the model is that it permits one to state something at a high level of generality and then go on to qualify or restrict, to moderate or modulate, what one has just said. Indeed, in every act of self-commenting, such as writing a footnote, this way of expressing oneself is exploited.[32] As an exegetical mode of thinking, it exhibits a distinctive type of rationality intrinsic to the commentarial approach. Wilfred Sellars has observed that whenever we have a model of some aspect of reality, we also need a commentary, 'which qualifies or limits—but not precisely nor in all respects—the analogy between the familiar objects and the entities which are being introduced by the theory' (1997: 96). A second reason for the power of the

[32] The structure of the *Tractatus* might be understood as a nested sequence of commentary, 'built up out of chains of self-commentaries (glosses on glosses), in which the commentary-structure has been deliberately left exposed' (Smith 1991: 2).

paradigm is that, as we have seen in some detail, it places structure and inter-relatedness in the foreground, encouraging creative association under the umbrella of a governing conception. For both these reasons, *reading* philosophically is a way of *thinking* philosophically. Similar observations can be made about other models of commentary, including the 'deep meaning' commentary.

The general conclusion from our study of commentary in Sanskrit is that within the genre of commentary many different sorts of philosophy are possible. There is much more to commentary than merely exegesis; it can also stand for a creative act of philosophy built around the text, a rejuvenation of the ancient in the present—and that is what I identified, in the Introduction to this book, as a key feature of early modernity in philosophy. I have emphasized that we will not appreciate the modernist developments if we are not careful to distinguish between these various types of commentary. In particular, we must distinguish between commentaries which are simply exegetical of the text, and commentaries which are creative or reconstructive with respect to it. An early modern philosophy seeks new articulations of a relationship with the past, and these find expression in the production of revisionary, creative, commentary upon it.

I suggest that just the same is the case even for early modern thinkers in Europe, thinkers like Leibniz, Spinoza, and Gassendi. Indeed, it is quite possible to analyse Descartes' *Principles of Philosophy* within the parameters of the theory I have outlined. For it is clearly a work in the *kārikā* form, with 207 *kārikās* embedded in a surrounding gloss. *Kārikā* 67, for instance, reads: 'That we are frequently deceived in our judgements regarding pain itself', the gloss providing an example of the sort of error he had in mind. It would certainly have been possible for someone to take the principles and provide them a quite different interpretation, for example one which purports to show that they all admit of a sound Aristotelian reading. Each of his *kārikās*—like a *sūtra*—is meant to be self-evidently true, but the causes of that self-evidence might vary considerably from one thinker to another. Moreover, the 'Preface', which Descartes subsequently provides in the form of a letter to his editor, is itself a commentary on the main text. He says that 'it will be a good idea to add a preface explaining the *subject* of the book, my *purpose* in writing it, and the *benefit* which may be derived from it' (AT ixb. 1; 1984: 179), thereby following Kumārila's advice in himself identifying the *abhidheya* and *prayojana* of the work by way of an act of self-commentary. Such acts are a distinctive mode of the intertextual 'illocutionary intervention' I spoke about in an earlier chapter.

The great advantage of the *kārikā* genre is that the author has complete control over the structure of the work; but even when starting with the ancient *sūtras* an early modern author in India finds plenty of room for manoeuvre, because those *sūtras* are themselves peculiarly elastic. In a later chapter (Chapter 11) I will look at an important example, Jayarāma's *Garland of Principles about Reason*. Choosing to build a new text around ancient *sūtras* rather than start afresh with a set of *kārikās* of one's own making is a sign of something; in Jayarāma's case, it signalled an intention to compose a work that constructed a modern theory on ancient foundations, and yet it is a text structurally and philosophically interestingly analogous to Descartes' *Principles*.

I have now finished putting in place a suitably rich theory of context, one in which both the *socio-political* context of a thinker and the *intertextual* context of their textual intervention are given due weight. I have already said a great deal to locate the 'new reason' philosophers within their social and historical contexts, including the contexts created by Islamicate and Persian authority and the networks of ṭol-based affiliations. The next step, if we are to put ourselves in a position where we can make sense of the works in the 'new reason' and evaluate their claims to be doing something radically new, is to reconstruct the *intellectual* context within which they occur, and in India what that means is to get a sense of how they situate themselves with respect to the history of the *śāstra* or discipline to which the author affiliates. Modernity is a happening that takes place against a backdrop, and we will only clearly be able to see it for what it is if we understand that backdrop in sufficient detail.

PART III

The Possibility of Inquiry

9

Inquiry: The History of a Crisis

The great Indian philosophical disciplines have overtly epistemological ambitions, ambitions which are typically formulated in the initial *sūtra* of their canonical texts. The claims for the possibility of knowledge with which these disciplines begin invite sceptical challenge, and this is readily witnessed within the Indian tradition itself. It is not always the case, however, that the force of that challenge is sufficiently acknowledged by the early discipline builders in their *bhāṣya* commentaries. Indeed, it is only with the new epistemology of the early modern period that there comes to be a full appreciation of the obligations incurred by a constructive epistemology of the sort envisaged within the traditional disciplines. A similar story is true of the history of metaphysics in India—the predisposition to help oneself to a default realism only gradually comes to terms with the substantive obligations that a defence of realism incurs, and with it eventually a sophisticated engagement with the task of accounting for the concept of a mind-independent physical world of objects.[1] This again is distinctive of the later philosophy, now already incorporating and appropriating the metaphysics of ancient Vaiśeṣika. In this chapter, I will describe the movements in epistemology that prepared the ground for the emergence of the new theory.

Inquiry in the knowledge disciplines

Consider how each of the five great *sūtra* compilations, the founding treatises of the Indian philosophical disciplines, begins. The initial statements of the *Mīmāṃsā-sūtra* and the *Brahma-sūtra* declare these two disciplines to be disciplines of 'inquiry' (*jijñāsā*), one into *dharma* or moral duty, and the other into *brahman*, the unifying cosmic principle:

Now, then, an inquiry into dharma (*athāto dharma-jijñāsā*: MS 1.1.1).
Now, then, an inquiry into brahman (*athāto brahma-jijñāsā*: BS 1.1.1).

The *Vaiśeṣika-sūtra* and the *Yoga-sūtra* reflect a perhaps more descriptive orientation in opening with statements that they are disciplines of 'explanation' and 'exposition' rather than inquiry, one into *dharma*, the term here probably signifying the 'real nature'

[1] See Part IV.

of things rather than moral duty, and the other into *yoga* 'spiritual-psychological discipline':

Now, then, we will explain dharma (*athāto dharmaṃ vyākhāsyāmaḥ*: VS 1.1.1).
Now, an exposition of yoga (*atha yogānuśāsanam*: YS 1.1.1).

The lost root-text of the Cārvāka school apparently began in a similar way: 'Now, then, we will explain *tattva* [reality]'.[2] The initial references to inquiry in the *Mīmāṃsā-sūtra* and the *Brahma-sūtra* invite philosophical discussion. Early commentators on these texts raise worries about the notion of inquiry itself, worries that resemble what has become known to European philosophy as Meno's Puzzle or the paradox of inquiry. Meno had wondered how inquiry is possible, since one cannot aim to search for what one does not know:

MENO: How will you look for it Socrates, when you do not know at all what it is? How will you aim to search for something you do not know at all? If you should meet with it, how will you know that this is the thing that you did not know?

SOCRATES: I know what you want to say, Meno. Do you realize what a debater's argument you are bringing up, that a man cannot search either for what he knows or for what he does not know? He cannot search for what he knows—since he knows it, there is no need to search—nor for what he does not know, for he does not know what to look for.

(Plato, *Meno* 80d5–e5).

Assuming the voice of an opponent, Śabara likewise says:

It must either be commonly known (*prasiddha*) what moral duty is, or else not commonly known. If it *is* commonly known, then there will be no inquiry. If, however, it *is not* commonly known, then all the more none. So this work of inquiry into moral duty is quite pointless.

(Śabara 1968: 14,20–15,2)

The word for 'inquiry' is *jijñāsā*, literally 'desire to know' and a desire to obtain or avoid something presupposes already knowledge of the thing in question. So the desire for knowledge of what one does not yet have knowledge seems paradoxical. A second Mīmāṃsā writer Kumārila Bhaṭṭa, reformulates Śabara's point in such terms:

It is possible to know that which is commonly known, but being commonly known there is no desire [to know it]. On the other hand, that which is not commonly known, being impossible [to know], is all the more not [a possible object of a desire to know].

(Kumārila 1926: v. 124)

In a very similar spirit, commenting on *Brahma-sūtra* 1.1.1, Śaṃkara presents the objector's worry:

[2] athātas tattvaṃ vyākhyāsyāma iti | (Jayanta 1982: 100,20).

It must, however, either be commonly known what *brahman* is, or else not commonly known. If it is commonly known, then there shall be no 'desire to know'; but if not commonly known, then it is impossible to inquire [into it].

(Śaṃkara 1917: 78–79)

As far as I am aware, no philosopher in the early Nyāya tradition has formulated the paradox of inquiry in such sharp terms. Indeed, it is taken for granted in early Nyāya that there is a method of investigation and inquiry, a method that begins with a doubt of some such form as 'Is yonder entity a man or a tree-stump?' and, appealing to observational examples and background principles, reasons to a final decision.[3] According to the Nyāya account of inquiry, then, a state of doubt is one in which an object is identified and delineated with enough detail to make it serve as the target for further questioning. Responding to the sceptical challenge, Śabara makes a not dissimilar move. He points out that different people do have ideas, albeit different ones, about the object in question, and the purpose of inquiry is to compare and decide between these differing notions. The different understandings make the object available as a target of inquiry, without it yet being fully and completely known:

On the contrary, [inquiry into *dharma*] does have a point. For different people have different understandings regarding the nature of *dharma*. Some say *dharma* is one thing, others something else. One who strives to perform an act without having considered this may take up any old thing and be thwarted and come to harm. Therefore one should inquire into the nature of *dharma*. For we insist that it connects a person with the highest good.

(Śabara 1968: 16,3–16,7)

Against this, one might wonder how one can be sure that these different conceptions are all conceptions of one and the same thing. Śaṃkara argues that we do have a common, residual, idea of *brahman*, even as we disagree over its more particular qualities:

We reply that *brahman* is [known]—his very nature is said to consist in what is eternal, pure and consciousness, bound up with the omniscient and the omnipotent. For the meanings such as 'being eternal' and 'being pure' are derived from semantic analysis of the word '*brahman*' these meanings following from the verbal root *bṛh*.

(Śaṃkara 1917: 79–80)

These manoeuvres are thought by the early authors to be sufficient to diffuse any sceptical challenge to the possibility of inquiry itself.[4] In the twelfth century, that challenge was formulated with considerably greater sophistication by Śrīharṣa. Before turning to his argument, let me consider the early Nyāya view.

[3] For the details, see Matilal 1986: 73–80; Ganeri 2001a: 7–41.

[4] See Carpenter and Ganeri 2010 for further discussion.

Inquiry in early Nyāya

The opening declaration of the *Nyāya-sūtra*, a statement that was to give birth to the formal discipline of epistemology in India, is considerably more complex than those of the other disciplines. *Nyāya-sūtra* 1.1.1 asserts that it is through an understanding of the 'truth' or 'reality' (*tattva*) about certain things that the highest good in life is to be achieved; an understanding, specifically, of the methods of conducting a debate, of performing an investigation, and of the sources of human knowledge as well as of all that can be known by means of them:

The highest good is reached through an understanding of the true nature of [the distinction between] honest, dishonest and destructive debate, of false reasoning, tricks and checks in debate, of [the pattern of sound investigation, whose components are] doubt, purpose, examples, assumed principles, syllogisms, suppositional reasoning and decision, and [initially] of the ways of gaining knowledge and the knowables.[5]

What is striking about this statement, first of all, is its epistemological optimism: there are things which it is beneficial to know, and there are ways of gaining knowledge about them. Each of us has a certain epistemic duty, to make sure that we are properly informed about the ways of investigating, debating, and gaining knowledge, a duty which follows directly from our wish to pursue that which is best for us, a pursuit that must be *informed* if it is to succeed. And yet it was apparent even to the earliest writers and certainly to Vātsyāyana, the author of the first major commentary, that the epistemological optimism of this opening declaration stands in need of its own philosophical defence. How does one know that there is indeed the stated instrumental relationship between possessing the specified competence in the acquisition of knowledge and the achievement of one's highest life goals? How, even if this be conceded, can one be sure that the alleged methods of acquiring knowledge—debate, investigation, and the individual ways of gaining knowledge like perception, reason, and testimony—really do lead to knowledge? Finally, what sort of knowledge is required by practical, goal-directed reason—knowledge of the world, knowledge of the goal, knowledge about our own epistemic capacities ('reflective knowledge'), or knowledge about ourselves and our mental states ('self-knowledge')?

In India, the Mādhyamika Buddhist Nāgārjuna presses one form of these worries in the direction of a sceptical doxastic ascent:

If such and such objects are established for you through the ways of gaining knowledge, tell me how you establish those ways of gaining knowledge. If the ways of gaining knowledge are

[5] pramāṇa-prameya-saṃśaya-prayojana-dṛṣṭānta-siddhāntāvayava-tarka-nirṇaya-vāda-jalpa-vitāṇḍa-hetvābhāsa-cchala-jāti-nigrahasthānānāṃ tattvajñānān niḥśeyasādhigamaḥ | (*Nyāya-sūtra* 1.1.1). Note that Praśastapāda incorporates the idea into his interpretation of *Vaiśeṣika-sūtra* 1.1.1: dravya-guṇa-karma-sāmānya-viśeṣa-samavāyānāṃ ṣaṇṇāṃ padārthānāṃ sādharmya-vaidharmya-tattvajñānaṃ niḥśreyasa-hetuḥ (Praśastapāda 1994: §2). See also Chapter 12 below.

established through other means of gaining knowledge, then there is an infinite regress. Neither the beginning nor the middle nor the end can then be established.

(Nāgārjuna 1968: 31–33)

I take it that a range of sceptical worries, including the sort introduced by Nāgārjuna, form the background to Vātsyāyana's 'preface' to *Nyāya-sūtra* 1.1.1, as well as to the 'critical examination' in *Nyāya-sūtra* 2.1.8–20, on which more below. The 'Preface' constitutes one of the most important and definitive passages in early Nyāya epistemology, this despite its presenting serious interpretative challenges. First of all, Vātsyāyana tells us that goal-directed intentional action succeeds only if the agent is well-informed, and that therefore success-in-action can serve as a guarantor for a way of gaining knowledge:

Ways of gaining knowledge (*pramāṇa*) are accurate (*arthavat*) [in hitting their goal] insofar as when there is an acquaintance (*pratipatti*) with something through a way of gaining knowledge, there is [also] a capacity to succeed in action (*pravṛtti-sāmarthya*). There is no capacity to succeed in action without [such] an acquaintance with things. Apprehending (*upalabhya*) something through a way of gaining knowledge, the knower indeed is either attracted to it or repulsed by it. 'Action' (*pravṛtti*) is the name given to the striving of someone filled with attraction or repulsion. 'Capacity to succeed' (*sāmarthya*) is the relationship of that action with a result. The one who [so] strives, being attracted or repulsed, either acquires the thing or avoids it. 'The thing' [in question] is happiness and the causes of happiness, and again sorrow and its causes. This is the object of a way of gaining knowledge, and it is of uncountable variety for uncountable are the differences between breathing things.

(Vātsyāyana 1997: 1,6–1,11)

Vātsyāyana, let us note, is a liberal in the matter of conceptions of the good towards which people strive. It is not that there is some one good, which knowledge happens to be instrumental in achieving. For then, if it were to turn out that having false beliefs or being misled were more effective methods of reaching that good, what could be the argument in favour of knowledge? Vātsyāyana argues instead that to be well informed about one's individual goal (that which is, for you, constitutive of happiness) is instrumental in achieving it. Read as a response to the sceptical regress, the point would be that a way of gaining knowledge is present when there is successful action, whether or not the agent of that action is able themselves to offer any justification for their success (other than citing the beliefs which led them to act). And, indeed, at this point in the discussion it seems as if the only knowledge the goal-directed practical agent needs is knowledge about the goal and the means to reach it, knowledge that includes self-knowledge because the goal has to do with happiness and sorrow, but not necessarily reflective knowledge.[6]

[6] One striking feature of the Nyāya theory of inquiry is that there is no sharp distinction between the methods of inquiry relevant to the mental and the physical, of the sort one finds in, for example, the work of Descartes. In Chapter 12 I will say more about the causes of this resistance to the idea that there are two epistemological realms.

Still, Vātsyāyana's first paragraph raises at least three other questions. First, are there any materials here for a distinction between knowledge and true belief? [7] After all, true beliefs are just as good in the matter of successful action as knowledge, so it might seem that all we have is an argument in favour of having true beliefs. Second, does an appeal to success help when it comes to knowing what the ways of gaining knowledge are, as *Nyāya-sūtra* 1.1.1 apparently demands? For that, does one not need to *know* success when one sees it, leading again to a doxastic ascent? Thirdly, how much weight is one meant to give to the talk of a 'capacity' for success in action, in contrast with success itself? Is it that employing a way of gaining knowledge sustains *actual* success in action, as the first sentence in the text seems to imply, or that it sustains a *capacity* for success in action, as the later discussion seems to suggest? Let me, however, continue with the text:

When a way of gaining knowledge is accurate, accurate too are the knower, the known, and the knowledge (*pramiti*). How so?—Because the goal cannot come about as separated from any one of them. Thus, when there is action by someone filled with attraction or repulsion, that person is the knower. He knows, comprehends, the thing by means of something, and that is the way of gaining knowledge. The thing which is known, cognised, is the known. The comprehension (*vijñāna*) of that thing is the knowledge. The truth is understood in the presence of these four ingredients.

But what is 'the truth' (*tattva*)? It is [to be defined as] the presence as being of what has being, and the presence as non-being of what has non-being. Truth is 'things as they are' (*yathābhūta*) and not the reverse, [as in] grasping as 'being' what has being; truth is 'things as they are' and not the reverse, [as in] grasping as 'non-being' what has non-being.

How, through a way of gaining knowledge, is the second of these to be apprehended? What is not is apprehended while apprehending things with, for instance, a lamp. Thus, in perceiving visible things by means of a shining lamp, what is not perceived is not there, for [one reasons] 'if it were there, it would be cognised; as it is not cognised, it is not there'. So it is that in grasping what is there through a way of gaining knowledge, that which one does not grasp is likewise not there; in that way, a way of gaining knowledge which reveals what is there also reveals what is not there.

(Vātsyāyana 1997: 1,12–2,4)

Success, Vātsyāyana now adds, is the guarantor of the entire epistemic situation, and not just of the way of gaining knowledge. Success in action shows that the agent is a knower, that the ensuing state of mind is one of knowledge. It is also what guarantees that the thing apprehended is genuinely known and not merely, for example, imagined. This seems to answer the third of our questions above—a way of gaining knowledge, by itself, sustains only a capacity for success; actual success needs the three other contributors too. Similarly, a lamp provides for a capacity to act in relation

[7] In what follows I will use the term 'belief' in the sense of 'occurrent belief,' that is a mental quality-particular with intentional content. Anyone who has qualms about the use of 'belief' as a translation of *jñāna* should construe my use of the term merely as shorthand for 'episodic awareness-event', 'cognitive occurrence', or whatever is their preferred rendering. The difference between occurrent and dispositional mental states is primarily relevant when discussing the psycho-dynamics. See Phillips and Tatacharya 2004: 13–16; Matilal 1986: 101–106.

to both what is present and what is absent. Of greater interest, in this passage, though, is the possibility that it provides for a distinction between truth (or true belief) and knowledge. Truth is defined, in a remarkably Aristotelian way, as grasping of what is that it is, and of what is not that it is not. Vātsyāyana then says that a way of gaining knowledge leads to knowledge of both. Perception, for instance, is a source of knowledge about what there is in one's surroundings. It is also a source of knowledge about what there is not, for one can deduce the absence of things from the fact of their non-perception. The implication of this seems to be that there is a distinction between a way of gaining knowledge as the *cause* and as the *ground* of knowledge. The lamp provides the grounds for one's knowledge of what is not there, distinct from the perceptions for which it is the direct cause. In other words, the relationship between knowledge and ways of gaining knowledge is more complicated than it might at first appear. It can be an evidential as well as a causal relationship. If knowledge is true belief in which a way of gaining knowledge is instrumentally implicated, what we now see is an expansion in the reach of instrumental implication, to include both being directly caused to see an object which is present, and being supplied with the evidence from which one can deduce an object's absence.

Ways of gaining knowledge

This point is further attested in the section comprising a 'critical examination' of the notion of a way of gaining knowledge, a section which falls at *Nyāya-sūtra* 2.1.8–20.[8] The first criticism dealt with is that there are no ways of gaining knowledge, because they cannot exist either before, at the same time as, or after, the object knowledge of which they are meant to produce (2.1.8–11). One answer—a standard anti-sceptical move—is that any argument that there are no ways of gaining knowledge is necessarily self-defeating or ineffective (2.1.12–14). Another, however, is that the relationship between objects of knowledge and ways of gaining knowledge is sometimes analogous to that between a musical instrument and the sound it makes (2.1.15): here, the sound occurs later but provides knowledge of the instrument, be it a lute or a lyre. Vātsyāyana's response to the 'three times' objection is to stress that there is no fixed temporal ordering, and he gives his own examples of all three relationships.[9] Given that the causal relation is temporally ordered but the evidential relation is not, it seems clear that Vātsyāyana here sees the relationship between a way of gaining knowledge and a thing known as an evidential one.

Vātsyāyana states that 'the term "way of gaining knowledge" denotes that which is a *hetu* of knowledge' (1997: 60, 3). The word *hetu* is notoriously ambivalent; it signifies both reason and cause, both evidence and origin. Given what Vātsyāyana has said about temporal sequence, perhaps the most reasonable understanding of his view is that the

[8] I discussed the structure of this section in Chapter 8.

[9] Vātsyāyana 1997: 59, 12–17.

evidence for something is also sometimes its cause, so that the primary signification of *hetu*, as the term is used here, is an evidential one. This, however, leaves open as a possibility that he has a non-cognitivist theory of evidence in mind, a theory in which 'having evidence' for something is not itself a matter of reflective knowledge. The sound gives me evidence of the presence of a lute, whether or not I acknowledge it as such. In the language of reasons, a *hetu* is a normative reason, a reason to believe that there is, for example, a lute. If I do come to believe that there is a lute, as a result of hearing the sound, then *my* reason for believing this is, presumably, the self-ascription 'I hear this sound'. This is a psychological ground for believing, the grounding reason as distinct from the normative reason. A way of gaining knowledge is a source of normative reasons.

Nyāya-sūtra 2.1.19 draws, finally, a controversial analogy between ways of gaining knowledge and sources of light, which are held to illuminate themselves and at the same time illuminate other things. We might see this analogy as providing a response to the sceptical regress, and certainly that is its role when Nāgārjuna considers it. On the other hand, we have already seen that success in action is the way a doxastic ascent is blocked by Vātsyāyana, and so it is also possible that the function of this analogy is a different one (as Vātsyāyana himself seems to think). I suggest that it again reinforces the idea that a way of gaining knowledge can provide evidence for beliefs other than the ones for which it is the direct cause. In particular, a way of gaining knowledge can provide evidence for its own accuracy: the normative reason for believing that one's eyes are working is just that one sees the things around one. Vātsyāyana will say that the case is similar to the one in which we test the purity of the water in a well by extracting a bucketful, and testing that. The point here is that a sample is evidence for the purity of the whole; similarly, one part of the entire epistemic process can be evidence for another part, without circularity. The example also illustrates another important strand in the thinking of the early Nyāya, which is that the application of the terms 'object of knowledge' 'way of gaining knowledge', etc., are situational and specific, and do not reflect any stable metaphysical distinction. What serves as the way of gaining knowledge in one epistemic situation can become the object of knowledge in another, and vice versa. They are functional terms, denoting specific roles to be fulfilled in any given act of gaining knowledge in situationally specific ways (see *Nyāya-sūtra* 2.1.16 and especially Vātsyāyana's comments, which draw a parallel with the thematic roles of case grammar, the *kārakas*). When my goal-directed actions are rewarded with success, it follows that the beliefs I had are of things as they are, and that those beliefs are instrumentally dependent on whatever has functioned for them, in that context, as an 'evidence' (*hetu*). This is a mitigated epistemological optimism, a far cry from any Cartesian vision of a first philosophy. It claims only that successful acts of gaining knowledge, like successful acts of cooking or driving or building, must include certain necessary functional ingredients.[10]

[10] I will return to this when discussing Jayarāma's *Garland of Principles* in Chapter 11.

In this mitigated account of inquiry, acquiring ordinary knowledge (knowledge of the world around the knower) does not engender a doxastic ascent. Reflective knowledge, that is knowledge of one's own epistemic capabilities and resources, is available if sought, but it is not a requirement. One sees an object and, in doing so, knows that it is there, and then pursues or avoids it; all this, without necessarily having to reflect upon the process or understand that the success or failure of one's subsequent action renders available a method of verification of the original way of gaining knowledge. But is such ordinary, non-reflective knowledge sufficient for the ambitions of *Nyāya-sūtra* 1.1.1, enough to realize one's highest life goals? Apparently not, for that same *sūtra* asserts that one must know the principles of debate, investigation and knowledge acquisition. Even if there is no doxastic ascent, still it is reflective knowledge, and not merely ordinary knowledge, which one needs in order to realize one's ambitions.[11] That further claim is a source of difficulty for the early Nyāya account, which later Nyāya seeks to resolve.

Śrīharṣa's 'refutations'

The attitude of epistemological optimism that seems to be a shared characteristic of all the Indian knowledge disciplines was to persist throughout the first millennium. It received, however, a dramatic and radical challenge in the highly original work of the independently minded twelfth-century thinker Śrīharṣa. In his *Amassed Morsels of Refutation* (*Khaṇḍana-khaṇḍa-khādya*), Śrīharṣa attacks both the epistemological complacency of the Nyāya school, and also the very idea of inquiry upon which the other disciplines had, as we have seen, come to rest.[12]

The problem is evident in an ambiguity in the formulation of *Nyāya-sūtra* 1.1.1. This *sūtra* tells us that knowledge is instrumental in reaching our goals, and Vātsyāyana therefore makes success the mark of knowledge. The problem is with the conceptual status of this claim. On one reading, what it states is that knowledge is to be analysed as

[11] In his comments on 2.1.19–20, Vātsyāyana goes still further, and adds that one also needs self-knowledge, that is to say, knowledge of one's own mental states. He argues that, although we must be careful to distinguish between, for example, perceiving and knowing that one is perceiving, the self-knowledge requires no additional way of gaining knowledge. He seems to hint at what would now be called a constitutive account of self-knowledge.

[12] Śrīharṣa has been claimed by later Advaita Vedāntins as one of their own, but the internal evidence is extremely weak and I will make no assumptions here as to his larger affiliations. The *Amassed Morsels* is an extended critique of constructive accounts of inquiry and knowledge: what remains if that critique is successful, what Śrīharṣa's motivation was in conducting it, and what the exact nature is of the 'illocutionary intervention' the text makes in the context of twelfth century Indian intellectual history, are all questions that require a great deal more exploration than has been done to date. Phyllis Granoff, noting various places where Śrīharṣa argues *against* Advaita doctrine, sums up the situation very well: 'Since so many of his texts have been lost and since the *Khaṇḍana* is a text with a very specific mission, to refute the tenets of anyone and everyone who would attribute reality to the visible world, we are not in a position to say much more about where exactly Śrīharṣa belongs in the as yet unwritten story of 12th century Indian philosophy' (Granoff, unpubl.). Phillips 1995 and Ram-Prasad 2002 argue the case for his being an Advaitin.

consisting in whatever mental states are required for success in action. On another reading, there is no such implication: knowledge is independently defined, and it is a further claim that it has the role it does in successful action. The trouble is that success seems to require only that one's beliefs are true—if I put money on the winning horse or buy the winning lottery ticket, then my self-confidence, however ill-grounded, is rewarded. The early Naiyāyikas have used 1.1.1 as the starting point for their epistemology, and are under pressure to identify knowledge with true belief. By the time of Udayana, this pressure had become irresistible. In the *Garland of Definitions*, Udayana presents a celebrated definition:

Knowledge (*pramā*) is an experience of the way things are.[13]

In his criticism of this analysis, Śrīharṣa first of all considers the case of a belief that is true by chance:

The definition of knowledge (*pramā*) as a non-mnemonic experience (*anubhava*) of the way things are (*tattva*) over-extends and covers beliefs which are true but [purely by chance], as in the maxim of 'the crow and the palm tree'.[14]

Another example: someone, closing five shells in his palm, asks, 'How many shells are there?' The person who has been asked the question says, 'five', as per the maxim of 'the goat and the sword'.[15] Then both the speaker and the respondent think that there are five shells.

Instances such as this are there to be seen. The expression 'the way things are' can't rule out this belief (*jñāna*), because there is no lack of accordance: the number five delimits what is actually the case.

Nor is it ruled out by the expression *anubhava* [implying *not a memory*], for it does not come after another such state, so the defining mark of recollection is not present.

Nor can they say that what results is just a doubt (*saṃśaya*: *p* or *not-p*?), lacking in commitment (*niścaya*), with only one side of the doubt articulated for the same reason that one finds in the practice of cultivation [one sows the seeds, uncertain but confident that they will grow]. That's because there must be only a pretence of certainty in one of the two sides of the doubt; for otherwise, we would make the mistake of thinking that a doubt is the conjunction of two certainties [*p* and *not-p*!].

Perhaps what is needed is a qualification [in the definition], to the effect that knowledge must be produced by such a cause as is 'faithful' (*avyabhicārī*). That can't be right, though, for it would make the expression 'the way things are' superfluous. If one wants to maintain that the belief that is as per 'the crow and the palm tree' is produced by a complex of causes that are collectively 'unfaithful' the unwelcome result would be that even the 'unfaithful' is true (*yathārtha*), because there is [still] no distinction among the causes [of the true].

[13] tattva-anubhavaḥ pramā | (Udayana 1963: v. 1). The next few paragraphs are extracted from my 2007: 135–138.

[14] A maxim (or *nyāya*), illustrating inexplicable coincidence: the crow alights in a palm tree at just the moment when its ripe fruit happens to fall, killing the crow. See Doniger O'Flaherty 1984: 265–268; Apte 1957: 58.

[15] Another maxim, illustrating an action's accidental and unintended effects: the sword is accidentally dislodged by the goat's rubbing against the post on which it is balanced; it falls and cuts the goat's throat. See Doniger O'Flaherty 1984: 266; Apte 1957: 52.

Nor can it be right to say that this 'accordance with how things are' is without any cause, for in the absence of any restricting principle (*niyāmaka*) there would be a serious over-extension [of the definition]. So, given that this 'faithfulness' is needed, one has to say that the instrumental cause [of knowledge] is indeed subject to a principle of restriction to what is 'faithful'.

'So what is then [this restriction to what is "faithful"]?' You must give an answer to this question yourself, an answer that shows either how to include this [luckily true] belief within the [somehow] restricted heaps of knowledge, or else how to delimit the general definition of knowledge.[16]

The possibility of the true guess seems to show that 'true awareness' or 'true belief' alone is not sufficient for knowledge. Adding the further condition, 'produced by a faithful cause' seems promising, but there are serious difficulties with the proposal. If it is meant to introduce a distinction *among* the causes of true mental states, so that we can say of some that they are not caused in the right way, then we cannot define a 'faithful' cause simply as one such as to produce as true beliefs. This is Śrīharṣa's challenge to traditional Indian theories of knowledge. It presented the tradition with a considerable difficulty, and would influence the renovation of epistemology among post-Gaṅgeśa 'new reason' thinkers.

Śrīharṣa goes on to argue that chance can be involved even when the belief is the result of one of the standardly approved sources of knowledge. The text continues as follows:

So too, it is possible that what merely appears to be the sign leads to an ascertainment of the signified in a place where, as chance would have it, the signified is present, either alone or with the sign. And there, even if as regards the mere appearance of the sign there is no knowledge (*pramā*), nor as regards the place it is located with the signified, nevertheless, as thus characterised [in the person's mind], the knowledge-hood (*prāmāṇya*) of the ascertainment has to be accepted, with respect to its being about the signified, for example, fire, either on its own or with a different sign. So there is no way to escape the fault [in the theory of knowledge] mentioned above.

Śrīharṣa identifies two places where a defect has crept into the inferential process: the person has misidentified the evidence, taking what is in fact fog to be smoke; and they have also misascribed it to the mountain, for there isn't (necessarily) any smoke on the mountain. The misascription is, of course, a consequence of the misidentification: once the fog is mistaken for smoke, then whatever is believed to be true of the fog will be taken to be a truth about the smoke. Still, the two beliefs, that *this* is smoke, and that there is smoke on the mountain, are distinct; and both are mistaken. Given the second belief as premise, it would indeed be rational to infer to the presence of fire, and, *by chance*, Śrīharṣa says, there is indeed fire on the mountain. Śrīharṣa the sceptic does not assert that the inference does not in fact lead to knowledge; his point is that the epistemological theory under discussion cannot agree that it is knowledge, and so the

[16] Śrīharṣa, *Amassed Morsels* 1.16, 1990: 241–244.

theory is defeated *on its own terms*. Śrīharṣa, indeed, thinks this is true of *all* theories of knowledge; he claims only to use others' epistemological criteria against themselves.

Finally, do we have in Śrīharṣa an anticipation of Edmund Gettier (1963)? Gettier's examples seem to show that the justification of a true item (state, episode, event, condition) of the mind is not sufficient for that item to be knowledge. In Gettier's cases there is a disconnect between the circumstances that make for truth and the circumstances that make for justification: I have a false but justified belief that Jones owns a Ford, and a true and justified belief that Jones either owns a Ford or is in Barcelona (he drives by in a borrowed car on the way to the airport). To some, it has seemed that what these cases show is that knowledge cannot rest on a 'false lemma'. I infer that Jones either owns a Ford or is in Barcelona from the false lemma, namely, that Jones owns a Ford. It is not entirely clear, however, if any of the Indian theories operate with a notion of justification that would entitle us to call the example a 'Gettier case', although it certainly has the form of a counter-example to the sufficiency of an analysis of knowledge. The Indians do not typically say that what these examples show is that I am in an inferentially justified and coincidentally true mental state. What they say is that I have *tried* to infer, but done so unsuccessfully. There has been, as we might say, a 'performative misfire' in my attempted act of coming to know. The notion of a 'performative misfire' is due to J. L. Austin (1962: 14–18). He says a couple might go through all the motions of getting married, but fail to do so for various reasons. One reason, which he calls a *mis-invocation* of the ceremony, is simply that one of the couple is already married, and so it is impossible for the performance to succeed, however well it is otherwise conducted. It might even be the case that both parties think, mistakenly, that the performance has been successful (the member of the couple who is already married wrongly believing, for example, that the old marriage has been annulled). That is how the 'fire–fog' case will be described—there is an attempt at the performance of an inference, an attempt that fails because the person involved mistakenly thinks that a condition on the successful performance of the inference has been met, whereas in fact it has not (the condition here being the one identified by Śrīharṣa, that there is smoke on the mountain). The 'ceremony' of inference has been misinvoked.

10

Challenge From the Ritualists

Scepticism and truth in the *Gemstone*

Gaṅgeśa Upādhyāya (c. 1325 CE) makes the problem of grounding the possibility of inquiry into the central question for philosophy. His only work, the *Gemstone fulfilling one's desire for the Truth* (*Tattva-cintāmaṇi*), is so structured as to place epistemology at the fore, giving one chapter to each of the ways of gaining knowledge acknowledged by the mainstream Nyāya tradition. The very title of the book implies that it is to be a method for pursuing inquiry, a technique for satisfying one's desire for knowledge and truth. After a short discussion of the reasons for having a benedictory verse (*maṅgala*) at the start of any literary work, the first chapter opens with three sections that deal with the key issues in Nyāya epistemology: (1) how is it possible to *know* when a belief is true or false? (*prāmāṇya-jñapti-vāda*); (2) what *produces* truth or falsity in belief? (*prāmāṇya-utpatti-vāda*); and (3) what *defines* true belief and/or knowledge (*pramā-lakṣaṇa-vāda*)? Gaṅgeśa's way of treating these issues, and indeed all philosophical issues, is to give voice to an opponent through the formulation of a sequence of disjunctive alternatives which are refuted one by one, before a statement or series of statements of the correct position is offered, together with the consideration of *prima facie* objections to the correct position and ways of responding to them. The texture this gives to the work is highly dialectical and abstract, Gaṅgeśa rarely making it easy to correlate some given opponent or objection, or particular formulation of what he regards as the correct position, with an actual historical philosopher. Gaṅgeśa nevertheless begins by presenting his work as if it is a kind of reconstructive commentary on the first verse of the *Nyāya-sūtra*:

> Now, the extremely gracious sage composed a critical philosophy which is the most respected amongst all the eighteen sciences, wanting to raise up the world[1] that is immersed in the mud of suffering. Therein, in order that discerning persons may take an interest in studying the work, he laid down the sūtra beginning 'The highest good is reached through an understanding of the real nature of the ways of gaining knowledge and so on' [*Nyāya-sūtra* 1.1.1]. Of these, fixing all the others rests on (*adhīna*) the ways of gaining knowledge. Therefore, the real nature of the ways of gaining knowledge will be discussed here.[2]

[1] I discussed Raghunātha's interpretation of the term 'world' in this statement in Chapter 4.
[2] Gaṅgeśa 1888: 114–116. Cf. Mohanty 1966: 73; Phillips and Tatacharya 2004: 69.

As we saw in the previous chapter, the opening text of the *Nyāya-sūtra* lists sixteen topics, and says that one needs to understand each of them in order to achieve the highest good. Gaṅgeśa collapses the list into the phrase 'the ways of gaining knowledge and so on' (*pramāṇādi*), and asserts that without an understanding of the nature of the ways of gaining knowledge, no understanding of the others is possible. Metaphysics (*prameya*) and the theory of debate (*vāda*) are made secondary to epistemology. And having done that, Gaṅgeśa gives to his first opponent the voice of scepticism:

However, it is not correct that a treatise which discusses the real nature of the ways of gaining knowledge and so on is linked by a chain relation with the highest good, for it is not possible to discern the real nature of the ways of gaining knowledge.

The sceptic does not deny that the highest good is achievable, but disputes the possibility of understanding the ways of gaining knowledge, and therefore rejects a cardinal ancient claim, that the study of philosophy is required on soteriological grounds. There are, this sceptic implies, other routes to the highest good. What grounds the sceptical doubt? Gaṅgeśa continues:

For [to discern the real nature of the ways of gaining knowledge] rests on discerning the real nature of true belief (*pramā*), and this is possible neither intrinsically nor extrinsically because of a heap of difficulties about to be mentioned.[3]

The scepticism from which Gaṅgeśa sees the greatest threat is one which argues that we shall never know what is a way of gaining knowledge, or indeed if there are any ways of gaining knowledge, because the determination of something as a way of gaining knowledge is dependent on determining states of true belief. If there is no means to discriminate between true and false belief, then there is no prospect identifying a source of belief as a 'way of gaining knowledge' as opposed to a source of untruth. Gaṅgeśa does not tell us whether he has in mind some particular sceptic, or whether this is for him a purely formal possibility. 'New reason' thinkers will identify the sceptical voice with one strand of Buddhism, Madhyamaka, the strand which flourished in Tibet in the second millennium, but began with Nāgārjuna, whose strong critique of the Nyāya account of inquiry is approximately contemporaneous with the compilation of the *Nyāya-sūtra* itself (Nāgārjuna 1986; Ganeri 2001a: 58–62). The 'new reason' philosophers see Gaṅgeśa as having retrieved an ancient scepticism in order to motivate his reformulation of the theory, in a moment of renewal not wholly dissimilar to the recovery of, and reaction against, Pyrrhonic scepticism by the *nouveaux pyrrhoniens* of Europe.

Ironically, as I will argue in the next chapter, the reformed epistemology is still unable to offer a convincing reply to Śrīharṣa, who combines scepticism about the possibility of inquiry with a quietist epistemology grounded in the idea that knowledge is a by-product of the refusal to engage in self-defeating attempts to acquire it (Carpenter and Ganeri 2010). It is only after Gaṅgeśa that an attempt is made to

[3] Gaṅgeśa 1888: 119. Cf. Mohanty 1966: 76; Phillips and Tatacharya 2004: 70.

exploit Gaṅgeśa's ideas in the construction of a genuinely post-Śrīharṣa epistemology.[4] Several Mithilā philosophers—including Vardhamāna, Śaṃkara Miśra, Vācaspati Miśra II, and Pragalbha—recognize the need, and write 'refutation-commentaries' on Śrīharṣa. Among 'new reason' philosophers, Raghudeva and Raghunātha Sārvabhauma Bhaṭṭācārya are keen to do so as well (the latter's *Bhūṣāmaṇi* is often but incorrectly attributed to Raghunātha Śiromaṇi). At the end of the seventeenth century and early in the eighteenth, when Mithilā enjoys a new lease of life, Gokulanātha will extend this important genre. What its distribution suggests is that there is a disagreement about whether an effective answer to Śrīharṣa can be constructed out of Gaṅgeśa alone, or whether it requires a departure from his *via antiqua* and a new willingness to go beyond ancient doctrine.[5]

In order to defend knowledge and inquiry against ancient scepticism, Gaṅgeśa has to make one large concession. He ends up admitting that success in action in many cases does not require knowledge. The successful performance of an elaborate and expensive ritual does not require that one *knows* that it will be a means to reach heaven; and likewise the successful performance of an act of gaining knowledge does not require that one *knows* what the ways of gaining knowledge are. That is what blocks the sceptical regress, which is now made to terminate in epistemically ungrounded basic acts.[6] Given that this is, in effect, to abandon the original soteriological justification for the study of philosophy (which justification is now seen as the door through which scepticism was able to enter), what Gaṅgeśa's concession amounts to is a realignment of philosophy as an autonomous discipline. The 'new reason' will begin to conceive of itself as a system of investigation not subservient to soteriological ends. In a work such as Mahādeva's *Precious Jewel of Reason*, the shift is evident in the way he paraphrases Gaṅgeśa's opening lines (see next chapter), while in Mādhavadeva's large *Essence of Reason*, we find the discussion of theological matters relegated to a single paragraph (1903–4: 162). Seventeenth-century Nyāya thinkers achieve a separation of philosophy far more thorough than their European counterparts, with even the topic of liberation (*mukti*) treated mainly as an exercise in the logic of negation rather than as of independent soteriological interest.[7]

[4] The precise nature and degree of Śrīharṣa's influence on Gaṅgeśa himself is very unclear. See Phillips 1995 for the most extended discussion available to date. Phillips concludes that although Gaṅgeśa 'very often had Śrīharṣa in mind,' 'the extent of his dependence is decidedly less than has been suggested by some.' Phillips stresses that 'the context of the emergence of Navya Nyāya was philosophically rich; there was much more on the agenda than Śrīharṣa's objections' (1995:4).

[5] Phillips 1995 likewise finds in Gaṅgeśa a continuation of the *via antiqua*. He also wants to claim that post-Gaṅgeśa thinkers do not innovate significantly over Gaṅgeśa: 'If there is a revolution sparked by [Śrīharṣa], it is a revolution in precision and analytic tools, not in fundamental outlook. Gaṅgeśa . . . defends inherited positions in all but a few instances; his followers are similarly conservative' (1995: 4–5). Phillips' reference to Gaṅgeśa's 'followers' seems to be directed to the Maithilī scholastics (cf. his translations of Śaṃkara Miśra and Vācaspati II; 1995: 269–309), for he also says that 'Raghunātha's achievements (and failures) and those of still later Naiyāyikas, lie outside the scope of this study' (1995: 121).

[6] Gaṅgeśa 1888: 281–283. Cf. Mohanty 1966: 203–204; Phillips and Tatacharya 2004: 135–136.

[7] Daya Krishna 2006: 232 makes a similar observation.

More precisely, what Gaṅgeśa will do is to distinguish two grades of epistemic warrant, a weak grade which attaches to true beliefs if no doubt or suspicion (*saṃśaya*) has ever arisen with regard to their veracity, and a strong grade which attaches to true beliefs about which a doubt has arisen and then been dissolved through a process of evidence-based investigation. The technical term for this strong grade is *nirṇaya* or *niścaya* ('decided belief'):

Cognising the inferential mark is what leads to a decided belief about the object signified, if there is no hint of a doubt as to its falsity, but if there is such a hint, then one proceeds just as stated [namely, by introducing further processes of verification].[8]

Gaṅgeśa's view seems to be that while mere true belief is adequate for successful activity, a state of greater epistemic warrant is the outcome of a process involving the resolution of doubt. Such a state is the ascertainment of truth in belief; to achieve such a state, one needs in addition to have undergone a process of doubt and confirmation. Thus

We do not hold that only from certainty about a cognition's truth is there certainty about an object. Rather, where doubt does not occur concerning (truth or) falsity, there an original cognition itself is an ascertainment (*niścaya*) of an object, for example, a cognition about an *āmalaka* fruit in the palm of one's hand. Just from that is there unhesitating action. But where, in unfamiliar circumstances, doubt about an object occurs—defeating any certainty—through doubt about truth, there one makes unhesitating action to proceed only after having become certain about the object from a cognition dependent on certainty about truth, not otherwise—so everyone's experience.[9]

That is to say, certainty about something in the world (*artha-niścaya*) may or may not rest upon a process of doubt resolution (*prāmāṇya-niścaya*). There are two grades of epistemic warrant associated with the idea of worldly certainty. This is what blocks the sceptical infinite regress, which Gaṅgeśa has already introduced, the worry, familiar from Nāgārjuna, that 'a cognition whose truth is grasped by another cognition could not assume the form of an ascertainment of the truth of another, because of an infinite regress'.[10]

For Gaṅgeśa, then, there is warrant which attaches to a truth about which no question has been raised, something which is simply not subject to suspicion, and there is warrant which attaches to a truth about which a suspicion has been raised and subsequently resolved, a truth for which a process of verification has taken place. If we call these grades of warrant 'weak' and 'strong', then the warrant attaching to the English verb *know* is of a middle grade: it seems to refer to something stronger than Gaṅgeśa's weak grade but weaker than his strong grade. Perceptions, for example,

[8] Gaṅgeśa 1888: 282. Cf. Mohanty 1966: 204; Phillips and Tatacharya 2004: 135.
[9] Gaṅgeśa 1888: 277–278. Cf. Mohanty 1966: 197; trans. Phillips and Tatacharya 2004: 130.
[10] Gaṅgeśa 1888: 276. Cf. Mohanty 1966: 195–196; trans. Phillips and Tatacharya 2004: 129.

count as states of knowledge, even if no process of doubting and resolving doubt has taken place. Gaṅgeśa uses the term 'way of gaining knowledge' (*pramāṇa*) both to refer to the causal production of true beliefs in the weak grade, and to the procedures of evidence-based investigation that underlie the strong grade, and this has been the source of considerable confusion about the nature of his epistemology. I will argue later that there are lacunae and equivocations in Gaṅgeśa's own thinking, permitting later philosophers ample scope for theoretical innovation.

Two models of inquiry

The deep threat to any epistemology which bases itself on the concept of a way of gaining knowledge is that we seem to need a prior method of deciding which beliefs are true and which false. As Gaṅgeśa has clarified, this threatens to be regressive, for a method of deciding which beliefs are true and which false seems just to be a way of gaining knowledge. A methodological principle endorsed by, and in part definitive of, the ancient Indian philosophical disciplines is, as we have seen, that a sound grasp of the ways of gaining knowledge is a necessary prerequisite in the fulfilment of life's aims, mundane or ultimate. The opening *sūtra* of the *Nyāya-sūtra* is programmatic: attainment of the highest good in life derives from knowledge of the true nature of the categories and methods enunciated in the Nyāya system. The principle rests on a pair of assumptions: first, that a person's projects and plans depend for their success on a grounding in a stable body of knowledge; and, second, that the possession of a stable body of knowledge requires a sound understanding of the ways of gaining knowledge. Gaṅgeśa asks a searching question of the ancient principle. We cannot, he says, possibly demand that a sound understanding of the ways of gaining knowledge is a prerequisite for the accomplishment of our highest ends unless we also have at least the capacity to identify and distinguish true beliefs from false—a capacity to discern the property of truth (*prāmāṇya*) in a belief. A key theoretical issue for the new intellectuals is whether any sense can be made of the attribution of such a capacity. Gaṅgeśa proceeds by introducing at this point a second philosophical dialectic, one which pitches two models of inquiry against each other—the Nyāya epistemology of inquiry against the Mīmāṃsā ritualists' advocacy of Vedic authority. The question is whether the identification of a belief as true is intrinsic (*svataḥ*) or extrinsic (*parataḥ*) to the belief-process itself. Gaṅgeśa will set the pattern for all future discussion by arguing in cases against three formulations of intrinsicism, which others will identify as originating with three eighth-century thinkers, Kumārila Bhaṭṭa, Prabhākara Miśra (aka 'the Guru'), and Murāri Miśra. Each of these philosophers is responsible for a distinct variety of ritualist epistemology.

Let us try to get clear what is at issue. Gaṅgeśa claims that my knowledge of the ways of gaining knowledge rests upon an ability to classify my beliefs as true or as false, and he has his sceptic argue that this is impossible:

[Objection:] It is impossible to determine the real nature of a way of gaining knowledge, for that wholly depends on determining the real nature of an item of true belief, and this cannot be done whether it is intrinsic or extrinsic.[11]

Presumably, some form of inquiry such as the following is envisaged. First, I survey the totality of my beliefs, and identify among them, those that are true. Then I examine the causes of each of my true beliefs, the specific manner by which each one came into existence. Finally, I search for commonalities in those specific aetiologies, underlying general patterns of causation common to the production of true beliefs and absent in the production of false ones. The result of the inquiry is a set of generalizations about the causal origins of my true beliefs. If this is the picture, then it is clear, first of all, that the claim cannot be that knowledge of the ways of gaining knowledge is necessary for the *production* of true belief, for that knowledge is itself the result of a survey and study of my true beliefs. The claim is rather that it is the *identification* of my beliefs as true which makes possible my knowledge of their sources. My ability to identify my beliefs as true or false is prior to and necessary for my acquisition of knowledge of the sources of true belief. At this point, however, the concept of inquiry threatens to unravel. For if I must already be able to identify my true beliefs, in advance, as it were, of a knowledge of the general causes of true belief, then how can that knowledge be required for the possession of a stable body of true belief? This was, recall, the leading methodological principle to which the ancient epistemology is committed.[12]

The move made by the ritualists here is an appealing one, and I will spend most of this chapter trying to motivate it. Their basic idea is that there is no further need to *identify* a belief as true or false. Rather, in some sense, its truth comes along with it. Gaṅgeśa looks for the essential thesis that underpins all three forms of intrinsicism. The fundamental intrinsicist thesis, he claims, is that *whatever makes me grasp one of my beliefs is sufficient to make me grasp the truth of that belief.*[13] This thesis might seem to be a straightforward consequence of two mundane but important facts about the nature of belief. First, believing that *p* and believing that *it is true that p* are one and the same thing—it is of the nature of belief that it is an attitude of commitment to the truth of

[11] Gaṅgeśa 1888: 117. Cf. Mohanty 1966: 76; Phillips and Tatacharya 2004: 70.

[12] There is a strong echo in all this of the 'problem of the criterion.' Montaigne, drawing on ancient sources, presents it as follows: 'To judge the appearances we have of objects, we must have an instrument for adjudicating (*instrument judicatoire*); to verify this instrument, we must give a proof of it; to verify the proof, an instrument is required: we are caught in a circle.' (Montaigne 1946: 544). Chisholm 1973: 3 paraphrases the argument: 'To know whether things really are as they seem to be, we must have a *procedure* for distinguishing appearances that are true from appearances that are false. But to know whether our procedure is a good procedure, we have to know whether it really *succeeds* in distinguishing appearances that are true from appearances that are false. And we cannot know whether it does really succeed unless we already know which appearances are *true* and which ones are *false*. And so we are caught in a circle.' Intrinsicism and extrinsicism might thus be regarded as two rival attempts to solve the problem of the criterion.

[13] jñānaprāmāṇyaṃ tadaprāmāṇyāgrāhakayāvajjñānagrāhakasāmagrīgrāhyaṃ na vā | (Gaṅgeśa 1888: 121–122). Cf. Mohanty 1966: 84; Phillips and Tatacharya 2004: 73.

what is believed.[14] Second, a suspicion about the truth of a belief is *fatal* to that belief, in the sense that one cannot sustain a belief and simultaneously entertain a question about its truth.[15] As soon as such a doubt arises, the belief ceases to be a belief, and is replaced instead by something else, a wish or hope or hypothesis. The intrinsicist thesis looks to be nothing more than a second-order version of these facts: my believing that I believe that *p* is sufficient for my believing that my belief that *p* is true. What the intrinsicist theory seems to insist is that there is no intelligible form of inquiry which begins with my first forming beliefs and proceeds by my then asking myself whether those beliefs are true or false. My commitment to the truth of my beliefs is part and parcel of what it is to have the belief at all. There is no *further* project, the project of identifying which of my beliefs are true and which false, over above and additional to the base-level project of forming the beliefs themselves.

There are more substantive readings of the intrinsicist thesis than this. I have said that it is the thesis that whatever makes me *believe* that I have a belief is sufficient to make me *believe* the truth of that belief. According to one stronger reading, what the thesis claims is rather that whatever makes me *know* that I have a belief is sufficient to make me *know* the truth of that belief. If we concede that it is possible, in principle, for me to know that I have any belief which I do in fact have, the stronger reading entails that all my beliefs are true! This need not be as implausible a proposal as it first seems, but it is revisionary and restrictive of the term 'belief'. We are owed now an account of cognitive error, which does not analyse error in terms of states of false belief. One way to pursue that possibility is to claim that so-called 'false beliefs' are not mental items of the same kind and type as true beliefs. They are 'false' in the sense of being mock or phoney, like a false promise or a false friend. The inquiry might be in order to ascertain of some mental item whether it was a real belief or a phoney, and this might be discernible from the shape and form of the item within the realm of the mental. Prabhākara, for instance, argues that what is referred to as a 'false belief' is not a single item in mental space at all, but a pair of cognitions, a memory and a sense impression. Falsity is the result of a complex of mental items coalescing to produce something that masquerades as a belief (Prabhākara 1929). A condition on action is that there is a non-perception of a difference between what is presented and what is remembered as desirable. I see a face in front of me, and remembering a good friend, go towards the person whose face it is, failing all the while to notice that this person is not in fact my good friend at all. No attribution of a false belief along the lines 'here is my good friend' seems required for the explanation of my mistake in action. Since Prabhākara's theory plays a very important role in the development of 'new reason' epistemology, and

[14] Cf. Bernard Williams 1973: 137, 'To believe that so and so is one and the same as to believe that that thing is true.'

[15] Cf. again Williams 2002: 67, 'It is an objection to a belief that it is false. In fact, in the case of a belief, it is a fatal objection, in the sense that if the person who has the belief accepts the objection, he thereby ceases to have the belief, or at least it retreats to the subconscious: if a person recognizes that the content of his belief is false, in virtue of this alone he abandons his belief in it.' The Indian term is *pratibandhaka*.

given indeed that Prabhākara exercises a good deal of influence on Raghunātha, I will take time to elaborate this thought further below.

Kumārila Bhaṭṭa (Kumārila 1926) has an ingenious alternative. He argues that when something is cognised, it is marked by the property 'being-cognised' *(jñātatā)*. I can investigate the things themselves and see if they have this among their various properties. That way I can find out which among the things in the world are the things believed by me. And that inquiry does not involve any simple recapitulation of the process of belief, for being-cognised is a secondary quality and a so-called 'Cambridge' property—a property that can change without there being any real change in the object to which it belongs. When I infer that I believe that *p* on the grounds that the 'fact' *p* is marked by the property 'being-believed-by-me' it follows that I am in a position to infer too that my belief that *p* is true—that is what is meant by saying that *p* is a 'fact'. By this method, therefore, I could never discover within myself a false belief, because, being false, there is no 'fact' that the false belief could mark as believed-by-me. So the implication of Kumārila's theory would seem to be that false beliefs, if there are any, never come to the surface of consciousness. Here again the cost of intrinsicism is to incur an obligation, this time to a substantive account of the sub-doxastic.

There is a second, perpendicular, way to derive a more substantive reading of the intrinsicist thesis. On this reading, the claim is that whatever makes me grasp that I have an *awareness* is sufficient to make me grasp the truth of that *awareness*. This reading turns on the use of the Sanskrit term '*jñāna*'. Nyāya classifies under this term any mental state or event that is not one of desire, aversion, or volition; in other words, any *attitudinal* rather than *motivational* state. The category includes memories, doubts, true beliefs, illusions, dreams, conjectures, and hypotheses. In particular, it includes states of *hesitation* (*saṃśaya, tarka*) as well as states of *commitment* (*niścaya*). The intrinsicist thesis now is that to be aware of being in any attitudinal mental state at all is to be aware that that state is one of commitment.

I said that a certain conception of the project of inquiry is untenable, the conception according to which I first form my beliefs and then inquire into their truth or falsity. If we continue with the idea that the term *jñāna* should be construed as referring to any attitudinal state and not only to states of belief, then one might envisage a rather different conception of inquiry, one in which the formation is not, initially, of beliefs (states of commitment), but rather of doubts, hypotheses, conjectures—states of hesitation. There is then a project distinct from and additional to the project of hypothesis-formation, and that is the project of hypothesis-confirmation: establishing whether my hypothesis is true calls for an inquiry whose causes and conditions do not overlap with those of hypothesis-formation. If the first move is taken to be one of doubt rather than belief, room is made for a distinct project of inquiry into the truth.

Familiar though it is, this 'hypothesis and confirmation' model does not exactly accord with the viewpoint of an Indian epistemologist. For it does not give due weight to the centrality and primacy of the belief-forming processes, and to the fact that the first move is one of belief production and not hypothesis formation. In their daily life, human beings are not scientists; our first reflex is to believe what we hear or see or infer. Gaṅgeśa has a far more fluid and 'psychologically real' account of the dynamics of belief-formation and revision.[16] If the first moment is to *believe*, the second is to *question*. Questioning a belief is, as we have seen, fatal to its persistence as a belief—our attitude shifts from one of commitment to one of hesitation. At the third moment, we reflect upon the grounds available, a reflection that will typically consist in cross-verification against subsequent behaviour. If all goes well, the attitude shifts again, from hesitation back to commitment, and so on, in an interplay of spontaneous acceptance and reflective questioning. When I infer that an initially uncritical belief is true on the basis of subsequent successful behaviour, I distance myself from that belief. In this model, a model in which I continually monitor the beliefs arising within me, commitment lasts only for a moment. Gaṅgeśa's account of the psychodynamics of belief is in important respects richer than a mere 'conjectures and refutations' model of inquiry.

There are here two models, then, of the way inquiry aims at the truth. On one model, truth regulates inquiry by imposing obligations on the formation of belief and the giving of assent; on the other, the obligations fall on confirmation, verifying that our assent was worthily given. One model constrains the act of assenting, the other the persistence of assent, one embodies an ethics of commitment and implies epistemic caution, the other embodies an ethics of trust, and implies an obligation to cross-check, and a readiness to withdraw one's consent. In the background to this dispute over the nature of inquiry is a fundamental disagreement about the epistemological status of scripture. The ritualists affirm that the statements of the Veda are authoritative, that they admit of no further question about their truth and no further need for any project of verification. Such an attitude towards scripture is an anathema to the naturalistically inclined Nyāya philosophers. They say that the scriptures are to be treated as sources of knowledge in just the same way as all other testimony, and equally open to issues of verification should the need arise.

An intrinsicist theory of error in action

In its response to scepticism, Gaṅgeśa's epistemology rejects the older principle that success in action necessarily requires knowledge (with 'strong grade' epistemic warrant). What about the converse of this principle, that failure in action necessarily presupposes false belief? Is there always a cognitive error in the background of practical mishap? A cardinal Buddhist principle claims that 'ignorance' (*ajñāna*) always lies upstream in the causal history of immoral action, and the ancient Nyāya philosophers seem to commit Nyāya to the same principle in the interpretation they give of *Nyāya-sūtra* 1.1.2, which refers to 'erroneous belief' (*mithyā-jñāna*) as necessarily implicated in

[16] Gaṅgeśa 1888: 194–215. Cf. Mohanty 1966: 116–128; Phillips and Tatacharya 2004: 86–90.

immoral acts and suffering.[17] An important virtue of intrinsicism, in Prabhākara's formulation, is that it leads to greater clarity about this principle. For what Prabhākara points out is that there can be error in action *without* false belief. If that is right, then a defence of the principle demands that we be careful to disambiguate the term 'ignorance'. It should not be understood as 'false belief' but rather as 'lack of belief'. There are beliefs which, had we had them, we would not have committed error in our deeds; but from this it does not follow that we believe anything false. Given the manifest importance of this argument, let me sketch how a defence of Prabhākara's claim might go.

If somebody I have never met before comes up to me and slaps me on the back, the explanation, it would seem, is that he mistakenly believes that I am somebody else, someone of his acquaintance. Likewise, if somebody sincerely asserts something when the facts are otherwise, the explanation appears to be that he is expressing his mistaken belief. Driving the thought is the idea that one must be able to give a unitary explanation of action, whether successful or not. But perhaps that is wrong; perhaps one will do better to account *disjunctively* for success and for error.[18] Suppose that the person mistakes me [JG] for a friend of his [CD]. He slaps me on the back and says 'You were here last week'. We can attribute to him the following pair of true beliefs:

(1) You [= JG] are here now.
(2) You [= CD] were here last week.

The indexical in the first sentence has its reference fixed perceptually: it refers to the person now standing before him. The indexical in the second sentence has its reference fixed through memory: it refers to a person remembered, a memory that might be prompted by some perceptual likeness. Prabhākara's proposal is that what explains the misguided conduct is not that my new acquaintance has a further *false* belief, that

(3) You [JG] are you [CD],

but rather that the explanation lies in a *cognitive lacuna*, the absence of a (true) belief that

(4) You [JG] are not you [CD].

There are many situations where the explanation of a person's action is very naturally in terms of a cognitive lack rather than a false belief. For example, if somebody walks straight into a tree, it is better to explain their action by saying that they failed to see the tree than that they falsely believed there was no tree. The attribution of a false belief in such a case would be otiose; here the explanation in terms of cognitive lack is simpler. Moreover, even in cases of 'mistaken identity' where the attribution of a false belief is more tempting, there is a reason to think that such an attribution would fail to be

[17] duḥkha-janma-pravṛtti-doṣa-mithyā-jñānānām uttarottarāpāye tadanantarāpāyād apavargaḥ | (Gautama 1997: 6, 7–8).

[18] On disjunctivism as a philosophical position, see Byrne and Logue 2009.

genuinely explanatory. Inferences involving proper names or demonstratives trade on the identity of occurrences of those singular terms across premises. For example, the validity of the inference from '*a* is *F*' and '*a* is *G*' to '*a* is both *F* and *G*' depends on the assumption that '*a*' has the same reference in each occurrence (Campbell 1987–8). It will not help to add an additional premise '*a* = *a*' for the problem will recur when we come to combine this new premise with the original ones. Rather, what we want to say is that in the explanatory inference '*a* is *F* & *G* because *a* is *F* and *a* is *G*' the identity is exploited in the *structure* of the explanation. The name '*a*' is the tag for a file of information into which is placed first the predicate '*F*' and then the predicate '*G*'. Now we look into the file and see that both *F* and *G* are there. The premises *place* information into labelled files, and the conclusion *retrieves* information from a file (see Table 10.1).

Table 10.1 The belief bank

a	b
F	*H*
G	

Suppose now that a labelling error has occurred and two different files are given the same label '*a*'. One contains the information '*F*' the other '*H*' (see Table 10.2). So far, we should not say that there is any mistake in the information: it is true that the object which the first file concerns is *F*, and the object which the second file concerns is *H*. An error only occurs when the information retrieval system operates. Asked to get the information about *a*, it will return with both *F* and *H*. There is no false belief here about the identity of the two files, but rather the *absence of correct labels* on the files. The explanation of misguided inference here refers to an error in the retrieval system, rather than to a misplacement of information in the belief-bank.

Table 10.2 Retrieval error—mislabelling

a	b	★a★
F	*H*	
G		
		H

This is one sort of example of how cognitive lack can explain inferential error. The same pattern is at work in the explanation of misguided action. We want to say that my new acquaintance slaps me on the back because he believes (1) and (2) above. Both beliefs are true; the error occurs in the translation of belief into action. As in the 'mislabelling' example, it is not the presence of a false lemma which explains the error but a structural lacuna in the belief-action system. The explanation of error exploits a directness or spontaneity in the relation between belief and action; in normal circumstances, action issues from belief (in the presence of background plans and projects) without further reflection.

Other kinds of error can be explained the same way. There are situations, for instance, where the retrieval system mistakenly flips from one column to another—asked to bring information from the file '*a*' it returns a piece of information from file '*b*'. Another sort of retrieval error is 'misreading', which occurs when the retrieval system returns the wrong value from a cell in the belief bank. I act as if *a* is *not* G because my retrieval system misreads the entry under the column for '*a*'.

Prabhākara's claim is that the thesis that error in action entails a background of cognitive error should be understood as requiring that cognitive error consist in lacunae in one's set of true beliefs rather than in the possession of states of false belief. Gaṅgeśa's epistemology consists in an attempt to find a way to defend the possibility of inquiry which does not rest on a commitment to intrinsicism, and that gives us reason enough to want to understand it. What I have tried to show, in addition, is that intrinsicism is not merely a 'straw-man'; in fact, it is a philosophical position of considerable power and explanatory strength.

I want now to consider the alternative Gaṅgeśa proposes. I am suggesting that one of the key debates of the period was a debate over the question of what it means for the norm of truth to govern our epistemic practice, a debate about whether the apprehension of truth is 'instrinsic' or 'extrinsic' on some interpretation of those terms. I have seen this as a debate over the question 'What do we mean when we say that our beliefs aim at the truth?' It is no surprise that in this debate, the Mīmāṃsakas, guardians of the absolute authority of Vedic scriptural truth, are pitched against the Naiyāyikas, who represent Bacon's third way—between empiricism and rationalism—in the pursuit of knowledge.

Knowing naturalized

The most telling objection to intrinsicism is that, if true, there will be no possible opportunity to doubt what one believes. Gaṅgeśa observes that such a consequence renders the intrinsicist position untenable. 'Did I really just see that?' 'Did that really just happen?' are all too natural questions to ask, particularly in situations that do not resemble past circumstances of belief-formation:

> If the truth of a belief is apprehended intrinsically, there could be no doubt about it [even] when a cognition arises in unfamiliar circumstances—for when the cognition itself is apprehended, its truth will be known. If one does not think that the truth is known then it is not apprehended intrinsically.[19]

The objection highlights an important contrast, and confirms how underpinning the debate is a difference in conceptions of the nature and function of inquiry. If to believe

[19] Gaṅgeśa 1888: 184. Cf. Mohanty 1966: 116; Phillips and Tatacharya 2004: 86.

is precisely to believe in the truth of what one believes, it necessitates no further inquiry or testing: the desire to test reveals that one does not, after all, believe. That does not rule out the possibility that one's belief will be defeated—if I later find out or begin to suspect that the source of my belief was subject to a fault or misfire (*doṣa*), I will begin to question its truth, a circumstance that is fatal to the persistence of the belief.[20] This leaves open, of course, the possibility that for certain beliefs there are no and never will be circumstances in which a fault can be disclosed. Such would be the case, for instance, with authorless testimony, on the supposition that human error alone is the source of testimonial misfire, a possibility which the ritualists exploit to account for the credibility of scripture. If the norm of truth is intrinsic and so forestalls inquiry, if beliefs once formed live unchallenged except by adventitious defeat, then the *entire* burden of epistemic responsibility lies in the formation of belief. What follows is a conservatism of assent: guard yourself against giving your assent too easily, because once given, it is not easily withdrawn. A belief is withdrawn only if a fault in the original process of production is later discovered. The old idea that some beliefs are self-evident and self-certifying is also transformed into a new claim, that certain beliefs are 'super-assertible'—immune to the possible uncovering of a condition that would necessitate the withdrawal of assent.

If the norm of truth is extrinsic, the burden of epistemic responsibility falls on the other side, with the revision of beliefs. False beliefs come and go; the important thing is to make sure they don't survive for long. One way to do this is to be on guard for any signs that one is entertaining false beliefs, specifically by attending to the success or failure of one's activities based on them. The monitoring of outcomes is one aspect of an extrinsicist epistemology of inquiry. Another is the monitoring of the methods of belief-formation. One must be vigilant for errors in the procedures being used in the conduct of inquiry. Gaṅgeśa says, for example: 'inasmuch as any veridical cognition is generated by some epistemic excellence' (*evaṃ pramāyāḥ guṇa-janyatvena*); and again that 'because of the difference between true and false belief, they are produced by excellences and defects' (*pramāpramāyor vaicitryāt guṇa-doṣa-janyatvam*).[21] Much debate occurs among the later 'new reason' philosophers about these notions of excellence and defect, and we can read that debate as an attempt to wrestle with the question of naturalism in epistemology. What naturalism claims, first of all, is that 'epistemic value is anchored in descriptive fact, no longer entering the world autonomously as brute, fundamental fact' (Maffie 1990: 284). The theory of excellences and defects is part of

[20] Gaṅgeśa 1888: 207–208. Cf. Mohanty 1966: 125; Phillips and Tatacharya 2004: 89–90. The examples cited by Gaṅgeśa are interesting. In both the examples—that of seeing a (white) conch-shell as yellow because of jaundice, and of seeing a face reflected in a mirror—the illusion persists even if we know that it is an illusion, produced by explicable causes. Nevertheless, although I may continue to *see* a face in front of me, my *belief* that there is a face in front of me does not survive the discovery that there is a mirror. This is what Gareth Evans has called the 'belief-independence' of informational states: 'the subject's being in an informational state is independent of whether or not he believes that the state is veridical.' Evans 1982: 123.

[21] Gaṅgeśa 1888: 287. Cf. Phillips and Tatacharya 2004: 141. See also Gaṅgeśa 1897–1901: 100–106 for comparable ideas about testimony.

an attempt to give a naturalistically respectable account of the epistemic properties of ways of gaining knowledge, an explanation in natural terms of what makes some belief-producing process carry the normative weight of a *pramāṇa*, a way of gaining knowledge.

A conceptual confusion lurked within the ancient epistemology. They thought that one could investigate the truth and falsity of one's beliefs by, as it were, taking one's belief in one hand, and the world in the other, and comparing the two. They forgot that belief itself *is* the way one takes the world in one's hand. Śrīharṣa is perhaps the one who first exposes the myth. In any case, Gaṅgeśa's renovation consists in large measure in an attempt to think through again the ancient understanding of the nature of inquiry. In his epistemology, attributions of truth are always provisional and go hand in hand with assessments of the worth of belief-forming processes. A constant mutual adjustment leads in time to a condition of reflective equilibrium (cf. Ganeri 2001a: 162–167). The myth of the side-on glance is decisively cast aside.[22] Gaṅgeśa's account requires that we are able to assume a 'reflective stance' with respect to the workings and deliverances of our epistemic apparatus. This is what it is to be a human knower and not an epistemic automaton or merely a sort of measuring instrument.

What sort of naturalist is Gaṅgeśa? Scholars have found in Gaṅgeśa the view that epistemic properties are natural properties in the causal web, and specifically the idea that ways of gaining knowledge are infallible causal processes.[23] Gaṅgeśa seems not to have been able to find a better way to reconcile his naturalist instincts with a refutation of scepticism; but the difficulties in making such a view plausible give very good reasons for later thinkers to want to explore new possibilities. It is to these new ideas that I now turn.

[22] In a similar vein but on different grounds, Matilal credits Gaṅgeśa with having 'struck at the root of what is called the third dogma of empiricism... the dualism of scheme and content' (2002, vol. 1: 145).

[23] Phillips and Tatacharya 2004: 7.

11

Interventions in a New Research Programme

Difficulties in Gaṅgeśa's theory

That Gaṅgeśa has made a decisive contribution in the direction of the defence of constructive epistemology against a rejuvenated scepticism is beyond question. It remains the case, however, that the epistemology of the *Gemstone* presents many problems and challenges. For all Gaṅgeśa's brilliance, there are ambiguities, lacunae, and difficulties in his epistemology. I will try to establish their principal source, before moving to a consideration of two important works in 'new reason' epistemology.

A way of gaining knowledge (*pramāṇa*) is now an instrumental cause of true belief (*pramā*). Gaṅgeśa's use of the expression is such that nothing other than true belief can be produced by a way of gaining knowledge. What this means is that, if we translate 'pramāṇa' as 'knowledge source' then we are using the word 'source' not in the way it is used when we speak of a mine as a source of diamonds (since the same mine can also be the source of things that are not diamonds) but rather in the way we speak of a spring as being a source of pure water (implying that no impure water comes from it). Verbs like *knows*, *perceives*, *infers* are factive, in the sense that one knows, perceives, infers that *p* only if *p* is true. Cases of perceptual or inferential error are then to be thought of as cases in which one tries to perceive or infer, but fails. They aim at the truth but miss their target, or, in other cases, hit their target but just by chance. In permitting such a notion of epistemic failure, Gaṅgeśa's account differs from that of the Mīmāṃsaka for whom the only way to miss the target is to fail to form a belief at all. In terms of J. L. Austin's (1962) doctrine of infelicities, they are 'performative misfires' rather than 'mis-invocations' of the ceremony of knowing.

Attractive as it is, Gaṅgeśa's model seems still to have a difficulty drawing a distinction between true belief and knowledge. He defines 'pramā' as a cognitive state whose content is veridical, a definition which does not itself distinguish between knowledge and accidentally true belief.[1] It would be natural to say that the difference lies in the manner of production, i.e. in the source. But Gaṅgeśa has taken it to be

[1] yatra yad asti tatra tasya anubhavaḥ pramā | tadvati tat-prakārakānubhavo vā | (Gaṅgeśa 1888: 401). Cf. Phillips and Tatacharya 2004: 236.

definitive of a way of gaining knowledge that it is instrumentally productive of true belief, and so it would seem that a 'way of gaining knowledge' lies in the causal ancestry of *any* true belief. There is a tension in his thought between wanting to give a purely causal account of the processes of true belief, and wanting to preserve the evaluative nature of epistemic assessment. That tension is most evident in the handling of problems about epistemic luck.

We have already seen that Śrīharṣa refers to cases of true beliefs formed by luck or chance, and denies that such beliefs are knowledge. The phrase he uses is 'as per the crow and palm-cabbage' (*kākatalīya)*, a reference to a 'maxim' (*nyāya*) involving a situation in which a crow lands on the branch of a palm tree at precisely the moment when the ripe palm-cabbage in any case falls. There is here the appearance—but just that—of a causal connection between the two events, and the implication seems to be that the same is true of, for example, the lucky guess. Gaṅgeśa uses the same phrase with reference to the possibility that the association between the occurrence of smoke and the occurrence of fire is just chancy,[2] and extends the point to true beliefs which are the product of the imagination (*utprekṣa*) (Saha 2003: 11, 46, 61). We see here that Gaṅgeśa will not allow that chance alone can produce states of knowledge, but without having any clear way to rule it out.

The way Gaṅgeśa appears to handle a particular case, the so-called 'inference from mist' (*bāṣpānumāna*), seems to be especially unsatisfactory. This is the case in which someone infers to the true conclusion that there is a fire on the hill on the basis of mist *misperceived as smoke*. The example has a long history, having been discussed by Kumārila, Maṇḍanamiśra, Rāmānuja, and others.[3] In this example, the belief that there is fire on the hill is the product not of guesswork or chance but is due instead to an apparently justifying inference (with a false but justified premise). Sukharanjan Saha has drawn attention to the surprising fact that Gaṅgeśa insists that this inference is knowledge-yielding (Saha 2003: 44, 66). What explains Gaṅgeśa's curious difficulty with regard to the inference from mist is, Saha, suggests, his commitment to a very rigid version of the causal theory of knowledge, which leads him to say that the false belief (that this is mist) is causally too remote from the final production of the inferential belief (that there is fire on the hill) for its falsity to infect the latter (Saha 2003: 44–52, 66–68). Whatever the details, the fact does seem to be that Gaṅgeśa's theoretical pre-commitments threaten to lead him to a counter-intuitive stance with respect to such cases. Certainly, he appears to lack anything like Maṇḍanamiśra's elaborate philosophical defence of their epistemological value. One explanation might be that he regards the inference as delivering true beliefs with weak but not strong epistemic warrant, and Anglophone intuition has it that this is a level of warrant insufficient for knowledge.

[2] Gaṅgeśa 1892: 188; cf. Saha 2003: 11, 30, 62, 123.

[3] Ganeri 2007: 125–144. Praśastapāda describes this inference as suffering from the fallacy of *tadbhava-asiddha*, a category on which early Nyāya philosophers are strangely silent.

The fundamental difficulty is that Gaṅgeśa's account of the methods of inquiry continually veers towards treating them as 'sources of truth' in a sense that leaves no gap between truth and knowledge. He wants a naturalistic account of the methods of inquiry, but a naturalistic account that leaves room for their fallibility seemingly evades him.[4] However brilliant his resolution of the paradox of 'doxastic ascent' and the 'problem of the criterion'—as retrieved from the ancient scepticism of Nāgārjuna—Gaṅgeśa appears at first sight not to have a plausible answer to Śrīharṣa's telling criticism of Udayana.

I now turn to an evaluation of texts in 'new reason' epistemology. I might have chosen to delve into the deep commentarial literature on the first chapter of the *Gemstone*, or else to explore the important genre of 'refutation-commentary' on Śrīharṣa's *Amassed Morsels*; but instead I have decided to examine two rather extraordinary and unusual works whose authors are both trying to do something exceptional.

The Precious Jewel of Reason: a genealogical state-of-research review

Towards the end of the seventeenth century, the Vārāṇasī-based philosopher Mahādeva Puṇatāṃakara composed a work which, in structure, closely parallels the *Gemstone*. His *Precious Jewel of Reason* is similarly divided into four chapters, one for each of the methods of gaining knowledge. Each chapter too is divided into sections in a sequence which departs from that of the *Gemstone* only occasionally. Thus, if we compare the first chapter of each of the two texts, we see that Mahādeva has eliminated sections on non-perception as a way of gaining knowledge (*anupalabdhi*) and on introspection (*anuvyavasāya*), but has added distinct sections on doubt (*saṃśaya*) and mental content (*viṣayatā*). He emulates Gaṅgeśa too in the manner in which he begins his discussion of epistemology, quoting *Nyāya-sūtra* 1.1.1 and raising the spectre of scepticism:

> Now, the master and great sage Akṣapāda described the categories starting with 'ways of gaining knowledge', when he said that 'the highest good is reached through an understanding of the real nature of the sixteen categories beginning with ways of gaining knowledge'. Here, fixing all the others rests on proof (*māna*). Therefore, the real nature of the ways of gaining knowledge will be discussed first.[5]

This is a close paraphrase of the opening paragraph of the *Gemstone*, but it is worth noting that reference to 'raising up the world that is immersed in the mud of suffering' has been dropped. There is no longer a soteriological justification for the philosophical

[4] Cf. Stephen Phillips' reading of Gaṅgeśa as an infallibilist about sources of knowledge: Phillips and Tatacharya 2004: 8.

[5] athaḥ pramāṇādi-ṣoḍaśa-padārtha-tattvajñānān niḥśreyasādhigama iti bhagavato mahāmuner akṣapādasyoktyā pramāṇādipadārthā nirūpaṇīyāḥ | tatra mānādhīnā sarveṣāṃ vyavasthitir iti prathamaṃ pramāṇa-tatvaṃ nirūpyate | (Mahādeva 1930: 31).

project. Unlike Gaṅgeśa, Mahādeva leaves us in no doubt about the identity of the sceptical opponent:

> Here the Mādhyamakas say that an attempt to determine the true nature of the ways of gaining knowledge is futile, for since the property of being true cannot be grasped either intrinsically or extrinsically, the idea that a way of gaining knowledge is the instrumental cause of true belief cannot be proved. Nor can one say that at least the idea that a way of gaining knowledge is a source of beliefs can be [proved]. For a conviction about truth of the premise is what motivates [one to proceed with the proof], and without that there can be no proof, since it cannot be used in the attempt to determine the true nature of a way of gaining knowledge.[6]

Mahādeva considers at some length the possibility that one does not need to be convinced of the truth of the premise in order for a proof to go through, but concludes that the sceptical argument against the possibility of determining the real nature of a way of gaining knowledge is 'extremely difficult to remove' (*duruddhara*).

Mahādeva uses the new technical language here to draw an important distinction. He employs an interesting construction in order to express the notion of a content which is being entertained and for which proof is sought: an abstract noun followed by the term 'cognition' (*jñāna*). Thus 'a cognition concerning the property of a way of gaining knowledge having the nature of being the instrumental cause of true belief',[7] which I have translated as 'the idea that a way of gaining knowledge is the instrumental cause of true belief'. This use of an abstract noun to express a cognitive content is a typical example of the way that 'new reason' thinkers develop an innovative technical language with great sophistication during our period. A few paragraphs on, Mahādeva uses a different technique to specify the content of a belief: he uses the formula 'a cognition having a qualificand, *x*, qualified by a qualifier, *f*'.[8] This is how a distinction is drawn between *entertaining* and *judging* a thought-content. The inability precisely to draw such distinctions is one reason that earlier philosophers had ended up in difficulties of the sort I have described.

Continuing to follow the pattern of the *Gemstone*, Mahādeva briefly canvasses the three rival Mīmāṃsā views, attributing them explicitly, before saying that in the debate with the Naiyāyikas a single common counter-proposition is required, and that the dispute is whether or not the truth of a cognition is grasped by the same collection of causes as bring about the cognition itself. This is what Mīmāṃsakas akas affirm and Naiyāyikas deny (1930: 34, 15). Up to this point the main difference has been the care taken by Mahādeva to attribute views to named authors, and the new use of the early

[6] atra mādhyamakāḥ pramātvasya svataḥ parato vā durgrahatayā tadgrahe sādhyasya pramākaraṇatva-rūpa-pramāṇatva-jñānasayāpy 'saṃbhavena pramāṇatattva-nirūpaṇaṃ niṣphalam | na ca bodhakatvarūpapramāṇatvajñānaṃ sambhavatyeveti vācyam | tathāpīṣṭa-sādhanatājñāne prāmāṇya-niścayasya pravarttakatayā taṃ vinā pramāṇatattvanirūpaṇe pravṛttyasambhavena tadasambhavāt | (1930: 31–32).

[7] 'pramā-karaṇa-tva-rūpa-pramāṇa-tva-jñāna.'

[8] 'tadvat-viśeṣyaka-tva-viśiṣṭa-tat-prakāraka-jñāna' (1930: 35,11). I will say more about the new technical language of the early modern thinkers in Chapter 15.

modern technical language. From this point on, however, there is an important difference between Mahādeva and Gaṅgeśa. For what Mahādeva proceeds to do is to describe, in great detail and rehearsing all the argumentation for and against, not simply *the* Naiyāyika view, but rather a whole range of Naiyāyika views. Mahādeva makes use of a vocabulary indicative of the relative modernity of the views, and it will be illuminating to examine this vocabulary in some detail. There is clear evidence here of an extremely dynamic ongoing conversation among the various leading Nyāya philosophers of the time.

Who else identifies the sceptic with the Mādhyamika Buddhist? The identification is already made by the fifteenth-century Mithilā philosopher Jayadeva Miśra, in his commentary, the *Āloka*, on Gaṅgeśa.[9] Mathurānātha, in the seventeenth century, makes the identification too, and interestingly characterizes the sceptic's position as a rejection of the claim that true belief is sufficient for knowledge, since the presence of truth in belief is impossible to ascertain.[10]

Self-conscious modernities

The first distinction is between the views of the older Navya Nyāya, meaning Gaṅgeśa and the philosophers who succeeded him in Mithilā, on the one hand, and Raghunātha and his followers on the other.[11] Mahādeva speaks of 'the author of the *Light-Ray*' (*dīdhitikāraḥ*), and he refers to 'the followers of the author of the *Light-Ray*'.[12] These followers of Raghunātha are reported as rejecting the view put forward by 'the new thinkers' (*navyāstu . . . iti cet*); and their view in turn is rejected by 'the modern thinkers' (*navīnāstu . . . prāhuḥ*). These moderns are elsewhere said to be hostile to the old theory.[13] To complicate matters still further, Mahādeva in one place uses the phrase 'the new followers of the author of the *Light-Ray*' (*dīdhitikārānuyāyino navyāḥ*). He sometimes rejects the view of the 'new thinkers' (e.g. 1930: 100, 222), and distinguishes between some 'new thinkers' and others (*apare tu*; 193), as well as between them and the 'ancients'.[14] He mentions both Gaṅgeśa, 'the author of the *Gemstone*' (*maṇikāraḥ*) as well as the 'followers of the author of the *Gemstone*' (*maṇikārānuyāyinaḥ*, 1930: 157, 216). There are also 'followers of the Teacher' (*ācāryānuyāyinaḥ*), who disagree with what is written in the *Gemstone* (1930: 161; 1982: 832). That seems to

[9] mādhyamikaḥ pratyavatiṣṭhate–nanu pramāṇādīnām iti (Jayadeva 1991: 125). His prolific pupil Rucidatta follows suit in his *Prakāśa*.

[10] mādhyamakaḥ pratyavatiṣṭhate, nanv iti, etanmate jñānamātrasyaiva tadvati tatprakārakatvarūpaṃ na pramātvaṃ tatra tasya niścetum aśakyatvena tatra tatsattve mānābhāvād iti dhyeyam (Mathurānātha, in Gaṅgeśa 1888: 116–117).

[11] Gaṅgeśa also uses the terminology to speak of original thinkers from his times. He uses 'navya' with reference to the view of Sondaḍa Upādhyāya (Kaviraja 1961: 33), and 'navīnāḥ' to refer to those who are, in the words of Kṛṣṇakānta Vidyāvāgīśa, 'navya-mīmāṃsakas' (Gaṅgeśa 1897: 35). See also Phillips 1995: 119.

[12] dīdhitikārānuyāyinaḥ; 1930: 169, 177, 185.

[13] prācīnavidveṣiṇāṃ navīnānām, 1930: 276.

[14] prāṃcaḥ, 1930: 193, 1982: 443, 550, 636, 826; prācīnaḥ, 1930: 2, 253; 1982: 793, 865.

indicate the existence of thinkers who continued in the tradition of Udayana even after Gaṅgeśa. He speaks of 'newer thinkers' (1930: 191; 1982: 486), and the 'extremely modern' thinkers (*atinavīnaḥ*, 1930: 164; 1982: 739), neither of whose views he always endorses. Then there are the views of the 'new logicians' (*navya-tārkikāḥ*, 1930: 79), the 'new followers of Prabhākara' (*navya-guravaḥ*, 1930: 91), the 'new Mīmāṃsakas' (*mīmāṃsaka-navyāḥ*, 1930: 102), the followers of Kumārila (1930: 158) and the 'new followers of Kumārila'[15] not to mention the 'new grammarians' (1982: 579), or the 'modern grammarians' (1982: 651. 684). There is a mention of 'new Vaiśeṣikas' (1982: 45), and even 'new Maithilis' (1982: 804). The views of the 'contemporaries' (*ādhunikāḥ*, 1920: 38), however, are not rejected.

Among the claims of the 'modern' thinkers is the thesis that inherence is not a unitary relation but rather multiple.[16] This is certainly the view of Raghunātha (*Inquiry* 1957: 76.1–3), though it could also have been in circulation as a possibility even earlier, Śaṃkara Miśra mentioning it apparently with approval (Potter and Bhattacharya 1993: 46). Another 'modern' opinion is that mental content is a separate metaphysical category, and not a special sort of self-linking relation.[17] They are also said to have a view about content (*viṣayatā*) different from that of Jayadeva (Mahādeva 1930: 276), a view in fact always associated with Raghunātha (*Inquiry* 1957: 78,1). So it is clear that by the 'modern thinkers' Mahādeva means Raghunātha's 'new reason' movement. The 'extremely modern' thinkers are mentioned only once, and the point of disagreement they have with the 'modern' thinkers has to do with the perceptibility of absences, which they deny (1930: 163–164).

What emerges from all this is the following scheme:

New	(*navya*)	Gaṅgeśa *et al.*
Newer	(*navyatara*)	Later Mithilā thinkers
Modern	(*navīna*)	Raghunātha
Very modern	(*atinavīna*)	Post-Raghunātha thinkers
Contemporary	(*ādhunika*)	Contemporaries of Mahādeva.

Among his near contemporaries, therefore, Mahādeva distinguishes between those who are 'very modern' and those who are 'contemporary'. Some of these thinkers will be people like Raghudeva and Jayarāma, as well as the literary theorist Jagannātha whom he quotes (1982: 252). His teacher Bhavānanda must be here somewhere, perhaps he is among the 'very modern', newer than Raghunātha and his followers.

At the end of the first chapter of the *Precious Jewel*, Mahādeva describes his work as a distillation of the conclusions about the nature of perception which have been reached in the commentaries on Gaṅgeśa's *Gemstone*, mentioning the *Āloka* of Jayadeva and the *Light-Ray* of Raghunātha in particular. Clearly, the 'intervention' which Mahādeva

[15] bhaṭṭānuyāyino navyāḥ, 1930: 131; abhinavabhāṭṭamīmāṃsakāḥ, 1982: 280.

[16] navīnāstu samavāyo naikaḥ kintu nānā; 1930: 128.

[17] navīnāstu viṣayatātiriktaiva | na tu svarūpasambandhaviśeṣaḥ (Mahādeva 1930: 238).

intends to make with this work is to present a synoptic account of the current state of debate, a 'state of the art' report. That the work contains its own original contributions is evidenced by the fact that its views are cited by others, including Mādhavadeva (1903–4: 225). Mahādeva, as is clear, goes to great lengths to record accurately the many different positions being assumed. His aim is not to close down and systematize but to represent the contours of a very active research programme, conducted by many participants.

There is another reason for us to take an interest in Mahādeva's treatise. It has recently been mentioned, albeit in passing, as evidence for the thesis that the originality of the new intellectuals of the seventeenth century was an originality of style but not of substance (Pollock 2001a,b). Pollock describes the mode of exposition of the *Precious Jewel* as 'dominantly historicist', and sees it as exemplary of a new 'modality of understanding how knowledge is to be organised'. He correctly points out that 'the many complications in [its] identifications remain to be fully disentangled' (Pollock 2001b: 8). I believe that he is wrong, however, in his further assertion that Mahādeva's treatise lacks originality of content, an assertion which he uses as one piece of evidence for his much larger and well-known claim about a lack of innovativeness among seventeenth-century intellectuals, which he has described dramatically as 'the death of Sanskrit'.[18] In making his case, Pollock does Mahādeva an injustice by selecting a relatively obscure and rather parochial passage (1930: 122) dealing with a metaphysical issue about the mind, which harks back to a discussion Gaṅgeśa had somewhat anomalously included in the *Gemstone*.[19] Clearly, the *Precious Jewel* is primarily a work in epistemology, and the question of Mahādeva's conceptual innovativeness must be addressed with respect to his programmatic ambitions in this field. In order

[18] The proposal appears first in Erich Frauwallner's work on the 'new reason' during the 1960s. Thus: 'Through Raghunātha's activity the Bengal school was given a definite direction, which it maintained till contemporary times. Numerous commentaries continued further what he had begun. The terms and viewpoints with which he had worked were systematically applied to all individual cases and worked through. In this way the system was brought to a kind of completion. There was, however, nothing basically new created. More independence is evident, at the most, in the field of language philosophy which at this time came stronger into the foreground and on which also major independent works were written. It is not surprising that such an activity gradually led to a kind of paralysis. This actually began at the end of the seventeenth century, and the situation was not changed by the work of individual, competent scholars, who with a full command of the material, sought to continue working on the usual lines. What was predominant, and remained so, was that the terms and their application which were handed down, were taught and practised as something given.' (Frauwallner 1994a: 55–56). I have argued at length that the notion that the 'new reason' came to a halt for purely internal reasons, having nothing to do with the political disintegration of structures of scholarship, is a myth.

[19] The topic is the theory of *manas*. Pollock says, 'The exposition itself, the sophisticated conception of logical relationships, and to some degree the autonomy of judgement . . . are strikingly new; the philosophical question itself, the method of analysis of the problem, and the actual judgement rendered, are archaic' (2001b: 13). To say this, however, is to fail to notice how greatly the 'new reasoners' modify the doctrine of *manas*. Early modern thinkers in Europe continue to write in ways that conceal their originality; for example, of Daniel Sennert's often pioneering *Epitome Scientiae Naturalis*, it has been said that 'we can find in it a deduction of the minima theory which could without any change be inserted in the commentary on Aristotle of some medieval commentator' (van Melsen 1952: 82).

to evaluate the question of innovativeness in the *metaphysics* of the Indian intellectuals of the seventeenth century, one needs to look at works that primarily have metaphysics as their subject matter, such as Mādhavadeva's *Essence of Reason*, Veṇīdatta's *Embellishment of the Categories,* or Jayarāma's *Garland of Categories*. I will look precisely at such texts in Chapter 14. Selecting a small passage that has little to do with Mahādeva's overall philosophical project threatens to distort and misrepresent the significance of his work.

In my earlier survey of the networks of individuals and ṭols, we saw that Mahādeva was an unusual individual in at least two respects. First of all, he was unusually willing to move between Vārāṇasī and Navadvīpa and to study with philosophers in both places. Secondly, he was an avid scribe, making his own personal copy of a great many works. These facts reinforce my suggestion that his project, in the *Precious Jewel,* is to construct a sort of state-of-the-art review of the current debate, for we see in Mahādeva an industrious collector of ideas. It seems to me that intellectual traditions which are in their death throws do not produce state-of-the-art research surveys of this sort; quite the contrary, in fact—the production of such a work is symptomatic of a culture needing to take stock in the face of breathless innovation.

What is true is that the early modern Indian intellectuals use terminology and frames of reference that had in many cases an ancient provenance. In earlier chapters of this book I have described the distinctive modalities of intellectual activity that explain this, the way, for instance, that commentary serves as a vehicle for a creatively philosophical reading of the text commented on, and the way that an original text such as Gaṅgeśa's might deliberately leave 'open spaces' as a resource for later philosophers in new circumstances. Descartes' debt to scholastic concepts and vocabulary, for example, has been very well documented (e.g. Cottingham 1993; Ariew 1999; Secada 2000). European thought of the early modern period had not left behind scholastic and medieval terminology and categories to any greater degree. Just as with the Sanskrit thinkers, they used more ancient frameworks as a vehicle with which to fashion conceptual innovation.

The fate of the *Precious Jewel* is representative of much of the philosophical literature produced in our period, in that it disappeared without trace for two centuries. When Umesh Mishra published the chapter on perception in 1930, he brought to light a work that had been completely forgotten, a single manuscript of which he had stumbled upon in the Government Sanskrit College Library in Vārāṇasī. A second manuscript came to light in the private collection of the son of Baccā Jhā, and there is also one in the India Office (IO 1981). V. S. Shastri edited a manuscript of the chapter on language, and published it from Thanjavur in 1982. Two manuscripts of this chapter survive in the Calcutta Sanskrit College (CSC 247; 888). A valuable manuscript of the chapters on inference, analogy and language is located in the Ganganatha Jha Institute, Allahabad (Jha 2996). The chapter on analogy, of which this is the only known manuscript, has still not been published. So it is that one of the best works on epistemology to be written in seventeenth-century Vārāṇasī teetered on the brink of extinction barely 200 years after it was written. There is nothing unusual about the story of this text; the same is true elsewhere, for instance in the important commentaries on Raghunātha's *Inquiry*. That works like this were written at all is a sign of the vibrancy of the time; that within a few years they had been forgotten, the only texts still to flourish being the training manuals and the canons of the teaching curriculum, is a sign of the swiftness and thoroughness with which its innovative philosophical culture collapsed. Pollock writes that 'when colonialism made the norms of Europe the norms of India the Sanskrit intellectual formation melted like so much snow in the light of a brilliant, pitiless sun' (2001b: 24). I fail to see in contemporaneous European epistemology ideas so superior to the Indian ideas surveyed by Mahādeva as to have been powerful enough in and of themselves to accomplish this: what caused the dissolution of Sanskrit culture under colonialism was the dismembering of the systems of education and patronage that held that culture together, along with the simultaneous creation of well-funded colonial universities and colleges. More importantly, it was precisely the 'norms of India', the modern model of engaging the new in a dialogue with the old, of the outsider with the insider, which enabled India to emerge from British colonialism uncrushed.

The weight of evidence

I will now look in some detail at one core element in Mahādeva's review of post-Gaṅgeśa research in epistemology. What I will claim is that in this later work we find what was missing in Gaṅgeśa, a notion of evidence both naturalistically respectable and able to ground a distinction between truth and knowledge.

Gaṅgeśa had argued that it is a precondition of inquiry that it has a target, an object of focal attention (*dharmi-jñāna*). With respect to this target, alternative possibilities (*koṭi*) present themselves in the form 'Is this thing an X or not?'. A state of mind in which incompatible alternatives are entertained of a common locus is called a *saṃśaya*, a 'doubt' or 'uncertainty'. Inquiry consists in a procedure aiming at the resolution of uncertainty. The procedure is called a 'way of gaining knowledge' (*pramāṇa*), and the resolution is a state of firm resolve (*nirṇaya*) reached by the process of first entertaining and then eradicating a doubt. Such states are to be contrasted with states of true belief for which no doubt has arisen. Gaṅgeśa's fundamental argument against Mīmāṃsā intrinsicism is that if the truth of a state is presented along with the state itself, then no doubt can arise, and that in turn entails that no inquiry is possible. Later thinkers scrutinize this model of epistemic practice.

Gaṅgeśa claims that the cognition of a single object to serve as the target is a precondition for inquiry. To reply to a sceptic, however, who denies that inquiry is possible, independent reasons must be given for thinking that doubt has the claimed structure.[20] One of Gaṅgeśa's key arguments is that the different alternatives can

[20] A structure which is, we might note, incompatible with radical Cartesian doubt. I will say more about this later in this chapter.

present themselves with different 'strength' (*balatva*), and this requires that they bear upon a common place. The background metaphor is that of a set of weighing scales, with two pans and a common fulcrum. Gaṅgeśa's point seems to be that if the two alternatives simply presented themselves as '*p*' and '*q*' they could not be balanced against each other and there could be no 'weighing up' of one against the other. He also affirms that the 'strength' of one alternative does not negate the 'strength' of the other:

From an assembly of two sets of conditions sufficient each for one of two incompatibles, there can be attribution of both to a single thing, which attribution would be doubt. But it is not the case that because of the set of conditions sufficient for the one attribution the set sufficient for the other attribution would be blocked (*pratibandha*), since the acts of attribution are not incompatible.[21]

And then:

Moreover, cognition of a target is the ground (*hetu*) for doubt. Otherwise, there would be neither regulation by the target in a doubt, nor would there be unevenness between the alternatives.[22]

These notions of strength and unevenness of strength are epistemological: the resolution of a doubt consists in the cancelling or lessening of the strength attaching to one of the alternatives. What the 'new reason' discussion adds, as Mahādeva's survey of that discussion in the *Precious Jewel* reveals, is a reinterpretation of this notion of increasing or decreasing epistemic weight as a concept of evidence. It is in these later discussions of the concept of unevenness (*utkaṭatva*) of epistemic strength (*balatva*), and related concepts, that one finds the crucial materials for a distinction between mere true belief and knowledge, and so a reply to Śrīharṣa.

Raghunātha already moves beyond Gaṅgeśa in arguing that evenness or unevenness of relative strength does not have to be, as Gaṅgeśa seems to think, a causal primitive.[23] Mahādeva begins by considering the argument that the cognition of the target object, which is a condition for doubt, must itself be given as veridical if inquiry is not to be blocked at the outset, and that this presentation must be intrinsic (*svataḥ*) (1930: 62–63). He claims that it is sufficient that there is no presentation of the cognition as non-veridical. He then clarifies the principle governing the 'regulation' of the doubt by the target, pointing out that it cannot apply if the different alternatives attach to a plurality

[21] viruddhobhayāropa-sāmagrī-dvaya-samājād ubhayāropa eka eva bhavati | sa eva saṃśayaḥ | na tv ekāropa-sāmagryā aparāropa-sāmagrī-pratibandhaḥ avirodhāt | (Gaṅgeśa 1888: 202–203). Trans. Phillips and Tatacharya 2004: 88.

[22] dharmi-jñānaṃ ca saṃśaya-hetuḥ | anyathā saṃśaye dharmi-niyamaḥ koṭy-utkaṭatvaṃ ca na syāt | (Gaṅgeśa 1888: 207). Cf. Mohanty 1966: 121–122; Phillips and Tatacharya 2004: 88.

[23] Raghunātha: tathā hi utkaṭatvaṃ ca yadi jātis syāt tadā kalpyetāpi tanniyāmakam | tatkoṭi-sahacarita-bhūyodharma-viśiṣṭa-dharmijñānam | bhūyastatkoṭisahacarita-dharma-viśiṣṭa-dharmijñānaṃ vā kāraṇam | tadbalāc ca saṃśayasāmānye dharmijñānasāmānyam | na ca tattathā cākṣuśatvādinā saṅkarāt āṃśikatvāc ca | parantu tādṛśa-dharma-viśiṣṭadharmi-viṣayatvaṃ, na ca tadeva tatra niyāmakam iti | (Raghunātha 1985: 148–149). Cf. Mohanty 1966: 125.

of target objects, nor if they apply to some parts and not others of a single object (1930: 64). He considers the nature of 'unevenness' with respect to the distribution of the alternatives within a complex target object, or a target group, arguing that it is enough for differential weighting that some of one alternative is distributed in some of the target, not that the whole of the alternative is spread over all of the target. From such remarks, there can be perceived the beginnings of a move towards a *quantitative* and non-subjective conception of evidence.

The nature of resolution (*nirṇaya*), Mahādeva asserts, is the opposite of that of doubt (1930: 224). A doubt as to whether some thing is a pillar or not leads one to reflect to oneself 'I am not sure if it is a pillar' and that is what proves that I was in doubt. But doubt does not constitute a type of mental state of its own (a *jāti*) because it overlaps with visual perception and other forms of perception. If I doubt whether the mountain has fire on it or not, it is still the case that I am aware that I see the mountain. The relationship between doubt and hypothetical reasoning (*tarka*) is more complicated (1930: 224–225). In hypothetical reasoning, one entertains the alternative in order to eliminate it by reductio. Was one initially then in a state of doubt? With the sophisticated resources of the new technical language, Mahādeva is able to explain that a doubt in the shape of a thought 'Is the mountain a possessor of fire or not?' has the following logical form:

A cognition the qualificandumness of which is, as delimited by mountainness, conditioned by a qualifierness delimited by fireness, being also one the qualificandumness of which is, as delimited by mountainness, conditioned by a qualifierness delimited by absence-of-fireness.[24]

This description ensures that the two incompatible predicates are jointly attributed to a single subject, thereby distinguishing the logical form of doubt from that of a disjunction. Mahādeva continues by noting that there are philosophers who think that the logical form of a doubt has to be analysed in a different way. They say that the logical form is:

A cognition whose qualificandumness as conditioned by a qualifierness delimited by absence-of-fireness is qualified by a qualificandumness as conditioned by a qualifierness delimited by fireness.[25]

This formulation is meant to be able to apply as well to a conjunctive doubt of the form 'Does the mountain have fire or not *and* the ground have fire or not?'.

In these descriptions, the technical terms used are 'delimited by' (*avacchinna*), 'conditioned by' (*nirūpita*), qualificandumness (*viśeṣyatā*), qualifierness (*viśeṣanatā*) and 'absence of' (*abhāva*). I will explain how these technical terms are used in detail in Chapter 15. Overenthusiastic use of such formulations are what gave the 'new reason' a

[24] parvatatvāvacchinna-viśeṣyatā-nirūpita-vahnitvāvacchinna-prakāratā-śālitve sati parvatatvāvacchinna-viśeṣyatā-nirūpita-vahnyabhāvatvāvacchinna-prakāratā-śāli-jñānatvaṃ saṃśayatvam (1930: 226).

[25] vahnitvāvacchinna-prakāratā-nirūpita-viśeṣyatā-viśiṣṭā yā vahnyabhāvatvāvacchinna-prakāratā-nirūpita-viśeṣyatā tacchāli-jñānatvam eva tatra saṃśayam (1930: 227).

reputation for an obsession with complex jargon, but used judiciously, as Mahādeva does, they are clearly very helpful. After a further discussion, Mahādeva concludes by noting that there are some who say that doubt is indeed a distinct type of mental state and do not accept that there is a fault of overlapping (1930: 237).[26]

In the last chapter, I distinguished two grades of epistemic warrant. One of these attaches to the concept of a 'resolution', implying the removal of a doubt on the basis of an appeal to evidence. The other sort of epistemic warrant attaches to states of true belief insofar as they arise directly from the exercise of a way of gaining knowledge. Mahādeva says

True belief (*pramā*) is of four kinds: perceptual, inferential, analogical, and testimonial. Its instrumental cause is also of four types: perception, inference, analogy and testimony. A 'way of gaining knowledge' (*pramāṇa*) is defined as the instrumental cause (*karaṇa*) of true belief (*pramā*). The word 'true belief' is used in order to avoid the application of the definition to the case of faulty vision, which is the instrumental cause of a false belief such as mistaking a tree for a man. The word 'instrumental cause' is used in order to avoid application of the definition to the sensory link and so on. An instrumental cause is in fact the operative special cause (*vyāpāra*). The sensory link is a direct cause but is not the operative one, so the definition does not apply. The word 'special' is used in order to avoid application of the definition to the body and so on. Even though the connection between the self and the body is operative, since it is the generic cause of all cognitions, the definition does not apply [to it either].

(1930: 95)

Mahādeva is reporting standard theory when he says that the concept of *pramāṇa* qua 'way of gaining knowledge' is defined as the instrumental cause of a true belief, and that there are four fundamental types of true belief, and therefore also four kinds of 'way of gaining knowledge'. What is interesting to notice about this formulation, however, is the logical priority of 'true belief' with respect to 'way of gaining knowledge'. In the definition of a 'way of gaining knowledge' the use of the factive term 'true belief' is now indispensable. In an infallibilist naturalism, it ought to be possible to describe 'way of gaining knowledge' independently of the notion of 'true belief'; and that is just what Mahādeva disputes.

In the course of an article originally published under the title '*Pramāṇa* as evidence', B. K. Matilal says that

I am inclined to treat *pramāṇa* as evidence for knowledge but not in the sense (at least not entirely in the sense) of the justificatory ground for knowledge . . . *Pramāṇa* is what 'makes' knowledge. Since knowledge is always an episode (an inner event in Indian philosophy, in fact, a sub-category of mental occurrence), *pramāṇa* has also a causal role to play. It is the 'most efficient' cause of the knowledge-episode. Knowledge yields determination of an object *x* or a fact that *p* (*artha-pariccheda*) as the result, and a *pramāṇa* is 'instrumental' in bringing about that result. This is

[26] For further discussion of the contrast between the earlier and later theories of doubt, see Prabal Kumar Sen 2006: 250–251; Mohanty 1970.

the causal role of a *pramāṇa*... Hence a *pramāṇa* is both a cause and a 'because'—it has both a causal and an evidential role.

(2002: 368)

That is to say, 'new reason' naturalism might be one in which the notion of evidence and evidential support is given a naturalistically respectable externalist interpretation.[27] We can certainly hear this usage in statements like 'And the proof (*pramāṇa*) for reflexivity is perception itself'.[28] The term is also used evidentially when it is asked 'What is the proof?' (*kiṃ pramāṇam*?), or when a conjecture is rejected with the words 'No,... because there is no evidence/proof?' (*na,... pramāṇābhāvāt*). Gaṅgeśa distinguishes a weak and a strong grade of epistemic warrant. What he lacks is a clear is disambiguation of the term 'pramāṇa' into its causal and evidential meanings, for what has become clear is that the concept is being put to two distinct uses. In making a firm distinction between a naturalized concept of evidence and the 'causes of true belief', partly with the help of more sophisticated techniques of analysis that allow for a clearer understanding of the logical form of doubt qua mental content, a decisive advance has taken place. What I have been particularly keen to stress is that we need to look to other aspects of the discussion, especially the discussion of unevenness of epistemic strength, if we are to see the emergence of this new concept of evidence, a concept which can then be used to clarify and disambiguate the term 'pramāṇa' itself. Only with the emergence of this new concept does a response to Śrīharṣa become available: for one can now say that the distinction between luck and knowledge is a matter of the availability of concrete, objective, evidence.

A method for rightly conducting reason in the *Garland of Principles*

Jayarāma's *Garland of Principles about Reason* is an extremely unusual and important work. Textually it is very strange and quite unique: it is a new commentary on certain selected sections from the *Nyāya-sūtra*, specifically the parts that describe the nature of reasoned inquiry, how to construct arguments which are truth-conducive and rationally compelling, the various ways in which public discourse can go wrong, and how it is adjudicated.[29] The *Garland* passes over the first eight *sūtras*, those dealing with general epistemology and the ways of gaining knowledge. It also ignores the metaphysics in the second, third, and fourth books. The choice of material clearly indicates an intention to write about the method of discovery, while the decision to approach the topic by writing a commentary on the ancient sources rather than a separate treatise is suggestive

[27] Stephen Phillips correctly points out that Matilal's understanding of the theory is based on the later, post-Gaṅgeśa, tradition. Matilal does not always resist the temptation to read later ideas back into Gaṅgeśa himself.

[28] pramāṇaṃ ca svaprakāśe pratyakṣam eva | (Gaṅgeśa 1888: 788). Cf. Phillips and Tatacharya 2004: 581.

[29] *Nyāya-sūtra* Book 1, except for 1.1.1–8; Book 5.2, except 5.2.2, 3, 5–11, 15–17, 19.

of a desire to present a work that carries a certain sort of authority among its users. Another notable feature of the *Garland* is that it includes as an appendix Śaṃkara Miśra's survey of alternative philosophical debating positions, including Cārvāka, Buddhist, Jaina and Mīmāṃsā, in that order.

As a whole, then, Jayarāma's book looks as if it intends to be an authoritative aid to evidence-based truth-conducive reasoning, including situations of multi-agent inquiry. It refers to the *Garland of Categories* and is therefore written either in or perhaps a little after 1659. It is striking indeed that such a work should have been written by someone who was one of the most public of the 'new reason' intellectuals. Jayarāma, let us recall, was a close acquaintance of Kavīndra Sarasvatī, probably Bernier's 'paṇḍit', and perhaps a member of the circle that met between 1658 and 1661. He engaged in a high profile act of public reason, the meeting of Vārāṇasī brahmins and their issuing of a 'letter of judgement' in 1657.

I think that it will be revealing to read this work in juxtaposition with two Cartesian works, the 1637 *Discourse* and 'Part I' of the 1644 *Principles of Philosophy*. The *Garland* might fairly be described as providing 'a method of rightly conducting one's reasoning and seeking truth in the sciences', which is the subtitle of the *Discourse*. The *Garland* and the first part of the *Principles* have a common aspiration and a common structure: both rest on the idea that a 'complete knowledge of the truth of all things' is the highest good (*Principles*, 1984: 180; cf. *Nyāya-sūtra* 1.1.1); and both are texts in which a series of 'principles' or '*sūtras*' (in both cases roughly seventy in number)—whose truth is beyond question—are listed along with detailed surrounding exegetical apparatus. Both promote a real distinction between self and body, and explore the consequences of the possibility of doubt. Juxtaposing the texts brings into immediate relief, however, a very evident fact: that the philosophy of inquiry in the *Garland* is quite contrary to that of Descartes. As a sort of philosophical experiment, I will try to read the *Garland* as if it were a 'new reason' response to the *Discourse* and the *Principles*. I will mention three ways in which Jayarāma's method is anti-Cartesian: his understanding of the nature of doubt and his exclusion of the radical sceptic; his insistence on empirical demonstration and diminution of the purely a priori; and finally a rejection of Cartesian individualism in the importance he attaches to collaborative inquiry in the search for truth.

The first section of the *Garland* (following *Nyāya-sūtra* 1.1.9–1.1.21) presents 'principles' about the objects of all inquiry, which are the self, the body, the senses, and the material world. It relates directly to a theme in both the *Discourse* and the *Principles*, the existence of a 'real distinction' between the mind and the body. The 'principle' here is that desire and repulsion, will, pleasure and pain, and cognition are 'signs' (*liṅga*) of the self. Jayarāma's first claim, however, is that the distinctively mental qualities are not inferential signs of the reality of the self but rather constitute its definition (*liṅgaṃ lakṣaṇam*; 1927: 3,4), i.e. that the word 'sign' in the principle does not mean what it might seem to. Against this, he notes that other philosophers say that perception only apprehends objects which have a shape or a colour (the term *rūpa* is ambiguous), and that we should read the principle that mental qualities are 'signs' of a self straightforwardly.

Praśastapāda, for example, says that only what is made out of the elements earth, fire, and water is perceptible. Jayarāma defends his non-inferentialist construal by considering an experience of the form 'I am thinking', and rehearsing the following argument: the 'I' in this experience must be something distinct from the body, because it is that which is experiencing, whether or not that experience is one in which 'I' is the subject term in a demonstration or the object of a perception.[30] Having canvassed that argument, he wonders whether there can after all be a demonstration that the self is distinct from the body, one running along the following lines. Things like cognitions are qualities and so reside somewhere; and it is both simpler and blocks 'growing' if they are qualities of a self distinct from the body ('growing' presumably refers to the problem that the self could grow or contract if it were identical to the body).[31] This first discussion, about the real distinction, is a weighing up of two alternatives, with echoes of a discussion that has taken place over whether the *cogito* ('I think therefore I am') is a demonstration or a non-inferential act. In entertaining two readings of *Nyāya-sūtra* 1.1.0, one as saying that cognition and the rest are what define the self, and the other as saying that they are signs of the self, he is noting the possibility of two views about a statement like 'I exist because I am thinking, desiring, feeling pleasure, pain, willing'.

The *Garland*'s anti-Cartesianism about philosophical method is apparent in the discussion of doubt and doubt-resolution (based on an interpretation of the principles stated in *Nyāya-sūtra* 1.1.23–1.1.31). The radical sceptic enters in the guise of a Mādhyamika Buddhist, 'someone who does not accept that anything can be established as proven or as a method of proving'.[32] Jayarāma argues that such a person falls foul of a fundamental principle, that all inquiry is necessarily based on some 'truths' (*siddhānta*) to which all parties in the inquiry agree (i.e. *Nyāya-sūtra* 1.1.27). So radical scepticism is not a starting point for any inquiry. Furthermore, to be in a state of doubt is to wonder of some given thing, which one of two contrary attributes it possesses.[33] The very idea of testing or examining (*vimarśa*) implies a state of mind in which contrary properties are entertained of a single object.[34] So the very possibility of doubt presupposes or entails, not the existence of the self, as it does for Descartes, but some object to serve as the focal point of doubting.

From what Jayarāma has said, it follows that while it might be true that any given thing can be doubted, it cannot be the case that one can doubt everything all at once. That contradicts what Descartes says under *Principle* 75, that 'In order to philosophize seriously and search out the truth about all the things that are capable of being known,

[30] ahaṃ jānāmītyādyātmāṃśe mukhyaviśeṣyatva-laukikatvayor ānubhavikatvād bhāṣye dehādi-bhinnatvenetyarthaḥ | (1927: 3, 13–15).

[31] parantu dehādibhinnatvam anumānagamyam eva | jñānādikaṃ kvacid āśritaṃ guṇatvāder lāghavād vakṣamāṇabādhāc ca | dehādibhinnātmaviṣayakatvāt | (1927: 3, 16–17).

[32] māna-meya-vyavasthānaṅgīkartṛ-śūnyatv[av]ādi-mādhyamikādi . . . | (1927: 21,10).

[33] ekadharmiṇi viruddhobhayāvamarśaḥ saṃśaya iti tadarthaḥ | ekadharmitāvacchedakāvacchedenānyatara-koṭi-prakārakatve sati tadviśiṣṭe viruddhobhaya-koṭi-prakāraka-jñānatvaṃ saṃśayatvaṃ phalitam | (1927: 14, 7–10).

[34] ekadharmika-bhāvābhāvaprakārakatvarūpaviśeṣavān vimarśo jñānam iti tadarthaḥ | (1927: 17, 6–7).

we must first of all lay aside all our preconceived opinions'. One might say that both have a method of doubt, but Jayarāma's method is very much of the 'Neurath's ship' type (doing repairs while the ship is afloat) rather than a Cartesian first philosophy.

Another anti-Cartesian element is Jayarāma's denial that any purely a priori method can give knowledge (interpreting *Nyāya-sūtra* 1.1.32–1.1.41). There are two strands to this denial. First, it is another fundamental principle that all inquiry is necessarily based on 'observational examples' (*udāharaṇa*) (*Nyāya-sūtra* 1.1.36). A method of inquiry must be evidence-based. So Jayarāma says that purely hypothetical reasoning (*tarka*) cannot serve independently as a way of reaching certainty, because it is not as such a method of inquiry.[35] Jayarāma rejects the thought that inquiry can proceed by first raising some imaginary or fictitious doubt (*āhārya-śaṅkā*), and then use hypothetical reasoning to settle it. That seems flatly to contradict Descartes' *Principle* 2: 'What is doubtful should even be considered false'. Dreams and evil demons have no place in the evidence-based method of inquiry Jayarāma recommends.

Jayarāma looks finally at collaborative inquiry, its proper (*vāda*) and improper (*jalpa*) forms, the idea of infelicitous moves (*jāti*), and conditions under which it can be judged to have reached a conclusion (*nighrahasthāna*). The theory is based on foundational principles drawn from two chapters in the *Nyāya-sūtra,* Chapter 1.2 and the supplemental Chapter 5.2. Jayarāma has a very succinct analysis of what a many-agent inquiry is. It is not simply a matter of several speakers making statements supporting or refuting some claim, because that would apply equally well to a group of people who, having met up, go about their individual examinations of the topic.[36] Rather, a many-agent inquiry consists in a mutual conversation with a single purpose and conducted in a structured, sequential manner. The result of such an inquiry is the production of a definite view, as well as the preservation and dissemination of the definite view reached.[37] The idea that the search for truth might be a collaborative venture is wholly at odds with Descartes' thoroughly individualistic conception of first philosophy: 'The seeker after truth must, once in the course of his life, doubt' (*Principle* 1).

The main point of juxtaposing the *Garland* with the *Principles* in this way is that we can appreciate just where Jayarāma's originality lies. It is not in constructing the individual arguments to which he appeals, for they invariably have long histories; it is in the marshalling of the material into a single, coherent, method of inquiry built around principles, in this case selected *Nyāya-sūtras*, so as to constitute something akin to what Descartes called 'a method of rightly conducting one's reasoning and seeking truth in the sciences'.

[35] tathāpi tarkasya na svātantryeṇa nirṇayaphalatvaṃ pramāṇatvābhāvāt | (1927: 47,4–5).

[36] atha kiṃ kathātvam | na tāvan nānā-vaktṛka-sādhana-dūṣaṇa-viṣaya-vākyatvaṃ, militvā nānā-puruṣa-praṇīta-vicāre 'tivyāpteḥ | (1927: 54, 1–2).

[37] prayojanaikyān mithaḥ sākāṅkṣatvāc ca kathaikyam | ata eva nānā-sthāpanāpratisthāpanābhinnaikā kathā | kathāphalāni cānupanna-nirṇayotpādanam, utpannasya pālanaṃ, pālitasyābhyāsaḥ, parapratipādanaṃ ceti catvāri | (1927: 54, 12–15).

Jayarāma concludes the *Garland of Principles* with a final, bold statement of intent. He has written the *Garland*, he says, for the intelligent to destroy darkness and find a way to certainty. With proofs based on good arguments, he will tame the pride of those who are full of bad reasoning. Echoing Gaṅgeśa's introduction to the *Gemstone*, he says that wise Gautama wrote the *Nyāya-sūtra* out of compassion for the world, and that he has now, with clear eyes purified by reason, brought out the deep meaning of the *sūtras* after studying the useless words that fill many books (1927: 178, 21–179, 6).[38] This 'studied pose' does strike me as a little reminiscent of the bold self-depiction as lone innovator and dismisser of tradition Descartes offers in the *Discourses*. Even the language, with its talk of eyes cleared by reason (*viśadaiḥ sat-tarka-śuddhākṣair*) and of intelligence destroying darkness (*sumanasā mantas tamo-nāśinī*), is similar. However, in building the method around the *sūtras*, Jayarāma combines this affirmation of a new beginning with a renovation of the most ancient past.

The method of inquiry proposed by Jayarāma in the *Garland* is strongly anti-Cartesian: the overall manner of presentation, and the centrality given to doubt and the self, not to mention the affirmation of his own break from tradition, have a quite Cartesian tone. The *Garland* is a courageously innovative work, very much in the spirit of the *via moderna* thinker. It is Jayarāma's promise of a new method for philosophy in the seventeenth century Vārāṇasī of Dārā Shukoh, Yaśovijaya Gaṇi, Kavīndra Sarasvatī and François Bernier.

[38] There is an echo too of Uddyotakara: 'In order to abolish the errors of the false reasoners, I will prepare a description of that *śāstra* which the best of sages, Akṣapāda, articulated for the peace of the world' (yad akṣapādaḥ pravaro munīnāṃ śamāya śāstraṃ jagato jagāda | kutārkikājñānanivṛttihetuḥ kariṣyate tasya mayā nibandhaḥ | (Uddyotakara 1997: 1, 3–4).

PART IV

The Real World

12

Realism in Question

I have suggested that the 'new reason' philosophers in the sixteenth and seventeenth centuries, especially in Vārāṇasī, had a distinctive interest in the consequences of Raghunātha's reappraisal of ancient Vaiśeṣika metaphysics, as the ancient theory had been articulated by Praśastapāda and in the classical commentaries on him, especially those of Udayana and Vallabha. There was a fundamental shift in their understanding of what a commitment to realism involves. In this chapter, I will describe the realism of ancient Vaiśeṣika, and I will argue that it is what I will call an ameliorated realism rather than, as it has normally been portrayed, a variety of metaphysical realism. Traditional Vaiśeṣika is not a tightly knit system but a rambling garden of metaphysical thought, and it will be from this that Raghunātha selects some parts and rejects others, in such a way as to give metaphysics a unified and coherent philosophical foundation. Raghunātha's new realism consists, in the first instance, in the rejection of a variety of reductionist hypotheses. Later early modern thinkers seek to demonstrate that reductionism is compatible with realism, their realism being a type of what Michael Dummett (1991a: 324) has called 'sophisticated realism'.[1]

The reach of Vaiśeṣika realism

Realism is the commitment to a world in which questions of existence are matters independent of the reach of our human epistemic resources—our capacities to verify, ascertain, or establish what is and what is not the case. It is moot whether, however it might look from a 'God's eye' perspective, we human beings are capable of such a commitment. Even if we can understand, as we seem to be able to, what would be *required* of us to be realists, it is not clear that in fact we are able to satisfy the requirement. What would underwrite the thought that some world of which we can conceive is a world in which the question of being is not a question that refers to us? What would make 'manifest' that this is the sort of world to which our concepts point? It is one thing to claim to be a realist, quite another to demonstrate how it is possible actually to be one.[2]

[1] For a clear statement of the distinction between reductive and non-reductive realism in application to general metaphysics, and a defence of 'nonreductionism' about physical wholes, see Baker 2008.

[2] The appeal to a manifestation requirement in arguments about realism is due to Dummett (e.g. 1978, 1996). See also Nagel 1986.

Among the Indians the Vaiśeṣikas are usually considered to be the most robust advocates of an across-the-board realism.[3] They admit all of the following:

- unobservable as well as observable substantial objects (*dravya*),
- the particular qualities (*guṇa*) and motions (*karma*) of those objects including their spatial and temporal position,
- a hierarchy of generic universals (*sāmānya*; *jāti*) under which the particular substances, qualities, and motions fall,
- a uniquely identifying 'distinguisher' (*viśeṣa*) for each non-composite particular,
- a single real connecting relation to bind the objects to their qualities, motions, universal features, and distinguishers (*samavāya*; 'inherence'),
- finally, and only from the twelfth century, a domain of real particular and generic absences (*abhāva*), such as the real absence in a room of a certain particular man or of any man at all.

Embedded within this expansive ontology is a metaphysics of mind that embraces real individual selves (*ātman*) that host a portfolio of specifically mental qualities including positive and negative affective states, cognition, desire, aversion, and volition. Each self is thought to have an accompanying but distinct 'mind' (*manas*), responsible for performing a range of subconscious executive functions including the regulation of respiration and the relay of signals between the body and the self.

The realism of the ancient Vaiśeṣika incorporates a range of less thoroughgoing realisms. It embeds a *scientific realism*, that is a commitment to the reality of unobservable entities postulated by our best theory of the world. The unobservable entities towards which traditional Vaiśeṣika shows an uncompromising commitment include atoms, space, time, and a pervasive aether-like substance called *ākāśa*. Vaiśeṣika realism also embeds, however, a *common-sense realism*, a realistic commitment to the 'middle-sized' objects of everyday experience, specifically to those composite wholes that are made out of smaller—ultimately atomic—parts. Halbfass (1992: 94) comments aptly that

> Whereas the Vaiśeṣika considers the noneternal substances to be effects of, and derived from, the eternal substances, it does not regard them as less real. They, too, are real substrates of real qualities and other attributes. They have their irreducible identity and reality as long as they last. The Vaiśeṣika tries to explain and defend their precarious ontological status in its peculiar and controversial theory of the 'whole' (*avayavin*) as an entity over and above its constituent parts (*avayava*).

In its metaphysics, old Vaiśeṣika embeds a *property realism* that seems to be more Aristotelian than Platonic (the monadic universals and the dyadic binding relation seem to be metaphysically dependent on being instantiated, just as a dent is metaphysically dependent on a surface). This is later extended to a realism about negative properties, which is, however, configured in terms of a commitment to a *sui generis* type of

[3] See, for example, Thakur 2003: 182; Bhaduri 1975: 2–3.

negative entity. Only in the early modern period is there a consideration of the metaphysical status of conjunctive and disjunctive properties. Realism about universals is, however, strongly tied by Udayana (1925: 67–70) to the reality of scientific causal law, which is seen to consist in relations between actual universals as opposed to merely nominal kinds (*upādhi*).

The explicit intention, at least according to Vyomaśiva and Udayana at the end of the first millennium, is 'to enumerate everything in this world that has the character of being'.[4] For Praśastapāda, whose thought these later philosophers are elaborating, knowing the truth about the six categories of being is of soteriological value in itself.[5] That seems to be said in an echo of the programmatic claim of *Nyāya-sūtra* 1.1.1, that it is knowledge of the truth about the methodology of inquiry which leads to the highest good. What Vaiśeṣika offers instead is a unified model of both the inquirer—the individual human subject—and the domain of inquiry, which consists of the natural world including those very inquirers themselves, of nature and mind's place within it. As I have mentioned before, the illocutionary intervention made by Udayana and other Vaiśeṣikas takes place in an intellectual context largely structured by Buddhist advocacy of a soteriology committed to the denial of realism. In one form or another, the fundamental Buddhist position is that the only therapy for human suffering is to undermine the commitment to a world of enduring subjects and objects, a commitment that is seen as presupposed by our needs, cravings, and attachments (Burton 2004; Ganeri 2010). One response is to find within ancient Hindu scripture the resources for an equivalent soteriology, so as to diminish the attractiveness of Buddhism as an alternative to Hinduism; and some such strategy is arguably at work for those Advaita Vedānta thinkers who offer a 'non-realist' interpretation of the Upaniṣads (Ram-Prasad 2002; Ganeri 2007: 208–209). For Vaiśeṣika philosophers, however, and perhaps they were comparatively never very many in number, a better response is to demonstrate that realism is true; for if realism is true, then Buddhist therapy rests on a mistake. The intervention that Praśastapāda and his end-of-millennium exponents make, through their commentarial retrieval of the ancient realism of the *Vaiśeṣika-sūtra*, is to put realism about the objects of inquiry firmly back on the philosophical map. There is the world as it would have to be if Buddhist therapy is to be effective; and then there is the real world.

Later in this chapter, I will argue that the search for a unified metaphysics of the objects of inquiry—including inquirers themselves—without a proper engagement with the epistemology of inquiry, leads old Vaiśeṣika into considerable difficulty. There are clear reasons why an accommodation of Nyāya and Vaiśeṣika, which is one of the hallmarks of 'new reason' philosophy, has a purely philosophical rationale.

[4] yad iha bhāvarūpaṃ tat sarvaṃ mayā upasaṃkhyātavyam (Vyomaśiva 1983: 21); yad bhāvarūpaṃ tat sarvam abhidhāsyāmi (Udayana 1989: 482). Both are cited in Halbfass 1992: 69, 82.

[5] dravya-guṇa-karma-sāmānya-viśeṣa-samavāyānāṃ ṣaṇṇāṃ padārthānāṃ sādharmya-vaidharmya-tatt-vajñānaṃ niḥśreyasa-hetuḥ (Praśastapāda 1994: §2).

But one sort of difficulty Vaiśeṣika doesn't seem to feel any pressure to confront is the problem about the relationship between mind and body that so plagued early modern philosophy in Europe. Of the radical Cartesian separation between the two realms there is little trace in their all-encompassing metaphysical picture. Nor is there any attempt to make spatial extension the mark of the material. Indeed the various ways of subdividing substances cut across the mental–non-mental distinction. One grouping divides substances into those which are 'material' (*bhūta*) and those which are not, but in a sense which makes the material world consist of everything made from the atomic elements (of which there are five types) as well as the ubiquitous *ākāśa*. That excludes various things which have spatial extension, including space itself and *manas*, which is thought to be of extremely small but finite extent. Another division groups together those substances which are 'shaped' (*mūrta*), or have limited spatial boundaries, a grouping which includes everything material apart from *ākāśa,* and also includes *manas*, but leaves out space, time, and selves. There of course remains a difficult problem of explaining the relationship between psychological and physical properties, but not a problem generated by the complete extrusion of the mind from the physical world. For what is sought is a *single* account of all possible objects of inquiry, and that necessarily includes inquirers themselves.

Realism and reference

What common thread underpins these various realist commitments? The Sanskrit term 'padārtha' is used by those philosophers in India who wish to signal their espousal of a commitment to realism, a term that is often loosely translated as 'category' or 'division of reality'. The category of universals is one, the category of substances another. A philosopher who claims that some class of entities constitutes a distinct category (*padārthāntara*) is advancing an irreducibility thesis: talk of the entities in this class is not reducible to talk of entities of any other type. What is rejected thereby is a reduction, for example, of a substance to a bundle of qualities or a human self to a continuum of mental events. As I will show later, Raghunātha is firmly anti-reductionist, wanting to preserve the metaphysical autonomy of a variety of phenomena, including for example intentionality.

Here it is helpful to recall the etymology of the term 'padārtha': it literally means the 'object for which a word stands' *(padasya arthaḥ)*. When the Vaiśeṣikas decide to count substance as a distinct category, the point of doing so has to be understood as one about reference: it is to assert that the use of substance words, such as 'pot' and 'pan' belongs to a distinct referential class. Every term is associated with a condition governing its use (a *pravṛtti-nimitta*), a condition that an object must satisfy in order to be a referent of the term. Different types of term are associated with different types of condition. The characterization of realism as a thesis about reference is considerably facilitated by the Sanskrit language itself, with its arsenal of syntactic tools for generating singular nominal terms, including abstraction and specification suffices. Then it is easy to formulate

Vaiśeṣika realism about universals as the doctrine that singular abstract terms denote objects, in this case universals. Sanskrit syntax is also what makes possible the characteristic late Vaiśeṣika commitment to realism about absences: the use of negative prefixes and suffices to form nominals from nominals is entirely unrestricted in Sanskrit, as unrestricted as, for instance, the use of conjunction in English. So the sentence 'the absence-of-Cat is in this room' can easily be parsed as predicating something of a singular negative subject. This is one reason why it would be important, in the early modern period, that philosophers develop a new technical language, one in which such constructions are regimented and freed from possible ambiguity (whether the sentence is consistent with a cat other than some particular one being in the room, for example).

In order to clarify the nature of Vaiśeṣika realism, it will be helpful to compare it with Meinong's. Meinong's realism, says Dummett, 'consisted in his treating singular terms as always denoting objects—actual ones, merely possible ones, or even impossible ones' (1991a: 324). So if 'Cyclops' is a singular term then Cyclops is an object. Dummett observes that there are two escape routes from such a commitment. One is to deny that singular terms for merely possible objects denote anything at all, the other is to deny that the terms in question really are singular terms. The first route does not deny that statements made with the help of those terms are intelligible, but does deny that they must be either true or false; the second route paraphrases the statements in such a way that there is no troublesome invocation of objects. So Dummett says,

> Integral to any given version of realism are both the principle of bivalence for statements of the disputed class, and the interpretation of those statements at face value, that is to say, as genuinely having the semantic form that they appear on their surface to have. Rejection of either one of these will afford a means of repudiating realism and will constitute a form of anti-realism, however restrained, for statements of the disputed class.
>
> (1991a: 325)

We find Udayana pursuing the second escape route, thereby sidestepping Meinong's realism about the merely possible and the impossible (*tuccha*, *alīka*). Udayana argues that the expression *śaśa-viṣāṇa* 'rabbit's horn' admit of a paraphrase that shows it not to be a genuine singular term; it falsely predicates horn to a rabbit and does not refer to some entity which does not actually exist (Matilal 1971: 123–145, 1985b: 76–111; Chakrabarti 1997; Ganeri 2006: 62–67). The same is true of names of impossible objects. Vaiśeṣika thinkers, then, are anti-realists in at least one domain.

It might seem like ultra-realism in another guise, however, to maintain realism with respect to the negative, for surely the same paraphrasing strategy would always let us parse a sentence containing a negative singular term as one with a normal singular term and a negative particle. The sentence 'Absence-of-Cat is in this room' might easily, it seems, be held to have the deep semantic form 'It is not the case that Cat is in this room'. For this reason, no contemporary philosopher I know of is a Meinongian realist about negative objects. It is not clear that any Vaiśeṣika thinker is either before the twelfth century. Well before Gaṅgeśa, however, Śivāditya insists that a new category of 'non-being' (*abhāva*) must be acknowledged, and this quickly became the accepted view. As I will explain in more detail in a later chapter, one reason is that many other sorts of thing, which one might otherwise have to accept as ontologically distinct, can effectively be reduced to types of non-being; so the proposal paradoxically achieves a considerable ontological economy.

Why, though, should one take the 'escape route' for the merely possible but not for the negative? The intuition seems to be that one cannot simply build an object by putting together any old properties, such as horn and hare: the 'creation' of such monsters is possible only in thought. Correspondingly, one cannot build a genuine *singular* term simply by conjoining various other terms. There is no fiction other than through construction out of what does exist, and therefore all fictional terms are the result of composition. On the other hand, there is nothing wrong with taking a genuine singular term and analysing it; the process of analysis does not reveal the term to have been less than genuinely singular after all. To give Udayana's example, the term 'beast' (*paśu*) is analysable as 'animal with hair and a long tail' (see Ganeri 2006: 53–72). What the analysis tells us is that the condition of use for the term is a complex one, stating something like 'The term "beast" refers to an object just in case that object is an animal with hair and a long tail'. If the parsing of negative terms can be shown to be nothing more than a similar sort of analytical expansion of the condition of use of the term, then we preserve their status as genuine singular terms. If one then also compares 'absence of a horn on the rabbit' with 'presence of a horn on the rabbit', one might say that the first attributes absence-of-horn to the rabbit just as the second attributes horn-ness, and in this way come to treat absence-of-horn as a category, just as one treats universals as a category. In sum, while the Buddhist strategy of analytical decomposition, as expounded for example by Vasubandhu,[6] proves nothing against the reality of the analysandum, no activity of imagination or mental creation can, of itself, bring an object into being.

Grades of existence

Ought it to count against the realism of the Vaiśeṣika that they are hesitant to accord the same relationship with existence to all the entities in their ontology? They make use of various terms: one is *sattā* 'existence' a second is *astitva* 'reality', and a third term is *bhāva* 'being' (the first two derived from the verb *as* 'is' and the third from *bhū* 'to be, to become'). Praśastapāda says that

> The three [categories] beginning with the substances have a 'bond with existence' (*sattāsambandha*)... the three beginning with the universals have an 'existence in their own terms' (*svātmasattva*).
>
> (1994: §§14–15)

[6] *Abhidharmakośa* 6.4; see Ganeri 2007: 169–175.

Let me reserve the term 'particular' for an object in any of the first three categories, that is the particular substances, along with their particular qualities and motions (better: objects, tropes, and events). The universals, the 'distinguishers' and the connective glue called 'inherence', Praśastapāda seems to say, have a degraded claim on existence, or at least a different claim. Later authors explicate the notion with the idea of 'own nature' (*svarūpa*; Śrīdhara actually glosses 'existence in their own terms' *svātma-sattva* as 'self-constituting existence' *svarūpa-sattva*). The thought seems to be that while particulars inherit their existence via their connection with a real universal 'existence' (*sattā*), the existence of non-particulars is self-constituting. Halbfass (1992: 157–158) comments that this idea 'is precarious and problematic and hardly suitable to vindicate the old realism of the Vaiśeṣika against reductionist and relativistic challenges'. But Udayana helpfully states that the idea of 'self-constituting existence' does not apply to the impossible or fictitious, and we have seen that he argues that the names of impossible objects, and of fictitious or merely possible entities, are susceptible to a semantic expansion which shows that they do not need to be treated as genuine singular terms at all. So the restriction of the term 'existence' to the three kinds of particular does not undermine the Vaiśeṣika claim to avow realism with respect to the other sorts of entity too. Dummett again:

> We cannot say that a realist about things of a certain category is one who believes that such things exist, for Meinong differentiated between actual and merely possible objects in that the former, but not the latter, existed; it is quite common for philosophers to distinguish, within reality, between those of its denizens which exist and those which only subsist, or are ideal, or the like.
> (Dummett 1991a: 324)

Vaiśeṣika, indeed, extends its realism still further when it accepts as real all manner of absence. Properly speaking, then, to be real is simply to be able to have a genuine name (*padārtha*). That is what the straightforwardly existent (*sattā-sambandha, bhāva*), the things whose existence is 'self-constituting' (*svarūpa*), and even the negative (*abhāva, nāsti*) have in common. That is what, allegedly, the impossible and the merely possible or fictitious lack.

Vyomaśiva offers another suggestion. He prefers to view the world of the non-concrete non-particular as a world to which the term 'exist' (*sat*) is indeed applicable, but only metaphorically.[7] Either way, the real world is pictured as comprising a principal domain of concrete particulars, partitioned into objects ('substances'), events ('motions'), and tropes ('qualities'), and two other domains, a domain of 'distinguishers' in one–one correspondence with the atoms and selves in the principal domain, and a domain of universals that is like a pyramid standing on the domain of particulars, moving in ever-increasing abstraction to an apex whose name is 'existence' (*sattā*). The cement that holds all this together is a single if distributed binary kind, designated by the relational mass term 'inherence' (*samavāya*). With this same cement, nested piles of wholes are fashioned out of ultimately atomic parts within the principal domain (Figure 12.1).

[7] Vyomaśiva 1981: 110ff; trans. Halbfass 1992: 248–255.

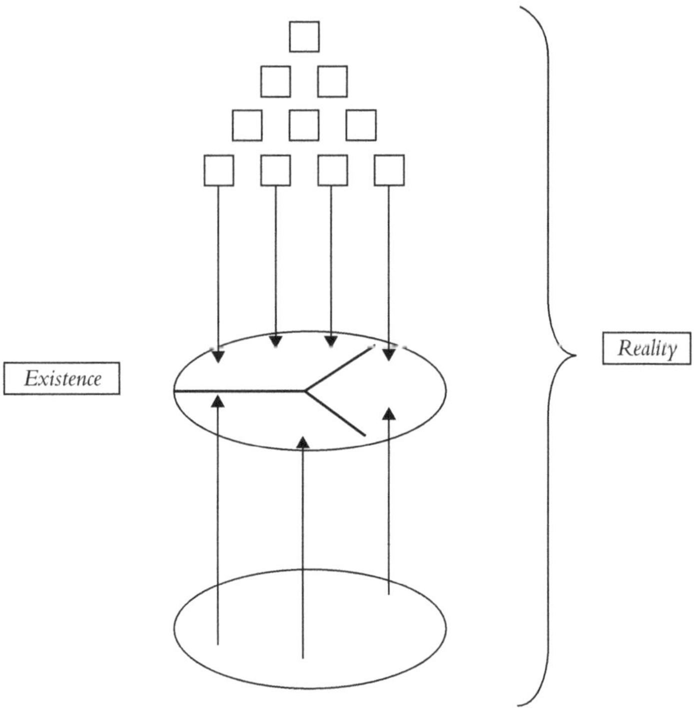

Figure 12.1 The Vaiśeṣika world.

The domains above and below (of universals and differentiators respectively) are metaphysically dependent on the tripartite domain of particulars (particular substances, qualities, and motions). This is exactly as, within the domain of particulars, the common-sense world is metaphysically dependent on the atomic world of physics (and for both, indeed, the metaphysical 'glue' is the same, inherence), as a wave is dependent on water, or a dent on a surface. Realism is content with such dependencies; its concern is to deny a conceptual dependence between domains of any sort and their human cognizers.

Epistemic constraints on the concept of truth

In Dummett's characterization, a realist is someone for whom

> the condition we associate with a name, as that which must be satisfied by an object for it to be the referent, need not be one whose satisfaction by an arbitrary object we should have any effective means of deciding, however favourably placed: our use of the name is mediated solely by the knowledge that, objectively, the condition is satisfied by at most one object in the history of the universe.
>
> (Dummett 1991a: 310)

An anti-realist holds that

> reality itself is indeterminate; it has gaps, much as a novel has gaps, in that there are questions about the characters to which the novel provides no answers, and to which there therefore are no answers.
>
> (1991a: 318)

The entire Vaiśeṣika theory, including even its doctrine of 'distinguishers' is geared up to making available a condition associated with a name, a condition whose satisfaction is what gives the name its reference. Yet, while they would certainly reject a picture of the world as having gaps in the way a novel or a dream might, it is not certain that Dummett's characterization of realism is one they will endorse. Given the existence of formidable objections to a conception of realism that makes it rest on an epistemically unconstrained notion of truth, it would be unsurprising if exponents of realism sought ameliorated understandings of the realist commitment. Dummett's characterization of realism unfairly tilts the scales in favour of the anti-realist.

One clear area where Praśastapāda tries to combine realism with epistemic constraint is the metaphysics of number. This topic is as central for Vaiśeṣika as John Locke's distinction of primary and secondary qualities was for early modern empiricism. Locke's account of secondary qualities is sometimes seen as affording a way to circumvent a full-blown metaphysical realism. Locke argued that colours, unlike weight or shape, are not simply in the things themselves, but depend on a relationship between the thing and the perceiver. The thought is that biconditionals such as the following are true: *x* is yellow iff *x* is disposed to look yellow to standard subjects in standard conditions (Pettit 1991; Johnston 1998). It has sometimes been suggested that this is also the right way to understand the reality of moral and other normative properties. The Vaiśeṣika discussion of colours does not give any hint of a primary–secondary quality distinction, but there is something analogous in their treatment of at least one other sort of quality, number. Praśastapāda states that the quality twoness arises in a pair of objects, cognized individually, when in dependence on a 'combinative cognition' (*apekṣābuddhi*):

> Next, two-ness arises from the two unit-qualities in their substrata, in dependence on a combinative cognition.
>
> (1994: §131)

According to Praśastapāda, it is the act of counting out the two objects which makes them two. We might formulate his view in terms of a biconditional: $\{x, y\}$ are two iff *x* and *y* are mentally counted out together. Śrīdhara comments that 'the thesis that an object can be produced by cognition is not outlandish (*alaukika*), for we do observe the production of pleasures and so on from cognitions' (Śrīdhara 1977: 275). He adds that in both cases, being produced by my prior cognition is what guarantees that the resulting awareness is private to me. The duality which I isolate by mentally counting out these two objects is analogous to the pleasure which I feel as a result of thinking of something pleasant: in both cases, what explains my privileged access to the ensuing state of affairs is my ownership of the preceding creative mental act. In other words, the hypothesis that numbers are 'counting-dependent' (just as colours, for Locke, are 'response-dependent') is justified by considerations from the epistemology of number, specifically the privacy of the counter's knowledge of the number. There would, presumably, be nothing to prevent a Vaiśeṣika extending this account to any aspect of perceptual appearance that varies in dependence on the perceiver; Matilal (1986: 290–291) recommends its application to certain cases of perceptual illusion. On such an account, the statement 'there are two objects' has no determinate truth-value independent of human capabilities; not, to be sure, our capacity to ascertain or verify it, but rather our capacity to constitute the statement's truth through our acts of counting.

What is striking is that the 'counting-dependence' of numbers is not held against their status as entirely real. Realism about numbers, the suggestion goes, is not incompatible with the existence of an epistemic constraint on mathematical truth. If the truth that there are two objects here is partly constituted by my having counted out, in my mind, two objects, then knowledge of that fact is in some sense already available to me, in a way that knowledge of other kinds of external object or event or fact is not. The fact that there are two objects, and the fact that I know that there are, has, as it were, a common cause in my act of mentally counting. There is a strong disanalogy between statements about numbers and statements about the merely possible, one which rests on a sharp distinction between mental acts of *counting* and mental acts of *imagination*. Vaiśeṣika realism defines itself in part as a rejection of the thesis that imagination has an object-constituting role. Using the mind to put a rabbit and a horn together in such a way as to fashion a creature with the body of a rabbit and a horn on its head is to be sharply differentiated from putting the rabbit and the horn together in the mind in such a way as to get a mentally delineated collection of two objects.[8]

What our contrastive study of number, the merely possible and the negative have shown is that Praśastapāda is operating with a realism that is fundamentally semantic but does not exclude the possibility that there may be certain types of epistemic constraint. Dummett argued that realism must meet two conditions at the same time when he said that 'Integral to any given version of realism are both the principle of bivalence for statements of the disputed class, and the interpretation of those statements at face value, that is to say, as genuinely having the semantic form that they appear on their surface to have' (1991a: 325), linking bivalence with the idea that we might not have an 'effective means of deciding' whether the condition associated with a name is satisfied or not. If that is a fair characterization of 'naïve' or 'metaphysical' realism, then Praśastapāda is not a metaphysical realist. His ameliorated realism claims that a sufficiently robust conception of the reality of the world is gained just from the second of the two conditions claimed by Dummett to be constitutive of realism.

[8] That differentiation is effected, in later Nyāya, through the asymmetrical use of the concepts of 'qualificative cognition' (*viśiṣṭa-jñāna*) and 'combinative cognition' (*samūhālambana-jñāna*); cf. Guha 1966.

'Whatever is, is knowable and nameable'

My interpretation of Vaiśeṣika realism is further supported by Praśastapāda's much quoted assertion that every being is real (*asti*), knowable and nameable:

All six categories possess reality, nameability and knowability.
(ṣaṇṇām api padārthānām astitvābhidheyatvajñeyatvāni; 1994: §11).

The claim that every real is nameable is a simple consequence of the semantic conception of realism, and the fact the Praśastapāda makes this claim is further evidence that Vaiśeṣika realism is a semantic conception. One might wonder how names could be given to the unobservable atoms; certainly not by ostensive definition. But several Vaiśeṣikas show us how unobservables can be named with the help of uniquely identifying definite descriptions: the name '*ākāśa*' is introduced as a name for that which is the substratum of sounds, and the means by which a theoretical name is introduced by way of an introducing description is sharply distinguished from the role of composite descriptions in the construction of fictional terms (Ganeri 2006: 181–184). Bhartṛhari's argument, that the nameability relation is not itself nameable, on the grounds that no relation can have itself as a relatum,[9] points, however, to a deeper worry, one that I will return to. Perhaps no language can say everything about itself.

On the other hand, the claim that every real is knowable threatens to collapse Vaiśeṣika realism into a type of verificationism.[10] Global knowability, or weak verificationism, does seem at first sight to be incompatible with realism. For if realism is characterized as the thesis that matters of being are independent of the reach of our epistemic resources, then there could be truths which transcend our ability to verify them, either now or in the future, and statements whose truth or falsity is something we cannot and never will be able to decide. But if everything is knowable, then there are no 'verification-transcendent' truths. Dummett (1991a: 315) states that undecidable sentences are principally the result of three features of our language: our ability to refer to inaccessible regions of space or time, such as the past or the spatially remote; the use of unbounded quantification over infinite totalities; and the use of the subjunctive conditional, for example in describing how an object would behave if subjected to a certain test, when that test is never performed. If realism is a commitment to the claim that such statements do nevertheless have a determinate truth-value, then it is precisely the *unrestricted* reach of language that makes realism possible.

One defence would be to invoke divine knowledge. That all is knowable only threatens realism if divine cognition is exempt; for otherwise, the claim might simply be that *if* realism is true, and *if* God is omniscient, then whatever is real is knowable.[11]

[9] See Parsons 2001; H. and R. Herzberger 1981; Houben 1996.

[10] Daya Krishna 1994 asked if global knowability is consistent with realism in Vaiśeṣika, in a discussion note which led to a flurry of indignant reaction among scholars. Their reactions are collected in Krishna 2004, along with his detailed and interesting response.

[11] See e.g. Balcerowicz 2010.

Some early modern thinkers do seek to defend the knowability claim this way, thereby implicitly conceding that human knowledge is bounded. Here is Mādhavadeva's explanation:

> The seven [categories], beginning with substance, are nameable and knowable, and such properties as being cognizable are what they have in common. To be nameable is to be the target of the semantic power of a word, for every object is the target of the semantic power of a word like the pronoun 'that'. The property of being knowable, in the shape of being the content of a knowledge episode, and the property of being cognizable, in the shape of being the content of a cognition, occur everywhere, for everything is the content of a cognition of God.
>
> (1903–4: 12)

It is interesting to note, however, that Raghudeva, in the *Survey of What is Essential about Substance,* does not appeal to the idea of God in defence of the doctrine. He says, instead, that knowability is a matter of being an object of knowledge and being a cause of knowledge, and that it is possible for any object to be a cause of *inferential* knowledge.[12] And there is a persuasive argument that the context of Praśastapāda's slogan is one in which it is human, not divine, knowledge that is in play. The argument is that knowledge of the categories of existence is meant to have a soteriological value for human beings (Praśastapāda 1994: §2; cf. Perrett 1999: 402; Krishna 2004: 282–283). If there were things that we humans might not know, and if knowledge of the true nature of things is essential for attaining the highest good, then it would be at best contingent that we should be able to do so. Indeed, knowing the truth about everything might itself *constitute* the highest good. The better defence of Praśastapāda is, I think, simply to note that he separates out the semantic and the epistemic components in the characterization of realism. In what I am calling the ameliorated as opposed to the naïve or metaphysical conception of realism, there is no particular difficulty with acknowledging the existence of epistemic constraints on 'the real'. All that must be kept clearly in mind is that such constraints do not *constitute* our conception of the real; that conception is based on issues about reference. His statement that every being is knowable is not part of an *analysis* of 'being'.

Even if not incompatible with realism, the thesis that everything is knowable might simply be false. This thesis, like the thesis that everything is denotable, admits of several interpretations. One is that it is possible to know every truth; another is that it is possible to think about every object and so to have discriminating knowledge of every object; a third is that it is possible to know of every object that it exists. F. B. Fitch has reported a proof, due to Alonzo Church, that the thesis that it is possible to know every truth entails a falsehood.[13] His proof has become known as the 'paradox of knowability'.

[12] evaṃ dravyādiṣadpadārthānāṃ jñeyatvābhidheyatve sādharmye | jñeyatvaṃ jñāna-viṣayatvaṃ jñāpakatvaṃ ca jñāyamāna-liṅga-karaṇatā-vādināṃ vaiśeṣikānā[ṃ] ca | vastu-mātrasyaivānumityātmaka-jñāna-karaṇatayā jñāpakatvopapatteḥ | (Stein 1253, fol. 26r, 3–5).

[13] Fitch 1964. See also Salerno 2009. Perrett 1999 is the first to see its relevance for Vaiśeṣika. He concludes that the 'doctrine that whatever exists is knowable and nameable must be judged rationally unacceptable.' I try to show here that this conclusion does not have to be drawn.

With two very plausible additional principles, Fitch proved that knowability entails the falsehood that *everything is actually known*. The first principle is that knowledge is factive, the second principle is that knowledge distributes over conjunction. Suppose now that there is a truth *p* which is actually unknown. This is another truth, and so should be knowable. That is, one should be able both to know *p* and to know that *p* is unknown. But if one knows that *p* is unknown, then *p* is unknown. So it follows, paradoxically, that one both knows *p* and that *p* is unknown.[14] The proof therefore seems to show that the original assumption is false, i.e. that every truth is *in fact* known. Something has gone wrong; for many people, the problem lies with the thesis of global knowability.

There have been a number of attempts to save the knowability thesis from this paradox. Timothy Williamson (1982) has pointed out that reductio arguments work only in a classical bivalent logic; under an intuitionist logic, in which double negation elimination does not hold, we can infer only it is not the case that nothing is unknown, not that everything is known. This will not help the Vaiśeṣika, however. It is a consequence of the Vaiśeṣika treatment of negation that a property and its absence can co-occur in a single substratum, and the effect of this is to surrender double negation introduction rather than double negation elimination.[15] Daniel Ingalls (1951: 68 n.) therefore made a mistake when he compared the Indian theory with intuitionism. A variety of attempts to deny Distribution also fail.[16]

I think, nevertheless, that there is a solution to our puzzle. Consider what would happen if we tried to run Fitch's proof with assertibility in place of knowability. The thesis now is that every truth is assertible, and the assumption would be that there is a truth which is not asserted. So it is possible to assert that something is true and that one is not asserting it; for example asserting 'It is raining and I do not assert that it is raining'. This is similar in form to Moore's Paradox ('*p* but I don't believe that *p*') and is paradoxical for similar reasons. Assertion is governed by principles whose net effect is that one cannot cancel an assertion one makes simply by asserting that one has not asserted it. So not everything is assertible; in particular, one cannot make certain assertions about one's assertions. This is the point foreseen by Bhartṛhari in his paradox

[14] [1] p & ~ K p. Assumption.
[2] ◊ K (p & ~ K p). Knowability Thesis.
[3] ◊ (K p & K ~ K p). By Distribution.
[4] ◊ (K p & ~ K p). By Factivity.

[15] The doctrine of *avyāpya-vṛttitva* 'nonpervasive occurrence' allows for an object to possess a property and simultaneously possess the absence of that property. But it is always a fully determinate matter whether it possesses the property or does not possess it. For details, see Ganeri 2001a: 89–91. One has to be careful not to turn every theory based on a many-valued logic into a version of anti-realism. Such a theory does not regard a statement as false whenever it is not true, (because it treats a statement as false when its negation is true), but can, nevertheless, regard every statement as determinately either true or *not true*. Dummett introduces the term 'objectivist' to describe a many-valued theory for which this is the case (1991: 326). Some later developments of Vaiśeṣika are objectivist in precisely this sense. Their logic of negation is many-valued but realist.

[16] Williamson 2000. See also Williamson 1987a,b and the essays in Salerno 2009.

of nameability. A language makes assertions about itself only at the risk of sliding into self-contradiction.

Fitch's proof likewise shows that the thesis that everything is knowable cannot coherently be maintained in an unrestricted form. I suggest that it also indicates the nature of the appropriate restriction. For what the proof shows is that if *p* is a truth that is unknown, then one cannot know that this is so.[17] Let us therefore restrict the knowability thesis to all those truths about the world that do not refer to our epistemic condition. In our restriction of the thesis, the quantifier 'everything' is allowed to range only over propositions the content of which makes no reference to our epistemic condition, so the first step in Fitch's proof is blocked. This move, of course, would beg the question against an antirealist, for whom all facts in some sense refer to our epistemic condition, but it is available to someone who is *already* a realist and who wishes *then* to maintain the knowability thesis in a restricted form. So restricted, the knowability thesis is that every 'non-epistemic fact' is knowable; it leaves it open for there to be at least some 'epistemic facts' which are not.

The paradox of inquiry, which I described in Chapter 9, shows that specifications of the target of a search for knowledge must not presume that the inquirer already knows that which the inquiry is meant to discover, but yet must have at least some conception of what is being sought, enough to get the inquiry going. Inquiry aims at the unknown, but 'the unknown' is a description and not a proper name. It is a black box—one cannot say of some given truth that it is included within it. The thought of the unknown, therefore, guides inquiry only insofar as we reflect on what we do know and become aware of the gaps. Since the 'unknown' is an absence or non-being (*abhāva*), the restriction is even consistent with Praśastapāda's statement that everything in the six categories of being is knowable. The absence-of-knowledge in a certain self is a fact which falls into the seventh category.

Reflecting on the paradox of knowability, and how to escape it, has served to throw new light on the nature of Vaiśeṣika realism. It is a realism that can remain coherent as long as no attempt is made to include within our conception of 'the world' *all* our own efforts to comprehend and describe it. The Vaiśeṣika willingness to endorse global principles of knowability and nameability reveals the influence of a conception of 'the world' that situates knowers and speakers *outside* itself, a conception reminiscent of Wittgenstein's Tractarian conception of the self as a limit of the world (*Tractatus* 5.633). This conception, however, is in tension with another one. The second conception is holistic, and thinks of 'the world' as that totality which includes knowers and speakers, knowledge, and language. In particular, a theory of such a world includes itself, for any such theory is itself a part of the totality it seeks to describe. Vaiśeṣika metaphysics, as I mentioned at the beginning, embeds human inquirers, along with all they know and think, within its own folds as further objects of inquiry. And, of course, that compre-

[17] Crispin Wright 2000: 356 makes a similar point: he says that 'rational acceptance of either conjunct under "sufficiently good" epistemic circumstances precludes rational acceptance of the other'.

hensive metaphysics is itself one of the things human beings seek to know; indeed, they must know it if the Vaiśeṣika soteriological claims are given their due, claims to the effect that it is precisely knowledge of the whole of reality, including ourselves within it, which leads to the highest good. What remains to be seen is whether there is any way to reconcile these two conceptions.

Realism and reduction

Is there also a tension between the common-sense realism and the scientific realism in Praśastapāda? He maintains that wholes, ordinary middle-sized objects, are real, but also that they are constituted by parts, ultimately unobservable atomic parts. Halbfass thought that there was, saying that the Vaiśeṣika wholes have a 'precarious ontological status' (Halbfass 1992: 94). Halbfass is not alone in thinking that the possibility of reduction puts pressure on realism, that because a whole is reducible to its parts its claim on reality is vulnerable. Praśastapāda finds nothing problematic in the idea that wholes are real, however, because there are perfectly genuine singular terms which refer to them. The existence of metaphysical dependences, of the sort that are seen between an object and the parts which constitute it, or a dent and the surface it occurs in, do not of themselves imply anything about the reality of the entities involved. Dummett himself argues very clearly that one can be both a realist and a reductionist so long as one continues to hold that for every statement in the disputed class there are statements in the reductive class that render it determinately true or not true:

> If it is his rejection of the principle of bivalence that marks the reductionist's divergence from realism, then the realist may continue to be a realist, despite espousing even a full-blooded reductionism, as long as he continues to adhere to the principle of bivalence.
>
> (1991a: 327–328)

Such a realist will be, in Dummett's phrase, a 'sophisticated realist' (1991a: 324) and in David Lewis's phrase a 'cautious reductionist'.[18] The sophisticated realist might admit the possibility of reduction without translatability (weak reductionism) or even the possibility of reduction through an actual translation (strong or full-blooded reductionism), as long as he or she continues to treat singular terms in the disputed class as genuinely referential. A Vaiśeṣika, it seems to me, could be a sophisticated realist about wholes, if he or she concedes that such an object admits of decomposition into parts, and so that statements about wholes can be translated into statements about their

[18] 'A supervenience thesis is, in a broad sense, reductionist. But it is a stripped-down form of reductionism, unencumbered by dubious denials of existence, claims of ontological priority, or claims of translatability. One might wish to say that in some sense the beauty of statues is nothing over and above the shape and size and colour that beholders appreciate, but without denying that there is such a thing as beauty, without claiming that beauty exists only in a less-than-fundamental way, and without undertaking to paraphrase ascriptions of beauty in terms of shape etc. A supervenience thesis seems to capture what the cautious reductionist wishes to say.' (Lewis 1998: 29.)

structural arrangements, but maintains realism about wholes nevertheless. This is how one might hope to adhere to both common-sense realism and scientific realism at the same time, in the teeth of strong Buddhist argumentation that such two-tier realism is incoherent.[19] One again sees a conflict between reductive and non-reductive realism in the debate over whether the colour of a whole piece of cloth is reducible to the various colours of its threads. Here some Vaiśeṣikas seem to veer towards a non-reductivist realism when they affirm that the colour of the piece of cloth is a new colour (*citra-rūpa*) distinct from that of the threads. What makes the doctrine of wholes a 'precarious' one in thinkers like Praśastapāda is that he seems to feel pulled towards insisting that wholes are irreducibly distinct entities, over and above their parts.

Among the older Vaiśeṣika philosophers, I detect an ambiguous stance on the issue of the relationship between reduction and realism. This is perhaps the key area where the early modern thinkers achieve greater clarity and in doing so put realist metaphysics on more coherent foundational principles. While Raghunātha rolls out a non-reductive realism across the board, as the best way to construct a coherent metaphysics out of the diverse strands within early Vaiśeṣika, the later Vārāṇasī philosophers are 'cautious' or 'sophisticated' reductionist realists. Buddhist argument strongly insists that if something can be taken apart or analytically reduced then it is less than fully real, and one response is to affirm a non-reductive realism. The availability of middle ground, in the form of a cautious reductionist realism, only becomes clear, perhaps, with sufficient intellectual distance from the heat and rhetoric of the traditional debate, which oscillates between two extremes because of a shared but false presupposition that reductionism and realism are incompatible.

The metaphysics of number is one of the key areas where these debates were played out within Vaiśeṣika. In the next chapter I will examine the movement, from the ancient doctrine of Praśastapāda, through its Mithilā rejuvenation in Śaṅkara Miśra, and on to the 'new reason' ideas of Raghunātha Śiromaṇi. A detailed examination of this evolving discussion will help to clarify the semantic and epistemic dimensions in the Vaiśeṣika conception of realism. Indeed, it is within this discussion that the traditional conception comes under the greatest pressure.

[19] See also Dummett 1979, and the discussion in Matilal 1986: 13–16.

13

New Foundations in The Metaphysics of Mathematics

The metaphysics of number illustrates Raghunātha at his most original. His new theory marks a radical and sharp dividing line. In the philosophers who precede him, what we find are ever more ingenious and sophisticated attempts to repair the ancient theory from increasingly grave difficulties. After Raghunātha, the work is on developing and extending the new theory he has introduced. One reason for examining the Indian metaphysics of mathematics is thus that it brings into greater clarity just what makes it the case that Raghunātha is the first modern philosopher. A second reason is that the topic of number seems to be where the internal strains that are present in the pre-modern theory express themselves most sharply; in particular, the attempt to give a semantics for the expression 'many' ends up severely testing the syntactically grounded realism I described in the previous chapter. It is only when new ideas about quantification are developed in connection with the particle 'only' that a solution becomes available.

The theory of number therefore serves as a highly instructive example of the nature of rationality, theory-change, and philosophical thinking. We will see how the processes of theory rejection and modification are driven by perceived explanatory failure rather than by discovery of foundational incoherence. I will argue that the source of structure, order, and pattern is seen to reside in the natural world, and not in any domain of abstract objects or in the empirically unconstrained working of a priori reflection. The discussion of number broaches fundamental questions about the nature of objectivity and the correspondence theory of meaning, and it explores the basic principles underlying the construction of a formal ontology. I will chiefly examine the contributions of four thinkers: Praśastapāda, the voice of classical Vaiśeṣika; Bhāsarvajña, an independently minded pre-Gaṅgeśa thinker; Śaṃkara Miśra, a fifteenth century 'new' (*navya*) Naiyāyika from Mithilā; and Raghunātha Śiromaṇi, founder of the Navadvīpa 'modern' (*navīna*) movement within Navya Nyāya.

Mathematics and the philosophical theory of number

The philosophical study of number in Vaiśeṣika belongs with the analysis of the structure of empirical knowledge. This theory of number is an account of the semantics and epistemology of contingent numerical judgements, judgements whose subject matter concerns questions of numerical quantity. Such judgements are typically expressed by statements like 'there are two pots in this room' or 'there are nine planets in the solar system'. The study of number is therefore an enquiry into the role of number within empirical and scientific knowledge. The Vaiśeṣika theory of number is broadly empiricist: number is part of the natural world. While these philosophers generally do not explicitly discuss the nature of mathematical truth, they implicitly favour an empiricist philosophy of mathematics, according to which the laws of arithmetic are of the same kind as the laws of nature, differing only in the degree of generality they possess.

Numerals have three distinguishable grammatical roles. They function as *adjectives* in sentences like 'There are nine planets,' as *predicates* in sentences like 'The planets are nine', and as *substantives* in sentences like 'Nine is the square of three'. Because the numerals are not treated as names of numbers, but rather as numerical predicates, there was no reason to introduce numbers into the ontology as objects; there is no tendency, for example, to analyse number set theoretically. The adjectival and predicative roles of the numerals, on the other hand, are analysed in depth. It is a result of modern semantic theory that the adjectival use of the numerals can be expressed in a first-order language with identity, and this result is partly anticipated by Bhāsarvajña. The dominant approach, however, is to treat numbers as properties of objects, exactly as colour adjectives stand for colour properties. A semantic conception of realism among these philosophers leads to the treatment as an object of anything which is referred to in thought or language (see Chapter 12). However, in their treatment of vagueness and the term 'many', the Vaiśeṣika philosophers press the limits of this conception.

Counting and construction

Praśastapāda supplements the *Vaiśeṣika-sūtra* account of number with a detailed description of the ontogenesis of numbers, and of the psychological process by which they come to be cognized. The entire process is supposed to take eight moments of time:

When [1] the eye of the cogniser contacts with a pair of substances of a similar or a dissimilar type, a cognition arises [2] of the generic oneness which inheres in those [qualities] which inhere in the objects of contact, and then [3] a single awareness arises of the two unit-qualities from the cognition of the relation between them and the generic oneness. Next [4] twoness begins to form from the two unit-qualities in their substrata, in dependence of that [single awareness]. But then [three things happen] at a single time [5]: a cognition of the universal twoness arises in this; the start of the decline of the combinative cognition (*apekṣā-buddhi*) due to that cognition of the universal twoness; and the beginning of the emergence of a cognition of the duality-quality from the cognition of the relation between it and the generic twoness. And now, [three more things happen] at a single time [6]: due to the destruction of the combinative cognition, the duality-quality begins to decline; the cognition of the duality-quality causes the destruction of the cognition of the universal twoness; and there begins to emerge a cognition of the two substances, in the form '[there are] two substances' from the duality-quality and its relation to the cognition. Following this, [four things happen] at a single time [7]: the [full] arising of the cognition of the two substances in the form '[there are] two substances;' the destruction of twoness; the beginning of the decline of the cognition of the duality-quality; and the beginning of the emergence of a dispositional memory trace from the cognition of the two substances. Following this [8], [there is] the destruction of the cognition of the duality-quality from the cognition of the two substances, and the [full] dispositional memory state also from the cognition of the two substances.

(1994: §§131–134)

This intricate description of the process is distilled by later writers into the following sequence of stages:[1]

(1) Sensory connection with the two objects.
(2) Awareness of the general property oneness.
(3) Combinative cognition (*apekṣā-buddhi*).
(4) Production of twoness in the objects.
(5) Awareness of the general property twoness.
(6) Awareness of a duality-quality.
(7) Knowledge of the two substances as qualified by such a duality.
(8) Dispositional memory trace.

Praśastapāda's theory of the production of number and numerical knowledge is as follows. One first perceives two separate objects. On perceiving an object, one can become aware of the sorts of qualities it possesses. Technically, this type of awareness is called *saṃyukta-samaveta-samaveta*, awareness of what inheres in what inheres in the object directly seen. In this case, what one becomes aware of is the universal property oneness, a property which inheres in every unit-quality (property-particular), and so in the particular unit-qualities which inhere in the two perceived objects. The third step is a mental act of counting or enumeration, a 'combinative cognition'. The thinker collects the two objects into a single awareness, judging '(here is) one and (here is) one'. The mental counting up of the objects produces in those objects a new feature, the property of being two. Although produced by the cognizer's counting, and depending for its continued existence on the continuing existence of that act, the number is an objective property of the objects themselves. Once the number two has come into existence, it is possible for the cognizer to become aware of it. He becomes aware, first of all, of the universal property twoness which inheres in all duality-qualities, then of the particular duality-quality which inheres in the two perceived objects, and finally of the two objects as qualified by that particular duality-quality. This episodic knowledge-event gives way to a dispositional memory trace, which preserves the knowledge for the cognizer after the episodic knowledge-event has faded away.

[1] Cf. Udayana 1956: 449, Śaṅkara Miśra 1923: 177.

The doctrine that numbers are created by mental acts of counting is important but difficult. Karl Potter regards the doctrine as 'a very dangerous admission' for a school that 'wishes to maintain a sure-footed realism about the external world' (1977: 120). Among the Vaiśeṣikas, Śrīdhara is most aware of the danger, and he reasons as follows (1977: 274–275):

This [combinative] cognition produces the twoness of the two objects which are the substrata, from the two unit-qualities which [each] depend on [the] universal oneness. The two substrata are inherent causes, the two unit-qualities are non-inherent causes, and the cognition of both is another causal factor. . . . The thesis that an object can be produced by a cognition is not an unworldly one, for the production of pleasure etc. from [cognitions] is seen [to be similar]. Nor is it right to say that there is a disanalogy [between numbers and pleasures] in that the production of an *external* object in such a way is not seen, for there is no distinction here between the two cases in the manifestation of the correlation [between cognition and production of object].

[Objection:] Although it has been shown that the causal foundation (*ālambana*) of the two qualities is what makes manifest the twoness, it is not the case that the cognition is its immediate antecedent cause. [Reply:] No, [if that were so then there would be] no regulation. If twoness were not produced by the cognition, then other people could cognise it, as with colours and so forth, because there would be no regulating causal factor. When produced by the cognition, however, this regularity arises: that which is produced by a person's cognition is ascertainable by him alone. The demonstration runs as follows—

1 Twoness is produced by cognition,
2 Because it is restricted to being thought of by a single cogniser.
3 That which is restricted to being thought of by a single cogniser is produced by cognition; as, for example, a pleasure.
4 Twoness is restricted to being thought of by a single cogniser.
5 Therefore, it too is produced by cognition.

This is a very interesting passage. A number is an objective entity, even though it is both *private* (capable of being cognized by at most a single person) and also *mind-created*. The inference from privacy to being mind-created is relatively unproblematic—it is hard to imagine how something which can only be cognized by a single person can be entirely mind-independent. But how does this give any support to the claim that numbers are objective? The analogy with pleasures and pains is apt, for the Vaiśeṣikas entertain the curious theory that pleasures and pains are distinct both from their (mental) causes as well as from the perception of them (Matilal 1986: 295–308). Pleasures and pains are also private to individuals, but, unlike numbers, they reside in the person and not in the outside world.

In saying that numbers have mental acts of counting as their causes, Praśastapāda gives voice to an intuition that there is an element of arbitrariness or a 'strain of subjectivity' (Matilal 1985: 19) in the numerical description of the world. Faddegon suggests that the arbitrariness lies in choosing a 'standard of counting, measuring, weighing' (1918: 206–207). What is certainly true is that the question 'How many things are there here?' has no determinate answer until we specify the *sort* of thing to be counted. As Frege (1950: §22) said, 'While I am not able, simply to be thinking of it differently, to alter the colour or hardness of a thing in the slightest, I am able to think of the *Iliad* either as one poem, or as 24 books, or as some large number of verses.' Yet Praśastapāda does not seem to have the sortal dependency of counting in mind, when he says that numbers are produced in objects by mental acts of counting. For he explicitly says that the two things can be of similar or dissimilar kinds. The point seems rather to be that the mental act is one of collecting together a number of objects, thereby making a particular group salient to the cognizer. From all the objects in the surroundings, the cognizer picks out in his mental act a *selected* subset. Looking at a garden full of trees, one might think 'these four trees are tall'. What makes it true that the subject in such a thought is a group of four trees, when there are many more trees around, is that those objects have been selected mentally by the cognizer. In other words, counting up the objects produces the number because it produces the group to which the number belongs. This in no way detracts from the objectivity of the number of objects being thought about, nor does it make the truth-value of the thought depend on anything other than the state of those objects.

Mental acts of counting and processes of selective attention seem to have a place only in judgements with demonstrative plural subjects. If one asks how many planets are there in the solar system, on the other hand, the number is fixed in advance of any counting up. In many cases, it is more natural to say that the number of things falling under a description is *discovered* and not *created*. The Vaiśeṣikas broach this problem in the course of their discussion of indefinite pluralities, to which I will turn. Before doing so, I might note another argument that Śrīdhara has for the existence of numbers as external entities. It is that if numbers did not exist, then nothing would regulate our cognition of them:

> If the forms [cognitions] of 'one,' 'two,' etc. were not compliant with external objects, they would not appear according to a condition of occurring from time to time. So number too is to be admitted, because there is no difference between the arising of both [cognitions of number and cognitions of other external things].
>
> (1977: 270)

It is central to the concept of objectivity that external objects are thought of as capable of being perceived and of existing unperceived. A familiar neo-Kantian thought is that in order to make sense of the idea that one can perceive what can also exist unperceived, one must think of perception as having certain spatio-temporal 'enabling conditions' such that in order to perceive something one must be appropriately located—both spatially and temporally—with respect to it.[2] One can then make sense of the fact that a perceivable object is not actually perceived by thinking that the enabling conditions for its perception are not satisfied. Śrīdhara's argument is similar: if numbers were not objective, then what we perceive would not be accountable to what there is to be perceived in our surroundings. Even though numbers have mental causes

[2] See, in particular, the discussion of objectivity in Evans 1985: 261–262.

in the theory, the *perception* of a number is a distinct mental event with *external* 'enabling conditions'.

The first four steps in the 'eight moments' theory describe the origin of numbers greater than one as properties of a group of objects collected together by a mental act of counting. The second four steps describe the origin of our *knowledge* of those properties, once they have come into being. According to *Vaiśeṣika-sūtra* 4.1.12–13, numbers are themselves perceptible when they reside in perceptible substances. In seeing a group of objects, we see also their properties, one of which is their number. The claim that we come to know of the number of objects perceptually is a little surprising, for one might have thought that it would be more natural to think of the act of counting itself as our means of coming to know how many objects there are. We have already seen, however, that it is crucial to Vaiśeṣika realism to maintain a sharp distinction between the creative act of counting and the epistemology of numerical knowledge. Presumably when the collected objects are not perceptible, then the act of counting them is our primary epistemological access to their number.

Mathematical knowledge, as distinct from empirical knowledge of the number of things, is often considered to have a distinctive epistemological status. It is thought to be possible to know a priori, without recourse to any empirical enquiry, that $17 \times 27 = 459$. The early philosophers did consider the hypothesis that mathematical truths are known by a special means in the course of their discussion of the source of knowledge called 'inclusion' (*saṃbhava*). Inclusion is said to have been recognized as an independent source of knowledge by the Paurāṇikas. Vātsyāyana defines it as 'the cognition of the existence of one thing from the cognition of the existence of another thing never absent from the first' (1997: 97, 10–11). He cites, as an example, coming to know of an *āḍhaka* from a *droṇa*. *Āḍhaka* and *droṇa* are both measures of grain, the former being one-quarter of the latter. So the point is that one is in a position to know that one has a quantity x of grain if one knows that one has a quantity of grain that includes x. Later writers give an example more relevant to our present purposes: the inference that there are a hundred of a certain thing because there are a thousand. We must take 'there are a hundred' to mean 'there are at least a hundred' and not 'there are exactly a hundred'. However, although they mention 'inclusion', our authors do not recognize in it any distinctive epistemological features. They reduce it to the standard pattern of quasi-inductive inference, in which one infers that something is F because it is G, on the basis of one's knowledge that F never occurs without G. Knowledge of the invariable concomitance between F and G is, however, taken to be derived from a search for counter-examples, cases where F is present without G. As long as one can find no such counter-example, one has a good reason to believe that the properties are concomitant. The inference that there are a hundred because there are a thousand, on the other hand, is based on the inclusion of a hundred in a thousand, something which one can come to know without searching for counter-examples or performing any empirical enquiry. This example shows how the empiricism of these philosophers deterred them, rightly or wrongly, from accepting the existence of a priori mathematical truth.

Numbers as properties of objects

Numbers are mentioned by Kaṇāda in *Vaiśeṣika-sūtra* 1.1.9 as one member in a list of seventeen kinds of 'quality' (*guṇa*). The Vaiśeṣika concept of a quality is a technical one. Qualities are distinguished, on the one hand, from substances and movements, and on the other, from universals and the so-called basic 'differentiators' (*viśeṣa*). A quality is a non-repeatable property-particular, a trope. The specific shade of grey a cloud has at a moment in time is in this sense a quality, something which is different from, and yet belonging to the same general type as, every other shade of grey. The Vaiśeṣika qualities are defined further as properties of substances alone. An immediate corollary (*Vaiśeṣika-sūtra* 2.1.16) is that qualities do not themselves have qualities. The category of quality is not restricted, however, to monadic property-particulars; some qualities, for example contact and disjunction, are *relation*-particulars.

Ancient Vaiśeṣika theory assimilates numbers into the category of qualities. There is, in a given pair of objects, a specific quality of duality. This duality is different from the duality in any other pair, and yet all such dualities belong to the same universal kind of twoness. As *one* is a number, every object possesses a unit-quality, distinct from but of the same kind as every other unit-quality. The theory is based on a reasonable intuition that when several objects are collected together, the number of objects in the collection is a fact about the objects over and above the facts about the individual objects. It is, however, highly problematic, as the authors were themselves well aware. Following the terse discussion in *Vaiśeṣika-sūtra* 7.2.1–6, the difficulty most strongly emphasized is the problem of accounting for our apparent ability to speak of numbers of things other than substances:

> 7.2.1 Because of its difference from colour, taste, smell and touch, oneness is a different [kind of] thing. 7.2.2 Similarly, separateness [is a different kind of thing]. 7.2.3 The absence of oneness and separateness-of-one in oneness and separateness-of-one is explained by minuteness and magnitude. 7.2.4 Oneness is not present in everything, because motions and qualities are devoid of number. 7.2.5 That [application of 'one' to motions and qualities] is an error. 7.2.6 In the absence of oneness, there is no derivative application [of the word 'one' to motions and qualities].
>
> (Thakur 2003: 98–99)

The principal objection rehearsed here is that individual substances each have the numerical quality of being one, and yet, since qualities do not inhere in qualities or motions, individual qualities and individual motions cannot be said to be numerically one. We might call this the 'number of qualities' problem.

The *Vaiśeṣika-sūtra* solution to the problem is disarmingly simple. It consists in denying that it is literally and properly correct to speak of a number of qualities. It would be an error to do so. The explanation for the use of the term 'one' to objects other than substances is that it is a derivative use, a metonymic extension of the term beyond the domain of its proper application. *Vaiśeṣika-sūtra* 7.2.6 is to be understood in this context as pointing out that if the term 'one' were not properly applicable somewhere, i.e. to substances, then it could not be used metonymically either. According to the standard analysis of derivative meaning (*lakṣaṇā*), a term may refer derivatively to objects that are in some way related to the literal reference of the term (see Raja 1963: 231–233; Ganeri 1999b: 91–94). One may say 'The platform is shouting' meaning that the people *on the platform* are shouting. The point of 7.2.6 is then that without a base use of the numeral 'one' to substances, there could be no metonymic application of the term to other categories of thing.

At face value, this attempt to solve the problem has little to recommend it. There is nothing about the use of numerals in statements about quality and motion to distinguish it from the use in application to substances.[3] The expression 'two' has precisely the same meaning in 'There are two pots on the ground' as in 'There are two shades of blue in this painting' or 'There are two movements in that dance-step'. Some writers took the idea to be that such statements are indirect ways of talking about the number of objects. Bearing in mind that qualities are non-repeatable properties of objects, it follows that there are exactly as many shades of blue as there are blue things. We might hope, then, to paraphrase a statement about the number of blue qualities as a statement about the number of blue objects. The idea is that the phrase 'two (shades of) blue' does not attribute a quality (two) to a quality (shade of blue), but attributes both qualities to an objects. It is paraphrased as 'two blue (objects)'. The relation between numbers and qualities is not one of inherence but rather one of 'co-inherence in a single substratum'.

Bhāsarvajña (c. 950 CE) rejects the classical Vaiśeṣika theory that numbers are qualities. His discussion of number is astute and insightful, and contains some important innovations. His theory is that number adjectives do not stand for qualities of substances, but for relations of identity and difference:

> Identity and difference depend on sameness and distinctness in colour and so on, and so are not considered to be qualities. Further, it is a verbal repetition (*paryāya*) to say 'the one is identical' or 'the many are different'.
>
> (1968: 159)

Bhāsarvajña's idea is simplest to see in the case of the predicative use of numerals. The statement '*a* and *b* are one' is, he claims, synonymous with '$a = b$'. To say that Hesperus and Phosphorus are one is just to assert the identity 'Hesperus = Phosphorus'. On the other hand, the statement '*a* and *b* are two' asserts that $a \neq b$. The adjectival use of numerals admits of a similar analysis. Indeed, it is now standard to formalize sentences of the form 'there are n *F*s' in terms of non-identity. The analysis varies, depending on whether we read the sentence as asserting that there are at least n *F*s or as asserting that there are exactly n *F*s. 'There are at least n *F*s' is paraphrased as (see Sainsbury 1991: 160):

[3] The point is made by Udayana 1956: 459.

$$(\exists x_1)(\exists x_2)\ldots(\exists x_n)(Fx_1 \,\&\, Fx_2 \,\&\ldots\&\, Fx_n \,\&\, x_1 \neq x_2 \,\&\, x_2 \neq x_3 \,\&\, x_1 \neq x_3 \,\&\ldots\&\, x_{n-1} \neq x_n).$$

The problem of the 'number of qualities' presents no particular difficulty for this account. For to say that there are two shades of blue in the painting is to assert that the two shades are different from each other. As long as we can refer to and quantify over qualities, the analysis is the same as before. The analysis of statements involving 'one' as identity statements is the source of some unclarity, however. Udayana objects to the account on the grounds that identity is something unique to each thing, but we can say 'one pot' 'one cloth' and so on. Since the identity of the pot is not the same as the identity of the cloth, it cannot be the meaning of the adjective 'one' here (Udayana 1956: 442; cf. Potter 1977: 597). The objection seems to be that if '*a* is one' means '*a* = *a*' then the predicate '. . . is one' means '. . . = *a*' and '*b* is one' then comes to mean '*b* = *a*' rather than '*b* = *b*'. This objection has some force if Bhāsarvajña's claim is that 'one' means identity in the sense of the individuating essence of a thing. But we need not read him this way. It is not after all very clear what we *are* doing when we say that something is one, but Bhāsarvajña's proposal is that we are not attributing a property to the object, but asserting, trivially, that it is identical to itself.

After presenting his radical analysis, Bhāsarvajña goes on to claim for it a much greater degree of generality than possessed by the old account:

> Now the application of twoness to qualities etc. is unproblematic. Moreover, even its use in arithmetic, as when one says 'a hundred and a half a hundred by six hundred' goes through. So it is said that one is the initial integer, two is that [one] together with another identical, three is [those] two together with another identical, four is those [three] together with another identical, and so on. The convention for the grounds for the use of 'twoness' etc., established by the treatises on arithmetic, is explicable [in this way].
>
> (1968: 159)

Bhāsarvajña reveals here a clear awareness that the integers can be defined recursively, and sees his theory as applicable to arithmetic. He says that one is the first whole number, two is one together with another identical, three is two together with another identical, and so on. The Sanskrit term for 'integer' is *abhinna* which means 'undivided' or 'whole' as well as 'identical' and Bhāsarvajña plays on the ambiguity in order to switch from the adjectival to the substantival use of numerals.

Vaiśeṣika thinkers generally assume that there is a maximal finite integer, which they call 'parārdha' (Praśastapāda 1994: §130). *Parārdha* is mentioned in many non-Vaiśeṣika works as the largest available decimal place name,[4] but only the Vaiśeṣika take it to be the highest number. There is no room for the idea of a maximal finite number if one

[4] Its precise value varies: in the *Taittirīya Saṃhitā* (4.40.11.4, 7.2.20.1) and the *Maitrāyaṇī Saṃhitā* (2.8.14), it is given as 10^{12}, while the *Kāṭhaka Saṃhitā* records both 10^{12} (17.10) and 10^{13} (39.6). For the mathematicians it is always 10^{17}. There are names for higher decimal powers in Buddhist and Jaina texts, *Abhidharmakośa* 3.93–94 naming powers up to 10^{59}, for example.

thinks of the number series as generated by recursive application of the successor function, the only Vaiśeṣika author other than Bhāsarvajña to do so being Bhaṭṭa Vādīndra (c. 1225 CE). Vādīndra (1985: 128) explicitly argues that the series of integers is infinite because we can add 1 even to *parārdha* (*'eka-parārdha'*).[5] Within a conception of numbers as qualities of substances, indeed, it seems that there would have to be a largest number if the number of things in the cosmos is finite. Once that theory is abandoned, so is the commitment to finitism.

As later authors are well aware, the 'number of qualities' problem is only a special case of some more general difficulty. For Śaṅkara Miśra, the post-Gaṅgeśa Mithilā thinker who wrote a fresh commentary on the *Vaiśeṣika-sūtra*, the real problem is one of self-inherence. The trouble is with talking about the number of numbers, and it presents the same difficulty as talking about the movement of movements or the qualities of qualities. He therefore explains *Vaiśeṣika-sūtra* 7.2.3 in an original way:

> [Objection:] Since one can say such things as 'oneness is one' or 'separateness is separate from colour and so on', surely oneness is in oneness and separateness is in separateness. Because of this, it is said [7.2.3] that 'the absence of oneness and separateness-of-one in oneness and separateness-of-one is explained by minuteness and magnitude'. [The meaning is that] just as minuteness and magnitude do not possess minuteness and magnitude, the application of which [characteristics] to them is derivative, so oneness and separateness do not possess oneness and separateness, the application of which to them is derivative. Two later *sūtras*, viz. 'by motions, motions' [7.2.24], and 'by qualities, qualities' [7.2.25] exhibit the same derivative meaning as this earlier one. The meaning is that just as motions do not possess motions and qualities do not possess qualities, so too oneness and separateness do not possess that [oneness and separateness].
>
> (1923: 174)

Śaṅkara Miśra's argument is that because nothing can inhere in itself, apparently acceptable talk of self-inherence must be non-literally construed. In particular, when we say that there is *one* number one, we are not really saying that the number one inheres in itself, any more than when we say that minuteness is minute, we are saying that minuteness inheres in itself. The point does not apply to numbers other than one, since we would not say that there are two number twos, even if we want to say that there is one number one. So for Śaṅkara Miśra, the non-literal use of numerals is restricted solely to the use of 'one' to itself.

Śaṅkara Miśra is right to be worried about the idea of self-inherence. It is a straightforward matter to modify Russell's Paradox and show that the property of *non*-self-inherence is incoherent. For let R be the property of being a non-self-inherent property. Is R self-inherent or not? If it is self-inherent, then (by the definition of R) it is a non-self-inherent property—which is a contradiction. If it is not self-inherent, then (by the definition of R) it is not a non-self-inherent property—again

[5] Thakur 2003: 135 suggests that Vādīndra is the last pre-Navya, that he 'draws a line of distinction between the ancient and modern Vaiśeṣikas.' It is indeed informative to compare his commentary on the *Vaiśeṣika-sūtra*, the *Nibandha*, with that of Śaṃkara Miśra, one of the first of the Navya thinkers.

contradictory. Russell's solution in his Theory of Types was to block the paradox by ruling as insignificant the application of a property to itself, so that the incoherent property cannot be formulated (cf. Sainsbury 1979: 315, 1995: 111). It is a little surprising that none of the Nyāya-Vaiśeṣika authors discovered the paradox. There is, however, some hint of it in Gaṅgeśa's account of 'non-pervasive' location (see Matilal 1975: 455–457). And, as I noted in the last chapter, Bhartṛhari hit upon a paradox of a rather similar type when he argued that the naming relation is unnameable, on the grounds that no relation can have itself as a relatum.

Indefinite pluralities

An interesting and revealing discussion arises with respect to the meaning of sentences like 'There are many trees in the forest' or 'The army is composed of many soldiers'. In such statements, the adjective 'many' has, formally, a role quite like a numerical adjective. Śrīdhara is said indeed to argue that 'many' is itself a number, distinct from any number in the cardinal series. As Śaṅkara Miśra reports him:

> Since in the case of a forest or an army, there is no definite combinatory cognition [i.e. counting up of the number of trees or men], a mere manyness comes into being, but not the number a hundred or a thousand—this is the view of the teacher Śrīdhara.[6]

If numbers are created by mental acts of counting, then the uncounted army or forest has no definite number of men or trees. The perceiver merely surveys the entirety, and judges 'there are many men' or 'there are many trees'. Śrīdhara's view, it seems, is that in such a case an 'indefinite' act produces in the objects the 'indefinite' number, many. That Śrīdhara is forced into such a move indicates the presence of a deep fault-line in the Vaiśeṣika theory. The problem arises whenever one has a clearly delineated but uncounted collection of objects. The collection might, as in these cases, be a perceptible aggregate, or it might be picked out under a description, for instance 'planets in the solar system'. There seems in such cases to be an inconsistency between the common-sense intuition that the collection has some definite if unknown number, and the Vaiśeṣika thesis that number is the result of a mental act of counting up the objects in the collection. Clearly, realism about numbers is at issue.

Udayana ridicules Śrīdhara's attempt to solve the puzzle by substituting a definite if unknown number with the known but indefinite number 'many'. He says:

> Perhaps twoness is produced by a pure combinative cognition, threeness by a [combinative] cognition of a oneness with a twoness, fourness by a [combinative] cognition of a oneness with a

[6] 1923: 179. All Śrīdhara actually seems to say on the matter is this: 'If it is said that there is no number apart from substances, because a difference is not grasped, then that is not right. For when a close arrangement of trees is seen from a distance, even though oneness etc. is not grasped, one can still grasp their nature. Thus too is explained the difference [of number] from colour etc. Although from a distance the colour is not grasped, there is still an awareness of the substance [=the forest?].' (1977: 270).

threeness, etc. How about the army and the forest? It might be thought that there is here no [combinative] cognition of a oneness with some definite number, and moreover that no definite number such as a thousand comes into being. But still a mere 'manyness' comes into being without a specific universal [numerical property] from a combinative cognition, because it can have as its foundation an indefinite [number of] onenesses.

This [theory of Śrīdhara] is false. One could not then have a doubt [about the number of things] without there being a specific number of [things qualified by] pothood or [things] delicately distinguished, nor could there be such statements as 'the large army is larger' at the time of becoming aware of the addition of another group of men.

(1956: 458)

Śaṅkara Miśra summarizes Udayana's argument in the following way: 'No doubt could arise as to whether [the army] has a hundred or a thousand parts, nor could one judge "the large army is larger"; so this is not right—this is the view of the teacher Udayana' (1923: 179). Udayana insists on the validity of common-sense: a doubt about the number of men in the army can arise only if one thinks of it as having a definite but unknown number. Still more devastating is his objection that if *many* is a number, we could not compare one group of many with another, or judge one group to be larger than another—for both would have the same number, *many*.

There is, however, a way to make sense of the idea of a definite but unknown number, if we clearly distinguish between the ontogenesis of numbers and their epistemology. In a normal case, the mental act of counting which produces the number will also manifest that number to the cognizer. That is to say, the means by which one comes to know how many objects there are will be precisely that act of counting them which produces the number in them. This need not always be the case. It is conceivable that some definite number can be produced in the objects by an indefinite mental act of counting, an act which will not itself supply the cognizer with any knowledge of the number of things. A definite or precise mental act of counting is both the cause and the 'manifestor' of the number. An indefinite or imprecise mental counting is the cause but not the manifestor of a number (Udayana 1956: 459). There is room in the theory for a gap between the creation and the discovery of numbers.

The meaning of the term 'many' presents another puzzle. Nyāya-Vaiśeṣika semantic theory is by and large realist or referential: the meaning of a word is the object for which it stands (see Ganeri 1999b: 82–107). The word 'many' cannot however stand for the actual number in the army (a thousand, say), for the sentence 'there are many men in the army' does not mean that there are a thousand men in the army. So 'many' must apparently denote, as Uddyotakara clearly states, the distinct number manyness:

What does the phrase 'large army' mean? The phrase 'large army' designates those very elephants etc. which are the abode of number, when increasing with the addition of new groups. So when the elephants etc. are described as 'large' the word 'large' denotes the number manyness which is the cause of the increase.

(Viśvanātha 1985: 211)

Śaṅkara Miśra grapples with the same problem:

Is manyness nothing but number [beginning with] three and ending at *parārdha*, or a number different from them? Not the first, since even in the case of an army and a forest, there must be a definite number such as a hundred or a thousand. Nor the second, since a manyness distinguished from three etc. is never observed. So [Udayana says that] manyness is indeed a number such as a hundred, produced by a combinative cognition which does not have as its foundation a definite [number of] units; but [the number] a hundred is not revealed there because its manifestor is absent.

We, on the other hand, say that manyness is indeed a number different from but colocated with three etc., and produced by the combinative cognition that produces the threeness etc. It is different, because there is a difference in prior absence. How else could one say 'There are many, but I do not know if there are precisely a hundred or a thousand'? If asked the question 'Shall I bring a hundred or a thousand mangoes?' one replies 'Bring some large amount – why do you want to know the exact number?' Three is due to a combinative cognition [of one] with two; four is due to a combinative cognition [of one] with three; and so on higher and higher and higher. When manyness arises without a combinative cognition, it does not depend on specific earlier numbers. In the case of the army or the forest, manyness alone comes into being and not any other number. So the above dilemma has false horns.

(1923: 180)

Śaṅkara Miśra's point is that what 'many' denotes is neither a particular number in the cardinal series, nor the series in totality, but rather a property that co-exists with the definite number the objects possess. It is, perhaps, the property of being large in number. 'Many' is in fact a vague predicate, and it is easy to see how a version of the Sorites paradox can arise. For if there are many men in the army, and one is taken away, there are still many men in the army. Repeating the process, however, one would eventually reach the situation where there are just two men in the army, and two is not many. Uddyotakara does indeed link 'many' with processes of increase, but none of the philosophers formulate the Sorites paradox in this form.

In the discussion of the semantics of 'many', the philosophers explore the limits of the attempt to treat numerals as predicates, or names of properties. The discovery of the problems involved with indefinite pluralities is, for these thinkers, a bit like the discovery of the irrationality of the square root of 2 for the ancient Greeks. Frege's (1950) remarkable insight was that numerals are not predicates but quantifier expressions. Statements like 'There are seven *F*s' really belong in the same semantic category as 'There are no *F*s' and 'There are some *F*s'. If '$/F/$' stands for the cardinality of the extension of 'F' then the semantics for such sentences follow a uniform pattern:

'There are no *F*s' is true iff $/F/ = 0$.
'There are some *F*s' is true iff $/F/ > 0$.
'There are at least seven *F*s' is true iff $/F/ \geq 7$.
'There are exactly seven *F*s' is true iff $/F/ = 7$.

When the numerals are recognized to be quantifier expressions, 'many' no longer causes any special difficulty:

'There are many *F*s' is true iff $/F/ \geq n$.
'There are more *F*s than *G*s' is true iff $/F/ > /G/$.

The early modern philosophers do offer this binary quantifier type of analysis, if not for 'many' (*bahu*), then at least for the particle 'only' (*eva*). According to the 'new reason' thinkers, 'only' is an expression with the following semantics:

'Only *F*s are *G*' is true iff $G \subseteq F$ & $F \wedge G$.
'*F*s are only G' is true iff $F \subseteq G$ & $F \wedge G$.

In offering this univocal semantics, as I will show in greater detail in Chapter 16, they disagree with the earlier analysis of the Buddhist philosopher Dharmakīrti, who claimed that 'only' has several distinct semantic roles. In the seventeenth century, furthermore, Gadādhara gives a quantificational semantics for the word 'one' (*eka*). He is discussing the adjectival use of the term, and he states that the meaning of 'one *F*' is an *F* as qualified by being-single, where 'being single' means 'not being the counter-positive of a difference resident in something of the same kind' (Gadādhara 1929: 189). Translating out of the technical language, according to a method I will describe in Chapter 15, 'one *F*' is to be analysed as saying of something which is *F* that no *F* is different to it. This is paraphrasable in the predicate calculus as '$Fx \& \neg (\exists y)(Fy \& y \neq x)$', and it is formally equivalent to the Russellian uniqueness clause '$Fx \& (\forall y)(Fy \rightarrow y = x)$'. In other words, Gadādhara's semantics for 'one' is

'There is one *F*' is true iff $/F/ = 1$.

It is clear that Gadādhara's analysis of 'one' is very similar to Russell's theory of the definite article.

Raghunātha's non-reductive realism

Raghunātha Śiromaṇi, in a decisive break from the ancient tradition, declares in the *Inquiry* that numbers constitute a new category altogether:

Number is a separate category, not a quality, for we make the judgment that there is possession of number in qualities, etc. And this judgment is not an erroneous one, for there is no other judgement which contradicts it. If you argue that judgments of this kind occur when there is inherence of two qualifiers in one individual, I say no, for inherence and inherence-of-two-qualifiers-in-one-substratum are two different relations, from which one cannot derive the homogenous idea of possession.

(*Inquiry* 1915: 75.1–5. Potter's translation, slightly altered)

Raghunātha's thesis is that the *is-the-number-of* relation is not reducible to the relation of inherence or any relation constructed out of it. The fact that each quality is unique to the object in which it inheres means that there is a one-to-one correspondence between objects and qualities. So we might hope to paraphrase talk of the number of qualities with talk of the number of objects. But this will not solve the cross-categorial problem because we can also count universals:

Just as the judgement of oneness in potness, etc., is to be explained by the opponent through inherence-of-two-qualifiers-in-one-substratum, so there ought to be a judgment of twoness in colourhood, etc., explainable through inherence-of-two-qualifiers-in-one-substratum, and that is not possible.

(*Inquiry* 1915: 75.6–8.)

The point is that while ordinary properties inhere in each of their loci, numbers do not. As Matilal puts it:

If, for example, duality inheres (i.e. resides by inherence) in two things counted as two then it must inhere also in either of them separately, and hence we must tolerate the oddity of saying that, of a pair, say the sky and the earth, the sky has duality.

(Matilal 2002, vol. 1: 133)

To put it another way, we cannot infer from 'The table's legs are four' to 'Each of the table's legs is four', although we can infer from 'The table's legs are wooden' to 'Each of the table's legs is wooden'. The crudest form of the adjectival theory, in which numbers are entirely analogous to other attributes, offers no explanation of the inadmissibility of such inferences, and hence, considered as a proposal about the logical form of number statements, must be mistaken.

Raghunātha's second contribution lies in his further account of the relation between numbers and things numbered and its distinction from the inherence relation. The further account occurs in the course of a note on the concept of 'limitor', the *Explanation of Limitorship* (Raghunātha 1977), which he inserts into his commentary on the *Gemstone*. He observes that while inherence is a distributive relation, the number-of relation has to be collective. The distinction occurs in the context of sentences with plural subjects. An attributive relation is distributive if it relates the attribute to every subject: if *the trees* are old, then each individual tree is old. A relation is collective if it relates the attribute to the subjects collectively but not individually. Thus, 'The trees constitute a forest' does not imply that each tree constitutes a forest. Number attributions are collective. If one says that there are two pots here, one does not imply that each pot is two. Inherence, however, is a distributive relation, and so cannot be the relation of attribution for numbers. Raghunātha therefore posits a new relation, which he calls the 'collecting' (*paryāpti*) relation:

The 'collecting' relation, whose existence is indicated by constructions such as 'This is one pot' and 'These are two', is a special kind of self-linking relation.[7]

Jagadīśa provides an explanation:

It might be thought that the 'collecting' relation is [in fact] nothing but inherence . . . So [Raghunātha] states that 'collecting' [is a special kind of self-linking relation] . . . In a sentence

[7] paryāptiś ca ayam eko ghaṭaḥ imau dvau iti pratītisākṣakaḥ svārūpasaṃbandhaviśeṣa eva | (Raghunātha 1977: 38).

like 'This is one pot', 'collecting' relates the property pot-hood by delimiting it as a property which resides in only one pot, but in a sentence like 'These are two pots', the 'collecting' relation relates the property two-hood by delimiting it as a property which resides in both pots. Otherwise, it would follow that there is no difference between saying 'These are two' and 'Each one possesses two-hood'.[8]

We may note here that in contemporary discussions of number, the theory that numbers are properties of objects is considered refuted by the simple observation that, in a statement like 'There are two people in the room', no one person is said to be two (Sainsbury 1991: 159). Raghunātha's new idea is that 'collecting' is a one-to-many relation which obtains between numbers on the one hand and objects on the other. It relates numbers to pluralities of objects, but not to objects taken individually. Suppose we let '**I**' stand for inherence, and '**C**' for the collecting relation. Inherence shares the formal properties of the class-membership or class-inclusion relations. So the analysis of a sentence like 'Venus and Mars are planets' would be:

I (planet-hood, Venus) & **I** (planet-hood, Mars),

which says that Venus is a planet and so is Mars. From this it trivially follows that each of Venus and Mars is a planet. Similarly, the sentence 'The table's legs are wooden' says the class comprising the legs of the table is a subset of the class of wooden things, and from this it follows that each of the legs of the table is wooden. Introducing a new logical relation of 'collecting' enables Raghunātha to analyse a sentence like 'Venus and Mars are two' in a new way. Its logical form is now:

C (2; Venus, Mars),

which, by hypothesis, does not entail that the number 2 resides in each planet individually. Similarly, 'The table has four legs' asserts that the number 4 is related by the 'collecting' relation with the four table legs. In effect, what Raghunātha claims here is that there is an ambiguity in the 'are' of predication for sentences with plural subjects. As well as standing for the class-inclusion relation, it can also stand for a relation which relates a property jointly with a multiplicity of objects.

Raghunātha's motive is to account for the distinction between collective and distributive properties. For the recognition that the inference from 'These are two pots' to 'Each pot is two' is invalid is just the recognition that the predicate 'two' does not distribute over plural subjects. The new idea is to analyse collective predicates, not as one-place predicates of aggregates or sets, but as n-place relational predicates, true of n objects jointly. Since such relational predicates still take objects as subjects, this indeed shows that recognizing the distinction between distributive and collective predicates does not force us to abandon the adjectival view. Later philosophers systematize the

[8] nanu paryāptiḥ samavāyaḥ. . . . paryāptiś ceti | ayam eko ghaṭa iti eka-mātra-vṛtti-dharmāvacchedena ghaṭatvasya paryāptiṃ darśayitum, imau dvau ity ubhaya-mātra-vṛtti-dharmāvacchedena dvitvasya paryāptiṃ darśayitum, anyathā dvau dvitvavān iti pratītyor aviśeṣaprasaṅgād iti bhāvaḥ | (Jagadīśa 1977: 38–39).

idea by introducing a term for collective properties: they call them *vyāsajya-vṛtti-dharma* or properties 'which occur jointly' (*Nyāyakośa* 1928: 778).

If it were the case that collective relations have to be analysed as relations to classes, and not to the members of classes, then Raghunātha's idea would come to resemble Frege's analysis of numbers as properties or classes of classes (cf. Ingalls 1951: 77; Shaw 1982). This is, however, premature, for we are not forced to analyse collective relations as relations to classes. Indeed, the idea that numbers relate to objects collectively is quite consistent with Bhāsarvajña's idea that number statements are statements of the mutual distinctness of a plurality. John Bigelow, whose account of number is among the nearest in the recent literature to that of Raghunātha, notes that since 'The planets are (at least) three' is 'logically equivalent' to '$(\exists x)(\exists y)(\exists z)$[Planet($x$) & Planet($y$) & Planet($z$) & $x \neq y$ & $y \neq z$ & $z \neq x$]', numbers are, in his phrase, 'n-fold relations of mutual distinctness' (Bigelow 1988: 121). The significance of Raghunātha's innovation is that the domain of numbers is seen now to relate to the world of objects in a way very different from that of the domain of universals and qualities. Numbers thereby acquire a distinct ontological status, although there is no reason to suppose that he takes them to be Platonic objects. Most recently, Antonelli has developed a nonreductionist accout in which numbers 'are abstract entities introduced for the purpose of counting' (2010: 191).

One of Frege's strongest arguments against the adjectival theory is that true statements involving the word 'zero' cannot be accommodated by the adjectival hypothesis, since there is nothing for zero, conceived of as a property, to be attributed to:

> If I say 'Venus has no moons', there simply does not exist any moon or agglomeration of moons for anything to be asserted of; but what happens is that a property is assigned to the concept 'moon of Venus', namely that of including nothing under it.
>
> (1950: §46)

This argument has considerable force when directed against the aggregate theory of Mill and Husserl, for there is no such thing as an aggregate of no things. David Bell, in his study of Husserl, acknowledges this, but thinks that there is a reply. Since 'There are zero moons of Venus' means the same as 'There does not exist any moon of Venus', we might regard the word 'zero', not as a name at all, but as standing for the negation particle (Bell 1990: 69–70).

I am aware of no 'new reason' text in which the problem of zero is discussed. Yet if the reconstruction of the theory I have offered is correct, it is clear what could have been said. If the number n is an n-place relation, then the number zero is a zero-place relation, or, in other words, a complete sentence. But note that a sentence like 'Venus has zero moons' can be read as equivalent to 'If there is a moon of Venus, then $\wedge$' (where '$\wedge$' is the absurdity symbol, standing for any self-contradiction), because 'if p, then $\wedge$' is logically equivalent to 'not p'. So by taking the term 'zero' to stand for $\wedge$, we can recover that equivalence of zero-sentences and negative existentials which Bell exploits. Zero, then, is a no-place relation which can never obtain.[9] The advantage of this over the Bell–Husserl theory is that it retains a univocal account of all number-sentences: the word 'zero', as with all other number-adjectives, is analysed as standing for a relation.[10] Frege presents several other arguments against the adjectival theory, which Raghunātha's version of that theory is equally able to answer (see Ganeri 1996).

Conclusion

It should be evident that Raghunātha's contribution is one of philosophical substance, and not merely of expressive style. Sheldon Pollock says that

> In the eyes of many seventeenth-century writers, Raghunātha represents the new scholar par excellence, and his metalinguistic innovations in the search of ever greater precision and sophistication of definition and analysis were enormously influential. These innovations sometimes produced—as readers of say, Heidegger would appreciate—the opposite of the intended result: Raghunātha's style makes his work undoubtedly the most challenging to read in the whole of Indian philosophy.
>
> (2001b: 12)

Behind the apparent praise there is here an ever-so slight insinuation that Raghunātha's cleverness consists in a certain obfuscation. Pollock describes Raghunātha's contribution as a 'transformation in discursive style'. What I hope that our case study has established is that such a judgement does not engage with the real philosophical content of Raghunātha's thought, an originality of content that in turn led him to invent new modalities of articulation. Nor is it correct to describe his style as 'the most challenging to read in the whole of Indian philosophy'—it is difficult, laconic, and technical, but no more so than work in any specialist field of inquiry. I detect in Pollock's assessment the unfortunate influence of Frauwallner, who said of Raghunātha that

> Not only does he strive for brevity but he takes pleasure in contrived and artificial obscurity. He does not speak clearly but gives hints, so that different interpretations are possible. Often important links in the train of thought are left out and the reader has to guess the omissions. It is also characteristic that he avoids saying openly what his own view is. That is why his work is unusually difficult to read. But this obscurity which pretends to be depth of thought, may have contributed, not in a small way, to the reputation which his work enjoyed subsequently.
>
> (Frauwallner 1994a: 55)

[9] My proposal that $0 = \Lambda$ might appeal to those who see a connection between the Mādhyamika theory of emptiness (Sanskrit: *śunyatā*) and the mathematical notion of zero (Sanskrit: *śunya*).

[10] It is now true, of course, that zero-sentences are conditionals while all other number-sentences are relational predications, but this is not unusual: the standard reparsing of 'Some men are mortal' and 'All men are mortal' treats the first as conjunctive and the second as conditional.

Frauwallner is clearly quite unable to appreciate Raghunātha's work in appropriate terms, and his criticism is reminiscent of those critics of Wittgenstein who berate his unsystematic style and likewise make unwarranted and *ad hominem* accusations of intellectual dishonesty. The publication in 1968 of Matilal's annotated translation and analytical study of Raghunātha's *Treatise on Negation* decisively undermined Frauwallner's view.[11]

Raghunātha's solution to the problem of number is symptomatic of his larger willingness to introduce new categories into metaphysics, that is to say, to be a non-reductive realist about new types of entity. This is the foundational principle on which he builds a wholly refashioned ontology, one which does not dismiss the ancient theory completely, but draws certain strands from within it in the construction of something new. He writes the *Inquiry* as an act of provocation, and what he wanted to provoke his readers into doing was to examine the facts themselves—in this case the facts about the logical form of number statements—and to begin to develop solutions based on those facts, rather than defensive exegesis of the ancient texts. The illocutionary force of the *Inquiry*, its 'intervention', consists in a call for a reorientation of gaze, away from the texts and onto the facts themselves. If you don't like the idea of treating number relations as a new type of entity, he seems to be saying, then show me how to do better and still be true to the facts about the logical form of number statements. This is typical of the challenge Raghunātha's work had. It is also typical that we have had to collect together his comments from various texts, in contexts not clearly marked as having to do with the subject in hand. This left his followers, and his critics, with plenty of work to do.

[11] See also Stuchlik 2009. I should add that, although I have not been able to agree with the claims Pollock made in his 2001 publications about Raghunātha and the 'new reason,' he has since then done more than anyone to demonstrate the importance of the early modern period particularly through his later project on Sanskrit knowledge systems on the eve of colonialism, the results of which themselves considerably complicate his earlier story.

14

Metaphysics in a Different Key

Raghunātha's challenge

A seven-category ontology came to be established as standard only in the work of Śivāditya (c. 1100 CE), incorporating the six categories of 'being' (*bhāva*) affirmed by Praśastapāda along with a metaphysically distinct category of 'non-being' (*abhāva*). This establishment can be seen as the stabilization of various revisionary currents, some pressing in the direction of expansion, others for contraction. The only work of classical Vaiśeṣika to have entered the Chinese tripiṭaka is a text arguing for ten categories, the standard six together with non-being, power, impotence, and 'particular universal' (*sāmānya-viśeṣa*).[1] Bhāsarvajña (c. 860–920 CE), on the other hand, argues for an amalgamation of the categories of motion and quality, as well as for systematization within the category of quality. Though certainly indicative of the existence of dynamic internal criticism, neither of these works achieved a significant position within the mainstream of discussion. The work which did was Raghunātha's *Inquiry*. In this work Raghunātha affirms eight new categories: legal ownership (*svatva*), intentionality (*viṣayatā*), number (*saṃkhyā*), the qualifying relation pertaining to absence (*vaiśiṣṭya*), power (*śakti*), being-a-cause (*kāraṇatva*), being-an-effect (*kāryatva*), and temporal moment (*kṣaṇa*). At the same time, he dismisses the ancient category of distinguisher and takes motion into a sort of quality. The list is open, and elsewhere other new categories, such as locushood (*ādhāratā*), are entertained. Raghunātha's decision to abandon the idea that there is a fixed list of categories can be read as a robust commitment to the idea that the phenomenon under study itself determines what types of thing there are, not the authority of any canonical text.

I examined Raghunātha's theory of number at length in the last chapter, as an exemplary illustration of the significance and motivation of his non-reductive realism. The new categories, most of which are like numbers in being relational, fall into three broad groups. One group has to do with the nature of time and causation, Raghunātha rejecting the old view that causation is reducible to a relationship of invariable temporal succession between things of the same type.[2] A second group includes new relations

[1] Candramati's *Treatise on the Ten Categories* (*Daśapadārthaśāstra*) was translated into Chinese by Yuan Chwang in 648 CE. See Ui 1917; Thakur 2003: 169–170.

[2] *Nyāyakośa* 1928: 197–199; Mohanty 2006: 44; Matilal 1985: 284–293.

invoked by the philosophical study of quantity and negation, specifically the relations which sustain the logics of absence and enumeration. Finally, there are the relations of mental content and of legal possession, which Raghunātha again claims have their own categorial standing. From a modern perspective, it is striking that the new categories are all related to normative properties or laws of nature. Raghunātha, we would now say, has insisted that there are several distinct types of normative relation, none of which is reducible to any of the others or to any non-normative type, and also that the laws of nature do not admit of Humean reduction. The normative relations he acknowledges are those belonging to logical form, mental representation, and legal rights. He does not, however, speak here about moral or aesthetic norms.

Raghunātha's fundamental criticism of the orthodoxy might therefore be said to consist in the thought that Praśastapāda's view of the world is myopic and flat, seeing only a mechanistic space of objects, compounded from atoms, bearing qualities of various sorts, and moving about in various ways. The inclusion into this picture of human inquirers has them fall under an identical descriptive model, located in space and time, displaying a range of qualities, many of which overlap with those of ordinary physical objects. That might seem like an attractively naturalistic picture, and later 'new reason' thinkers are keen to preserve the naturalism, but I have already given reasons why the very flatness of the model produces serious fault lines within it. What it fails to see, according to Raghunātha, are the irreducibly normative structures introduced by the presence of thinking beings who represent and reason about the world they inhabit, and have duties and rights with respect to each other.[3] To say that we therefore need new categories is just a way of claiming that the old model cannot accommodate this fact; and I have suggested that the point of doing so is to throw down a challenge to his contemporaries to show how, if at all, a naturalistic reduction is to be achieved.

Naturalism and reductionism in the *Essence of Reason*

Metaphysicians of the sixteenth and seventeenth centuries, mostly Vārāṇasī-based, take up Raghunātha's challenge. We find a reaffirmation of the seven-category ontology in several of the most important metaphysical works of the time, especially Jayarāma's *Garland of Categories*, Mādhavadeva's *Essence of Reason*, and Raghudeva's *Survey of What is Essential about Substance.* Jayarāma's pupil Laugākṣī tells us explicitly that Jayarāma's intention is to demonstrate that there are indeed exactly seven categories and to refute the claim that power and the others are additional.[4] Mādhavadeva begins the *Essence of Reason*, a work that seems to be a sort of advanced textbook in the new epistemology and metaphysics, with a reaffirmation of the seven-category ontology:

[3] The question about whether there are irreducibly normative properties continues to be a live issue of debate. Many agree with Raghunātha that there are; for example, Moore 1903, Dancy 1993, Scanlon 1998, Shafer-Landau 2003.

[4] śaktyādīnām atiriktatva-nirāsena padārthāḥ saptaiva iti vyavasthāpya ... | (Laugākṣī 1985: 181, 10–11).

The categories are seven only, and they fall into two types, being and non-being. Among them [the types of] being are six, due to the division into substance, quality, motion, universal, differentiator and inherence. Non-being is of two types, due to the division into relational absence and non-identity.

(1903–4: 3)

The plan of the book is dictated by a desire to show that the doctrine of ways of gaining knowledge (*pramāṇa*) can be incorporated within the seven-category ontology. The simple expedient by which this is done is to insert a discussion of epistemology within the category of quality, because formally mental states are qualities of the self, and among mental states, some are truth-evaluable (*buddhi*) and others not; thus, a way of gaining knowledge is the instrumental cause of a true mental quality. Mādhavadeva discusses the categories of substance and quality first (5–101), then the various qualities of mind (102–116), before devoting the rest of the book to the three principal Nyāya sources of true mental states, perception (117–131), inference (132–162), and language (163–241). He concludes by restating his basic thesis, that 'there are only seven categories, since the categories called universal, differentiator, inherence and non-being are as described' (241). There is a very brief discussion of the particle 'only' (241), and a short discussion of the claim that being-owned (*svatva*) is another category (242–246). The book concludes:

Since the [*Nyāya-sūtra* list] beginning with the ways of gaining knowledge, the things known and so on are indeed included (*antarbhāva*) here, and since the distinctness (*atiriktatva*) of [the new categories] power, similarity and so on has been refuted, the categories are just seven.

(1903–4: 246)

This summarizes the key ambition of seventeenth-century metaphysics in Vārāṇasī. The *Essence* is, nevertheless, curious in that a discussion of the metaphysical claim with which the book begins and ends constitutes a rather small proportion of the total text, the much greater bulk of which is a discussion of the sources of knowledge, of perception, reason, and language. One might note that properly analysing the logical form of 'The categories are only seven' draws upon the full resources of the 'new reason' containing as it does both a number adjective and the domain-restricting particle 'only'. One needs all the theoretical apparatus I have assembled in Chapters 13, 15, and 16 of this book to give a proper analysis of that simple yet fundamental declaration!

A work which shares this same structural arrangement is Annambhaṭṭa's *Survey of [what can be known through] Reason* (*Tarka–saṃgraha*). Annambhaṭṭa rather curiously glosses the word 'tarka' in the title as signifying the seven categories: 'The seven categories, namely substance and so on, are *tarka* in the sense that they are reasoned about, deliberated on'.[5] He too then argues for a reduction of the sixteen categories of the *Nyāya-sūtra* to the seven categories of classical Vaiśeṣika:

[5] tarkyante pratipādyanta iti tarkā dravyādisaptapadārthāḥ (Annambhaṭṭa 1918: 2, 5–6).

Since everything is included under one or another of the above-mentioned categories, it is proven that the categories are seven precisely. 'Given that *Nyāya-sūtra* 1.1.1 speaks of sixteen categories, how can you say that there are just seven?' It is said in reply: 'Since everything...', meaning that everything is included in the seven.[6]

He goes on to provide reductive definitions of the sixteen Nyāya categories. For example, a principle (*siddhānta*) is 'a thing accepted by epistemologists', a firm belief (*nirṇaya*) is 'a decision, the result of a way of gaining knowledge', and good public reason (*vāda*) is 'a discussion among those who desire to know the truth'. As the commentator Nṛsiṃha explains, the purpose of these definitions is to show that principles are included in the categories, for each is a 'thing' of a certain sort, namely something which has been accepted by epistemologists, while firm belief and public reason are shown to be included in the category of quality, the first as a cognition, being a quality of the self, the second as a piece of speech and therefore a quality of *ākāśa*, the substratum of all sounds. The strategy of incorporation is set out most fully in Dinakara's seventeenth-century commentary on the *Pearl-necklace of Principles about Reason,* a text which also contains a reaffirmation of the seven-category ontology and an indication that what is at state is the question of the compatibility between Nyāya and Vaiśeṣika.[7] Dinakara says:

What is meant here is that the categories are exactly seven, namely substance, quality, motion, universal, differentiator, inherence and non-being, for the sixteen [of the *Nyāya-sūtra*] are included in this list.

(in Kṛṣṇadāsa 1923: 50–51).

Dinakara goes on systematically to set out a mapping of the sixteen onto the seven. He mainly agrees with Annambhaṭṭa, clarifying however that a way of gaining knowledge is a substance, because it is something like a sensory faculty (*pramāṇasyendriyādeḥ dravye*).

I take this whole manoeuvre to be a very elliptical and compressed assertion of the naturalism about epistemology that I discussed in an earlier chapter. Given that many of the Nyāya topics have to do with either epistemology or the logic of reasoning, the problem of their assimilation to the seven metaphysical categories is just another instance of the more general problem about the normative. What we see here are attempts to construct texts the very architecture of which affirms such an 'inclusion'. As illocutionary interventions in the early modern discourse about metaphysics, they constitute acts of consolidation in a reductivist agenda. What I find interesting about this response to Raghunātha is not so much the defence itself of the seven-category metaphysics as the new engagement with the deeper philosophical problem concerning just what it means to assert or deny that entities of some type belong to a

[6] sarveṣāṃ padārthānāṃ yathāyatham ukteṣv antarbhāvāt saptaiva padārthā iti siddham | | nanu [1.1.1] iti nyāyaśāstre ṣoḍaśapadārthānām uktatvāt kathaṃ saptaivety ata āha—sarveṣām iti | sarveṣāṃ saptasvevāntarbhāva ityarthaḥ (1918: 64, 3–9).

[7] ete ca padārthāḥ vaiśeṣika-naye prasiddhāḥ naiyāyikānām apy aviruddhāḥ | (Kṛṣṇadāsa 1923: 50).

new category of existence. These thinkers fully appreciate the need to acknowledge the reality of laws of nature and norms of thought and conduct, but deny that they constitute additional categories. Early modern metaphysics in Vārāṇasī is an attempt to develop what I earlier called a 'sophisticated realism' or 'cautious reductionism' about the entities in question.[8] It is therefore by no means merely a retrenchment into the traditional view. In the well-known terminology of John McDowell, the move, in response to Raghunātha's challenge, is a new affirmation of a relaxed naturalism. McDowell's most recent explanation of how the concept is to be understood is particularly helpful:

> [T]he point of the labels is captured by this thought: by dint of exploiting, in an utterly intuitive way, ideas like that of the patterns characteristic of the life of animals of a certain kind, we can insist that such phenomena, even though they are beyond the reach of natural-scientific understanding, are perfectly real, without thereby relegating them to the sphere of the occult or supernatural. We can accept that a distinctively human life is characterized by a freedom that exempts its distinctive phenomena from natural-scientific intelligibility, without thereby being required to push it back into the region of darkness, the region supposedly occupied by phenomena that resist the light cast by natural science because they are occult or supernatural . . . What 'natural' means, as the root of 'naturalism' in, say, 'relaxed naturalism' as I use that phrase, is: not supernatural (not occult, not magical, . . .).
>
> (2008: 217–218)

The force of Raghunātha's challenge is to call for an account of just how to achieve an acknowledgement of the reality of features of human life which Praśastapāda's model seems ill-equipped to accommodate without abandoning naturalism as that model conceives of it (a unified explanation of all objects of inquiry including inquirers). It will come as no surprise if what we find is that the reduction of Raghunātha's new categories to the traditional seven turns out to involve a considerable liberalization and relaxation of the terms of reference of the original framework. To that extent, there is certainly a resemblance between the programmes of the new Vārāṇasī metaphysicians and the progressive neo-Aristotelians of early modern Europe. McDowell himself, who vociferously calls for a re-introduction of scholastic Aristotelian ideas about 'natural powers' and 'modes of being', might even be counted as among them (see McDowell 1996).

The overall contours of this movement tend to be obscured by several factors. One is that these same philosophers also wrote commentaries on Raghunātha's *Inquiry*, and that might give the impression that they endorse his revisionary ontology. The fact that an author writes such a commentary cannot be taken as definitive evidence of his or her personal endorsement of the views expressed in the commented upon text, although it is evidence that the work is important in setting the philosophical agenda. If the

[8] Among contemporary writers, Jackson 1998 argues influentially that there are normative properties but that they are reducible. For further defence of Jackson's reductive realism, see Streumer 2008.

commentary is of the expository kind, aimed at explaining and clarifying the text, perhaps for a student audience, it cannot be used as evidence of the commentator's own views—the 'illocutionary intervention' is not to state one's own view but to explain those of the original author. The name of a commentary can itself signal this intention, if it is a *ṭīkā* or a *vyākhyā,* for example (see Chapter 8). Indeed, there are cases of a single individual writing commentaries on two different texts and apparently arguing in favour of diametrically opposite views in each of them, as Udayana does in defending the Nyāya claim that testimony is a way of gaining knowledge in his Nyāya commentaries but the Vaiśeṣika doctrine that it is not in the *Row of Lightbeams.* In fact, however, we will find later thinkers offering revisionary readings of Raghunātha even in their commentaries on the *Inquiry*; I will give an example below.

A second reason for obscurity is that the category of quality in the traditional system is a sort of catch-all, and contains within it a great array of disparate elements. The fact that it is so disparate and heterogeneous means that a defence of the seven-category ontology can easily become trivial, for given any allegedly new category of entity, a defender of the seven-category ontology might always try to identity it in one of the types of quality. In short, the rambling disunity of the category of quality in the work of Praśastapāda threatens to make possible an assimilation of Raghunātha's revisionary metaphysics into the traditional schema without engendering a substantive disagreement with him. It is no accident, therefore, that Raghunātha, and before him Bhāsarvajña, saw it as an important part of their project to systematize and rationalize the contents of this category, and so to prevent it from being used as a rug under which to sweep all manner of metaphysical debris. As we saw in the last chapter, the demonstration that number is not a quality required a great deal of leverage to accomplish, a demonstration eventually exploiting the fundamental principles that qualities do not themselves have qualities and that inherence is a distributive relation. It was part of Raghunātha's brilliance to see that a new articulation of fundamental principles like these was needed.

A rather different sort of response can be seen at work in the *Embellishment of Categories*, whose author Veṇīdatta invents a single new category, which he calls *dharma*, in which to shepherd all the new types of entity for which Raghunātha has argued (Veṇīdatta 1930: 36). Veṇīdatta also includes within this new category the traditional Vaiśeṣika categories of universal and differentiator, thereby ending up with a five-category ontology: substance, quality, motion, and *dharma*, along with non-being. Given that the basic sense of 'dharma' is 'property', what Veṇīdatta's move amounts to is an exploitation of the fact that Raghunātha's new types are relational to offer an ontology whose categories are objects, tropes, events, properties and absences. Veṇīdatta's reaction to Raghunātha's challenge is thus quite different from that of his contemporaries.

I will conclude this section by returning to the *Essence of Reason*. I believe that we can find a new epistemological naturalism emerging as part of a general theory of experience:

True experience is of four types, due to the division into perception, inferential experience, analogical experience and testimonial experience ... A true experience ascribes a qualifier to what does possess it. [More accurately,] it is an experience of a thing in a thing via a particular relation when that thing does possess that thing via that very relation. So a cognition of fire as inhering [in something] when the fire is located by contact is not a true experience (*pramā*). Nor is a cognition true which disjoins pearl and white to a white pearl. Nor is a true memory a true experience. One should not claim that it would be good to treat memory as *pramā*. For what is proper to say is that it is good to treat only experience as *pramā*.

Should one think that the unacceptable idea that a *pramāṇa* is the instrumental cause of a falsity is thereby contradicted? But the unacceptable idea that a *pramāṇa* is the instrumental cause of a memory is thereby contradicted too. And is it the case that even if it is agreed that an instrumental cause of a falsity is a *pramāṇa* the division of *pramāṇas* is not contradicted? Since it [falsity] is included in perception etc. [the four types of experience], it is correct to say that its instrumental cause is included in the *pramāṇas* such as perception [the four types of instrumental cause]. But if memory is a *pramā*, its instrumental cause will not be included in the instrumental causes of *pramā*, such as perception etc. So then there would be the unacceptable consequence that the division of *pramāṇas* is contradicted ... False experience is of four types because of the very division into perception etc. Some people say that the non-conceptual is excluded from both.

(1903–4: 116–117)

It seems to me that we have, in this passage, a clear movement beyond infallibilism about methods of inquiry. Mādhavadeva says that there are four distinct types of knowledge, and four corresponding 'sources' of knowledge. He then considers the possibility that these 'sources' are not infallible, but that they sometimes generate false cognitions, and he points out that such a possibility would not be in conflict with the fourfold typology. What would be in conflict with that typology would be the claim that memory-experience too is a type of knowledge, because the cause of memory-experience would then have to be regarded as a new, fifth, source of knowledge. Mādhavadeva is willing to say, as well, that there are four sorts of false cognition, corresponding to the four sources of knowledge: there are perceptual errors, inferential errors, and so on. So the 'sources' of knowledge are the sorts of thing that can malfunction or misfire; they are nevertheless our only sources of knowledge. To return to my earlier analogy, one might say that there are only four sources of diamonds in the world, four particular mines, without implying that these four mines are incapable of producing anything other than diamonds. In discussions such as this there is a clear development of ideas that are left open or unsatisfactorily resolved in the *Gemstone* in such a way as not to renege on its naturalist ambitions.

Escaping the oscillation between eliminativism and non-reductivism

I have observed that Raghunātha rejects the ancient category of differentiator. What, though, does this rejection consist in? His view, I think, is that differentiators are bogus pseudo-entities which a new metaphysics should discard. Raghunātha says:

And further, differentiator is not another category, because there is no proof. For [atoms and selves] the eternal substances discriminate by themselves, without a discriminating property—just as do the differentiators, according to others. 'Yogis see distinct differentiators' [it is said]. Well, then let them be asked on oath whether they see distinct differentiators or not.

(1915: 30,3–32,1)

It is clear that he rejects the claim of the old thinkers, that what distinguishes one atom (or self) from another is its possession of a unique discriminating property, conceived of as a special sort of property which the atom has in addition to all its other properties. Raghunātha notices that the postulation of differentiators is superfluous, and potentially regressive. For even those thinkers, the old Vaiśeṣika metaphysicians, who claim that they exist do not also claim that every differentiator has another differentiator to distinguish it from all the others. Given that the threatened regress has to be stopped somewhere, it may as well stop with the atoms themselves. His claim is that there are no differentiators, and that it was a mistake of the old school to think that any such category of thing exists. He scoffs at the idea that there is any empirical evidence of their existence.

Raghunātha is clearly an *eliminativist* about differentiators. His rejection of the category is therefore quite different in kind from the rejection of his own new categories by philosophers who came after him, for whom rejecting a category means showing how its members can be 'included in' (*antarbhāva*) some more basic category. This *reductionist* strategy is already visible in what the later philosophers say about differentiators. Raghudeva says, in his commentary on the *Inquiry*, that:

The meaning of the statement 'differentiator is not another category' is that it is not a [sort of] being different from the five beginning with substance.[9]

His words echo those of Rāmabhadra, who said that 'the meaning is that it is not a [sort of] being different from those beginning with substance'.[10] Raghudeva offers a reductionist, not an eliminativist, reading of Raghunātha's thesis. He takes the claim to be that differentiators are indeed real things, but that they are reducible to entities in the categories of substance, quality, motion, inherence and universal. Raghudeva does not say how the reduction should go, but presumably in the case of atoms, it will make use of the qualities of spatial and temporal separation of one from another, or the quality of contact between atoms and regions in space and time.

It seems more difficult to give a reductive account of the discrimination of one self from another, for the obvious suggestion that it is in virtue of their different mental qualities does not explain what discriminates two selves when they have become liberated, when, according to the standard theory, they no longer have mental lives. The apparently innocent rejection of differentiators thus comes to have surprisingly

9 viśeṣo 'pi na padārthāntaram iti | na dravyādipañcabhinno bhāva ityarthaḥ | (Raghudeva 1915: 30, 21–22).

10 dravyādibhinno na bhāva ityarthaḥ | (Rāmabhadra 1915: 91,11).

radical consequences for the ancient soteriology. We see early modern thinkers in the process of working through these problems in works like Mahādeva's *Examination of Selfhood as a Natural Kind*. Jayarāma seems to think that it is important to preserve differentiators as the ultimate grounds of distinction between individual human selves, given the absence of generic descriptive individuation.[11]

Veṇīdatta, for one, resists the elimination of differentiators. He does so on the grounds that the word 'differentiator' does not fail to refer, the way 'the rabbit's horn' (*śaśa-śṛṅga*) does (1930: 13; cf. Thakur 2003: 363). I mentioned in Chapter 12 that it is fundamental to Vaiśeṣika realism that a sort of entity is real if it is denotable by a genuine singular term, and that Meinongian ultra-realism about the merely possible is avoided by denying that fictional terms and names of merely possible objects *are* genuinely singular. The standard example of such a term is 'the rabbit's horn', which can be parsed as saying falsely of the rabbit that it has a horn. Veṇīdatta's argument, then, is that to be an eliminativist about differentiators, that is to deny that differentiators are real at all, one must claim that their names are not genuinely singular. Some followers of Raghunātha do indeed seem to have taken precisely this course, for Raghudeva himself refers to 'those who delight in reasoning' (*tarka-rasika*), who say that a differentiator is the same as a rabbit's horn (1915: 31,18). That comment is interesting and significant, because it confirms what I said earlier, that for these 'new reason' metaphysicians, the whole point is to show that reductionism and realism are compatible. Realism consists in the affirmation that names of differentiators are not like fictional terms; reductionism about differentiators consists in the claim that they are not different in being from entities of some other type.

While Raghunātha is an eliminativist about differentiators, his is a non-reductivist in many other domains. He says, for example, that legal ownership is a distinct category:

> Being-owned is another category. If you think that it is being-fit-for-use-as-one-wishes, [we answer] 'What is that 'use'?' If you say eating and such like, [we answer] 'no, for it is possible to eat the food of another'. If you say that this is prohibited by written law, [we answer] 'Which written law is that?'. If you say that it is the scripture beginning 'One may not take what belongs to another' [we answer] 'How does that apply if one does not yet have the notion of being-owned?' Therefore, being-owned is indeed distinct. And the proof is just the written law beginning 'One may not take what belongs to another'. It is produced by receiving as a gift, by purchasing, and on inheritance, and it is destroyed by giving away and so on.
>
> (1915: 62,1–64,2)

The claim is that one can describe the circumstances in which possession comes into being and goes out of existence, but that one cannot define possession in terms that do not presuppose it. Ownership is not a matter of what one *can* do with the object, but what one is *entitled* (for example by written law) to do with it. While we can specify the

[11] tathā caitramātravṛttitve sati sāmānyaśunyatvaṃ viśeṣalakṣaṇam | (Jayarāma 1985: 217). For a modern defence of the idea that persons have 'individual essences' or haecceities, see Chisholm 1976: 29.

circumstances in which such entitlement arises, one cannot reduce the entitlement itself to something else. The law books tell us that there is such a thing as ownership and under what conditions it comes into being and is transferred, but they do not, and cannot, tell us what ownership itself consists in. The attempt by some to reduce ownership to the property of being fit to be used as one wishes is in this way undermined.[12]

How do later thinkers react? To which traditional category does legal ownership belong? Jayarāma prepared a monograph on the topic, the *Meaning of Ownership.*[13] There are particularly interesting discussions in Mādhavadeva and Veṇīdatta. Mādhavadeva (1903–4: 282–286) begins by offering a rather different defence of non-reductionism to that of Raghunātha, but instead follows a pattern of argumentation familiar already from our review of discussions about number. He says that being-owned cannot be a substance, quality or action, because qualities too can be owned! The implicit premise here is the Vaiśeṣika principle that substances, qualities and actions inhere only in substances. To support the rather surprising idea that not only objects but even qualities can become somebody's property, he gives as an example the use of a particular red mark as proof of purchase. On the other hand, being-owned cannot belong within the categories of universal, inherence or differentiator, because unlike them it can be created and destroyed, here implicitly invoking another Vaiśeṣika principle. The whole 'proof' is an example of the semi-axiomatic method made possible by the newly regimented metaphysics. Mādhava does not think it is a sound proof, though, and seems to prefer a performativist theory of ownership, assimilating it to the category of action.

Veṇīdatta (1930: 33) considers a rather different proposal, due to Rāmabhadra, a proposal which is consistent with the soundness of the above proof. The proposal is to give the following reductive analysis of legal possession: I own something just in case (1) I purchased it in the past and have not yet sold it, or (2) I was given it in the past and have not yet given it away, or (3) I inherited it in the past and have not yet sold it. The anti-reductionist, Veṇīdatta continues, ought not to object to this analysis that it makes the word 'owned-ness' have a disjunctive meaning, since they too will have trouble explaining what the condition of use for that word is other than with reference to 'owned-ness-ness'. He doesn't come down in favour of one side or the other, but simply remarks that this analysis faces an epistemological difficulty which its proponents need to consider, namely that since one does not know the entire past or the future, one can never say if, according to this analysis, one owns something or not.

[12] 'Ownership is not an additional category, for it consists in the fitness of a thing to be used as one desires. Receiving gifts and so on is what delimits such fitness' svatvam api na padārthānaram | yatheṣṭaviniyogayogyatvasya svatvarūpatvāt | tadavacchedakaṃ ca pratigrahādilabdhatvam eveti | | (Annambhaṭṭa 1918: 65, 11–12).

[13] Anjaneya Sarma and Satyanarayana have kindly transcribed the only extant copy Adyar D 1401E (73879c) of Jayarāma's text, the *Svatva-vādārtha,* for me from the Telugu script. See also Derrett 1956. Kroll 2010 contains an extended analysis of the seventeenth-century 'new reason' *svatva* literature, with particularly helpful discussions of Raghunātha's further discussion in his *Light-Ray* on Vallabha, and Jayarāma's treatise, and clearly brings out the jurisprudential significance of the discussion.

This last analysis reveals how the new category of absence transforms reductionist strategies from attempts at naturalization into projects of logical analysis. A similar movement can be seen in the discussion about causal powers. Raghunātha had said that it is right to think that causal power is a new category because to do so is ontologically more economical. His example is the causal power to produce fire, which is found in dry grass, which bursts into flame when dry, in fire-sticks, which burn when rubbed together, and in translucent gems, which produce fire by focusing the sun's rays. It is simpler, argues Raghunātha, to describe this situation as one in which a single causal power is triply instantiated than to say that there are three distinct causal regularities involved (1915: 65,1–66,1). Raghunātha is not the only one to argue that causal power belongs to a separate category; this is also the view of the Mīmāṃsaka thinker Prabhākara. Prabhākara's argument is that objects have dispositional capacities which are not necessarily instantiated, something that laws between actual causes and actual effects cannot describe. When Mādhavadeva reconstructs the argument for non-reductivism, he makes it an argument from elimination rather than an argument from simplicity:

However [says the opponent], it is not the case that there are just seven categories, since causal power is in truth a distinct category. How, otherwise, is it that burning with fire does not [automatically] arise when there is a gem and instigating factor? So there is a causal power disposed to burning, which [burning] does not arise from the gem but from the instigating factor. This causal power is not a substance, since it does not possess qualities. Nor is it a quality, since it exists even without the cause of any prescribed quality. Nor is it another quality, distinct from [any of the prescribed ones], for to imagine such a quality is ontologically redundant. Nor does it belong to the category of motion, for it would then wrongly follow that motions like the capacity fire has will be perceptible, since that is the principle governing perceptibility. Nor does it belong to the categories of inherence and so on, since it will be destroyed when it arises. Therefore, it is a distinct category. If this is claimed, [we reply], no. Thinking about the causes [of fire] before it has arisen or after it has ceased to be in terms of a permanent causal power is redundant, for one can imagine the causality to be either with respect to the fire as qualified by the absence of the gem as qualified by the absence of the instigating factor, or with respect to the fire together with the absence of the gem as qualified by the absence of the instigating factor.

(1903–4: 3,12–4,11)

The argument that causal power is irreducible to any of the six categories is here not controverted; rather, what Mādhava provides is a reduction to a complex absence, an unexercised potentiality being analysed into the absence of appropriate triggering causes: 'A gem has the power to burn' is analysed as meaning that when the triggering cause is present it burns, and when the triggering cause is absent it does not burn. Mādhava in effect concedes that there were good reasons in the time of Prabhākara to treat causal power as an additional category, but that the inclusion of absence as a distinct category gives the Vaiśeṣika new scope for a successful reduction.

In alternating between eliminativism and irreductivism, Raghunātha reveals himself to be at best uncomfortable with the idea that one can be a reductionist and a realist at the same time. This is the position, however, which emerges as the most attractive in the seventeenth century. The ability to see that there is a way to escape the antinomy produced by the false dichotomy between realism and reductionism is one of the great 'conceptual breaks' of the period.

The *Garland of Categories*: naturalism and reduction

Jayarāma's *Garland of Categories* is by far the most thoroughly worked-out statement of the metaphysics of the new realism. No other work from the period is as comprehensive or as systematic. While reaffirmations of the seven-category ontology can be found in the beginners' manuals written in the seventeenth century, as well as in works like Mādhava's *Essence of Reason*, none can compare in detail of argument with Jayarāma's work, which is certainly the *opus magnum* in his large corpus of work. The text has a complex and revealing structure, one that it will be worthwhile to review. It is roughly divisible into four parts. Jayarāma begins by explaining that since a knowledge of the true nature of all the categories—along with their commonalities and differences—is the method for reaching the highest good, he will examine the categories and their features.[14] In saying this, he is strongly echoing Praśastapāda's more ancient claim. Jayarāma affirms that the categories are the standard seven only, namely the six categories of being described by Praśastapāda and the additional category of non-being (1985: 14–83). He uses this affirmation as the pretext for two extended discussions in philosophical logic, first of the logic of subject–predicate constructions with plural subjects, and second of the role of the particle 'only' in restricting the scope of subject or predicate phrase. The eventual outcome of this analysis is that the sentence 'The categories are substance and so on' means that everything belongs to at least one and at most one of the seven named categories. Since the architecture of Praśastapāda's metaphysics is based on enumeration and classification, the underlying function of this first part of the text is to provide the logical tools needed in the construction of a systematic metaphysics. It represents an important meeting of logic and metaphysics, of the sort found in the work of Peter Strawson or Michael Dummett in more recent times.

Jayarāma (1985: 81–180) next considers the new categories introduced by Raghunātha, in the *Inquiry* and other works (though not *svatva*, on which he has a separate treatise), as well as suggestions from other thinkers. The purpose of this section is to demonstrate that there are indeed exactly seven categories and to refute the claim that things like causal power are extra (Laugākṣī 1985: 181). As well as those already mentioned, he discusses similarity (*sādṛśya*), being-a-locus (*ādhāratā*), and being-an-absence (*pratiyogitva*). Similarity as a separate category has a long history stretching back

[14] atra sādharmya-vaidharmyābhyāṃ nikhila-padārtha-tattvajñānaṃ niḥśreyasopayogīti padārthāḥ tad-dharmāś ca nirūpyante | (Jayarāma 1985: 8,1–2).

to Prabhākara.[15] This section concludes with a detailed examination of the seven-category ontology.

The third part of the book is an analysis of the shared and unshared qualities of different types of substance. It attempts to organize the natural world on the basis of resemblance (1985: 181–332). A central problem is to explain how it can be, if atoms do not share all their properties with macroscopic objects, that 'macro-properties' come into being. A property which macroscopic objects and atoms don't share is the property of being sensible, and this leads directly to difficult issues about reconciling empiricism with atomism. Jayrāma rehabilitates an old distinction between a conception of the physical as 'material' (*bhūta*) and a conception of the physical as 'bounded' (*mūrta*) in spatial extent. The first, he now says, is the idea of something which possesses properties that render it perceptible, while the second is the idea of something which makes possible motion.[16] He claims that the second idea is the more basic of the two, constituting a natural classification rather than a merely useful one.[17]

The final part of the book is devoted to a searching discussion of the various sorts of substance (1985: 333–470). This fourth part has much that is similar in spirit to Raghudeva's tract, *Survey of What is Essential about Substance*. Both seem to be new attempts to recover a more ancient atomic theory (and in fact, Raghudeva's so-called 'Survey' is rather longer than Jayarāma's discussion). Jayarāma addresses himself to the problem of how an object can come to have new properties through processes of chemical synthesis or reaction. He speaks about kinematics, rejecting the theory, which he attributes to the Mīmāṃsaka, that 'momentum' (*vega*)—that in virtue of which an object keeps moving—is an interval-less (*nirantara*) sequence of individual motions (1985: 331, 5), on the grounds that this would leave unexplained the first motion of the arrow. He develops instead an 'internal impetus' theory, making reference to anticipations in the *Vaiśeṣika-sūtra* and in Praśastapāda. Jayarāma defends atomism, and discusses the problem of 'large' (*mahat*) and 'small' (*aṇu*) bodies, a 'large' body being one which can be perceived (1985: 341,11). Jayarāma rejects the idea that although atoms are not 'large' a heap of them could be, and that this explains how something can come into being with properties its parts do not possess. His reason is that a heap, by definition, is made of things which are partly in contact and partly not in contact with each other, and atoms cannot aggregate in that way because they do not have parts (1985: 342,1–3). He defends and develops the idea, again having its origins in the work of Praśastapāda, that a pair of atoms can generate an 'atomic secondary' (*dvyaṇuka*), three of which can then generate an 'atomic tertiary' (*tryaṇuka*), and only such a hypothesis

[15] Gaṅgeśa, in a rare excursion into metaphysics, had considered the possibility that similarity is an irreducible category in his third ('upamāna') chapter (1897: 7), but firmly rejected it and offered instead an analysis of it as the sharing of a common property by several objects (asādhāraṇānya-tadgatabhūyodharmavattvaṃ tatsādrśyam; 1897: 25). See also Kṛṣṇadāsa 1923: 50.

[16] bhūtatvaṃ bahirindriyaghāhyaviśeṣaguṇajātīyaguṇavattvarūpaṃ pṛthivyādau . . . (1985: 244, 4); mūr-tatvasyaiva kriyāsamavāyikāraṇatāvacchedakatayā jātitvāt (1985: 245, 7–8).

[17] na ca bhūtatvena sāṅkaryaṃ, bhūtatvasyoktopādhirūpatvāt (1985: 245,6–7).

will solve the problem. The tertiary particle is the smallest entity able to instantiate sensory properties. Next, therefore, comes a general discussion of how structural complexes can instantiate properties which are not instantiated by their constituents. Another suggestion, due it seems to Udayana, is that the number 'manyness' (*bahutva*) in a collection of atoms could constitute the 'largenesss' of an object (1985: 349,1–2). This reinforces my earlier observation about the significance of the discussion of indefinite pluralities, and Jayarāma's discussion brings together the theory of number with the question of magnitude.

The problem of explaining how 'large' objects can come to have sensible properties when the 'smaller' objects that constitute them do not is an extremely live one in India. Raghunātha offers a characteristically bold solution: he denies that the smallest perceptible object has any imperceptible parts, thereby it would seem rejecting atomism altogether (1915: 11,2–5; cf. Bhaduri 1947: 66–69). Vaiśeṣika atomism is not an empirical matter but a deduction, and for Raghunātha the deduction rests on a false premise to the effect that everything perceptible is partite. This was not an option the 'new reason' philosophers chose to explore. Jayarāma (1985: 351,9) considers more carefully the eliminativist thesis that there are no wholes as distinct realities, a view he ascribes to the Buddhists. He takes the preceding considerations to refute it: macro-objects have properties not instantiated by their parts.

Very interestingly, Jayarāma now turns to another group, whom he calls 'new deniers' (*navya-nāstikāḥ*; 352,9). They are new eliminativists about wholes. This new group argue as follows: let us grant that there are atoms, and say moreover that a secondary particle is made of two connected atoms, a tertiary particle is made of six connected atoms, a quadrad (*caturaṇuka*) is made of twenty-four connected atoms, and so on. Coming into contact with six-atom complexes or greater is what gives rise to perception. That is why neither atoms nor secondary particles are observable, and also why things like demons are not observable either.[18] For we need to explain why atoms are not observable in a way that does not assimilate them merely to the category of unobservable entities like ghosts or demons—it is their being very small, not their having strange properties, which the explanation must avert to. The thought is that there are two distinct sorts of unobservability, unobservability due to falling below the threshold of size, and unobservability due to 'interference' with the process of perception. The point of this new move is that we don't bring in wholes as distinct entities which have atoms as their parts, but keep the explanation at the level of aggregates. Secondary particles, which for Jayarāma are the smallest wholes, are treated instead as the smallest sort of aggregate. Perhaps too anything not made of atoms at all, such as space, will be unobservable in a third sense.

[18] atra navya-nāstikāḥ—santvaṇavo nityāḥ, tathāpi saṃyuktāṇudvayaṃ, dvyaṇukaṃ saṃyuktānuṣaṭkaṃ tryaṇukaṃ, saṃyuktāṅucaturviṃśatikaṃ caturanukam ityādayastu laukikaviṣayatayā dravya-sākṣātkāratvāvacchinne tryaṇukatvādighaṭakasaṃyogānāṃ piśācādighaṭakasaṃyogābhinnānāṃ vaijātyena kāraṇatvāt na kevalāṇudvyaṇukādeḥ pratyakṣatā | (1985 : 352,9–12).

Jayarāma's criticism of this new proposal seems to be that it must treat the production of macro-properties, ones which the aggregate has but not the aggregated elements, as *sui generis*, and in that sense is theoretically more extravagant than the Vaiśeṣika theory (cf. Laugākṣī 1985: 352,10–12). He continues by linking this discussion with one about causation, and the debate over whether an effect can come into being which did not exist already in the causes (*asat-kārya-vāda*; 1985: 361–366), and distinguishing a variety of senses of production (*kārya*; 366–370). There is a discussion of the problem of the first cause of falling, and whether one needs to give atoms weight in order to explain how wholes which they constitute have weight.[19]

Many individual elements of Jayarāma's theory can be found in earlier sources. Where Jayarāma's innovates is in the way he brings this theory together, and turns it into an explanatory account. The theory of secondary and tertiary particles, and of the emergence of macro-properties, is presented as an explanatory hypothesis, one which solves a particular philosophical problem, namely to reconcile atomism with empiricism. It is not intended to be a proto-scientific description of the natural world.

The *Garland* therefore comprises a general methodology for metaphysics, a cautious reductionism, a categorial ontology based on the reworking of ancient naturalism, and an atomic theory of material and immaterial substances. Jayarāma tells us that he has 'created the *Garland of Categories*, which strings together whatever is emancipatory because in accordance with reason (*yukti*), for the diversion of the learned' (1985: 7). Laugākṣī explains that reasons are proofs, refutations, and statements of evidence, and that these alone are emancipatory.[20] There is in the work of Jayarāma and his students a sort of research programme to reconfigure Vaiśeṣika metaphysics as a unified explanatory account based on a series of clearly articulated principles.

Mechanical philosophy in the *Garland of Categories*?

How does Jayarāma's theory compare with seventeenth-century thought in Europe? In particular, are there parallels for the distinction he draws between his own renewed Vaiśeṣika atomism and the ideas of the 'new deniers', who reject the theory of emergent wholes but are themselves atomists? As it turns out, in the now largely forgotten work of one of the most important early pioneers of the new mechanistic conception of nature, there are uncanny echoes of the theory Jayarāma rejects. The work in question is the *Natural Philosophy Directed Against Aristotle* of Sébastien Basso.[21]

[19] astu vā paramāṇāv eva gurutvam | . . . astu vā paramparayā saṃbandhaviśeṣeṇa vā paramāṇugurutvam eva patananiyāmakam | (Jayarāma 1985: 365).

[20] yuktayaḥ sādhaka-bādhaka-prāmāṇyopanyāsa-rūpāḥ tā eva mauktikāni taiḥ gumphitā grathitā | (Laugākṣī 1985: 7, 6–7).

[21] On Basso, see Lüthy 1997. The difficulty which Lüthy finds in establishing anything much about him, even his nationality, is reminiscent of what we have seen with respect to the Indians. It is worthy noting that the problem of lack of historical detail is also one for European philosophers, especially those who fell from view or from standard history.

Published in 1621, it was widely read, certainly by both Descartes and Gassendi. Descartes refers to Basso as a *novator*, an innovator.[22] Basso rejects the Aristotlian theory of forms, and the entire Aristotelian explanation of generation and chemical change. He replaces the peripatetic doctrine of *mixis*—according to which the ingredients in a mixture lose their old form and a new form comes into being (*eductio formae*; Meinel 1988: 91)—with one of aggregate juxtaposition, the elements remaining as they are in a compound, whose properties are then determined wholly by their arrangement, motion and individual qualities (Basso 1621: 37–42).[23] All perceptible objects are aggregate compounds of elements, of which there are four along with the space-filling *aether*, and which have individual attributes and powers, over and above mere extension (Ariew 1999: 133). Of particular importance to Basso is a doctrine of secondary and tertiary particles. Secondary particles are compounds of atoms, and tertiary particles are compounds of secondary ones (van Melsen 1952: 91). Clearly, however, for Basso a secondary particle is not an emergent entity with a new form, but an aggregate of the unchanged elements that constitute it.[24] The mechanical conception of the molecule, unlike a contemporary one, can avail itself only of contact and not of any non-mechanical binding forces: 'Basso argues... *contra* almost the entirety of the tradition, mixtion is nothing beyond mere aggregation' (Lolordo 2007: 138).

The claim that generation and qualitative change can be explained in terms of the gain, loss or movement of particles within aggregate compounds is the essence of the new mechanistic conception of nature, which was to be developed by Galileo, Leibniz and Newton later in the seventeenth century. The doctrine of secondary and tertiary particles, again conceived of as aggregate compounds and not as new substances, brings Basso's formulation into close similarity with that of the 'new deniers' referred to by Jayarāma. Let us remember that the *Garland* was written in 1659, right in the middle of the period when, after Dārā Shukoh's fall, Dāniṣmand Khān brought Kavīndra,

[22] 'Plato says one thing, Aristotle another, Epicurus another, Telesio, Campanella, Bruno, Basso, Vanini, and all the innovators (*novatores*) all say something different. Of all these people, I ask you, who is it who has anything to teach me?' (Letter to Beeckman, 17 October 1630; AT 1: 158). Ariew 1999: 85 comments that 'however much he may have sneered at them, the innovators were in fact preparing the way for Descartes' 'revolution'.' He shows that Descartes agrees with Basso's account of generation and alteration, but disagrees with him about the nature of the *aether*.

[23] Lolordo 2007: 137: 'Basso denies that any new form can or must be taken on in mixtion and argues that all the qualities of mixtures can be explained in terms of the qualities of the components.' Cf. Leclerc 1972: 285 (cf. 143–146): 'The early seventeenth century thinkers... rejected the [Aristotelian doctrine that a body is a single unitary whole, the principle of its unity being its form], maintaining that the organic body is a compound, an aggregation, and not a single substantial whole, and that the true substances are its ultimate constituents, the material atoms. It was clear to the early protagonists of this doctrine such as Basso, Galileo and Gassendi, that an immediate implication is that the unity which Aristotle had proclaimed is merely apparent.'

[24] Fisher 2005: 202: '[In Basso] we find an early molecular picture of material structure: elementary particles come together to form secondary aggregates and these in turn come together to form tertiary aggregates, the higher-order compounds having generally greater stability than the lower-order ones.' Cf. Leclerc 1972: 287: 'Basso earliest, then others, introduced the conception of groups of atoms in a particular structure, Gassendi giving them the name 'molecules' (little masses) which was thence-forward adopted.'

Bernier, and a host of 'learned scientists' together under his patronage, and Bernier explained Gassendi and Descartes to them in the medium of Persian. I do not find it inconceivable that Jayarāma gained an impression of the thought through Bernier. I am aware of no other reference to 'new deniers' (*navya-nāstikāḥ*) anywhere in the Sanskrit philosophical literature, which suggests that Jayarāma has some specific and new source in mind. And the reference to quaternary aggregates, which is again distinctive of Basso (Fisher 2005: 335 n.), is also not found in standard Vaiśeṣika discussions of atomic combination.

Basso's retrieval of atomism attempts to undermine the scholastic doctrine that generation and alternation require emergent forms: for him, change is explicable in terms of the local motion of atoms. Descartes, though not an atomist, uses the same pattern of explanation to account for macro-phenomena like visibility in terms of micro-phenomena:

> [Not only heat, cold, moistness and dryness] but all the others as well, including even the forms of inanimate bodies, can be explained without the need to suppose anything in their matter other than the motion, size, shape, and arrangement of its parts.
>
> (*Le Monde*, 1984: 89; AT 11: 26)

The question, however, is whether this claim is true. A theory of material substance which treats substances as mere aggregations of atoms and does away with substantial forms seemed even to many seventeenth-century atomists inadequate.[25] It is hard to be sure what Gassendi's view was on this crucial issue. Although the *Syntagma* begins with programmatic claims seemingly in favour of fully mechanistic explanation, he seems to have abandoned this by the time he gets to discussing inanimate compounds and animal bodies, and his overall account relies on a vague notion of 'texture', the arranging and ordering of aggregates of atoms.[26] However expansive the notion might end up being, Gassendi is admirably clear about the fundamental issue at the outset:

> [I]f it is true that the only material principles of things are Atoms, and that there are in Atoms no qualities other than Magnitude, Figure, and Weight or motion, as I explained above, how, I ask, may

[25] Leclerc 1972: 288: 'The question, which exercised the ingenuity of a good many thinkers in the seventeenth century, [was] how the atoms come to adhere into groups at all . . . In respect of these philosophical issues it is manifest that the theory of material substance is extremely inadequate. The basic reason for this inadequacy is that in this theory, given the nature of matter, it is impossible for the atoms to have relations to each other. For there to be groups of atoms which are more than mere aggregates, however, implies that there must be relations between the members of the groups.'

[26] Lolordo 2007: 153: 'Gassendian bodies are composites of atoms 'woven together' with a certain texture. The notion of texture is central to Gassendi's atomism. In theory he relies heavily on the claim that the qualities and behaviour of macroscopic bodies derive from the size, shape, and local motion of tiny particles, but in practice Gassendi almost always appeals to the notion of texture in providing explanations of particular bodily phenomena . . . The program outlined in the initial books of the *Syntagma* suggests that texture is not something over and above the arrangement of atoms in space. However, it is unclear how we could derive anything that does all the explanatory work Gassendi needs textures to do from patterns of atoms moving in space . . . Gassendi's programmatic reliance on local motion turns into practical reliance on the rather loose notion of texture.'

it happen that so many other qualities beyond these are created and exist in things? . . . [J]ust as the same letters are different in respect of seeing and hearing when they are positioned differently . . . so the same atom positioned differently affects sense in different ways, just as, if it were a pyramid, sometimes its edge might penetrate into the senses and sometimes it would apply itself through its base. . . . [And] as the same two or many letters, when they proceed or follow in different ways, suggest different words to the eye and the ear and the mind . . . so the same atoms, transposed in different ways, can demonstrate very different qualities or species to the senses.

(Gassendi 1658: 1.366a–1.367b; trans. Lolordo 2007: 155–156)

Returning to Jayarāma, his reply to the aggregativism of the 'new denial' is that one does need to posit emergent substances (*janya-dravya*) to explain how macroscopic objects have visible properties.[27] Such objects also have emergent qualities (*citra-rūpa*), determined by but not reducible to the qualities of the constituent parts. He is led to discuss how something can come out of nothing—how an 'effect' can come into being which did not already exist in the 'cause'. Jayarāma seems to admit that there is a difference between qualities like weight and sensible qualities like colour, insofar as he is willing to concede that a macroscopic object can have weight only if the atoms have weight. It is not clear whether his explanation of the fact that a macroscopic object can be visible even though its atomic parts are not consists in anything over and above the claim that, being a different object, it can have different properties. What is clear is that he rejects the sort of view proposed in the above passage of Gassendi, that the atoms can arrange themselves as if in pyramids, and so present different aspects to the senses. It is fundamental to Vaiśeṣika atomism that, lacking parts, atoms cannot come into partial contact with one another, and so that the idea of spatial arrangement is insufficient to explain the way in which they come to constitute composite bodies. Jayarāma (1985: 366,3–6) is, very unusually, willing to consider the idea that the way a collection of parts constitutes a whole is different from the way an object exhibits qualities; even though he does not agree with the suggestion, the fact that he even entertains it is significant. There might be an echo of this thought in Gassendi's alternative suggestion, that the structure of the world is essentially syntactic.[28] In his separate discussion of ownership, Jayarāma suggests that what makes a composite body perceptible is that, unlike the atoms or the tip of a thorn, it instantiates sensible properties co-extensive with the property 'largeness' (*mahattva*), rejecting an alternative view proposed by some other 'new reason' thinkers.[29] He also offers what is in

[27] phalamukhagauravasyāpi kvaciddoṣāt janyadravyam apekṣya dravyalaukikasākṣātkārasyaiva laghutvāt tvayodbhūta-rūpa-mahatvayoḥ tadavacchinna-hetutvasya kalpyatvāc ca | tādṛśasaṃyogaviśiṣṭavṛttitvādikaṃ tu guṇādipratyakṣe tantram iti kevalāṇu-dvyaṇukādi-guṇāpratyakṣatve 'pi na tryaṇukādiguṇāpratyakṣam | (1985: 353, 3–7).

[28] An idea already present in his *Animadversiones*: 'As letters are the elements of writing and from letters are formed first syllables and then successively words, phrases, and speeches, so also atoms are the elements of all things' (quoted in van Melsen 1952: 92).

[29] paramāṇvādeś ca kṣurādeś cāpratyakṣatvād bahirindriya-janya-dravya-pratyakṣe mahatva-samānādhikaraṇodbhūta-rūpaṃ kāraṇam iti sarvasiddhaṃ atra kecit mahatva-samānādhikaraṇodbhūta-rūpatvenaiva kāraṇatā na tūdbhūta-rūpa-samānādhikaraṇa-mahatvena nyāya-naya pākād rūpa-nāśottara-kāle prāṅmahatva-satvena

effect a new argument against aggregativism: that owning a 'large' body does not entail owning the atoms which constitute it.[30]

If one were to look for the closest parallel to Jayarāma's neo-Vaiśeṣika atomism among the various atomic theories of seventeenth-century Europe, it isn't certain that it would be Gassendi's, not least because it is not clear just what Gassendi's theory is. Jayarāma would certainly side with the critics of the Aristotelian doctrine of forms, because of that theory's claim that the elements lose their own form when they go to make the new substance, a view at odds with the Vaiśeṣika picture of composition and resolution. I think that the nearest view is that of Daniel Sennert, who looked for a theory of 'mixtion' that is somewhere between mere aggregation and Aristotelian substantial form. The term 'mixtion', in his usage, applies to 'a body composed of many things so that from all of them is made a certain one thing, different in nature from all the components and possessing a different form than the form of the components' (Sennert 1636: 119; trans. Lolordo 2007: 134–135). His claim is that a new supervening form is taken on in mixtion, but that 'bodies that are mixed retain their forms in mixtion' (ibid: 123). This doctrine, which Sennert attributes to Avicenna, is, he says, 'the key to the whole of physical science' (van Melsen 1952: 88).

The neo-Vaiśeṣika theory of composite bodies is that each one is a whole (*avayavin*), a single entity, made out of parts, and ultimately atoms, which do not lose their fundamental qualities when in composition. A dyad or secondary particle (*dvyaṇuka*) is a new entity, constituted by two atoms which continue to exist as parts of the dyad, and can potentially exist individually after its destruction. As I have noted, this theory is combined with a theory of projectile motion, according to which an initial *vega* is imparted to the arrow by the thrower, which then imparts a second *vega* so that the arrow keeps moving, and so on. The resemblance between this theory and the non-Aristotelian *impetus* theory of late scholasticism, due originally to Buridan (Ariew 1999: 130), is striking enough for me to translate *vega* as 'impetus'. If one were to seek to place this theory within the landscape of seventeenth-century theory of substance in Europe, it would fall between the aggregativism of a pure mechanical philosophy such as Basso's and a full-fledged Aristotelianism. The ideas of Sennert and possibly Gassendi, depending on exactly what his doctrine of 'texture' amounts to, do come closest. If we remember the way that Jayrāma rehabilitates the old distinction between a conception of the physical as 'material' (*bhūta*) and a conception of the physical as spatially 'bounded' (*mūrta*), one the idea of something which possesses properties that render it perceptible, the other the idea of something which makes possible motion, we see clearly his view about the issue which divided atomists from Cartesians in the seventeenth century.

pratyakṣāpatter iti | tanna | pākād rūpanāśottara-kāle pratyakṣasyeṣṭāpatti-saṃbhavena vinigamanāvirahāt aṇur api viśeṣoddhyavasāyakara iti cet tathāpy udbhūta-rūpa-viśiṣṭa-ma[ha]tvena kāraṇatve vinigamanāvirahāt viśiṣṭa-satvasya niyāmakatvāt kalpanam ato 'pi vinigamakam iti cet maivam || (Jayarāma, *Svatvavādārtha* lines 150–157).

[30] *Svatvavādārtha*, lines 73–82.

The broadly reductionist metaphysics of the 'new reason' philosophers leads them in the direction of a theory of the atomic constitution of material bodies that has many parallels with atomic theories under discussion in Europe. A view resembling mechanism is considered, but found wanting, and indeed found wanting for something like the reason that the mechanical theory of substance did run into trouble, the problem of explaining on purely aggregativist premises how macroscopic phenomena such as the instantiation of visible properties are related to the microscopic. This is not an empirical problem but a philosophical one; indeed, it is one with which contemporary work on emergentism continues to grapple. The new Vaiśeṣikas did not have all the answers either, but they understood the nature of the problem well enough to see very clearly which answers could not be right, and were in the process of making an extremely important intervention in the development of natural philosophy.

This brings to an end my examination of 'new reason' work in epistemology and metaphysics. As I have stressed before, the development of a new language for philosophy was a vital part of the overall project. I will argue that it constitutes a calculus of relations, and I will also examine in more detail the semantics of the particle 'only'. After these two studies, which are by their very nature somewhat technical, I will bring this book to a conclusion with a broad summary and assessment.

PART V

A New Language for Philosophy

15

The Technical Language Assessed

A key feature of 'new reason' philosophy is its gradual construction of a new technical language. This language, which evolved from initially scattered ideas in the writings of Udayana, Gaṅgeśa, and Raghunātha, emerged rapidly to become a standard idiom for academic works in philosophy. Nor was it limited only to philosophy: in early modern India it swiftly became the *lingua franca* for intellectual exchange—in grammar, poetics, law, theology, and the other knowledge disciplines.[1] A careful analysis of the conceptual framework and expressive power of the new language is therefore of the utmost importance for any study of the literature of this period. The 'new reason' philosophers recognize that a new method is needed for precision in thinking. It was as natural for them to turn to grammar and linguistics in search of such a model as it was for early modern Europeans to turn to Euclid, for the study of grammar has always played, in India, a role analogous to that of geometry in Europe.

There have been several excellent attempts to describe the technique over the course of the last fifty years.[2] At its heart is a logic of binary relations, expanded to include identity, several types of negation, and generalized quantification. The extensive use of abstraction gives the language an intensional feel; but there is nevertheless a strongly extensional strain in the theory, and to a large extent the use of abstraction is pleonastic. I have given examples of the expressive potential of the new language in earlier chapters, where I showed, for example, how it enables a clear distinction to be drawn between thought contents that are judged and those that are merely entertained, how it clarifies the analysis of self as the inherence cause of pleasure and pain, and how it permits a formulation of the logical form of 'The number of categories is only seven'. These examples highlight an essential feature of the language—its capacity to disambiguate where ordinary Sanskrit cannot. I have also emphasized that realism is tied to claims about reference, and so to questions about underlying logical form. The new language is precisely the tool for distinguishing between surface grammatical form and deeper logical

[1] Among notable writers to have made use of this technical language: the grammarians Bhaṭṭoji Dīkṣita, Kauṇḍa Bhaṭṭa and Nāgeśa Bhaṭṭa, the Vedāntin Madhusūdana Sarasvatī, the Jaina Yaśovijaya Gaṇi, the legal theorist Jagannātha, the polymath Vijñānabhikṣu.

[2] Ingalls 1951; Matilal 1968; Guha 1968; K. Bhattacharya 2006; Wada 1990, 2007; Krishna 1997a. Maheśa Chandra 1891 is a helpful article in Sanskrit, translated in Jha 2004.

form. My aim in this chapter is to establish the extent to which this newly invented technical language can be seen as forming the basis for a 'calculus' of relations.

The importance of disambiguation

Ordinary Sanskrit is regarded by the early modern philosophers as an imperfect vehicle for philosophical discourse, mainly because it is infested with ambiguity. It is not just the presence of ambiguities in the lexicon, homonymous words like '*saindhava*' (which can mean either salt or a horse), for it is always possible to eliminate such terms in favour of univocal expressions. The greater problem derives from the absence in ordinary Sanskrit of any systematic or compulsory use either of articles or quantifier expressions. In English, the combination of an 'applicative' (Geach 1980: 73), that is an expression like 'a', 'the', 'all', 'some', or 'most' with a substantival general term such as 'pot' or 'cow' forms a descriptive or quantified phrase. In Sanskrit, however, an inflected noun or noun phrase occurring by itself often has the same syntactic role. So, for example, the sentence *ghaṭo nīlaḥ* 'pot [is] blue' might mean either 'the pot is blue' 'some pot is blue' or 'every pot is blue'. Similarly, a phrase like *vahni-kāraṇa* 'cause of fire' might signify the cause of a certain fire ('The cause of [the] fire is unknown'), the cause of a fire ('carelessness causes fire'), or the cause of all fire ('a cause of every fire is heat').

In some contexts an inflected noun has the role of a definite description, as for example in '[The] doctor is coming'. A classical dispute in Indian philosophy of language is whether the semantic value of '(the) doctor' in a sentence like this is an individual or a universal. The former view represents a doctrine that nouns have a genuine referring use, and it is within discussions of this view that the theory of reference developed in India. The second view, on the other hand, whose approach is in some ways nearer to the standard Russellian treatment of definite descriptions explains the referential use of nouns by appeal to pragmatic constraints on the interpretation of sentences (for further discussion see Ganeri 1999b).

In other sentences, a noun can have an existential or universal force; for example, 'Bring [a] pen' or '[A] cow should not be kicked'. Faced with the problem of accounting for this use of nouns, those Indian semanticists who endorse a referring use argue that a noun has a systematic ambiguity in semantic role, sometimes taking an individual as its value, and sometimes a universal or class. This approach was shared by the early grammarians such as Patañjali as well as the early Naiyāyikas. I will try to show how this idea comes to be formalized in the new technical language.

When two or more nouns occur in the same sentence, there is a possibility of ambiguities of scope. Suppose one forms a phrase 'cause of smoke'. This might mean cause of a particular body of smoke, cause of some or other smoke, or else cause of all smoke. Now, when such a phrase is combined with another noun to form a sentence, e.g. 'Fire is cause of smoke' the threefold ambiguity of each noun leads to nine different readings of the sentence. In two of these readings 'All fire is (the) cause of some smoke' and 'Some fire is (the) cause of all smoke' there is a further ambiguity. The first, for example, might mean 'Each fire is (the) cause of some smoke or other' or 'There is a body of smoke which is the effect of every fire'. This scope ambiguity is not the result of any putative ambiguity in the nouns, but is due to an ambiguity in the syntax of the language.

When sentences contain relational expressions, there is room for still another sort of ambiguity. Compare the sentences 'Pothood is in a pot' and 'The cat is in the kitchen'. In the first case, the relational expression 'in' (or the locative post-noun) indicates the relation of inherence, but in the second it indicates the relation of containment. The English expression 'is' is similarly ambiguous, sometimes indicating identity, sometimes existence, and sometimes predication. This kind of ambiguity concerns the semantic role of the relational expression in the sentence (cf. Sainsbury 1979: 136).[3] Our philosophers claim that the negation particle *na* 'no' suffers from ambiguity in this way: it sometimes indicates a 'mutual absence' (*anyonyābhāva*), which is the negation of an identity, but sometimes a 'relational absence' (*saṃsargābhāva*), the negation of a predication.[4]

If an ordinary language 'with all its ambiguities and abominable syntax' (Bertrand Russell; quoted in Sainsbury 1979: 134) is ill-suited for the careful formulation of philosophical doctrines, the alternative is to construct a formal artificial language free from these defects. Authors such as Frege, Russell, and Quine, all of whom introduce artificial or formal languages, differ in their opinions as to the relation between the formal language and ordinary languages, and it is not entirely clear how the early moderns conceive of the relation between ordinary Sanskrit and their technical language (see Guha 1968: 9–15; S. Bhattacharyya 1998: 30–33; K. Bhattacharya 2006, 2007). Minimally, however, we might suppose it to be such that corresponding to each of the various possible readings of an ordinary Sanskrit sentence, there should be just one sentence in the formal language. The attitude seems to me to have most in common with the view expressed by the later Wittgenstein (1958: §19), that the relationship between a formal language and natural language is akin to the relationship between a new suburb, 'with regular streets and uniform houses' and the ancient city, 'a maze of little streets and squares'.

The new language includes a small number of logical words, especially 'substratum' or 'locus' (*adhikaraṇa, ādhāra*) and its inverse 'occurrence' (*vṛtti*), 'conditioner' (*nirūpaka*), 'delimitor' (*avacchedaka*) and 'absentee' or 'counterpositive' (*pratiyogin*), together with a non-logical vocabulary of terms and relation-expressions.[5] Accompanying the

[3] Or, if we agree with the later Nyāya view that the relational element is indicated, not by an explicit expression, but by grammatico-syntactic features (*ākāṅkṣā*) of the sentence, we must locate the ambiguity there.

[4] Raghunātha, *Treatise on Negation* 1968: 173, cf. Matilal 1968: 94–95; Ingalls 1951: 54–55.

[5] See Ingalls 1951: 28–85, Matilal 1968: 3–98, Nyāyaratna 1891, Sen 1924: 16–35, Guha 1968, Wada 2007: 24–35.

language, there is a formalized ontology. Modern interpreters disagree on whether this ontology is extensional or intensional.[6] On the one hand, various abstraction devices are exploited, so as, for example, to speak of pothood or (cause-of-fire)-hood where we might speak of the class of pots or the causes of fire. Yet, when one examines the role of such abstract properties in the theory, it is very often only their extension which is semantically relevant. When describing the new language, I shall follow the strategy of using an extensional ontology as far as possible. It seems that the early modern approach is to avoid disputes about ontology, and to develop a theoretical language which is available even to those who do not share the same metaphysical dispositions (Matilal 1971: 66; S. Bhattacharyya 1987: 201).

The mention of properties in the technical language seems then to be mainly pleonastic. In particular, the abstraction device *-tva* is used freely, not restricted to the naming of genuine properties alone: a Naiyāyika happily reparses the sentence 'the pot has a long neck and a conch-shaped handle' as 'long-neck-conch-shaped-handle-ness is located in the pot'. Its commitment to a principle of ontological parsimony (*lāghava*) blocks agreement that every such operation generates the name of a genuine property. Guhe (2008) argues that the attitude towards the ontology of properties is similar to that of George Bealer's property theory. I doubt, for the reasons just given, that the liberal ontology of Bealer's theory is necessary, but it is possible that a sparser intensional system will be called for fully to render the new language. We must first see how much can be understood on a purely extensionalist basis; we can then ask what is the leanest intensional addition necessary to handle the residue.

The technical language is not a symbolic one. It does not, for example, employ variables, although 'dummy singular terms' (Matilal 1968: 23) like *ghaṭa* ('pot'), as well as the pronouns *tat* 'that' and *sva* 'own-' sometimes function in the same way. The sentences in the language therefore resemble long-hand versions of symbolic formulae, and as a result are notoriously cumbersome. In principle, however, I see no reason why it cannot be symbolized, and as a step in that direction I will attempt to construct a symbolic notation for a fragment of the language here. We can denote this fragment 'NN'. As long as we restrict our attention to the sentences for which an extensional ontology is sufficient, this fragment should be equivalent to some part of first-order predicate logic, and it will be an interesting exercise to find out which part this is.

The syntax of the formal system

I shall now give an informal presentation of the fragment NN (for a more formal treatment, see Ganeri 2008b). Informally, we can say that a syntax for NN is built up from the following components.

[6] Sen 1924, Ingalls 1951, Bochenski 1961, Goekoop 1967, Matilal 1968.

1. There is a set of primitive terms, such as *ghaṭa* ('pot'), *go* ('cow'), etc. These are the nouns, or more precisely, the uninflected nominal stems (*nāman, prātipadika*). I will use the Roman letters '*a*', '*b*', etc., for these primitive terms.
2. There is an abstraction functor *-tva* or *-tā* ('-ness' '-hood'), the operation of which on a primitive term like *ghaṭa* 'pot' gives rise to an abstract term *ghaṭatva* 'pothood'. I will use the Greek letters 'α' 'β', etc., as abstract terms.[7]
3. There is a set of relational abstract expressions, such as 'locushood', 'causehood', 'cousinhood', 'pervadedness', some of which are logical and others non-logical. There is a corresponding set of inverse relational abstract expressions, 'superstratum-hood', 'effecthood', etc. I will use bold letters, e.g. '**R**', for these expressions.
4. There is a conditioning operator, which combines a relational abstract expression with a term (of any kind) to form a term, such as 'locushood-conditioned-by-pot' (*ghaṭa-nirūpitādhāraṇatā*) or 'causehood-conditioned-by-smokehood' (*dhūmatva-nirūpita-kāraṇatā*). I will call such expressions 'relational terms'. They are sometimes abbreviated as 'locushood-to-pot' (*ghaṭīyādhāratā*), etc. (cf. Ingalls, 1951: 83; Guhe 1968: 220). A conditioned relational abstract is represented here by writing the conditioner letter on the right-hand side of the relational abstract expression: thus '**R**β'.
5. There are two kinds of sentence-forming operator. One combines a relational term 'Rβ' with another term to form a sentence '*a*.**R**β' or 'α.**R**β'. This operator is named 'location' or 'residence' (*niṣṭhana*) if the term is primitive, and 'delimitation' (*avacchedana*) if it is abstract. For example, 'locushood-conditioned-by-pot is resident in ground' (*ghaṭa-nirūpitādhāraṇatā sā bhūtalaniṣṭhā, or ghaṭa-nirūpitādhāratāśrayaṃ bhūtalam*) or 'causehood-conditioned-by-smokehood is delimited by firehood' (*dhūmatva-nirūpita-kāraṇatā sā 'gnitvāvacchinnā*). The second sentence-forming operator, colocation (*sāmānādhikaraṇya*), represented here by a colon, combines an abstract term 'α' with a relational term '**R**β' to form a sentence 'α:**R**β'.
6. There is a negation functor '-absence' (*atyantābhāva*), which forms negative terms such as 'pot-absence' (*ghaṭābhāva*) from terms. By definition, the negative term 'pot-absence' is identical with the relational abstract term 'absenthood-conditioned-by-pot' (*ghaṭa-nirūpitānuyogitā*), where 'absenthood' (*anuyogitā*) is a logical relational abstract expression. I will write 'absenthood' as '**N**' and negative terms as '*a*-absence' or '**N***a*'. There is also a sentence negation 'not' (*na*). Thus, 'causehood-conditioned-by-smokehood is not delimited by firehood' (*dhūmatva-nirūpita-kāraṇatā sā 'gnitvānavacchinnā*). Nyāya avoids sentential negation

[7] Some Naiyāyikas employ a second abstraction functor *-vyaktitva* ('-individual-hood'), e.g. *ghaṭavyaktitva* 'pot-individual-hood'. This functor allows us to replace any particular use of a primitive term with a corresponding abstract term. Our philosophers sometimes use this device to eliminate primitive terms from their technical language. It partially resembles Quine's elimination of proper names like 'Socrates' in favour of predicates like '*x* Socratises' (Quine 1960: 181), or rather, 'to Socratise'.

wherever it can (cf. Matilal 1985b: 116), but cannot eliminate it altogether. I will isolate the point at which its introduction is required.

To summarize, then, the syntax of NN consists of relational abstract expressions, various different kinds of term expressions—primitive, relational, abstract, and negative—and a negation particle.

A semantics for the language

For the semantics of NN, I will, as I said, draw only upon an extensional ontology. The new theory does not use set-theoretic notions like set inclusion or set membership, but prefers to talk instead of properties occurring in objects, or co-occurring with other properties. It is for this reason that it is sometimes said to have a 'property-location language' (Matilal 1985b: 112). However, since its semantic vocabulary is often clearly extensional (properties which are equipollent (*samaniyata*) are in many cases identified), there is a justification in using a set-theoretic notation to describe it.[8] We can then assign, to each expression in the syntax, an element or set as follows.

(1 & 2) As noted above, nouns sometimes function like singular referring expressions. When thus used, they will share with indexicals the property of taking a different referent depending on the context of use. To each occurrence of a primitive term like 'pot' is therefore assigned an object P, such that P belongs to the set π of pots. And to the corresponding abstract term 'pothood' is assigned the property pothood.[9] In keeping with our simplifying restriction, let us assign to such an expression the set π of pots. It is now possible for any particular use of a noun-phrase in the ordinary language to be mapped either to a primitive term having a particular value, or else to the corresponding abstract term, whose value is a class.

Corresponding to each occurrence of a primitive term, there is an abstract term formed by the application of the individuality abstraction functor, for example the term 'pot-individual-hood' (*ghaṭavyaktitva*; Matilal 1968: 57). If the value assigned to a particular occurrence of the primitive term is P, then the set assigned to this abstract term is the unit set $\{P\}$, i.e. the property of being this very pot.

(3 & 4) Let us next introduce a number of relations. In set theory a relation is a subset of the Cartesian product of two sets, A and B, the former being the range and the latter the domain of the relation. In other words, a relation is a set of ordered pairs. Naturally, there is a degree of anachronism in using such a notion to explicate the early modern theory. Yet since this theory claims that a relation is made up of a collection of relation-particulars, each of which is individuated by specifying the two relata in order (cf. Matilal 1968: 33–34), the anachronism seems to me to be justifiable. Now given

8 Note, however, Ingall's reservation 1951: 50; S. Bhattacharyya 1987: 290; Guhe 2008.

9 The basis for this is Kātyāyana's aphorism under *Pāṇini-sūtra* 5.1.119: 'the abstraction suffixes [i.e. -hood, -ness, -ity] such as *-tā* and *-tva* (added to nominal stems) "express" (*abhi* +*dhā*) only those qualities (*guṇa*) on the basis of which the nominal stems are used to refer to things'. See also K. Bhattacharya 2006: 7.

any relation, we can form a series of sets, the extensions of relational properties, as follows. Suppose that an object *b* is in the domain B of the relation R. Then we can form the set of elements in A which are related by R to *b*. Similarly, given a set β in B, we can form the set of elements in A which are related by R to some element in β. In the standard terminology of relations, this set will be the image of β under the inverse of R. Now, if *b* is an object assigned to an occurrence of the primitive term '*b*' or β is the set assigned to an abstract term '*b*-hood' then we will say that the set thus formed is the set assigned to the relational abstract term 'R-hood-*conditioned-by-b*(-hood)'. For example, the set assigned to the relational abstract term 'causehood-conditioned-by-pot-hood' (*ghaṭatva-nirūpita-kāraṇatā*) comprises those objects which are the cause of a pot. Let such sets be assigned to '**R**b' or '**R**β'.

Given any relation R, it is possible to form an inverse relation R^{-1} such that $yR^{-1}x$ iff xRy.

(5) If '*a*' is a token of a primitive term, and '**R**β' is a relational abstract term, then the sentence '**R**β is *resident in a*' (or equivalently '*a* is *the locus of* **R**β'), i.e. '*a*.**R**β' is true iff the object assigned to '*a*' is a member of the set assigned to '**R**β'. Similarly, if '*a*-hood' is an abstract term, then the sentence '**R**β is *delimited by a*-hood' i.e. 'α.**R**β' is true iff the set assigned to '*a*-hood' is contained in the set assigned to '**R**β'.[10] For example, the sentence 'causehood-conditioned-by-smokehood is delimited by firehood' is true iff the set of fires is a subset of the set of causes of smoke.

The sentence 'a-hood is co-located with **R**β' is true iff the intersection of *a*-hood with **R**β is non-empty, e.g. iff there is a fire which is the cause of smoke.

(6) The treatment of negative terms is unusual, and gives a distinctive colour to the whole language. Navya Nyāya increases the number of categories so as to be able to include, for every object such as a pot *P*, an 'absentee' or 'anti-object' (*abhāva*), an absence of the pot *P*. It expresses the fact that *P* is not on the table by saying that the anti-object absence-of-*P is* on the table. Given a token primitive term such as 'pot' we can form a negative term 'pot-absence' by means of the relational abstract term 'absenthood-conditioned-by-pot': the set assigned to 'pot-absence' is the set of absences which are absences of the pot *P*. In fact, since the absence relation is one-one, there is only one such absence, and it is called a 'specific' absence (*viśeṣābhāva*) (cf. Ingalls 1951: 56). Given an abstract term such as 'pothood' we can form the negative term 'absenthood-conditioned-by-pothood' (unfortunately this is also written as 'pot-absence'), to which is assigned the set of absences which are absences of some pot or other. There are 'generic absences' (*sāmānyābhāva*), the absence of any pot, for example. We will see later how such generic readings of 'absence of pot' are obtained in the language.

This completes the semantics of NN, but I would like to note a frequently encountered extension. When the conditioner of the relational abstract term

[10] This is the definition of a limitor as 'that which occurs in no more [than the abstract]' (*anatirikta-vṛtti*). See Matilal 1968: 76.

'R-hood' is a primitive term '*b*' the new language sometimes reformulates 'R-hood-conditioned-by-*b*' as 'R-hood-conditioned-by-R^{-1}-hood-resident-in-*b*' (e.g. *ghaṭa-niṣṭha-kāryatā-nirūpita-kāraṇatā*). Similarly, when the conditioner is an abstract term '*b*-hood' the new language sometimes reformulates 'R-hood-conditioned-by-*b*-hood' as 'R-hood-conditioned-by-R^{-1}-hood-delimited-by-*b*-hood' (e.g. *ghaṭatvāvacchinna-kāryatā-nirūpita-kāraṇatā*) (cf. Ingalls 1951: 46; Matilal 1968: 80). The use of the terms 'conditioned by' 'resident in' and 'delimited by' in these neologisms are distinct from, although related to, their use above as term- and sentence-forming operators. The point to the reformulations is as follows. Suppose that an object *a* is in the domain *A* of the relation R. Then we can form the set of elements in *B* which are related by R to a. Similarly, given a set α in *A*, we can form the set of elements in *A* which are related by R to an element in α. Now, if *a* is an object assigned to a token primitive term '*a*' or α is the set assigned to an abstract term '*a*-hood' then we shall say that the set thus formed is the set assigned to the relational term 'R-hood-resident-in-*a*' or 'R-hood-delimited-by-*a*-hood' respectively. For example, the set assigned to the relational abstract term 'causehood-delimited-by-fire-hood' (*agnitvāvacchinna-kāraṇatā*) comprises those objects which are the effect of a fire. Let such sets be assigned to the terms '*a***R**' or 'α**R**' respectively. The reformulation relies on the identity of **R***b* with *b***R**$^{-1}$, and of **R**β with β**R**$^{-1}$. Sometimes the notion of delimitation in such a reformulation is called delimitation-by-conditioning (*nirūpitatva-saṃbandhāvacchinna*), to distinguish it from the sentence forming delimitation-by-residence (*niṣṭhatva-saṇbandhāvacchinna*) introduced earlier (Ingalls 1951: 50; Matilal 1968: 75). The reformulation leads to a pleasant simplification in certain cases. When the relation R is one–one, or when the relation restricted to the sets α and β is itself a subrelation, then α.**R** β iff β.**R**$^{-1}$ α. In such a case, we can say that **R** as conditioned by β**R**$^{-1}$ is delimited by α iff **R** as conditioned by α **R**$^{-1}$ is delimited by β (e.g. *ghaṭatvāvacchinna-kāryatā-nirūpita-kāraṇatā sā daṇḍatvāvacchinnā*, and vice versa). Having noted this extension, I will not mention it again in what follows.

Reparsing ordinary language

We are now ready to see how an ordinary sentence, for example 'pot is on table' (or '*bhūtale ghaṭaḥ*'), is disambiguated in the technical language. The ambiguity of semantic role in the relation expression 'on' is resolved by saying that contacthood, rather than inherencehood, etc., is the 'limiting relation' (*avacchedaka-saṃbandha*) of the sentence (Ingalls 1951: 51; Matilal 1968: 77). Having done that, the language needs to distinguish eleven distinct readings, which it does as follows.

1. 'A particular table *t* is the locus of a particular pot *p*'. This would be expressed by saying that the relational abstract locushood conditioned by the pot *p* is resident in the table *t*. In our symbolic notation, we write '*t*.**L***p*' where '*t*' represents the token primitive term 'table' whose value is *t*, '*p*' the term 'pot' whose value is *p*,

and 'L' the relational abstract locushood. '$t.Lp$' is true iff $t \in Lp$, the class of objects on which p is located.

2. 't is the locus of some pot'. The paraphrase is: the relational abstract locushood conditioned by pothood is resident in t. Symbolically, '$t.L\pi$' where 'π' represents the abstract term 'pothood' whose value is the class π of pots. '$t.L\pi$' is true iff $t \in L\pi$, the class of objects on which some pot is located. A sentence for which (2) might be the most natural construal is '[The] mountain possesses fire' (*parvato vahnimān*).
3. 't is the locus of all pots'. This is turned around to read 'Every pot occurs on t' and is paraphrased as: occurrenthood-to-t is limited by pothood, where occurrenthood (*vṛtti*, *ādheyatā*) is the inverse of locushood. In our notation, this reads as '$\pi. L^{-1}\ t$' which is true iff $\pi \subset L^{-1}\ t$, i.e. the class of pots is a subset of the class of things located on t. The new language will sometimes say that t is the 'generic locus' of pot (cf. Ingalls 1951: 50). Reading (3) is especially natural when absence is involved. As Ingalls notes,

An absence the [absenteehood (*pratiyogitā*, i.e. the inverse of absenthood)] to which is limited by a generic character or by a property common to several entities is termed a generic absence (*sāmānyābhāva*). Notice that generic absences have the effect of negating all particulars of a given class.

(1951: 56)

Clearly, we should not think of 'generic loci' or 'generic absences' as a special kind of entity.

4. 'Some table is the locus of p' (i.e. 'p is on a table'). The language says here that occurrenthood-to-tablehood is resident in p (p possesses the property of occurring on a table). Symbolically, '$p.L^{-1}\ \tau$' where 'τ' is the abstract term 'tablehood' which is true iff $p \in L^{-1}\ \tau$, the set of objects which occur on a table.
5. 'Every table is the locus of p'. Locushood-to-p is limited by tablehood, i.e. '$\tau.Lp$' which is true iff $\tau \subset Lp$. We find in the early Naiyāyika Vātsyāyana's discussion of semantics, the sentence '[A] cow should not be kicked [by you]' which may very well serve as an example of this reading.
6. 'Some table is the locus of some pot'. The language would say here that locushood to pothood is co-located with tablehood, that is, '$\tau{:}L\pi$' which is true iff $\tau \cap L\pi \neq \emptyset$.
7. 'Every table is the locus of some pot'. This has two readings: (7i) 'every table has some pot or other on it', and (7ii) 'there is a pot which is on every table'. The language expresses the first reading by saying that locushood to pothood is delimited by tablehood, i.e. '$\tau.L\pi$' which is true iff $\tau \subset L\pi$, (the set of tables is a subset of the set of things with pots on). We might borrow another of Vātsyāyana's sentences, '[A] cow is born of [a] cow' to illustrate this reading. It is also a reading closely connected with the notion of pervasion (*vyāpti*). For

example, 'fire pervades smoke' means that every locus of smoke is also a locus of fire. I will discuss (7ii) below.

8. 'Some table is the locus of every pot'. Again, there are two readings, (8i) 'every pot is on some table or another', and (8ii) 'there is a table which is the locus of every pot'. The first reading is naturally expressed by saying that occurrenthood to tablehood is bound by pothood, i.e. '$\pi.\mathrm{L}^{-1}\ \tau$'. (8ii) requires a treatment similar to (7ii), on which see below.
9. 'Every table is the locus of every pot'. This too needs to be treated with the second readings of (7) and (8).

The new language and the predicate calculus

The structure of the new language might be further clarified if we can set up a translation manual between NN and some fragment of the predicate logic, presumably a fragment containing dyadic predicates and quantifiers. The examples discussed above suggest the form such a translation manual might take. From readings such as (1), it is clear that each occurrence of a primitive term will translate into an individual constant. Consider now a sentence like 'fire causes smoke' (i.e. reading 7(i) above). The new language first forms the expression 'causehood-conditioned-by-smokehood' which translates into the open sentence '($\exists x$: smoke)(y causes x)' where ': f' indicates a restriction on the domain of quantification to things that are f. The original sentence is then paraphrased as 'causehood-conditioned-by-smoke is delimited by fire' which translates as

'($\forall y$: fire)($\exists x$: smoke)(y causes x)'.

So a conditioner maps to an existential quantifier, whose domain is restricted to the class assigned to the conditioner, and which binds the second place of a dyadic predicate. Similarly, a delimitor maps to a universal quantifier, whose domain is restricted to the class assigned to it, and which binds the first place of a diadic predicate. It is clear from the way sentences are constructed in NN that the universal quantifier corresponding to the limitor always has wider scope than the existential quantifier corresponding to the conditioner. Finally, the co-location operator will translate into an existential operator binding the first place of the dyadic predicate, for a sentence like (6), 'locushood-conditioned-by-pothood is co-located with tablehood' ('τ:Lπ') translates to '($\exists x$: τ)($\exists y$:π) (xLy)'. In this way the technical language formalizes an ambiguity in the semantics of an ordinary noun-phrase, by translating it into either a token primitive term or an abstract term, and assigning to it either an individual or a class.[11]

[11] The idea that nouns are ambiguous in this way was first clearly stated by Uddyotakara and Jayanta. See their comments under *Nyāya-sūtra* 2.2.66, and Matilal 1971: 67–69.

The ordinary sentence 'pot is not in the room' has three distinct readings. It might mean that a certain pot *p* is not in the room; or that there is a pot which is not in the room; or that no pot is in the room. The third reading is usually the most natural. In NN, we can form from a primitive term 'pot' a negative term 'pot-absence'. We can also form a negative term from the abstract term 'pothood', unfortunately also expressed as 'pot-absence'. These two terms are by definition equivalent to the relational terms 'absenthood-conditioned-by-pot' ('**N***p*') and 'absenthood-conditioned-by-pothood' ('**N**π'), where the relation of absence is a one-one relation between any entity and its negative entity or absentee. The first reading is now expressed as '*t*.**L**(**N***p*)' i.e. '*t* is a member of the set of loci of absentees of *p*' i.e. '$\neg tLp$'. The second reading is expressed as '*t*.**L**(**N**π)', i.e. '*t* is a member of the set of loci of absences of a pot', i.e. '*t* is a member of the set of objects which are such that there is a pot for which it is not the locus', i.e. '$(\exists y{:}\pi)\ (\neg\ tLy)$'. Note how this shows that the absence relation, with its corresponding negative terms, is equivalent to a negation which always takes narrowest scope. To catch the third, and most natural, reading of the sentence, i.e. 'No pot is on the table' or 'The table is the locus of the absence of all pots', the new language makes pothood the delimitor of absenteehood (*pratiyogitā*), the inverse of absenthood (cf. Matilal 1968: 80–81). The obvious candidate is 'π. $\mathbf{N}^{-1}(\mathbf{L}^{-1}t)$', i.e. 'absenteehood-conditioned-by-superstratumhood-conditioned-by-table is limited by pothood' (*bhūtala-nirūpita-ādheyatā-nirūpita-pratiyogitā sā ghaṭatvāvacchinnā*). This expands as 'the set of pots is a subset of absentees for which there is an absence in the set of superstrata of *t*', i.e. 'the set of pots is a subset of the set of objects whose absence is located on *t*' or '$(\forall x{:}\pi)(\neg tLx)$'.

We might note that, as long as negative terms are only used for the adjunct of another relation, the negative objects are 'virtual' entities; they are always quantified out of the final sentence. Matilal exploits this fact to construct a semantics in which every property has a 'presence-range' and an 'absence-range' corresponding to the set of loci of the property and the set of loci of the absence of the property (Matilal 1985: 112 *sqq*).

The problem of scope ambiguity is usually illustrated by a sentence like 'Everybody loves somebody'. It is possible to read this sentence in two ways, as saying that given any person, there is someone who loves them, or as saying that there is a person who is loved by everybody. In this second reading, the existential quantifier precedes the universal quantifier. It therefore poses a problem for the new language, in which the universal quantifier or limitor always has widest scope. However, suppose we consider the third 'generic' reading of 'pot is not on a table'. The NN expression of this is 'π. $\mathbf{N}^{-1}\ (\mathbf{L}^{-1}\ \tau)$', i.e. 'absenteehood-conditioned-by-superstratumhood-conditioned-by-table is limited by pothood' that is, 'the set of pots is a subset of the set of objects whose absence is located on t' or '$(\forall y{:}\pi)(\exists x{:}\ \tau)\ (\neg tL^{-1}x)$'. If this is *not* true, then there is a table which is not the locus of the absence of any pot, i.e. a table which is the locus of every pot. So the second reading can be expressed as 'not $\pi.\mathbf{N}^{-1}\ (\mathbf{L}^{-1}\ \tau)$' i.e. 'absenthood-conditioned-by-occurrenthood-conditioned-by-pothood is not delimited by tablehood'. In the predicate calculus, this result can be expressed via the theorem: $(\exists y{:}\beta)(\forall x{:}\alpha)(xRy) = \neg(\forall y{:}\ \beta)(\exists x{:}\ \alpha)(\neg xRy) = \neg(\forall y{:}\ \beta)(\exists x{:}\ \alpha)\ (\neg yR^{-1}x)$. So with the help of a negation which always takes narrowest scope (the term negation) and one which always takes widest scope (the sentence negation), we can actually express the mixed readings. An exactly analogous tactic will obtain (9) from (6). It seems that only in such cases is a sentential negation ineliminable.

The language NN is therefore equivalent to a quantified language (call it NN★) in which each sentence is constructed as follows. (1) Begin with a dyadic predicate '. . . *R* . . .'. (2) A negation (¬) taking narrowest scope optionally occurs next. Thus '(¬)(. . . *R* . . .)'. (3) The next step is to fill the second place of the relational predicate, either with a constant or with a variable bound by an existential quantifier, whose range is restricted to a certain set β. We might, for simplicity, use the individualization device to eliminate the constants in favour of bound variables. This quantifier has wider scope than the negation in (1) but narrower scope than anything else. Thus '$(\exists y{:}\pi)$ (¬) (. . . Ry)'. (4) Next, the left-hand place is bound, either by a constant, or by a restricted universal quantifier or by a restricted existential quantifier. Thus '$(\forall x{:}\tau)(\exists y{:}\pi)$ (¬) (xRy)' or '$(\exists x{:}\tau)(\exists y{:}\pi)$ (¬)(xRy)'. (5) The last step is the optional insertion of a negation which takes largest scope. These five steps correspond to forming a relational abstract, conditioning it with a term (possibly negative) to form a relational term, and forming a sentence using delimitation or co-location, possibly negated. It follows that every sentence in this language (NN★) has the structure (¬)(∀/∃)(∃)(¬)(. . . R . . .). The order of the various components is fixed. However, it seems possible to show that every sentence composed from a dyadic predicate, one or two quantifiers, and negation, with no restrictions on the order in which these elements occur, is equivalent to a sentence having the structure of the sentences in NN★. For the formula (¬∀ = ∃¬) permits any sentence of the form (∃∀) or (∀∀) to be transposed into one of the form (∀∃) or (∃∃) respectively, and also permits the transformation of any sentence in which a negation occurs between two quantifiers into one having only narrow or wide scope negation, appropriately inverting the dyadic predicate if necessary. Also, a restricted quantifier can be replaced by an unrestricted quantifier together with an appropriate predicate. It follows that the language NN★ is equivalent to that fragment of the predicate calculus whose sentences take the form '(Fx&Gy & xRy)' quantified and negated according to taste.[12]

NN encodes some of the logical apparatus used by early modern thinkers. The authors themselves do not draw such a sharp distinction between terms and sentences as is done in NN. Nor do they show much interest in the problems of scope ambiguity, and hence they understate the need for a sentence negation. Many other technical notions are introduced, many having to do with the concatenation of relations and terms and with the treatment of identity. In earlier chapters of this book, I have alluded

[12] Uckelman 2009 notices a remarkable congruence between this formalization and the truth conditions for the square of opposition given by Peter Abelard.

to several of them: *paryāpti* (collective rather than distributive predication), *samūhālambana* (conjunctive predication), and *vyāsajya-vṛtti* (pervasive predication). Moreover, the use of the technical vocabulary varies a little from one author to another. And often the language is used in only a semi-formal way, especially when not used by philosophers. Thus NN is itself a 'regimentation' of the new technical language.

One of the insights which marked the advance from scholastic or medieval logic to the quantifier theory was the realization that sentences should be seen as constructed in a series of stages, and not as constructed simultaneously from their component elements (Geach 1980; Dummett 1981: 10ff). The two readings of 'Someone loves everyone' cannot be distinguished if we regard the two expressions of generality and the relational expression as simultaneously synthesized; instead, we should see the sentence as built up from the relational expression '. . . loves . . . ' in two steps. First, we form a predicate 'someone loves . . . ' or a predicate '. . . loves everyone' and then we fill in the remaining place. Dummett (1981: 12) notes that in an ordinary language, there is an '*ad hoc* convention' that

> The order of construction corresponds to the inverse order of occurrence of the signs of generality in the sentence.

This convention works because every sentence has both an active and a passive form, in which the order of the signs of generality are reversed. Thus, the active form 'someone loves everyone' and the passive form 'Everyone is loved by someone' are most naturally heard as expressing different readings of the sentence, even though strictly both are ambiguous.

The new technical language seems, as I have tried to show, to encode the insight that sentences are constructed in stages, and for this reason sidesteps the need for a counterpart of the medieval doctrine of *suppositio*. It is true that this language, systematizing the '*ad hoc* convention', lacks the elegance or clarity of a quantifier-variable system. Moreover, when a sentence is such that, in the quantifier system, several argument-places are filled by the same bound variable, it resorts, as does ordinary language, to the use of pronouns in order to generate an equivalent sentence in which the sign of generality occurs only in a single place (Matilal 1968: 23; Dummett 1981: 13). On the other hand, Dummett's (1981: 20) criticism of natural languages, that they

> work by means of principles which are buried deep beneath the surface, and are complex and to a large extent arbitrary,

is far less applicable to the early modern technical language than to the ordinary Sanskrit of earlier philosophical discourse, for the principles to which it appeals are generally systematic, explicit, and, most importantly, unambiguous.

I conclude from this study that we do find in the 'new reason' technical language the elements necessary for a 'calculus' of relations. It was to be highly effective in the formulation of logical arguments which are not just sound but *can be seen to be* sound. It is the basis for a new vehicle for reasoning, representing to early modern India what the appeal to geometrical methods and diagrams represented in the work of early modern thinkers in Europe. I will finish this book by looking, in still further detail, at the treatment of quantification in this language, for the ability of any technical language to serve as a calculus will is fundamentally dependent on how well it handles quantification.

16

Rival Logics of Domain Restriction

Early modern philosophy in India is very interested in the logic of quantification, and in particular in the semantics of the Sanskrit particle *eva*, which can mean something like 'only', 'alone', 'exactly', 'indeed', or 'just' depending on the exact context of use.[1] Raghunātha again is responsible for this interest, having remarked on the particle in the course of his commentary on Vallabha. Bhavānanda, who extended the genre of writing of short treatises on particular parts of speech, a genre Raghunātha had introduced with his work on the negative particle and the verbal endings, was the first to write a separate treatise, the *Elucidation [of Raghunātha's comments] about the Particle Eva* (*Evakāraṭippaṇī*). Laugākṣī composed his *A Study of the Particle Eva* (*Evakāravicāra*), and Harirāma, Mathurānātha and Gadādhara all did likewise.[2] The importance of *eva* as a device of quantification was noticed first by the Buddhists, and Dharmakīrti made much of it in his development of Buddhist logical theory. Early modern writers analyse some of the same examples on which Dharmakīrti bases his analysis, but bring to bear a much broader range of linguistic data in support of their new theory. Recently attention has been drawn to the fact that Dharmakīrti's theory continued to be discussed in early modern Tibetan manuals of dialectics (specifically, the dGe lugs pa's *bsdus grwa* texts), and a comparison with contemporaneous 'new reason' discussion would be very illuminating.[3]

I will begin by reconstructing Dharmakīrti's influential analysis, so that the innovation that this description introduces can better be appreciated. The early modern criticism rests on two claims. First of all, Dharmakīrti bases his analysis on a small number of examples, ones which are in certain respects atypical of the general behaviour of the particle. Moreover, he presents a theory in which the particle is semantically ambiguous, and what the early modern philosophers attempt to provide is a semantically unified account, one which is applicable to the particle wherever and whenever it is used.

[1] Gillon 1999: 118 says that '[i]n Classical Sanskrit, the very same particle, *eva*, has both [restrictive and emphatic] uses.' Monier-Williams suggests that it can be rendered 'by such adverbs as just, exactly, very, same, only, even, alone, merely, immediately on, still, already, &c.,' while Apte offers '(1) just, quite, exactly; (2) same, very, identical; (3) only, alone, merely (implying exclusion).'

[2] See NCat 3: 78 for references. See also the text in Gadādhara *et al.* 1913–31: 67–68.

[3] On the Tibetan discussion, especially in the *Sras bsdus grwa* of Ngag dbang bkra bshis (1678–1738 CE), see Nemoto (forthcoming).

Analysis from Buddhist sources

According to Dharmakīrti, the meaning of the restrictive particle is 'exclusion' *(vyavaccheda)*. Depending on the position of *eva* in the sentence, the exclusion is of one of three kinds: 'exclusion from connection with something else' *(anyayoga-vyavaccheda)*, 'exclusion from non-connection' *(ayoga-vyavaccheda)*, and 'exclusion from permanent non-connection' *(atyantāyoga-vyavaccheda)*:

The restrictive particle excludes the non-connection, the connection with something else, or the permanent non-connection of the predicate-property, when attached to the predicate term, the subject term or the verb [respectively]. Even when not actually used, its role is understood from the speaker's intention, for [any] sentence has exclusion as its outcome. Examples [of the three cases] are: 'Caitra is an archer', 'Pārtha is an archer', and 'A lotus is blue'.[4]

Dharmakīrti follows Diṅnāga in using this particle as a means to introduce quantification into the clauses of the logical formulae defining valid inference. Kajiyama records how later Buddhist logicians applied the theory to the analysis of negative statements, general terms and causal relations (Kajiyama 1966: 57; 1973). In another place, Dharmakīrti seems not to regard the distinction between impermanent and permanent as *semantically* relevant:

There are two kinds of exclusion—from non-connection and from connection to something else.[5]

The contribution of *eva* to the meaning of a sentence lies in the restriction it places on the relation between subject and predicate.[6] The effect of its insertion is to make explicit which of several sorts of exclusion a sentence exemplifies, something that depends on whether it attaches to the subject, the non-verbal predicate, or the verb or copula. Dharmakīrti offers an example of each cases:

1a. (Pārtha eva) dhanurdharaḥ 'Pārtha alone is an archer'.
1b. Caitro (dhanurdhara eva) 'Caitra is an archer indeed'.
1c. Nīlaṃ sarojaṃ (bhavaty eva) 'A lotus is surely blue'.

The meaning he assigns to each of these sentences is:

2a. Being-an-archer is excluded from connection with **other than** Pārtha.
2b. Being-an-archer is excluded from **non-connection** with Caitra.
2c. Being-blue is excluded from **permanent non-connection** with a lotus.

4 ayogaṃ yogam aparair atyantāyogam eva ca | vyavacchinatti dharmasya nipāto vyatirecakaḥ | | viśeṣaṇaviśeṣyābhāyāṃ kriyayā ca sahoditaḥ | vivakṣāto prayoge 'pi tasyārtho 'yam pratīyate | | vyavacchedaphalaṃ vākyaṃ yataś caitro dhanurdharaḥ | pārtho dhanurdharo nīlaṃ sarojam iti vā yathā | | (*Prāmāṇavārttika* iv: 190–192).

5 dvividho hi vyavacchedo viyogāparayogayoḥ vyavacchedād (*Prāmāṇavārttika* iv: 38a–c).

6 As Katsura 1986: 8–9 notes, the grammarians were the first to link the meaning of *eva* with the notion of 'restriction' (*avadhāraṇa*). See *Pāṇini-sūtra* 8.1.62, and Vyāḍi's meta-rule: yata evakāras tato 'nyatrāvadhāraṇam 'when the restrictive particle *eva* occurs with reference to one linguistic item, the other is subject to restriction'. Later analyses concern, in effect, the proper expansion of the notion of restriction.

I will follow Dharmakīrti in not attaching sematic weight to the distinction between the second and third cases here. A number of authors have drawn attention to the fact that, given these semantic assignments, the particle is being treated as a quantifier.[7] We must note, however, that it does not behave like the Aristotelian determiners, 'all' 'some' 'no' and 'not all'. For, first, it can be inserted into sentences with singular subjects: sentence 1a. is well-formed, but we cannot say 'all Pārtha is an archer' or 'no Pārtha is an archer'. In this respect, the role of *eva* resembles the cross-categorical behaviour of expressions like 'only' and 'even' in English (Horn 1989; Lycan 1991). Second, the contribution the particle makes to the truth-conditions is sensitive to context. Indeed, from the standpoint of modern theory about generalized quantifiers (Barwise and Cooper 1981; Westerståhl 1988), the context neutrality of the Aristotelian quantifiers, their failure to distinguish between focus and scope, places them in a rather special category. Attempts to translate sentences involving *eva* directly into sentences involving the standard quantifiers of a first-order language tend to be insensitive to such questions.

For the purposes of this overview, however, I too will ignore issues about context.[8] What I want to emphasize, instead, are difficulties in deciding exactly what Dharmakīrti's theory asserts. There are two sorts of difficulty. Let us start with his first example, 'Pārtha alone is an archer'. According to the analysis he offers, what this says is that nobody who is not Pārtha is an archer. The problem is that this analysis does not, in itself, affirm that Pārtha actually is an archer. It leaves it open whether this is something stated by the sentence, or whether it is something that the sentence implicates but does not state, or else something that the sentence only presupposes. If I say, for instance, that 'No non-members will be admitted' that certainly implicates that members will be admitted; but does it actually state it?

A second difficulty about interpreting Dharmakīrti's theory arises because two of his examples involve proper names. The problem is that it is not clear how to generalize the account from cases of singular predication to cases where the subject is expressed by a general term. The sentence 'Caitra is an archer indeed' asserts, according to Dharmakīrti, that there is no lack of connection between Caitra and being an archer; in other words, that Caitra is in the class of things which are archers. Suppose, though, we consider the sentence 'Men are archers indeed'. What the theory tells us is that this states that there is no lack of connection between the class of men and the class of archer—but does that mean that all men are archers or only that at least some men are archers?

These two sorts of ambiguity have left interpreters unsure what Dharmakīrti's theory actually is (see Kajiyama 1973; Gillon and Hayes 1982; Ganeri 1999a). One of his early commentators remarks that his view is that the statement 'S-*eva* P' is made when it is 'well-known' that S is P, but there is a doubt about whether things other

[7] For references, see Gillon and Hayes 1982: 194, n. 1.

[8] I have shown how to treat the particle as a context-sensitive quantifier in Ganeri 1999a.

than S are P as well.[9] This suggests that the view is that the fact that S is P is a *presupposition* for asserting 'S-*eva* P'. A statement presupposes a state of affairs just in case the statement only has a truth-value if the state of affairs obtains. Given that the presupposition is a precondition for the statement to assert anything, it is generally held that that statement does not literally assert that the presupposition obtains. However, that the presupposition obtains will usually be conversationally implicated by the statement. In this way, one might deny that 'S-*eva* P' literally states that S is P, although it is presupposed and implicated.

Dharmakīrti's view, in any case, is that the particle has two different logical functions. When attached to the subject, it denies a connection of the predicate with what is other than the subject; when attached to the predicate, it denies non-connection between subject and predicate. The most likely hypothesis, therefore, is that his theory is as summed up in Table 16.1.

Table 16.1 Dharmakīrti's analysis

'S-*eva* P'	'S P-*eva*'
$P \subseteq S$	$S \wedge P$

The early modern theory: a unified account

What do the early modern 'new reason' philosophers say about the logic of domain restriction? Jayarāma, as I have already noted, begins the *Garland of Categories* with just such an extensive discussion (1985: 30–83). He tells us that Raghunātha's view was that the particle never means exclusion from permanent non-connection, but only exclusion from non-connection and from connection with another, or merely exclusion from connection with another.[10] Mādhavadeva wrote a commentary, the *Panicle of What is Essential in the Light-Ray about the Particle Eva* (*Evakāra-dīdhiti-sāramañjarī*), on the section of Raghunātha's work where the particle is discussed.[11] In his *Essence of Reason*, he provides a helpful summary of the old and the new view. The old view is clearly identifiable as that of Dharmakīrti:

This is the old view. The particle *eva*, in a sentence like 'A lotus is certainly blue' (*nīlaṃ sarojaṃ bhavatyeva*) when joined with the verb, means exclusion from permanent non-connection. In a sentence like 'A conch-shell is white indeed' (*śaṅkhaḥ pāṇḍura eva*), when joined with the predicate, it means exclusion from non-connection. In a sentence like 'Pārtha alone is an archer' (*pārtha eva dhanurdharaḥ*), when joined to the subject, it means exclusion from connection with something else.

[9] pārthe dhanurdharatvaṃ prasiddham eva | kintu tādṛśam anyasyāpi kim astīti sandehe 'nyayogavyavacchedaphalaṃ viśeṣaṇam | (Manorathanandin, in Dharmakīrti 1989: 402).

[10] dīdhitikṛtastu nātyantāyogavyavacchedako vācyaḥ | kintu ayogānyayogavyavacchedau, anyayogavyavaccheda eva vā ityāhuḥ | tathā hi nātyantāyogavyavacchedo 'rthaḥ | (1985: 32).

[11] Hz. 14148, p. 133. Luck. Uni. p. 42 (-*arthavivṛtti*; author called Mādhava Godāvari). Mithilā. PUL. II. p.3.

The new philosophers, however, say that the particle *eva* never leads to a cognition of exclusion from non-connection, because it always gives rise to a cognition of expulsion from connection with something else, following the example of a sentence like 'He is the brother only of Caitra, and he only of Maitra'. It does not have a denotative power. I have considered the matter at great length in my treatise on *eva*.[12]

Mahādeva Puṇatāṃakara says that in the view of the modern thinkers, the particle *eva* always and only means 'exclusion from connection with another'.[13]

Another helpful source is the entry in Bhīmācārya Jhalakīkar's *Nyāyakośa,* which presents a standardized version of the early modern account in a succinct form. Jhalakīkar summarizes an emerging consensus about the 'new reason' position:

In actual fact, the meaning of *eva* is [always] exclusion from connection with another. An exclusion is a constant absence or a mutual absence. In a case like 'In earth alone (*eva*) is there smell' the meaning is that there is smell in earth and absence of smell in what is other-than-earth. In a case like 'A conch-shell is white indeed (*eva*)' the meaning is that that which is identical to a conch-shell is white and that there is mutual absence from a conch-shell in what is other-than-white. In a case like 'Pārtha alone (*eva*) is an archer' it is understood that that which is identical to Pārtha is an archer and that there is exclusion from being an archer in what is other-than-Pārtha.[14]

A more detailed investigation of the primary texts would be of great value in reaching an understanding of the internal debates about the logic of domain restriction among the later 'new reason' authors. There is clear evidence in this discussion of an evolving rapprochement between linguistic analysis and philosophical theory. The sources I have presented are, however, sufficient for our present purposes.

The issue which divides Dharmakīrti and the Naiyāyikas is the positive existential force of sentences containing *eva*: does the sentence *state* that some/all S are P or *presuppose* it? It is most interesting to note that exactly the same issue is the major source of contemporary dispute about the semantics of the English quantifier 'only'. Horn (1989: 248) notes that

The essential issue is: is *only* α negative in meaning and positive only by presupposition or implicature, or does it abbreviate a conjunction (*only* α = 'α and nothing {other/more} than α')?'

[12] evakārasya nīlaṃ sarojaṃ bhavatyetyādau kriyāsaṅgatasyātyantāyogavyavacchedaḥ śakyaḥ | śaṅkhaḥ pāṇḍura evetyādau viśeṣaṇasaṅgatasyāyogavyavacchedaḥ | pārtha eva dhanurdhara ityādau viśeṣyasaṅgatasyānyayogavyavaccheda iti prāñcaḥ | navyāstu caitrasyaivāyaṃ bhrātā maitrasyaivedam ityādyanurodhenānyayoga-vyavacchedabodhasyāvabodhāt tenaiva sarvatropapattau nāyoga-vyavacchedādi-bodho evakārād iti na tatra śaktiḥ | vistarastv asmatkṛta evakāravāde draṣṭavyaḥ | (Mādhavadeva 1903–4: 241).

[13] navīnanaye sarvatraivakārasyānyayogavyavacchedakamātrārthakatvāt | (Mahādeva 1930: 61,9).

[14] vastutastu anyayogavyavaccheda eva-kārārthaḥ | vyavacchedaś cātyantābhāvaḥ anyonyābhāvaś ca | pṛthivyām eva gandhaḥ ityādau pṛthivyāṃ gandhaḥ pṛthivyanyasmin gandhābhāvaś ca iti bodhaḥ | śaṅkhaḥ pāṇḍura eva ityādau śaṅkha-tādātmyavān pāṅduraḥ pāṇḍurānyasmiñ śaṅkhānyonyābhāvaś ca iti bodhaḥ | pārtha eva dhanurdharaḥ ityādau pārtha-tādātymavān dhanurdharaḥ pārthānyasmin dhanurdharatvavyavacchedaś ca pratīyate iti | *Nyāyakośa*, sv. '*eva*'. The Nyāya view that particles contribute to semantic content (*vācaka; sārthaka*) is rejected by grammarians, who treat particles as having a merely 'indicative' (*dyotaka*) role (P. Chakravarti 1933: 175–177).

The early moderns think that there is assertion and nor merely presupposition. Though based, in the first instance, on an analysis of the linguistic data, they regard this account as having an important theoretical advantage, which is that they can now offer a *univocal* account of the role of the particle. Whether it attaches to the subject or not, it denies a connection with what is other, and simultaneously asserts a connection. So the sentence 'Men alone are archers' asserts that some men are archers and no non-man is an archer, while the sentence 'Men are archers indeed' asserts that some men are archers and no non-archer is a man (Table 16.2):

Table 16.2 The new analysis

'S-*eva* P'	'S P-*eva*'
$P \subseteq S \;\&\; S \wedge P$	$S \subseteq P \;\&\; S \wedge P$

A promising way to decide which semantics is the right one is to look at what is syntactically permissible. For example, is it permissible to delete the particle:

3a. S-*eva* P $\vdash$ S P, or
3b. S P-*eva* $\vdash$ S P?

Both parties will claim these transitions to be valid. For Dharmakīrti, it is the move from an unambiguous sentence to an ambiguous sentence, one which has as one of its meanings the meaning of the first sentence. For the Naiyāyika, the transition is valid because the sentence on the right expresses the existential implication of the sentence on the left.[15] Transitions which are validated by Dharmakīrti's semantics but not by the 'new reason' semantics are these:

4a. S-*eva* P $\vdash \neg$ (non-S P-*eva*), and
4b. P-*eva* S $\dashv \neg$ (non-S-*eva* P).

This pair partly corresponds to the inter-definability of the existential and universal quantifiers. For 'S-*eva* P' states that all P are S, which is equivalent to the proposition that it is not the case that some non-S is P. The question at issue is one about the existential import of universal quantification.

Another issue has to do with monotonicity. Barwise and Cooper (1981: 184) give the following tests for monotonicity. Suppose $P_1 \subseteq P_2$, and QS is a quantifier (e.g. 'some men'). Then QS is monotone increasing if QS $P_1 \rightarrow$ QS P_2, and QS is monotone decreasing if QS $P_2 \rightarrow$ QS P_1. If it is neither, QS is non-monotone. For example, 'some men' is monotone increasing, as shown by the validity of the inference from 'some men are running' to 'some men are moving' while 'no men' is monotone decreasing. Horn (1989: 248) observes that if 'only' is negative in meaning and positive

[15] The same question arises in the analysis of 'only'. Lycan remarks that 'for convenience, I have fallen in with the common view that *Only S is P* non-cancellably implies *S is P*, but that claim is highly questionable' (1991: 135 n. 12).

only by presupposition, then it will be monotone decreasing, while if it has a conjunctive meaning, then it will be non-monotone. Clearly, an inference like 'Socrates alone is running ⊢ Socrates alone is moving' is invalid; so 'only' is not monotone increasing. The question is whether the inference 'Socrates alone is moving ⊢ Socrates alone is running' is valid. The inference is invalid on the conjunctive account, since it does not follow that Socrates is running from his moving. However, it is valid on the purely negative account, since if no one other than Socrates is moving, then no one other than Socrates is running.

Returning to the particle *eva*, what we can see now is that Dharmakīrti's position is that *eva* is a monotone decreasing quantifier, while the Naiyāyikas treat it as being non-monotone (the salient transition is 'S-*eva* $P_2 \vdash$ S-*eva* P_1'). Since there is no widespread agreement even among contemporary linguists about what natural language intuitions say about the monotonicity of 'only' it is hardly surprising that there is no general consensus about the Sanskrit particle *eva*. It is, however, remarkable how clearly the issue is already formulated in early modern India. Only with further study of examples in natural Sanskrit will we be in a position to decide which semantics best fits the actual use of *eva*. Such detailed examinations of actual constructions are exactly what we find in later Navya Nyāya treatises about the particle, and are the method by which they try to defend their analysis, which they also prefer on grounds of theoretical simplicity and elegance.

Let me conclude by affiraning that, in my opinion, the 'new reason' analysis of *eva* is the first properly systematic work in the theory of generalized quantifiers (on which, see Peters and Westertåhl 2006). A comparison with Latin scholastic discussions of *tantum* would be very illuminating, in treatises on syncategorematics by, for instance, William of Sherwood, John Buridan and the Oxford calculators (thanks to Stephen Menn for mentioning this).

Conclusion

Early modernity in India consists in the formation of a new philosophical self, one which makes it possible meaningfully to conceive of oneself as engaging the ancient and the alien in conversation. Dārā Shukoh is an exemplary early modern thinker, his belief that the Upaniṣads could be read as a commentary on the Qu'rān envisaged a relationship that was based neither on deference nor on rejection. For Dārā the Hindu text was not an authority to which Islam must defer but a partner in a single quest for truth—his sectarian contemporaries' inability to make that distinction cost him his life. Yaśovijaya is a quintessential early modern thinker too: in his case this was due to his search for a theory of individuals and community in which liberal political values occupy the centre stage. Yaśovijaya articulates a key feature of the early modern self when he says that public discussion must rest in balance, neutrality and an openness to the reasonable opinions of others.

What distinguishes the modernity of the 'new reason' philosophers is a new sense of one's duties towards the past. They saw themselves as engaging in 'dialogues with the dead' (Curley 1986), not in deference, but to collaborate in a new search for the truth. Interestingly enough, Descartes himself is by no means unfamiliar with the idea, even though he is typically dismissive of it:

> Conversing with those of past centuries is much the same as travelling. It is good to know something of the customs of various peoples, so that we may judge our own more soundly and not think that everything contrary to our own ways is ridiculous and irrational, as those who have seen nothing of the world ordinarily do. But one who spends too much time travelling eventually becomes a stranger in his own country; and one who is too curious about the practices of past ages usually remains quite ignorant about those of the present.
>
> (*Discourse* AT vi. 6; 1984: 113–114)

Descartes is right in his identification of the danger—that of being so drawn in to one's study of the past as to forget why one has undertaken it—and in so far as he was seeking 'rules for the direction of the mind', the policy he advocates, of turning away from the past altogether, an effective one (indeed, it is very similar to the method of radical doubt he would also recommend, to treat everything as false of which one cannot be certain). There is, however, also something of the 'studied pose' in Descartes' pretence to have given up travelling in the past altogether; and there are other ways to safeguard against the danger than the one he recommends. However captivating one's conversation partner might be, there are always ways to maintain one's own sense of self.

One effective method is to imagine that one is talking to a contemporary rather than hearing a voice with all the gravity of past tradition (and to a fellow human being rather than to the member of an alien race or religion). In introducing an opinion from the ancient past with the words, 'Some people think that...', or in saying 'Here is an old view and here is a new one', this is just what the early moderns do. There is a conscious and deliberate ahistoricism in such a strategy, which Jorge Luis Borges notes may either frustrate or delight the twentieth-century reader, depending on their frame of reference:

> I have read several histories of Indian philosophy. The authors (Englishmen, Germans, Frenchmen, Americans, and so on) always wonder at the fact that in India people have no historical sense—that they treat all thinkers as if they were contemporary. They translate the words of ancient philosophy into [their own] modern jargon. But this stands for something brave. This stands for the idea that one *believes* in philosophy or that one *believes* in poetry—that things beautiful once can go on being beautiful still.
>
> (Borges 2000: 114–115).

To treat a thinker as if they are contemporary means, first of all, to be willing to disagree with them, and it is this that comes strongly and clearly to the fore with first Raghunātha and then subsequent 'new reason' philosophers. Conversing with the past is not incompatible with originality and modernity, although it could be a good heuristic to pretend that it is. It is certainly brave to vow, as Descartes did, 'entirely [to] abandon the study of letters' (*Discourse* AT vi. 9; 1984: 115), but there is another form of intellectual bravery, to relate to the ancient—and the alien—as if it were a friend who can take criticism. This is an effective remedy against what Sarvepalli Radhakrishnan described, referring to the pre-moderns, as an 'anxiety to preserve continuity' with the past.[1] Radhakrishnan himself felt the pull of that anxiety, and it was right for his biographer to describe him as involved in a project of 'returning to the source' in the course of nationalist identity-building (Gopal 1989: Introduction). A return to the source is not, and can never be, a conversation among equals; it is escapism. Halbfass observes in a Weberian spirit that no romanticization or adulation of ancient India could alter the facts of Western dominance.[2] It goes without saying that

[1] 'While employing logical methods and arriving at truths agreeable to reason, they were yet anxious to preserve their continuity with the ancient texts. They did not wish it to be thought that they were enunciating something completely new. While this may involve a certain want of frankness with themselves, it helped the spread of what they regarded as the truth.' (1929: 21).

[2] 'Whatever the nature of the current crisis may be, we cannot return to the past, and we cannot escape into foreign traditions and ways of orientation... It does not help to invoke Eastern methods of meditation, or the cultivation of inner awareness, against objectification, instrumentalization, consumerization... No calculated importation and application of Eastern ways of thinking, or methods of meditation, will enable us to reverse history, or change the basic conditions of a world which is dominated by science and technology, driven by blind rationality, and over-powered by mechanisms of mastery and calculation.' (Halbfass 1988: 441).

he is equally scathing about what he describes as 'the exclusion of India from the history of philosophy' (1988: 145), seeing in this phenomenon an attempt by Europeans to define themselves in terms of their acceptance of a certain set of philosophical values; which then, of necessity, had to be denied to non-European cultures.

Historians of Indian philosophy have, however, been misled by this attitude of Indian philosophers towards their own philosophical past, and this has led to what we might call 'the paradox of Indian historiography': virtually without exception, standard 'histories' of Indian philosophy are *ahistorical*—instead, they describe and juxtapose monolithic systems of ideas using a manner of description which strips those systems of internal temporal texture. It is obvious, however, that one cannot recognize an idea as 'new' unless one can situate it against a backdrop sensitive to what came before and what came after; so the historiography produces—as an artefact of its own methodology—a refusal to acknowledge any distinction between the pre-modern and early modernity. Reading later developments back into the earlier texts has virtually the same result. My alternative method in this book, which is based on an expanded and adapted application of Skinner's contextualist approach to the history of ideas, in which the penning of a text is situated against a background of intertextual context or *śāstra*, and ṭol-oriented network or *sampradāya*, is a step in the direction of putting Indian intellectual historiography on a new foundation. The use of this method has enabled me sharply to distinguish between the incentives that motivate a thinker to be modern and what that modernity itself consists in.

The difficult *via moderna* respects the past *and* rebels against it. Another strategy for ensuring that the conversation is not one-sided is to make use of the full resources of commentary as a tool for mediating the discussion between the ancient text and the contemporary audience. Raghunātha's commentaries are more like asides and marginal notes, of the sort one makes not when one is trying to interpret the text so much as when one is thinking with it and beyond it. One's comments will then often take the form 'But this can't be right, because . . . ' 'What is really going on?' 'What is the deeper thought?'. In disseminating such commentaries, Raghunātha succeeded in showing his contemporaries that there is another way to read an ancient text. It became possible, for example, to take the textual material of the ancient text and use it as the foundation upon which to build a new philosophy, as Jayarāma does in the *Garland of Principles*, and as many others did with Udayana's verses in the *Offering*. Such a practice can hardly be described as deference; still less is it to 'entirely abandon' the ancient work. It is also no accident that the *Garland* contains a theoretical model of ideal conversation (*vāda*) between equals in a search for truth. Other sorts of commentary likewise have a constructive role in educating readerships in new strategies of appraisal and appropriation of the past.

I have characterized *early* modernity not as real modernity mixed up in a confused muddle with pre-modern habits, as many historians of early modern Europe do, but as the embodiment of a distinctive understanding of one's duties towards the past. It is true that early modern thinkers write for pre-modern audiences, but their appeal to the past is not merely one of expedience. The fundamental change is in how one intends the reader to react. Pre-modern works of philosophy in India are very often in the therapeutic mould. They aim to bring about a certain sort of transformation in the mind of the reader; they are what I have elsewhere called 'protreptic' (Ganeri 2007). In early modern works, the shift is from an intention to make the reader *live* well to an ambition to make them *think* well. Raghunātha is explicit enough about this in the *Inquiry*, addressing readers directly in an appeal to them to reflect (1915: 79,1–80,3; quoted in the Introduction); and his commentarial notes, whatever their ambition, certainly had this as their actual effect. The texts of 'new reason' philosophers are full of exhortations to the reader to direct their attention to what matters: 'this should be thought about' (*iti cintyam*); 'this needed to be pondered' (*iti dhyeyam*); 'this is the direction [the reader should go in]' (*iti dik*). The *Inquiry* is a challenge: deliberately provocative, it led other philosophers to a far-reaching and sophisticated reformation of realism. The new spirit is succinctly captured by Veṇīdatta at the end of his *Embellishment of the Categories*. He appeals to a model of reasoning as 'adaptation' (*ūha*), which has itself a long history in Indian thought, and claims that an adaptation of the ancient metaphysics is legitimate as long as it is done on the basis of a proper deliberation (*vicāra*; Veṇīdatta 1930: 36). This is the *via moderna*, working with the ancients but not hamstrung by them.

Central to the 'new reason' were three ideas. The first was that methods of inquiry have to be evidence-based and collaborative, relying on proof-strategies that are open to empirical confirmation or disconfirmation and involving reasoned decision-making mechanisms in multi-agent environments. The second idea was that of a stratified or layered conception of the world, in which atomism at the lowest level is compatible with the reducible or irreducible reality of other categories of entity, including composite bodies, at higher levels. The third was that a new philosophy needs a new language, one in which the underlying logical form of philosophical claims is exposed and transparent, and which can therefore serve the needs of demonstration in a calculus of relations. These key ideas—and the concomitant reworking of the ancient tradition they presumed—were all essentially in place by the middle of the seventeenth century. One will never know whether Kavīndra translated Descartes into Sanskrit from Bernier's Persian, but what I do claim is that we can read two very remarkable works of Jayarāma, the *Garland of Principles* and the *Garland of Categories*, as constituting a direct intellectual confrontation between the 'new reason' and Cartesian new philosophy. 'Cartesian' ideas are rejected in favour of a philosophy that could have held its own among any of the early modern philosophies of later seventeenth-century European thought.

I have argued in this book that the emergence of the 'new reason' depended on individuals whose relationship to centres of scholarly influence was somewhat oblique. These individuals were close enough to those centres to be able to benefit from their intellectual community, but distant enough not to be too deeply implicated in the perpetuation of the centres themselves. There needed to be patronage, sometimes from the Mughal court or the Bengali sultanates, sufficient for a network of centres to exist in a more-or-less stable and continuing form; and, crucially, there needed to be room for early modern individuals to work at arm's length from those centres. An individual who was too closely associated with the need to impress in virtuoso debating displays or otherwise to attract students, prestige, and income to his or her ṭol, could not be as free to think for themselves, directly and deeply, as someone on the periphery; but without the established networks, the more radical individuals could not have emerged. The story of Raghunātha going to Mithilā to study before distancing himself from it is emblematic of this double-sided relationship (and perhaps not so very different from Descartes' relationship to La Flèche). There were few institutions which brought together people of different intellectual persuasions, and certainly nothing like the Royal Society, but occasionally a liberal patron, such as Dāniṣmand Khān, Ḥusayn Shāh, or Kṛṣṇa Candra, would achieve this. Philosophers on the fringe and unusual sponsors define the emergence of early modernity in India. I was able to distinguish three ṭol-based networks, one rather conservative and well-established in Vārāṇasī, a second also in Vārāṇasī but much more marginal, and a third operating in the very unusual circumstances of seventeenth-century Navadvīpa.

I have tried to establish, through a careful examination of the texts, that the philosophy of the 'new reason' in the sixteenth and seventeenth centuries embodied a new spirit of inquiry. I have reviewed work on the concept of knowledge, the nature of evidence, the self, the nature of the categories, mathematics, and the idea of the real, and an entirely new language for philosophy. Vivekananda, writing at the end of the nineteenth century, evinced a continuing awareness of the power and influence of the movement:

> Transported from the soil of Mithilā to Navadvīpa, nurtured and developed by the fostering genius of [Raghunātha] Śiromaṇi, Gadādhara, Jagadīśa, and a host of other great names, an analysis of the laws of reasoning in some points superior to every other system in the whole world, expressed in a wonderful and precise mosaic of language, stands the Nyāya of Bengal, respected and studied throughout the length and breadth of Hindusthān.
>
> (1895: 336)

A few years later he had become less complimentary about the 'new reason', and gives voice to what was already a standard cliché. Speaking to a Bengali student, he says:

> Why do you not set about propagating Vedānta in your part of the country? . . . Rouse and agitate the country with the lion-roar of Advaita-vāda. Then I shall know you to be a Vedāntist. First open a Sanskrit school there and teach the Upaniṣads and the *Brahma-sūtras* . . . I have heard that in your country there is much logic-chopping of the Nyāya school. What is there in it? Only *vyāpti* [pervasion] and *anumāna* [inference]—on these subjects the paṇḍits of the Nyāya school discuss for months! What does it help towards the knowledge of the *ātman* [the self]?
>
> (1902: 256–257)

Hindu religion has now become the only thing worth studying, and 'new reason' philosophy is reduced to so many soteriologically irrelevant logical games. One finds the new assessment in many neo-Vedāntic writers from around the time, not least Radhakrishnan. For Vivekananda, the study of philosophy is of no help in that spiritual renaissance which would rejuvenate India. It was necessary, rather, to establish institutions in which the key texts of Vedānta—the Upaniṣads and *Brahma-sūtras*—could be taught.

The origins of this new attitude lie, I think, in the earlier imposition of colonial educational policies, which sought or served to undermine the traditional ṭol-based structures. Clearly a ṭol could not be portrayed—as the *madrasa* is today—as a house of religious fundamentalism, and instead the strategy seems to have been to describe their curricula as narrow and irrelevant (Minto 1811). Two investigations of the Navadvīpa ṭols, by H. H. Wilson in 1829 and E. B. Cowell in 1864 confirm the myth and call for an expanded, Western, curriculum. The enduring notion that the 'new reason' philosophers of early modern India were concerned only with logical trivia, with style but not substance, has its beginnings here. It represents another instance of a phenomenon Halbfass has identified: the wish to refuse to India anything which resembles that which nineteenth-century Anglo-European philosophers wanted to ring-fence as definitive of the Anglo-European mind. I have also suggested that the resources of the 'new reason' provided material for a powerful intellectual resistance to colonialism, and it is no wonder that they should have been actively undermined.

The construction in the nineteenth century of what I called in the Introduction the 'standard history' of early modernity had a not dissimilar effect. It too fabricated a mythology which served to exaggerate and dramatize the differences between India and Europe.[3] The standard history about the distinctively European origins of modern philosophy in the seventeenth century was shaped, it seems, by distinctly nineteenth-century needs.[4] It is actually rather shocking that this history of the birth of modern philosophy continues to be taught uncritically in university philosophy departments still today.

[3] Edmund Husserl, for example, identifies 'Cartesian freedom from prejudice' as what distinguishes 'European mankind' from India and the Orient (Halbfass 1988: 157). Gottlob Frege says that 'in arithmetic, if only because its methods and concepts originated in India, it has been the tradition to reason less strictly than in geometry, which was in the main developed by the Greeks' (1950: §1). See too van Fraassen's 2002 study of the history of the term 'empiricism.'

[4] Typical is the following: 'The Hindoo mind for a long period has been in what Whewell calls the 'commentarial stage,' a stage in which originality is forbidden and shunned. This would seem to present one of the occasions when a just appreciation of the history of an analogous period may be fairly expected to throw light upon the prospect of the future, on its undesirable probabilities, and its more desirable possibilities, possible only if they be properly anticipated.' (Ballantyne 1852: ix). Ballantyne prefers Bacon, and indeed he translated the *Novum Organum* into Sanskrit hoping thereby to persuade Nyāya paṇḍits of the superiority of European thought. Max Müller would comment that 'Till very lately the [Nyāya paṇḍits] entertained a very low opinion of European logic, some account of which had been supplied to them from the popular work of Abercrombie . . . By the exertions of Dr. Ballantyne, the Principal of the Sanskrit College at Benares, some of the best English works on logic have been made accessible to the paṇḍits, and at the present day we might hear the merits of Bacon's *Novum Organon* discussed in the streets of Benares' (Müller 1853: 300). For a study of nineteenth-century European ways of representing what they called 'Hindu logic,' see Ganeri 2001b.

In this book I have wanted to make a case for renewed attention to an overlooked and misunderstood episode in the history of thought. Although I too am writing about the past, I have not here tried to engage with it in a philosophical conversation.[5] The methodology I have used is instead one adapted from Quentin Skinner's contextualist 'theory and method'. I have tried to make sense of the illocutionary intervention that particular 'new reason' works make in their social and political context, and have reconstructed those contexts in as much detail as possible. Yet I have also argued that it is important to see these texts as making another sort of illocutionary intervention, one the context of which is defined by the *śāstra* and *sampradāya* within which the text falls. Taking these two sorts of intervention together gives us a surer grasp of the significance of the work than concentrating on either one alone.

I will conclude by mentioning a few of the areas where I think detailed further investigation would be very productive. In order better to understand the nature of the philosophical dynamism of the period, it would be fascinating to make comparative studies when there are several commentaries on a single root text. I have in mind, especially, the various commentaries on the verses of Udayana's *Offering*, the different commentaries on Raghunātha's *Inquiry* and the commentaries on Jayarāma's *Garland of Categories*. It would be revealing to study how different writers use the two rival manuals, namely the *Panicle of Principles* and the *Pearl-necklace of Principles*, and also to compare two manuals which resemble one another, the *Survey of [what can be known through] Reason* of Annambhaṭṭa and the *Lamp of Categories* of Kauṇḍabhaṭṭa. It will be important to study in more detail the way in which a new genre of commentary, the sort which discloses a deep or hidden meaning, functions across the disciplines in the modern period. The 'refutation-commentaries' written by new Nyāya thinkers on Śrīharṣa's *Amassed Morsels* in themselves constitute an important and little-studied body of work in epistemology. Proper studies of the various tracts on a range of semantical expressions, including especially the particle 'only' and the thematic case-roles, are very important for an understanding of the revolution that was beginning to take place in the use of language as a method for transformation in philosophy. Finally, much more detailed examination of the epistemology and metaphysics being elaborated in texts like the *Essence of Reason*, the *Precious Jewel*, the *Embellishment of Categories,* and the *Garland of Principles* is called for, for I have only barely scratched the surface of these highly unusual and important works.

[5] Much of Matilal's work is firmly in the spirit of promoting a conversation between his anglophone reader and the Indian text (and so is in our sense a 'commentary' on the Indian tradition). I might remark here that Halbfass's criticism of Matilal—which is that he uses analytical philosophy as a 'standard of evaluation' (1992: 82) or a 'measure' (1988: 158) of Indian thought—quite fundamentally misunderstands Matilal's philosophical enterprise. Matilal broaches a conversation between an Indian past and an Anglo-American present, and his writings are replete with occasions when it is the Indian voice which criticizes the analytical one. It would be similarly absurd to reduce the project of a contemporary philosopher who studies Kant to one of evaluating and measuring according to 'contemporary standards' (an idea which is itself suspect), rather than one of openness to philosophical possibilities brought out through new readings of him (cf. Wood 2000).

Daya Krishna concludes his survey of the 'new reason' in these words: 'All in all, one may say that here there is one of the richest modes of alternative epistemological analysis that the philosophical world has ever seen and which still awaits not merely intelligible articulation but also significant development within its own postulates of analysis' (Krishna 1997a: 162). I hope with this book to have made a beginning on that project, and also to have combined it with a larger one; for a study of early modernity in India has much to teach about the nature of modernity as such, about the reform of educational institutions and its relationship to creative research, and about cosmopolitan identities in circumstances of globalization.

Recommended Further Readings

Introduction. There are regrettably few reliable general studies of the history of philosophy in India. The older scholarship of Radhakrishnan, Frauwallner, and others is overly programmatic and best avoided, but the work of Dasgupta and Mishra continues to be valuable. Excellent recent examinations of European early modern philosophy include Lolordo (2007), Ariew (1999), Garber and Ayers (2003). See also Rosalind O'Hanlon, 'Contested Conjunctures: Brahman Communities and "Early Modernity" in India,' *American Historical Review* 118.3 (2013) 765–787.

Chapter 1, *The World and India*. Halbfass 1988 is an important analysis of philosophical engagements between Europe and India from a dialogical perspective. The historical studies of P. K. Gode (1954) are useful, as are D. C. Bhattacharya's (1952) and (1958) manuscriptological accounts of the 'new reason'.

Chapter 2, *Dārā Shukoh*. Azam (2004) provides a background to political Islam in India, while Hasrat (1982) is a study of the life and times of Dārā Shukoh. Ernst (2003) is a particularly fine study of Dārā's project of translating Hindu canonical works from Sanskrit into Persian. Also now William Chittick, *In Search of the Lost Heart* (Albany, 2012); Audrey Truschke (2012).

Chapter 3, *Yaśovijaya Gaṇi*. Desai (1910) and Qanungo (1952) are biographies of Yaśovijaya, while Dundas (2004) and Shastri (1991) have useful discussions of the later phase in his intellectual development.

Chapter 4, *Navadvīpa*. Easton (2000) and Tarafdar (1965) examine Navadvīpa in the context of Muslim Bengal, while Kaviraja (1961) and Sinha (1993) have information about the 'new reason' communities there. Krishna (1997b) is an excellent introduction to Raghunātha.

Chapter 5, *Contextualism*. Skinner's essays on method are collected in his 2002.

Chapter 6, *New Reason Networks*. Background sociological information about the Nyāya philosophers is available in Krishnan (1976) and M. Sen (1934–5), and about thinkers and texts in Kaviraja (1961) and Mishra (1966: 237–276).

Chapter 7, *Genres*. Chakravarti (1915), Thakur (2003) and Krishna (2001) all contain useful information.

Chapter 8, *Commentary*. An excellent theoretical analysis of commentary is Culter (1992). Culter's approach has been developed further by Clooney (1990, 1991). Smith (1991) and Jyväsjärvi (2010) contain useful discussion.

Chapter 9, *Inquiry*. The early Nyāya theory of inquiry is described further in Ganeri (2001a: 7–41) and Matilal (1986: 73–80). For a detailed examination of Śabara, Śaṃkara and Śrīharṣa, see Carpenter and Ganeri (2010).

Chapter 10, *Mīmāṃsā Ritualists*. Mohanty (1966), and Phillips and Tatacharya (2004), both have detailed studies of Gaṅgeśa and the role of the ritualists' alternative theory.

Chapter 11, *New Interventions*. There is little secondary literature, but Saha (2003) and Mohanty (1966) have some material.

Chapter 12, *Vaiśeṣika Realism*. Several good studies are available, including Bhaduri (1947), Halbfass (1992), Phillips (1995), Thakur (2003), and Matilal (1986: chapters 11, 12).

Chapter 13, *Mathematics*. Among several good studies, Matilal (1987) and Narasimha (2007, 2009) are particularly worthwhile.

Chapter 14, *New Metaphysics*. Again, there is little secondary literature. Gangopadhyaya (1980) is a helpful review of Indian atomism. Kroll (2010) studies the debate over ownership.

Chapter 15, *The New Language*. Krishna (1997a) gives a good sense of the importance and style of the technical language. Ingalls (1951) is a classic work, while Guha (1968) and Matilal (1968, 1985) are very valuable. Wada (2007) is a more recent study using diagrams to explain the language. Jha (2004) is a translation of a helpful nineteenth-century work.

Chapter 16, *Particles of Restriction*. I have said more about my approach in Ganeri (1999a), discussing the earlier Gillon and Hayes (1982) and Kajiyama (1973). Nemoto (forthcoming) looks at the Tibetan discussion.

Bibliography

I. Reference works

NCat *New Catalogus Catalogorum: An Alphabetical Register of Sanskrit and Allied Works and Authors*. V. Raghavan, K. Kunjunni Raja, N. Veezhinathan, E. R. Ramabai *et al.* (Madras: Madras University Sanksrit Series, 1968–1907). References in the form '[NCat 8: 322]' are to volume number and page. References to manuscript collections use the NCat abbreviation.

Potter *Bibliography of Indian Philosophies, Part I: Listed by Authors' Dates (15th c.—present)*. Maintained and updated online at http://faculty.washington.edu/kpotter/xtxt4.htm. References in the form '[P 948]' are to authors according to their numbered entry in the Bibliography.

NK *Nyāyakośa or Dictionary of Technical Terms of Indian Philosophy*, Bhīmācārya Jhalakākar [1874]; revised by Vasudev Shastri Abhyankar (Poona: Bhandarkar Oriental Research Institute, 1928).

II. Primary sources

Abū-l-Fażl (1873, 1894 [1597]). *The Ā'īn-i-Akbarī by* Abū-l-Fażl *'Allami,* translated from the original Persian by H. Blochmann (vol. 1: 1873), and H. S. Jarrett (vols 2, 3: 1894) (Calcutta: Baptist Mission Press).

Annambhaṭṭa (1918). *Survey of [what can be known through] Reason* (*Tarka-saṃgraha*), with auto-commentary *Dīpikā*, Y. V. Athalye ed. (Poona: BORI). Trans. Gopinath Bhattacharya (1983), *Tarka-saṃgraha-dīpikā on Tarka-saṃgraha* (Calcutta: Progressive Publishers).

Bacon, Francis (1857–74). *The Works of Francis Bacon*, J. Spedding, R. L. Ellis and D. D. Heath eds. (London: Longmans).

Basso, Sébastien (1621). *Philosophie naturalis adversus Aristotelem, in quibus abstrusa veterum physiologia restauratur, & Aristotelis errores solidis rationibus refelluntur* (Geneva: Pierre de la Rovière).

Bernier, François (1934 [1670–71]). *Histoire de la dernière révolution des États du Gran Mogol*, 4 vols (Paris: Claude Barbin, 1670–1671); edited as *Voyage dans les États du Grand Mogol*, France Bhattacharya (Paris: Fayard, 1981). Trans. Irvind Brock, *Travels in the Mogul Empire AD 1656–1668* (London: W. Pickering 1834; 3rd edn).

Bhartṛhari (1973). *Vākya-padīya,* K. A. Subramania Iyer ed. (Delhi: Motilal Banarsidass).

Bhāsarvajña (1968). *Nyāya-bhūṣaṇa*. Svami Yogindrananda ed. (Vārāṇasī: Saddarsan Prakasan Pratisthanam).

Bhaṭṭa Vādīndra (1922). *Rasa-sāra [Haraprasāda-kiraṇāvali-darpaṇaka]*. Ganganatha Jha and Gopinatha Kaviraja eds (Princess of Wales Saraswati Bhavana Texts no.5; Benares: Vidya Vilas Press).

Bhaṭṭa Vādīndra (1985). *Vaiśeṣika-vārttika*. Anantalal Thakur ed., *Vaiśeṣika-darśana with Three Commentaries* (Dharbhanga: Kameshare Singh Sanksrit University).

Buddhaghosa, Bhadantācariya (1991). *The Path of Purification (Visuddhimagga)*, translated from the Pali by Bhikkhu Ñāṇamoli (Kandy: Buddhist Publication Society).

Dārā Shukoh (1929 [1655]). *Majma'al-baḥrayn, or The Mingling of the Two Oceans by Prince Muhammad Dārā Shikuh*. M. Mahfuz-ul-Haq ed. and trans. (New Delhi: Adam Publishers, 1929; (2006) edn).

Dārā Shukoh (1957 [1656/7]). *Sirr-i Akbar: The Oldest Translation of the Upaniṣads from Sanskrit into Persian*. Tara Chand & S. M. Raza Jalali Nayni eds (Tehran: Taban, 1957).

Descartes, Rene (1984). *The Philosophical Writings of Descartes*, John Cottingham ed. (Cambridge: Cambridge University Press, vol. 1).

Dharmakirti (1989). *Pramāṇavārttika*, R. C. Pandeya ed. (Delhi: Motilal Banarsidass).

Gadādhara Bhaṭṭācārya *et al.* (1913–31). *Vādārtha-saṃgraha*. M. S. Bakre ed. (Bombay: Gujarati Mundralaya).

Gadādhara Bhaṭṭācārya (1927). *Gādādharī*. V. P. Dvivedi, V. Bhattacharya, R. S. Bhandari, and P. D. Shastri eds. (Benares: Chowkhamba Sanskrit Series Office), 2 vols.

Gadādhara Bhaṭṭācārya (1929). *Śakti-vāda*, with Kṛṣṇa Bhaṭṭa's *Mañjūṣa*, Mādhava Bhaṭṭācārya's *Vivṛtti* and Sāhitya Darśanācārya's *Vinodini*. G. D. Sastri ed. (Benares: Kashi Sanskrit Series no. 57).

Gadādhara Bhaṭṭācārya (1933–40). *Vāda-vāridhi*. Dhundiraja Shastri ed. (Benares: Chowkhamba Sanskrit Series Office, vols. 421, 446, 468).

Gaṅgeśa Upādhyāya (1888). *The Gemstone [which will fulfil one's desire] for Truth (Tattvacintāmaṇi)*. Kāmākhyānātha Tarkavāgīśa ed., *The Tattvacintāmaṇi by Gaṅgeśa Upādhyāya with extracts from the commentaries of Mathurānātha Tarkavāgīśa* and *Jayadeva Miśra. Volume 1: Pratyakṣa-khaṇḍa* (Calcutta: Bibilotheca Indica). Trans. Phillips, Stephen H. & Tatacharya, N. S. Ramanuja, *Epistemology of Perception: Gaṅgeśa's Tattvacintāmaṇi* (New York: American Institute of Buddhist Studies, 2004).

Gaṅgeśa Upādhyāya (1892). *The Gemstone [which will fulfil one's desire] for Truth (Tattvacintāmaṇi)*. Kāmākhyānātha Tarkavāgīśa ed., *The Tattvacintāmaṇi by Gaṅgeśa Upādhyāya with extracts from the commentary of Mathurānātha Tarkavāgīśa. Volume 2 Part 1: Anumāna-khaṇḍa: anumiti to bādha* (Calcutta: Bibilotheca Indica).

Gaṅgeśa Upādhyāya (1893). *The Gemstone [which will fulfil one's desire] for Truth (Tattvacintāmaṇi)*. Kāmākhyānātha Tarkavāgīśa ed., *The Tattvacintāmaṇi by Gaṅgeśa Upādhyāya with extracts from the commentary of Jayadeva Miśra. Volume 2 Part 2: Anumāna-khaṇḍa: īśvara* (Calcutta: Bibilotheca Indica).

Gaṅgeśa Upādhyāya (1897). *The Gemstone [which will fulfil one's desire] for Truth (Tattvacintāmaṇi)*. Kāmākhyānātha Tarkavāgīśa ed., *The Tattvacintāmaṇi by Gaṅgeśa*

Upādhyāya with extracts from the commentary of Kṛṣṇadāsa. Volume 3: Upamāna (Calcutta: Bibilotheca Indica).

Gaṅgeśa Upādhyāya (1897–1901). *The Gemstone [which will fulfil one's desire] for Truth (Tattvacintāmaṇi)*. Kāmākhyānātha Tarkavāgīśa ed., *The Tattvacintāmaṇi by Gaṅgeśa Upādhyāya with extracts from the commentary of Mathurānātha Tarkavāgīśa. Volume 4: Śabda-khaṇḍa* (Calcutta: Bibilotheca Indica).

Gassendi, Pierre (1658). *Syntagma Philosophicum*. In *Petri Gassendi Opera Omnia in sex tomos divisa*, vols 1 and 2 (Lyon: Laurent Anisson and Jean-Baptiste Devenet).

Gautama Akṣapāda (1997). *Nyāya-sūtra*. Anantalal Thakur ed., *Gautamīya-nyāya-darśana with Bhāṣya of Vātsyāyana* (Delhi: Indian Council of Philosophical Research).

Harirāma Tarkavāgīśa (1964). *Prāmāṇya-vāda*. Gaurinath Shastri ed., with Visvabandhu Bhattacharya's *Prabhā* (Calcutta: Sanskrit College).

Jagadīśa Tarkālaṃkāra (1908). *Jāgadīśī*. Somnathopadhyaya ed. (Benares: Chowkhamba Sanskrit Series 29), 2 vols.

Jagadīśa Tarkālaṃkāra (1977). *Avacchedakatva-nirukti-jāgadīśī*. Svami Dharmananda Mahabhaga ed. (Vārāṇasī: Chaukhambha Sanskrit Sansthan, Kashi Sanskrit Series 203).

Jagadīśa Tarkālaṃkāra (1980–85). *The Illumination of Semantic Powers (Śabda-śakti-prakāśikā)* (Calcutta: Sanskrit College).

Jānakīnātha Cūdāmaṇi Bhaṭṭācārya (1990). *Panicle of Principles about Reason (Nyāya-siddhānta-mañjarī)*. Gaurinatha Shastri ed. (Delhi: Sri Satguru Publications; 2nd edn).

Jānakīnātha Cūdāmaṇi Bhaṭṭācārya (2003). *Analysis of the Truth in Philosophical Method (Ānvīkṣikī-tattva-vivaraṇa)*. See P. K. Sen 2003.

Jayadeva Miśra (aka Pakṣadhara). *Tattva-cintāmaṇi-āloka*. See Gaṅgeśa 1888, 1893.

Jayanta Bhaṭṭa (1982). *Nyāya-mañjarī*. With the commentary *Granthibhaṅga* by Cakradhara, Gaurinath Shastri ed. (Vārāṇasī: Sampurnananda Sanskrit University).

Jayarāma Nyāyapañcānana (1927). *Garland of Principles about Reason (Nyāya-siddhānta-mālā)*. M. D. Shastri ed. (Benares: Vidya Vilas Press; Princess of Wales Sarasvati Bhavana texts 21), 2 vols.

Jayarāma Nyāyapañcānana (1985 [1659]). *Garland of Categories (Padārtha-mālā)*. With Laugākṣī Bhāskara's *Prakāśa*, N. Srinivasan ed. (Tanjore: Sarasvati Mahal Library, series no. 217).

Jayarāma Nyāyapañcānana. *The Meaning of Ownership (Svatva-vādārtha)*. Unedited [Adyar D 1401E (73879c).] Line numbers refer to a transcription made by Anjaneya Sarma and Satyanarayana.

Kaṇāda (1961). *Vaiśeṣika-sūtra*. With the Commentary of Candrānanda, Muni Sri Jambuvijaya ed. (Baroda: Oriental Institute, Gaekwad's Oriental Series 136).

Kauṇḍabhaṭṭa (1900). *Lamp of the Categories (Padārtha-dīpikā)*. Ramakrishna Shastri ed. (Vārāṇasī: Benares Sanskrit Series 14).

Kavīndracandrodaya (1938/9). Har Dutt Sharma and M. M. Patkar ed. (Poona: Oriental Book Agency).

Kṛṣṇadāsa (1923). *Necklace of Verses (Kārikāvalī)* aka. *Divisions of Language (Bhāṣā-paric-cheda)*, with the *Pearl-necklace of Principles about Reason (Nyāya-siddhānta-muktāvalī)*. S. R. Shastri ed. (Madras: Sri Balamanorama Press).

Kumārila Bhaṭṭa (1926). *Śloka-vārttika. The Śloka-vārttika of Kumārila with the Kāśikā of Sucaritamiśra*, K. S. Sastri ed. (Trivandrum: Trivandrum Sanskrit Series no. 90).

Laugākṣī Bhāskara (1886). *Moonlight of Reason (Tarka-kaumudī)*. Manilal Nabhubhai Dvivedi ed. (Bombay: Government Central Book Depot).

Laugākṣī Bhāskara (1985). *Prakāśa* on Jayarāma's *Padārtha-mālā*. In Jayarāma 1985.

Mādhavadeva Bhaṭṭa (1903–4). *The Essence of Reason (Nyāya-sāra)*. Nagesvara Pant Dharmadhikari ed., in *The Paṇḍit*, new series vol. 25: 455*ff.*, and vol. 26: 97*ff.*; pages also sequentially numbered 1–246. Reprinted Benares: Medical Hall Press 1905.

Madhusūdana Sarasvatī (1984–6). *Advaita-siddhi*. Yogindrananda ed. (Varanasi: Sad-darsanaprakasanapratishanam).

Mahādeva Puṇatāmakara (1930). *Precious Jewel of Reason (Nyāya-kaustubha), Pratyakṣa-khaṇḍa*. Umesh Mishra ed. (Benares: Vidya Mandir Press, Saraswati Bhavana Texts 33, Part I).

Mahādeva Puṇatāmakara (1967). *Precious Jewel of Reason (Nyāya-kaustubha), Anumāna-khaṇḍa*. Damodara Lal Gosvami ed. (Varanasi: Vidya Mandir Press, Saraswati Bhavana Texts 33, Part II).

Mahādeva Puṇatāmakara (1982). *Precious Jewel of Reason (Nyāya-kaustubha), Śabda-khaṇḍa*. V. Subrahmanya Sastri ed. (Tanjore: T. M. S. S. M. Library).

Mahādeva Puṇatāmakara. *Examination of Selfhood as a Natural Kind (Ātmatva-jāti-vicāra)*. Unedited. [Stein 1331].

Nāgārjuna (1986). *Vigrahavyāvartanī*. Johnston, E. H. and Kunst A. crit. ed., in *The Dialectical Method of Nāgārjuna: Vigrahavyāvartanī*; containing a translation by Kamaleswar Bhattacharya (Delhi: Motilal Banarsidass).

Nobili, Roberto de (1972 [1613]). *Ad patrem nostrum generalem informatio, de quibusdam moribus nationis Indicae*. Translated in *Roberto de Nobili on Indian Customs*, S. Rajamanickam ed. (Palayamkottai: De Nobili Research Institute).

Prabhākara (1929). *Bṛhatī*. A. Chinnaswami Sastri ed. (Benares: Chowkhamba Sanskrit Series Office).

Praśastapāda (1994). *Praśastapādabhāṣya* [aka *Padārtha-dharma-saṃgraha*] Johannes Bronkhorst and Yves Ramseier, *Word Index to the Praśastapāda-bhāṣya* (Delhi: Motilal Banarsidass, 1994).

Raghudeva Nyāyālaṃkāra Bhaṭṭācārya. *Survey of What is Essential about Substance (Dravya-sāra-saṃgraha)*. Unedited. [Stein 2766; Asiatic Society III.A.9].

Raghudeva Nyāyālaṃkāra Bhaṭṭācārya (1915). *Exegesis of the Inquiry (Padārtha-tattva-nirūpaṇa-vyākhyā)*. In Raghunātha 1915.

Raghunātha Śiromaṇi (1915). *Inquiry into the True Nature of Things (Padārtha-tattva-nirūpaṇa)*. V. P. Dvivedi ed. (Varanasi: Maha Mandalayantralaya).

Raghunātha Śiromaṇi (1927). *Light-Ray Shining on the Gemstone* (*Tattva-cintāmaṇi-dīdhiti*). See Gadādhara 1927.

Raghunātha Śiromaṇi (1932). *Light-Ray Shining on the Illumination of the Row of Light-beams* (*Kiraṇāvalī-prakāśa-dīdhiti*). Badrinath Sastri ed. (Benares: Princess of Wales Sarasvati Bhavana texts 38).

Raghunātha Śiromaṇi (1939). *Light-Ray Shining on the Discrimination of the Truth about the Self* (*Ātmā-tattva-viveka-dīdhiti*). In *Ātmā-tattva-viveka, with the commentaries of Śaṃkara Miśra, Bhagīratha Thakkura and Raghunātha Śiromaṇi*, V. P. Dvivedin and L. S. Dravida eds. (Calcutta: Royal Asiatic Society of Bengal [reprinted 1986]).

Raghunātha Śiromaṇi (1968). *Treatise on Negation* (*Nañ-vāda*). Text and trans. B. K. Matilal, *The Navya-nyāya Doctrine of Negation: The Semantics and Ontology of Negative Statements in Navya-nyāya Philosophy* (Cambridge, Mass.: Harvard University Press, 1968). Edited with Raghudeva's *Ṭīkā*, N. K. Ramanjua Tatacharya ed. (Tanjore 1972). Edited with Gadādhara's *Ṭīkā*, Lokanatha ed. (Banares 1899).

Raghunātha Śiromaṇi (1977). *Examination of Limitorship* (*Avacchedakatva-nirukti*). Svami Dharmananda Mahabhaga ed. (Varanasi: Chaukhambha Sanskrit Sansthan, Kashi Sanskrit Series 203).

Raghunātha Śiromaṇi (1979). *Treatise on Finite Verbal Forms* (*Ākhyāta-vāda*). With the *Ākhyātavāda-vyākhyā* of Rāmabhadra Sārvabhauma, Prabal Kumar Sen ed. (Calcutta: Sanskrit Pustak Bhandar, 1979); trans. K. N. Chatterjee, *Śiromaṇi's Ākhyātaśaktivāda* (Varanasi: Kishor Vidya Niketan, 1981). Edited with the commentaries of Mathurānātha, Rāmacandra, Jayarāma, Rudra, and Rāmakṛṣṇa, M. G. Bakre ed. (Bombay 1931). Edited with Raghudeva's *Ṭīkā*, N. K. Ramanuja Tatacharya ed. (Tanjore 1972).

Raghunātha Śiromaṇi (1985). *Prāmāṇyavāda* [on the *Gemstone*]. N. S. Ramanuja Tatacharya ed. (Tirupati: Kendriya Sanskrit Vidyapeetha).

Raghunātha Śiromaṇi. *Līlāvatī-vibhūti*. Unedited [Chandra Shum Shere, Oxford d.481. Cf. Hall, p. 73, Ben 172, NP I. 370 (ṭippaṇī), SB 296 (p. 160)].

Raghunātha Śiromaṇi. *Līlāvatī-prakāśa-ṭippaṇī*. Unedited. [India Office 1670. Cf. Hall p. 72; Ben. 185; L. 1997.]

Raghunātha Śiromaṇi. *The Light-Ray Shining on the Offering of Flowers* (*Kusumāñjalī-dīdhiti*). Unedited. [SB 297 (p. 160).]

Rāmabhadra Sārvabhauma (1915). *Comments on the Inquiry* (*Padārtha-tattva-nirūpaṇa-ṭīkā*). In Raghunātha 1915: 81–132.

Rāmabhadra Sārvabhauma (2003). *Nyāya-sūtra-rahasya*. See P. K. Sen 2003.

Roth, Heinrich (1988). *The Sanskrit Grammar and Manuscripts of Father Heinrich Roth, S.J. 1620–1668*, with an introduction by Arnulf Camps and Jean-Claude Muller. Includes *Grammatica linguae Sanscretanae* by Roth, *Pañcatattvaprakāśa* by Veṇīdatta, and *Vedāntasāra* by Sadānanda (Leiden: E. J. Brill).

Śabara (1968). *Śabara-bhāṣya*. Erich Frauwallner ed., *Materialen zur ältesten Erkenntnislehre der Karma-mīmāṃsā* (Vienna: Hermann Bölaus Nachf).

Śabdakalpadruma (2006 [1822]) (Delhi: Nag Publishers).

Śabdārthacintāmaṇi (1992 [1860]) (Jaipur: Printwell).

Śaṅkara Miśra (1915). *Vādavinoda.* Ganganath Jha ed. (Allahabad).

Śaṅkara Miśra (1923). *Vaiśeṣika-sūtra-upaskāra.* In *Vaiśeṣika-darśana, with Praśastapāda's Padārtha-dharma-saṃgraha and Śaṅkara Miśra's Upaskāra,* Dundhiraja Sastri ed. (Varanasi: Chaukhamba Sanskrit Series Office, Kashi Sanskrit Series 3); trans. *The Vaiśeṣika Sūtras of Kaṇāda,* with the Commentary of *Śaṅkara Miśra,* translated by Nandalal Sinha (Allahabad: The Panini Office, Bhuvaneswari Asrama, 1911).

Śaṅkara (1917). *Brahma-sūtra-bhāṣya.* With the commentaries *Bhāmatī, Kalpatarū and Parīmāla,* N. A. K. Sastri and V. L. Sastri Pansikar eds. (Bombay: Nirmaya Sagar Press).

Sennert, Daniel (1636). *Hypomnemata Physica* (Frankfurt: Clement Schleich).

Śrīdhara (1977). *Nyāya-kandalī.* With Hindi translation, Durgadhara Jha ed. (Varanasi: Sampurnanand Sanskrit Vishvavidyalaya, Ganganatha Jha Granthamala).

Śrīdhara (1984). *Nyāya-kandalī.* V. P. Dvivedin ed., *The Bhāṣya of Praśastapāda together with the Nyāyakandalī of Śrīdhara* (Delhi: Sri Satguru Publications).

Śrīharṣa (1990). *Amassed Morsels of Refutation (Khaṇḍana-khaṇḍa-khādya).* B. Dvivedi ed. (Varanasi: Sampurnanand Sanskrit University). Edited with Citsukha's *Bhāvadīpikā.* Śaṃkara Miśra's *Ānandavardhana,* Raghunātha's *Bhūṣāmaṇi,* Pragalbha Miśra's *Darpana* and the editor's *Ratnamālikā,* S. N. Śukla ed. (Benares: Chowkhamba Sanskrit Series 82, 1936).

Udayana (1925). *An Offering of Flowers (Kusumāñali).* Dhundiraja Shastri ed. (Benares: Chowkhamba Sanskrit Series 30).

Udayana (1956). *Row of Lightbeams (Kiraṇāvalī). With Vardhamāna's Prakāśa* and *Vādīndra's Rasa-sāra,* Narendra Chandra Vedantatirtha ed. (Calcutta: The Asiatic Society, Bibliotheca Indica no. 200, fasc. 4).

Udayana (1963). *Garland of Definitions (Lakṣaṇa-mālā.).* Sasinatha Jha ed. (Darbhanga: Mithila Institute Series, 13).

Udayana (1986). *Discrimination of the Truth about the Self (Ātma-tattva-viveka).* V. P. Dvivedin and L. S. Dravida eds (Calcutta: The Asiatic Society, Bibiotheca Indica No. 170).

Udayana (1989). *Row of Lightbeams (Kiraṇāvalī).* With the Commentary of Vardhamānopadhyāya, Siva Chandra Sarvabhouma ed. (Calcutta: The Asiatic Society, fasc. 1–3).

Uddyotakara (1997). *Nyāya-vārttika.* Anantalal Thakur ed. *Nyāya-bhāṣya-vārttika of Uddyotakara* (Delhi: Indian Council of Philosophical Research).

Umāpati Upādhyāya (1961). *Padārthīya-divya-cakṣuḥ.* Dhiranand Mishra ed. (Dharbhanga: Mithila Institute).

Vātsyāyana (1997). *Nyāya-bhāṣya.* Anantalal Thakur ed., *Gautamīya-nyāya-darśana with Bhāṣya of Vātsyāyana* (Delhi: Indian Council of Philosophical Research).

Veṇīdatta (1930). *Embellishment of the Categories* (*Padārtha-maṇḍana*), Gopala Sastri Nene ed. (Benares: Vidya Vilas Press; Princess of Wales Sarasvati Bhavana texts 30).

Viśvanātha Nyāyapañcānana (1985). *Nyāya-sūtra-vṛtti*. In *Nyāya-sūtra*, with Vātsyāyana's *Bhāṣya*, Uddyotakara's *Vārttika*, Vācaspati Miśra's *Tātparya-tīkā* and Viśvanātha's *Vṛtti*, edited by T. Nyayatarkatirtha and A. Tarkatirtha (Calcutta: Calcutta Sanskrit Series nos. 18–19; 2nd edn: Delhi: Munshriram Manoharlal, 1985).

Vyomaśiva (1983). *Vyomavatī*. Gaurinath Sastri ed. (Varanasi: Sampurnanand Sanskrit University).

Yaśovijaya Gaṇi (1938). *Treatise on the Hidden Teaching about the Self* (*Adhyātmopaniṣat-prakaraṇa*). Sukhlalji Sanghvi ed. (Ahmedabad: Sri Bahadur Singh Jaina Series).

Yaśovijaya Gaṇi (1938/42/97). *Jaina Language of Reason* (*Jaina Tarka-bhāṣā*). Sukhlalji Sanghvi, Mahendra Kumar & Dalsukh Malvania eds. (Ahmedabad: Sri Bahadur Singh Jaina Series).

Yaśovijaya Gaṇi (1966). *Jaina Amassed Morsels of Reason* (*Jaina Nyāya-khaṇḍa-khādya*). Badarinath Shukla ed. (Varanasi: Chowkhamba Sanskrit Series Office, Kashi Sanskrit Series no. 170).

Yaśovijaya Gaṇi (1973). *Essence of Knowledge* (*Jñāna-sāra*). Dayanand Bhargava ed. (Delhi: Motilal Banarsidas).

Yaśovijaya Gaṇi (1986). *Examination of Morality* (*Dharma-parīkṣā*). (Mumbai: Shri Andheri Gujarati Jain Sangha).

Yaśovijaya Gaṇi (1996). *Essence of the Self* (*Adhyātma-sāra*). Ramanalal C. Shah ed. (Sayala: Sri Raja Sobhaga Satanga Mandala).

III. Secondary literature

Alsdorf, Ludwig (1977). 'Jaina Exegetical Literature and the History of the Jaina Canon', in A. N. Upadhye ed., *Mahāvīra and his Teachings* (Bombay: Bhagavan Mahavira 2500th Nirvana Mahotsava).

Anacker, Stefan (1988). *Seven Works of Vasubandhu* (Delhi: Motilal Banarsidass).

Anquetil Duperron, H. (1801–2). *Oupnek'hat (id est, Secretum tegendum),* translated from the Persian (Paris: Levrault), 2 vols.

Antonelli, Aldo (2010). 'The Nature and Purpose of Numbers,' *Journal of Philosophy* 107.4: 191–212.

Apte, V. S. (1957). 'A Collection of Popular Sanskrit Maxims', in his *The Practical Sanskrit-English Dictionary, Revised and Enlarged*, Appendix E. (Kyoto: Rinsen Publishers).

Ariew, Roger (1999). *Descartes and the Late Scholastics* (Ithaca: Cornell University Press).

Austin, J. L. (1962). *How To Do Things With Words* (Cambridge: Harvard University Press).

Austin, J. L. (1979). 'Performative Utterances', in his *Philosophical Papers*, 3rd edn, J. O. Urmson and G. J. Warnock, eds (Oxford: Oxford University Press, 1979): 233–252.

Alam, Muzaffar (2004). *The Languages of Political Islam: India 1200–1800* (London: Hurst & Company).

Baker, Lynne Rudder (2008). 'A Metaphysics of Ordinary Things and Why We Need It', *Philosophy* 83: 5–24.

Balcerowicz, Piotr (2010). 'What Exists for the Vaiśeṣika?' in P. Balcerowicz ed., *Logic and Belief in Indian Philosophy* (Delhi: Motilal Banarsidass).

Ballantyne, J. R. (1852). *A Synopsis of Science from the Standpoint of the Nyāya Philosophy* (Mirzapore: Orphan Press).

Barwise, J. & Cooper, R. (1981). 'Generalized Quantifiers and Natural Language', *Linguistics and Philosophy* 4: 159–219.

Bell, David (1990). *Husserl* (London: Routledge).

Benson, James (2001). 'Śaṃkarabhaṭṭa's Family Chronicle: The *Gādhivaṃśavarṇana*', in Axel Michaels ed., *The Paṇḍit: Traditional Scholarship in India* (New Delhi: Manohar Publishers).

Bhabha, Homi, Carol Breckenridge, Dipesh Chakrabarty and Sheldon Pollock (2002). 'Cosmopolitanisms', in *Cosmopolitanism*, Carol Breckenridge, Sheldon Pollock, Homi Bhabha and Dipesh Chakrabarty eds (Durham: Duke University Press): 1–14.

Bhaduri, Sadananda (1947). *Studies in Nyāya-Vaiśeṣika Metaphysics* (Poona: Bhandarkar Oriental Research Institute [2nd edn 1975]).

Bhattacharya, D. C. (1937). 'Sanskrit Scholars of Akbar's Time', *Indian Historical Quarterly* 13: 31–36.

Bhattacharya, D. C. (1940). 'Vāsudeva Sārvabhauma', *Indian Historical Quarterly* 16: 58–69.

Bhattacharya, D. C. (1941a). 'Cirañjīva and His Patron Yaśavanta Siṃha', *Indian Historical Quarterly* 17.1: 1–10.

Bhattacharya, D. C. (1941b). 'Who Wrote the *Bhāṣāpariccheda*?' *Indian Historical Quarterly* 17: 241–244.

Bhattacharya, D. C. (1945). 'Bengali Scholars at Benares', *Indian Historical Quarterly* 21: 91–97.

Bhattacharya, D. C. (1946). 'More Light on Sanskrit Literature of Bengal', *Indian Historical Quarterly* 22: 144–147.

Bhattacharya, D. C. (1948). 'More Light on the Authorship of the *Bhāṣāpariccheda*', *Indian Historical Quarterly* 24: 156–161.

Bhattacharya, D. C. (1952). *Vāṅgālīr Sārasvat Avadān: Baṅge Navya-nyāya Carcā* (Calcutta: Sahitya Pariṣat, 1952). (References in the 'form 1952 [33]' are to the as yet unpublished translation by Nirmalya Chakraborty.)

Bhattacharya, D. C. (1958). *History of Navya-nyāya in Mithilā* (Darbhanga: Mithilā Institute).

Bhattacharya, G. (1983). Ed. and trans. *Tarkasaṃgrahadīpikā on Tarkasaṃgraha* (Calcutta: Progressive Publishers).

Bhattacharya, Gopikamohan (1966). 'Ratnakoṣakāra—A Forgotten Naiyāyika', *Ānvīkṣā* 1.1: 24–29.

Bhattacharya, Gopikamohan (1968–69). '*Tattvacintāmaṇiṭīkā (anumānakhaṇḍa)* of Vāsudeva Sārvabhauma', *Ānvīkṣā* 3.1 (1968: 95–111), 3.2–4.1 (1969: 171–205).

Bhattacharya, Gopikamohan (1976). 'Vāsudeva Sārvabhauma—The Naiyāyika', *Journal of the Oriental Institute Baroda* 26: 81–86.

Bhattacharya, Gopikamohan (1984). *Yajñapati Upādhyāya's Tattvacintāmaṇiprabhā (anumānakhaṇḍa)* (Vienna: Osterreichische Akademie der Wissenschaften, Philosophisch-Historische Klasse, Sitzungsberichte 423).

Bhattacharya, Kamaleswar (1977–2005). 'Le *Siddhāntalakṣaṇaprakaraṇa* du *Tattvacintāmaṇi* de Gaṅgeśa avec la *Dīdhiti* de Raghunātha Śiromaṇi et la *Ṭīkā* de Jagadīśa Tarkālaṃkāra', *Journal Asiatique* 265: 97–139; 266: 97–124; 268: 275–322; 283: 373–406; 293: 213–244.

Bhattacharya, Kamaleswar (2001). 'A Note on Formalism in Indian Logic', *Journal of Indian Philosophy* 29: 17–23.

Bhattacharya, Kamaleswar (2006). 'On the Language of Navya-Nyāya: An Experiment With Precision Through a Natural Language', *Journal of Indian Philosophy* 34: 5–13.

Bhattacharya, Kamaleswar (2007). 'On the 'Generosity' of a Natural Language', *Journal of Indian Philosophy* 35: 413–416.

Bhattacharya, Nilkamal (1924). '*Naiṣadha* and Srī Harṣa', *Sarasvatī Bhavana Studies*, vol. 3: 159–194.

Bhattacharyya, Sibajiban (1987). *Doubt, Belief and Knowledge* (New Delhi: Indian Council of Philosophical Research).

Bhattacharyya, Sibajiban (1998). *Language, Testimony and Meaning* (New Delhi: Indian Council of Philosophical Research).

Bhattacharyya, Sibajiban (2004). *Development of Nyāya Philosophy and its Social Context.* History of Science, Philosophy and Culture in Indian Civilization, vol. 3, part 3 (Delhi: Centre for Studies in Civilizations).

Bigelow, John (1988). *The Reality of Numbers* (Oxford: Clarendon Press).

Birajmohan (1963). *A Descriptive Catalogue of Sanskrit Manuscripts in the Collections of the Sanskrit College* (Calcutta: Calcutta Sanskrit College).

Bochenski, I.M. (1961). *A History of Formal Logic* (New York: Chelsea Publishing Co.).

Borges, Jorge Luis (2000). *This Craft of Verse*, edited by Calin-Andrei Mihailescu (Cambridge, Mass.: Harvard University Press.)

Burton, David (2004). *Buddhism, Knowledge and Liberation: A Philosophical Study* (London: Ashgate).

Byrne, Alex and Logue, Heather (2009). *Disjunctivism: Contemporary Readings* (Cambridge, Mass.: MIT Press).

Campbell, John (1987–88). 'Is Sense Transparent?' *Proceedings of the Aristotelian Society* New Series 88: 273–292.

Camps, Arnulf (1988). 'Father Heinrich Roth and the History of his Sanskrit manuscripts', in Roth 1988: 5–19.

Cardona, George (1975). 'Paraphrase and Sentence Analysis: Some Indian Views', *Journal of Indian Philosophy* 3: 259–281.

Carpenter, Amber and Ganeri, Jonardon (2010). 'Can You Seek the Answer to This Question? Meno in India', *Australasian Journal of Philosophy* 88.4: 571–594.

Chakrabarti, Arindam (1997). *Denying Existence: The Logic, Epistemology and Pragmatics of Negative Existentials and Fictional Discourse* (New York: Springer-Verlag).

Chakravarti, P. (1933). *The Linguistic Speculations of the Hindus* (Calcutta: University of Calcutta).

Chakravarti, Rai Monmohan Bahadur (1915). 'History of Navya Nyāya in Bengal and Mithilā', *Journal of the Asiatic Society of Bengal* New Series 11: 259–292.

Chand, Tara (1943). 'Dara Shikoh and the Upanishads', *Islamic Culture*: 397–413.

Chaudhuri, Roma (1945). *Sufism and Vedānta* (Calcutta).

Chaudhuri, Roma (1954). *A Critical Study of Dārā Shikoh's Samudra-sangama* (Calcutta).

Chisholm, Roderick (1973). *The Problem of the Criterion* (Milwaukee: Marquette University Press).

Chisholm, Roderick (1976). *Person and Object: A Metaphysical Study* (London: Routledge).

Clooney, Francis (1990). 'Vedānta, Commentary, and the Theological Component of Cross-Cultural Study', in F. Reynolds and D. Tracy eds, *Towards a Comparative Philosophy of Religions* (Albany: State University of New York Press, 1990): 287–314.

Clooney, Francis (1991). 'Binding the Text: Vedānta as Philosophy and Commentary', in Jeffrey R. Timm ed., *Texts in Context: Traditional Hermeneutics in South Asia* (Albany: State University of New York Press, 1991): 47–68.

Clooney, Francis (1996). *Seeing Through Texts: Doing Theology among the Śrīvaiṣṇavas of South India* (Albany: State University of New York Press).

Cottingham, John (1993). 'A New Start? Cartesian Metaphysics and the Emergence of Modern Philosophy', in Tom Sorell ed., *The Rise of Modern Philosophy: The Tension between the New and Traditional Philosophies from Machiavelli to Leibniz* (Oxford: Clarendon Press): 145–166.

Coward, Harold G. and Raja, K. Kunjunni (1990). *The Philosophy of the Grammarians*, Encyclopedia of Indian Philosophers, vol. 5 (Princeton: Princeton University Press).

Cowell, E. B. (1867). 'Memo to W.S. Atkinson: Nuddea Report', *Proceedings of the Asiatic Society of Bengal* (June 1867): 86–102.

Cox, Collett (1995). *Disputed Dharmas: Early Buddhist Theories on Existence* (Tokyo: The International Institute for Buddhist Studies).

Curley, Edwin (1986). 'Dialogues with the Dead', *Synthese* 67.1: 22–49.

Cutler, Norman (1992). 'Interpreting Tirukkuṟaḷ: The Role of Commentary in the Creation of a Text', *Journal of the American Oriental Society* 112.4: 549–566.

Dancy, Jonathan (1993). *Moral Reasons* (Oxford: Blackwell).

Das, Kumudranjan (1979). *Raja Todar Mal* (Calcutta: Saraswat Library).

De, Sushil Kumar (1934). 'Philosophy of Bengal Vaiṣṇavism', reprinted in *Indian Studies Past and Present* 2: 90–110.

De, Sushil Kumar (1942). *Early History of the Vaiṣṇava Faith and Movement in Bengal* (Calcutta: Firma K. L. Mukhopadhyaya; 2nd edn: 1961).

Derrett, J. Duncan (1956). 'An Indian Contribution to the Study of Property', *Bulletin of the School Oriental and African Studies* 18.3: 475–498.

Derrett, J. Duncan (1973a). *Dharmaśāstra and Juridical Literature* (Wiesbaden: Otto Harrassowitz).

Derrett, J. Duncan (1973b). *History of Indian Law (Dharmaśāstra)* (Leiden/Cologne: E. J. Brill).

Desai, Mohanlal Dalichand (1910). *Yashovijayaji: The Life of a Great Jaina Scholar* (Bombay: Meghji Hirji & Co.).

Deshpande, Madhav (1985). 'Historical Change and the Theology of Eternal Sanskrit', *Zeitschrift für vergleichende Sprachforschung auf dem Gebeite der indogermanischen Sprachen* 99: 122–149.

Dimock, C. Edward and Stewart, Tony K. (1999). *Caitanya Caritāmṛta of Kṛṣṇadāsa Kavirāja, a Translation and Commentary* (Cambridge, Mass.: Harvard Oriental Series).

Doniger O'Flaherty, Wendy (1984). *Dreams, Illusion and Other Realities* (Chicago: University of Chicago Press).

Donne, John (1953–62). *Sermons*. G. R. Potter and E. M. Simpson eds. (Berkeley: University of California Press).

Dreyfus, Georges (2005). 'Where do Commentarial Schools Come From?', *Journal of the International Association of Buddhist Studies* 28.2: 273–298.

Dummett, Michael (1978). *Truth and Other Enigmas* (Cambridge, Mass.: Harvard University Press).

Dummett, Michael (1979). 'Common-Sense and Physics', in G. F. Macdonald ed., *Perception and Identity* (London: Macmillan): 1–40.

Dummett, Michael (1981). *Frege: Philosophy of Language* (London: Duckworth; 2nd edn.).

Dummett, Michael (1991a). *The Logical Basis of Metaphysics* (Cambridge, Mass.: Harvard University Press).

Dummett, Michael (1991b). *Frege: Philosophy of Mathematics* (London: Duckworth).

Dummett, Michael (1996). *The Seas of Language* (Oxford: Oxford University Press).

Dundas, Paul (1992). *The Jains* (London: Routledge).

Dundas, Paul (1996). 'Somnolent Sūtras: Scriptural Commentary in Śvetāmbara Jainism', *Journal of Indian Phiolosophy* 24: 73–101.

Dundas, Paul (2004). 'Beyond Anekāntavāda: A Jaina Approach to Religious Tolerance', in Tara Sethia ed., *Ahiṃsā, Anekānta and Jainism* (Delhi: Motilal Banarsidas, 2004): 123–136.

Dvivedi, Sudhakara (1933). *Lives of Hindu Astronomers, or Gaṇaka-taraṅgiṇī* (Benares: Jyotish Prakash Press).

Easton, Richard M. (1992). 'The Bengal of Śrī Caitanya Mahāprabhu', in Steven Rosen ed., *Vaiṣṇavism: Contemporary Scholars Discuss the Gauḍīya Tradition* (New York: Folk Books).

Easton, Richard M. (2000). 'Who are the Bengal Muslims? Conversion and Islamization in Bengal', in his *Essays on Islam and Indian History* (Delhi: Oxford University Press, chapter 11).

Edgington, Dorothy (1985). 'The Paradox of Knowability', *Mind* 94: 557–568.

Ernst, Carl W. (2003). 'Muslim Studies of Hinduism? A Reconstruction of Arabic and Persian Translations from Indian Languages', *Iranian Studies* 36.2: 173–195.

Evans, Gareth (1982). *The Varieties of Reference* (Oxford: Clarendon Press).

Faddegon, B. (1918). *The Vaiśeṣika System, Described with the Help of the Oldest Texts* (Amsterdam: Johannes Müller).

Fish, Stanley (1980). *Is There a Text in this Class? The Authority of Interpretive Communities* (Cambridge, Mass.: Harvard University Press).

Fisher, Saul (2005). *Pierre Gassendi's Philosophy and Science* (Leiden: Brill).

Fitch, Frederic B. (1964). 'A Logical Analysis of Some Value Concepts', *Journal of Symbolic Logic* 28: 135–142.

Frauwallner, Erich (1966). 'Raghunātha Śiromaṇi I', *WZKSOA* 10: 86–207.

Frauwallner, Erich (1967). 'Raghunātha Śiromaṇi II', *WZKSOA* 11: 140–208.

Frauwallner, Erich (1970). 'Raghunātha Śiromaṇi III', *WZKSOA* 14: 161–208.

Frauwallner, Erich (1994a). 'Navyanyāyaḥ', in *Erich Frauwallner's Posthumous Essays*, translated by Jayandra Soni (New Delhi: Aditya Prakashan): 43–56.

Frauwallner, Erich (1994b). 'Navyanyāyaḥ: An Article for the *Wörterbuch der Philosophie*', in *Erich Frauwallner's Posthumous Essays*, translated by Jayandra Soni (New Delhi: Aditya Prakashan): 57–62.

Frege, Gotlob (1950). *The Foundations of Arithmetic.* Translated by J. L. Austin (Oxford: Basil Blackwell).

Ganeri, Jonardon (1996). 'Numbers as Properties of Objects: Frege and the Nyāya', *Studies in Humanities and Social Sciences, Shimla* 3: 111–121.

Ganeri, Jonardon (1999a). 'Dharmakīrti's Semantics for the Quantifier *Only*' in Shoryu Katsura ed., *Dharmakīrti's Thought and Its Impact on Indian and Tibetan Philosophy* (Vienna: Verlag der Österreichischen Akademie Der Wissenschaften): 101–116.

Ganeri, Jonardon (1999b). *Semantic Powers: Meaning and the Means of Knowing in Classical Indian Philosophy* (Oxford: Clarendon Press).

Ganeri, Jonardon (2001a). *Philosophy in Classical India: The Proper Work of Reason* (London: Routledge).

Ganeri, Jonardon (2001b). 'Introduction', to Ganeri, J. ed., *Indian Logic: A Reader* (London: Routledge).

Ganeri, Jonardon (2004). 'The Ritual Roots of Moral Reason', in Kevin Schilbrack ed., *Thinking Through Rituals: Philosophical Perspectives* (London: Routledge, 2004): 207–233.

Ganeri, Jonardon (2006). *Artha: Meaning* (Delhi: Oxford University Press).

Ganeri, Jonardon (2007). *The Concealed Art of the Soul: Theories of Self and Practices of Truth in Indian Ethics and Epistemology* (Oxford: Clarendon Press).

Ganeri, Jonardon (2009). 'Philosophy in Early Modern India', *Stanford Encyclopedia of Philosophy*, http://plato.stanford.edu/entries/early-modern-india/.

Ganeri, Jonardon (2010). 'A Return to the Self: Indians and Greeks on Life as Art and Philosophical Therapy', in Ganeri and Carlisle 2010: 119–136.

Ganeri, Jonardon (2011). '*Apoha*, Feature-Placing and Sensory Content', in Arindam Chakrabarti, Mark Siderits, and Tom Tillemans eds, *Apoha and Human Cognition* (Columbia: Columbia University Press).

Ganeri, Jonardon and Clare Carlisle eds (2010). *Philosophy as Therapeia* (Cambridge: Cambridge University Press).

Gangopadhyaya, Mrinalkanti (1980). *Indian Atomism: History and Sources* (Calcutta: Bagchi & Co.)

Ganguly, Krishna Chakravorty (1993). *A Bibliography of Nyāya Philosophy* (Calcutta: National Library, Calcutta).

Garber, Dan (1988). 'Descartes, the Aristotelians, and the Revolution That Did Not Happen in 1637', *The Monist* 71.6: 471–486.

Garber, Dan and Ayers, Michael (2003). *The Cambridge History of Seventeenth-Century Philosophy* (Cambridge: Cambridge University Press).

Geach, P.T. (1980). *Reference and Generality: An Examination of Some Medieval and Modern Theories* (Ithaca: Cornell University Press; 3rd edn.).

Gelblum, Tuvia (1960). *Perception and Inference in the Nyāyasiddhāntamañjarī* (London: University of London Ph.D. dissertation).

Gettier, Edmund (1963). 'Is Justified True Belief Knowledge', *Analysis* 23: 121–123.

Ghosh, B. (1970). 'A Study of Sanskrit Grammar in Tibet', *Bulletin of Tibetology* 7.2: 21–41.

Ghosh, Purnima (forthcoming). 'The Prābhākara Influence on Raghunātha Śiromaṇi's *Padārthatattvanirūpaṇa*', *Proceedings of the 14th World Sanskrit Conference, Kyoto*.

Gillon, B. S. and Love, M. L. (1980). 'Indian Logic Revisited: *Nyāyapraveśa* Reviewed' *Journal of Indian Phil*osophy 8: 349–384.

Gillon, B.S. and Hayes, R.P. (1982). 'The Role of the Particle *eva* in (Logical) Quantification in Sanskrit' *WZKS* 26: 195–203.

Gode, P. K. (1943/4). 'Some New Evidence Regarding Devabhaṭṭa Mahāśabde, the Father of Ratnākarabhaṭṭa, the Guru of Sevai Jaising of Amber', *The Poona Orientalist* 8.3&4: 129–138.

Gode, P. K. (1945). 'Some Evidence About the Location of the Manuscript Library of Kavīndracharya Sarasvatī at Benares in A.D. 1665', in C. Kunhan Raja ed., *Jagadvijayachandas of Kavindracharya* (Bikaner: Anup Sanskrit Library).

Gode, P. K. (1954a). 'Bernier and Kavīndrācārya Sarasvatī at the Moghal Court', in P. K. Gode, *Studies in Indian Literary History* (Bombay: Bharatiya Vidya Bhavan), vol. 2: 364–379.

Gode, P. K. (1954b). '*Samudra-saṅgama*, a Philosophical Work by Dārā Shukoh, Son of Shah Jahāṇ, Composed in A.D. 1655', in P. K. Gode, *Studies in Indian Literary History* (Bombay: Bharatiya Vidya Bhavan), vol. 2: 434–446.

Goekoop, Cornelis (1967). *The Logic of Invariable Concomitance in the Tattvacintāmaṃi* (Dordrecht: Reidel).

Gomez, Luis (1987). 'Buddhist Literature: Exegesis and Hermeneutics', *Encyclopedia of Religion* (New York: Mc Millan), vol. 2: 529–540.

Goodman, Nelson (1978). *Ways of Worldmaking* (Hassocks: The Harvester Press).

Gopal, S. (1989). *Radhakrishnan: A Biography* (London: Unwin Hyman).

Granoff, Phyllis (1978). *Philosophy and Argument in Late Vedānta: Śrī Harṣa's Khaṇḍana-khaṇḍa-khādya* (Dordrecht: Reidel).

Gupta, Sanjukta (2006). *Advaita Vedānta and Vaiṣṇavism: The Philosophy of Madhusūd-hana Sarasvatī* (London: Routledge).

Guha, D. C. (1968). *Navya-nyāya System of Logic* (Delhi: Motilal Banarsidass [2nd edn 1979]).

Guhe, Eberhard (2008). 'George Bealer's Property Theories and Their Relevance to the Study of Navya-Nyāya Logic', in Mihir Chakraborty, Benedikt Loewe and Madhabendra Mitra eds, *Logic, Navya-Nyāya and Applications: Homage to Bimal Krishna Matilal* (London: College Publications, 2008): 143–157.

Hadot, Pierre (1995). 'Philosophy, Exegesis, and Creative Mistakes', in *Philosophy as a Way of Life: Spiritual Exercises from Socrates to Foucault* (Oxford: Blackwell Publishing): 71–78.

Hahn, L. E. ed. (1998). *The Philosophy of P. F. Strawson* (Chicago: Open Court).

Halbfass, Wilhelm (1988). *India and Europe: An Essay in Understanding* (Albany: State University of New York Press).

Halbfass, Wilhelm (1992). *On Being and What There is: Classical Vaiśeṣika and the History of Indian Ontology* (Delhi: Sri Satguru Publications, 1992).

Hasrat, Bikrama Jit (1982). *Dārā Shikūh: Life and Works* (Delhi: Munshiram Manoharlal [1953]).

Hayes, Richard (1988). *Diṅnāga on the Interpretation of Signs* (Kluwer: Studies of Classical India, vol. 9).

Herzberger, H. and Herzberger, R. (1981). 'Bhartṛhari's Paradox', *Journal of Indian Philosophy* 9: 3–32.

Horn, L. R. (1989). *A Natural History of Negation* (Chicago: The University of Chicago Press).

Houben, Jan (1995). 'Bhartṛhari's Solution to the Liar and Some Other Paradoxes' *Journal of Indian Philosophy* 23.4: 381–401.

Hume, David (1990 [1780]). *Dialogues Concerning Natural Religion* (London: Penguin).

Hunter, William Wilson (1897). *The Annals of Rural Bengal* (London: Smith, Elder and Co.), 7th edn.

Husain, Yousuf (1928). 'Haud-ul-Hayāt', *Journal Asiatique* 213: 308–344.

Ingalls, Daniel H. H. (1951). *Materials for the Study of Navya-Nyāya Logic* (Cambridge, Mass.: Harvard University Press).

Ingalls, Daniel H. H. (1962). 'Cynics and Pāśupatas: the Seeking of Dishonour', *Harvard Theological Review* 55: 281–298.

Jackson, Frank (1998). *From Metaphysics to Ethics* (Oxford: Clarendon Press).

Jacob, G. A. (1900–04). *A Handful of Popular Maxims Current in Sanskrit Literature (Laukikanyāyāñjali)* (Bombay: Tukaram Javaji).

Jain, K. K. (2006). 'Kāśī, Yaśovijaya and Jaina Institutes', in R. C. Sharma & P. Ghosal eds, *Jaina Contribution to Varanasi* (New Delhi: D. K. Printworld): 133–145.

James, Susan (1993). 'Spinoza the Stoic', in Tom Sorell ed., *The Rise of Modern Philosophy: The Tension between the New and Traditional Philosophies from Machiavelli to Leibniz* (Oxford: Clarendon Press): 289–316.

Jani, A. N. (1996). *Śrīharṣa* (Delhi: Sahitya Akademi).

Johnston, Mark (1998). 'Are Manifest Qualities Response-Dependent?' *Monist* 81: 3–43.

Jyväsjärvi, Mari (2010). 'Retrieving the Hidden Meaning: Jain Commentarial Techniques and the Art of Memory', *Journal of Indian Philosophy* 38: 133–162.

Kahrs, Eivind (1998). *Indian Semantic Analysis* (Cambridge: Cambridge University Press).

Kajiyama Yuichi (1966). *An Introduction to Buddhist Philosophy: An Annotated Translation of the Tarkabhāṣā of Mokṣākaragupta* (Kyoto: Memoirs of the Faculty of Letters, Kyoto University, no. 10).

Kajiyama, Yuichi (1973). 'Three Kinds of Affirmation and Two Kinds of Negation in Buddhist Philosophy' *WZKS* 17: 161–175.

Kansara, N. M. (1976). 'The *Bhagavadgītā* Citations in Yaśovijaya's *Adhyātmasāra*, A Manual on Jaina Mysticism', *Annals of the Bhandarkar Oriential Institute* 57: 23–39.

Kant, Immanuel (1795). *Towards Perpetual Peace*, in Mary J. Gregor trans. and ed., *Practical Philosophy* (Cambridge: Cambridge University Press, 1996).

Kapadia, Hiralal Rasikdas (1966). *Yaśodohana* (Bombay: J. S. Javeri).

Kaplan, David (1989). 'Demonstratives: An Essay on the Semantics, Logic, Metaphysics and Epistemology of Demonstratives and Other Indexicals', in J. Almog, J. Perry, and H. Wettstein eds, *Themes From Kaplan* (Oxford: Clarendon Press).

Karim, Abdul (1985). *Social History of the Muslims in Bengal to AD 1538* (Chittagong: Baitush Sharaf Islamic Research Institute).

Katsura Shoryu (1986). 'On the Origin and Development of the Concept of *vyāpti* in Indian Logic', *Tetsugaku* 38: 1–16.

Kaviraja, Gopinath (1961). *Gleanings from the History and Bibliography of Nyāya-Vaiśeṣika Literature* (Calcutta: Sarasvati Bhavan; reprinted from the Sarasvati Bhavana Series, Benares, vols 3, 4, 5 & 7). Reprinted Benares (1982) with different pagination.

Kaviraja, Gopinath (1965). *Kāśī kī Sārasvata Sādhanā* (Patna: Bihara Rastrabhasha Parishad).

Krishna, Daya (1994). 'Is Nyāya Realist or Idealist?', *Journal of Indian Council of Philosophical Research* 12.1: 161–163.

Krishna, Daya (1997a). 'The Modes of Analysis and the Search for Precision: Developments in Navya Nyāya after Gaṅgeśa', in his *Indian Philosophy: A New Approach* (Delhi: Sri Satguru Publications): 155–162.

Krishna, Daya (1997b). 'Raghunātha the Rebel', in his *Indian Philosophy: A New Approach* (Delhi: Sri Satguru Publications): 174–180.

Krishna, Daya (1997c). 'The British Intrusion and the Great Apartheid', in his *Indian Philosophy: A New Approach* (Delhi: Sri Satguru Publications): 188–196.

Krishna, Daya (2001). *Developments in Indian Philosophy from Eighteenth Century Onwards*. History of Science, Philosophy and Culture in Indian Civilization, vol. 10 part 1 (New Delhi: Centre for Studies in Civilizations).

Krishna, Daya, ed. (2004). *Discussion and Debate in Indian Philosophy: Issues in Vedānta, Mīmāṃsā and Nyāya* (New Delhi: Indian Council of Philosophical Research).

Krishnan, Y. (1976). 'Role of the Nyāya-Vaiśeṣikas in Indian Religion and Society', *Prachya Pratibha* 4.1: 67–74.

Kristeller, P. O. (1984). 'Stoic and Neoplatonic Sources in Spinoza's *Ethics*', *History of European Ideas* 5.1: 1–15.

Kroll, Ethan (2010). *A Logical Approach to Law* (University of Chicago PhD. Dissertation).

Lambros, C. (1976). 'Are Numbers Properties of Objects?', *Philosophical Studies* 29: 381–389.

Leclerc, Ivor (1972). *The Nature of Physical Existence* (London: George Allen & Unwin).

Leibniz, G. W. (1956). *Philosophical Papers and Letters*, L. E. Loemker ed. (Chicago: University of Chicago Press).

Lewis, David (1998). *Papers in Philosophical Logic* (Cambridge: Cambridge University Press).

Locke, John (1975). *An Essay Concerning Human Understanding*, Peter H. Nidditch ed. (Oxford: Oxford University Press).

Lolordo, Antonia (2007). *Pierre Gassendi and the Birth of Early Modern Philosophy* (Cambridge: Cambridge University Press).

Long, Rev. D. J. ed. (1869). *Selections from the Unpublished Records of Government for the Years 1748 to 1767 Inclusive*. Appendix D: 'Lord Minto's Minute on Sanskrit Colleges in Tirhut and Nuddea'. (London: N. Trübner & Co.): 554–560.

Lüthy, C. H. (1997). 'Thoughts and Circumstances of Sébastien Basson. Micro-History, Questions', *Early Science and Medicine* 2.1: 1–73.

Lycan, W. G. (1991). 'Even and Even If', *Linguistics and Philosophy* 14: 115–150.

McDowell, John (1996). *Mind and World* (Cambridge, Mass.: Harvard University Press).

McDowell, John (2008). 'Responses', in Jakob Lindgaard ed., *John McDowell: Experience, Norm, and Nature* (Oxford: Blackwell Publishing).

McEvilley, Thomas (2002). *The Shape of Ancient Thought: Comparative Studies in Greek and Indian Philosophies* (New York: Allworth Press).

Maffie James, (1990). 'Recent Work on Naturalizing Epistemology', *American Philosophical Quarterly* 27: 281–293.

Maheśa Candra Nyāyaratna (1981). *Brief Notes on the Modern Nyāya System of Philosophy and its Technical Terms* (Calcutta: Calcutta Sanskrit College Studies Series). Trans. Ujjwala Jha, *A Primer of Navya Nyāya Language and Methodology* (Kolkata: The Asiatic Society 2004).

Majumdar, R. C. (1971). *History of Ancient Bengal* (Calcutta: G. Bharadwaj & Co.).

Mallik, Kumuda Nath (1912). *Nadīyā-kāhinī* (Calcutta; 2nd edn).

Marshall, John (1927). *John Marshall in India: Notes and Observations in Bengal, 1668–1672* (London: Oxford University Press).

Martin, Julian (1993). 'Francis Bacon, Authority, and the Moderns', in Tom Sorell ed., *The Rise of Modern Philosophy: The Tension between the New and Traditional Philosophies from Machiavelli to Leibniz* (Oxford: Clarendon Press): 71–88.

Matilal, Bimal Krishna (1968). *The Navyanyāya Doctrine of Negation* (Cambridge, Mass.: Harvard University Press).

Matilal, Bimal Krishna (1971). *Epistemology, Logic and Grammar in Indian Philosophical Analysis* (The Hague: Mouton).

Matilal, Bimal Krishna (1975). 'On the Navya-Nyāya Logic of Property and Location', in *Proceedings of the (1975) International Symposium of Multiple-valued Logic* (Bloomington: Indiana University): 450–461.

Matilal, Bimal Krishna (1977). *Nyāya-Vaiśeṣika.* A History of Indian Literature, vol. 6, fasc. 2, edited by Jan Gonda (Wiesbaden: Otto Harrassowitz).

Matilal, Bimal Krishna (1985a). 'On the Theory of Number and *paryāpti* in Navya-Nyāya', *Journal of the Asiatic Society of Bengal* 27: 13–21.

Matilal, Bimal Krishna (1985b). *Logic, Language and Reality: An Introduction to Indian Philosophical Studies* (Delhi: Motilal Banarsidass).

Matilal, Bimal Krishna (1986). *Perception: An Essay on Classical Indian Theories of Knowledge* (Oxford: Clarendon Press).

Matilal, Bimal Krishna (1989). 'Moral Dilemmas: Insights from Indian Epics' in B. K. Matilal ed., *Moral Dilemmas in the Mahābhārata* (Shimla: Indian Institute of Advanced Study): 1–19.

Matilal, Bimal Krishna (1991). *The Word and the World: India's Contribution to the Study of Language* (Delhi: Oxford University Press).

Matilal, Bimal Krishna (1998). *The Character of Logic in India* (Albany, NY: State University of New York Press).

Matilal, Bimal Krishna (2002). *Mind, Language and World*, Collected Essays, vol. 1 (Delhi: Oxford University Press).

Mehta, J. L. (1990). 'The Ṛgveda: Text and Interpretation', in his *Philosophy and Religion: Essays in Interpretation* (Delhi: Indian Council of Philosophical Research).

Meinel, Christoph (1988). 'Early Seventeenth-Century Atomism: Theory, Epistemology, and the Insufficiency of Experiment', *Isis* 79.1: 68–103.

Mercer, Christia (1993). 'The Vitality and Importance of Early Modern Aristotelianism', in Tom Sorell ed., *The Rise of Modern Philosophy: The Tension between the New and Traditional Philosophies from Machiavelli to Leibniz* (Oxford: Clarendon Press): 33–70.

Millikan, Ruth G. (1993). 'On Mental Orthography', in B. Dahlbom ed., *Dennett and His Critics* (Oxford: Blackwell): 97–121.

Minkowski, Christopher (2005). 'What Makes a Work "Traditional"? On the Success of Nīlakaṇṭha's *Mahābhārata* Commentary', in Federico Squarcini ed., *Boundaries, Dynamics and Construction of Traditions in South Asia* (Florence: Firenze University Press, 2005): 225–252.

Minkowski, Christopher (2011). 'Advaita Vedānta in Early Modern History', in R. O'Hanlon and D. Washbook eds, *Religious Cultures in Early Modern History* (London: Routledge).

Mishra, Umesh (1966). *History of Indian Philosophy*, vol. 2, chapter II, part II—'Navya-Nyāya' (Allahabad: Tirabhukti Publications): 237–476.

Montaigne, Michel (1946). *The Essays of Montaigne* (New York: Modern Library).

Mohanty, J. N. (1966). *Gaṅgeśa's Theory of Truth* (Santiniketan; revised 2nd edn. 1989).

Mohanty, J. N. (1970). 'Nyāya Theory of Doubt', in his *Phenomenology and Ontology* (The Hague: Martin Nijhoff, 1970).

Mohanty, J.N. (1992). *Reason and Tradition in Indian Thought: An Essay on the Nature of Indian Philosophical Thinking* (Oxford: Clarendon Press).

Mohanty, J. N. (2006). 'Categories (*padārtha*-s) in Indian philosophy', in Pranab K. Sen 2006: 29–46.

Moore, G. E. (1903). *Principia Ethica* (Cambridge: Cambridge University Press).

Müller, Max (1853). 'Indian Logic', appendix to W. Thomson, *An Outline of the Necessary Laws of Thought* (London: Longmans, Green and Co.; 3rd edn).

Nagel, Thomas (1986). *The View From Nowhere* (Oxford: Clarendon Press).

Narasimha, Roddam (2007). 'Epistemology and Language in Indian Astronomy and Mathematics', *Journal of Indian Philosophy* 35: 521–541.

Narasimha, Roddam (2009). 'The Chequered Histories of Epistemology and Science', in Bharati Ray ed., *Different Types of History*. History of Science, Philosophy and Culture in Indian Civilization, vol. 14, part 4 (Delhi: Pearson Longman).

Narayanan, T. K. (1992). *Nyāyasāra of Bhāsarvajña: A Critical Study* (Delhi: Mittal Publications).

Nasr, Seyyed Hossein (1999). *Sufi Essays* (Chicago: ABC International).

Nemoto, Hiroshi (forthcoming). 'Three kinds of *vyavaccheda* (*rnam gcod*) in Tibetan *bsdus grwa* Literature', *Proceedings of the 14th World Sanskrit Conference, Kyoto.*

Newman, J. H. (1845). *An Essay on the Development of Christian Doctrine* (London: Longmans Green; reprinted 1890).

Nietzsche, F. (1954). *The Portable Nietzsche*, ed. and trans. Walter Kaufmann (New York: Viking).

O'Connell, J. T. (1982). 'Vaiṣṇava Perceptions of Muslims in Sixteenth Century Bengal', in Milton Israel and N.K. Wagle eds., *Islamic Society and Culture: Essays in Honour of Professor Aziz Ahmad* (New Delhi: Manohar Publications, 1982): 289–314.

O'Malley, L. S. S. (1925). *History of Bengal, Bihar & Orissa under British Rule* (Calcutta: Bengal Secretariat Book Depot).

O'Hanlon (2010). 'Letters Home: Banaras Paṇḍits and the Maratha Regions in Early Modern India', *Modern Asian Studies* 44.2: 201–240.

Olivelle, Patrick (1998). *The Early Upaniṣads: An Annotated Text and Translation* (New York: Oxford University Press).

Osler, Margaret (1993). 'Gassendi's Epicurean project', in Tom Sorell ed., *The Rise of Modern Philosophy: The Tension between the New and Traditional Philosophies from Machiavelli to Leibniz* (Oxford: Clarendon Press): 129–144.

Pahi, Visvambhara and Kusuma Jain (1997). *Raghunātha Śiromaṇi's Padārtha-tattva-nirūpaṇam with Rāmabhadhra Sārvabhauma's Commentary* (Jaipur: Rajasthan University Press).

Pandeya, Srirama (1983). *Dīdhitikāropajñāvicārāṇām Ālocanam (Reflections on Works about Raghunātha's Novel Ideas)* (Varanasi: Sampurnanand Sanskrit University).

Parikh, Vasant G. (2001). *Guṇaratna-gaṇi's Tarka-taraṅgiṇī* (Ahmedabad: L. D. Institute of Indology).

Parsons, Terence (2001). 'Bhartṛhari on What Cannot be Said', *Philosophy East & West* 51: 525–534.

Perrett, Roy W. (1985). 'A Note on the Navya-Nyāya Account of Number', *Journal of Indian Philosophy* 13: 227–234.

Perrett, Roy W. (1999). 'Is Whatever Exists Knowable and Nameable?' *Philosophy East & West* 49: 410–414.

Peters, Stanley and Westertåhl, Dag (2006). *Quantifiers in Language and Logic* (New York: Oxford University Press).

Pettit, Philip (1991). 'Realism and Response-Dependence', *Mind* 100: 597–626.

Phillips, Stephen (1995). *Classical Indian Metaphysics* (Chicago: Open Court Publishing Company).

Pimputkar, R. S. (1926). *Citaḷebhaṭṭa Prakaraṇa* (Bombay, 1926); reproduced in C. Y. Mule *et al* eds, *Devarūkhe* (Bombay: Ramesh Visnu Nimbkar, 1973): 87–107, as well as in P. K. Gode (1943–4).

Pollock, Sheldon (1989). 'Mīmāṃsā and the Problem of History in Traditional India', *Journal of the American Oriental Society* 109: 603–610.

Pollock, Sheldon (2001a). 'The Death of Sanskrit', *Comparative Studies in Society and History* 43.2: 392–426.

Pollock, Sheldon (2001b). 'The New Intellectuals in Seventeenth-century India', *The Indian Economic and Social History Review* 38: 3–31.

Popkin, Richard H. (2003). *The History of Scepticism: From Savonarola to Bayle* (Oxford: Oxford University Press).

Potter, Karl (1957). *The Padārtha-tattva-nirūpaṇam of Raghunātha Śiromaṇi*. Text and trans. (Cambridge, Mass.: Harvard University Press, Harvard Yenching Institute Studies, vol. 17).

Potter, Karl (1977). *The Tradition of Nyāya-Vaiśeṣika up to Gaṅgeśa*, Encyclopedia of Indian Philosophies, vol. 2 (Delhi: Motilal Banarsidass).

Potter, Karl and Bhattacharyya, Sibajiban (1993). *Indian Philosophical Analysis: Nyāya-Vaiśeṣika from Gaṅgeśa to Raghunātha Śiromaṇi*, Encyclopedia of Indian Philosophies, vol. 6 (Delhi: Motilal Banarsidass).

Prahlada Char, D. (2001). 'Developments in Nyāya from Eighteenth Century Onwards', in Krishna (2001): 123–209.

Prahlada Char, D. (2004). 'On the *kroḍapatras*—A New Genre of Philosophical Writing in India', in Krishna (2004): 354–381.

Prajapati, Sweta (2001). 'Raghudeva Bhaṭṭācārya and his Unknown Works', *Journal of the Oriental Institute* 51.1–2: 65–84.

Prajapati, Sweta (2008). *Raghudeva Bhaṭṭācāryaviracitā Navyanyāyavādagranthāḥ (Eight Dialectical Treatises of Raghudeva Bhaṭṭācārya)*, critically edited with an introduction in English (Baroda: Sweta Prajapati, 62 Aksharadham Society).

Qanungo, Kalika-Ranjan (1952). *Dara Shukoh: Volume 1, Biography* (Calcutta: S. C. Sarkar).

Quine, W. V. O. (1960). *Word and Object* (Cambridge, Mass.: MIT Press).

Raghavan, V. (1940). 'Kavīndrācārya Sarasvati', in *D. R. Bhandarkar Volume*, edited by Bimala Churn Law (Calcutta: Indian Research Institute): 159–165.

Rahri, Kantichandra (1891). *Navadvīpa-mahimā* (Hoogly).

Raja, K. K. (1963). *Indian Theories of Meaning* (Madras: The Adyar Library).

Raja, C. K. (2007). *Cultural Foundations of Mathematics: The Nature of Mathematical Proof and the Transmission of the Calculus from India to Europe in the 16th Century*. History of Science, Philosophy and Culture in Indian Civilization, vol. 10, part 4 (Delhi: Centre for Studies in Civilizations).

Ramaiah, C. (1976–7). 'Nyāya-Vaiśeṣika Theory of Numbers (Sānkhyā)', *Indian Philosophical Quarterly* 4: 129–134.

Ram-Prasad, Chakravarthi (2002). *Advaita Epistemology and Metaphysics: An Outline of Indian Non-Realism* (London: RoutledgeCurzon).

Raychaudhuri, Tapankumar (1953). *Bengal Under Akbar and Jahāngīr* (Calcutta: A. Mukherjee & Co.).

Richards, John F. (1993). *The Mughal Empire*. The New Cambridge History of India, I, 5. (Cambridge: Cambridge University Press).

Rizvi, Sajjad (2011). 'Mīr Dāmād in India: Islamic Philosophical Traditions and the Problem of Creation', *Journal of the American Oriental Society* 13.1 9–23.

Rizvi, Saiyid Athar Abbas (1989). 'Shi'a Contributions to Philosophy, Science and Literature in India', in his *A Socio-Intellectual History of the Isna 'Ashari Shi'as in India* (Delhi: Munshiram Manoharlal Publishers).

Roy, N. B. (1941). 'The Muslim Conquest of Bengal', *Indian Historical Quarterly* 17: 92–96.

Ruegg, D. S. (1985). 'Purport, Implicature and Presupposition: Sanskrit *abhiprāya* and Tibetan *dgoṅs pa/ dgoṅs gzi* as Hermeneutical Concepts', *Journal of Indian Philosophy* 13: 309–325.

Saha, Sukharanjan (2003). *Epistemology in Pracīna and Navya Nyāya* (Kolkata: Jadavpur University Press).

Sainsbury, Mark (1979). *Russell* (London: Routledge & Kegan Paul).

Sainsbury, Mark (1991). *Logical Forms* (Oxford: Basil Blackwell).

Sainsbury, Mark (1995). *Paradoxes* (Cambridge: Cambridge University Press, 2nd edn).

Salerno, Joe ed. (2009). *New Essays on the Knowability Paradox* (Oxford: Oxford University Press).

Sankhyatirtha, Gopendu Bhusan (1964). *Navadvīpe Saṃskṛta Carcar Itihās* (Navadvipa).

Sarkar, Jadunath (1984). *A History of Jaipur c. 1503–1938* (Hyderabad: Orient Longman).

Sastri, Gaurinath (1968). 'Post-Gadādhara Naiyāyikas of Bengal (1600–1800 A.D.)', in *Pratidānam: Indian, Iranian and Indo-European Studies Presented to Franciscus Bernardus Jacobus Kuiper on his Sixtieth Birthday*, J. C. Heesterman, G. H. Schokker and V. I. Subramoniam eds (The Hague: Mouton): 516–522.

Scanlon, T. M. (1998). *What We Owe to Each Other* (Cambridge, Mass.: Harvard University Press).

Schmitt, Charles (1983). *Aristotle and the Renaissance* (Cambridge, Mass.: Harvard University Press).

Secada, Jorge (2000). *Cartesian Metaphysics: The Scholastic Origins of Modern Philosophy* (Cambridge: Cambridge University Press).

Sellars, Wilfred (1956). 'Empiricisim and the Philosophy of Mind', reprinted in Robert Brandom *et al.*, *Empiricism and the Philosophy of Mind* (Cambridge: Harvard University Press, 1997).

Sen, Amartya (1993). 'Positional Objectivity', *Philosophy and Public Affairs* 22: 126–145. Reprinted in *Rationality and Freedom* (Harvard: Belknap Press, 2002): 463–483.

Sen, Amartya (2005). *The Argumentative Indian: Writings on Indian History, Culture and Identity* (London: Allen Lane).

Sen, Amartya (2009). *The Idea of Justice* (London: Allen Lane).

Sen, Malati (1934–45). 'Some Literary Anecdotes and Stories about Naiyāyikas', *Calcutta Oriental Journal* 2: 247–249.

Sen, Prabal Kumar (2003). *Nyāyasūtras with Nyāyarahasya of Rāmabhadrasārvabhauma and Ānvīkṣikītattvavivaraṇa of Jānakīnātha Cūḍāmaṇi* (Kolkata: The Asiatic Society).

Sen, Prabal Kumar (2006), 'Saṃśaya', in Pranab Kumar Sen 2006: 243–255.

Sen, Pranab Kumar, ed. (2006). *Philosophical Concepts Relevant to Sciences in Indian Tradition*. History of Science, Philosophy and Culture in Indian Civilization, vol. 3, part 4 (Delhi: Centre for Studies in Civilizations).

Sen, P. K. and Verma. R. R. eds. (1995). *The Philosophy of P. F. Strawson* (New Delhi: Indian Council of Philosophical Research & Allied Publishers).

Sen, Saileswar (1924). *A Study of Mathurānātha's Tattva-cintāmaṇi-rahasya* (Wageningen: G. van der Hoogt).

Sen, S. N. (1995). 'History of Science in Relation to Philosophy and Culture in Indian Civilization', in D. P. Chattopadhyaya and R. Kumar (eds), *Science, Philosophy and Culture in Historical Perspective*, PHICPC Monograph 1 (Delhi: Munshiram Manoharlal).

Shafer-Landau, Russ (2003). *Moral Realism: A Defence* (Oxford: Clarendon Press).

Sharma, K. V., Ramasubramanian, K., and Sriniva, M. D. and Sriram, M. S. (2008). *Ganita-yukti-bhāṣā (Rationales in Mathematical Astronomy) of Jyeṣṭhadeva* (Dordrecht: Springer).

Shastri, Yajneshwar (1991). '*Adhyātmopaniṣad-prakaraṇa* of Yaśovijaya: a Study', in his *Traverses on Less Trodden Paths of Indian Philosophy and Religion* (Ahmedabad: L. D. Institute of Indology, 1991): 65–74.

Shastri, MM. Haraprasad (1912). 'Dakshini Paṇḍits at Benares', *Indian Antiquary* XLI: 7–13.

Shastri, MM. Haraprasad (1939). *A Descriptive Catalogue of the Sanskrit Manuscripts in the Collections of the Royal Asiatic Society of Bengal*, vol. 9 (Calcutta: Asiatic Society).

Shaw, J. L. (1982). 'Number: From the Nyāya to Frege-Russell', *Studia Logica*, 41: 283–291.

Shein, Sheila Sylvia (1963). *Akbar and the Fatwā of 1580* (University of Pennsylvania dissertation).

Shukla, K. S. (1959). *The Pāṭīgaṇita of Śrīdharācārya with an Ancient Sanskrit Commentary*, ed. Kripa Shankar Shukla (Lucknow: Lucknow University Department of Mathematics and Astronomy).

Sinha, Samita (1993). *Paṇḍits in a Changing Environment: Centres of Sanskrit Learning in Nineteenth Century Bengal* (Calcutta: Sarat Book House).

Sjödin, Anna-Pya (2006). *The Happening of Tradition: Vallabha on Anumāna in Nyāya-līlāvatī* (Uppsala: Uppsala University, Interfaculty Units).

Skinner, Quentin (2000). *Machiavelli: A Very Short Introduction* (Oxford: Oxford University Press).

Skinner, Quentin (2002). *Visions of Politics*, Volume 1: *Regarding Method* (Cambridge: Cambridge University Press).

Smith, V. A. ed. (1923). *The Oxford History of India* (Oxford: Oxford University Press, 2nd edn.).

Smith, Barry (1991). 'Textual Deference', *American Philosophical Quarterly* 28.1: 1–12.

Solomon, Esther A. (1976). *Indian Dialectics: Methods of Philosophical Discussion* (Ahmedabad: B. J. Institute of Learning and Research), 2 vols.

Solomon, Esther A. (1986). 'Trilocana—A Forgotten Naiyāyika', in *Sanskrit and World Culture* (Berlin: Akademie Verlag): 560–566.

Sorabji, Richard (2004). *The Philosophy of the Commentators 200–600 AD* (London: Duckworth), vol. 3.

Srinivas, M. D. (1992). 'The Methodology of Indian Mathematics and its Contemporary Relevance' in G. Kuppuram and K. Kumudamani eds, *History of Science and Technology in India*, vol. 2: 29–86.

Staal, Frits (1961). *Advaita and Neoplatonism* (Madras: University of Madras).

Staal, Frits (1962). 'Negation and the Law of Contradiction in Indian Thought: A Comparative Study', *Bulletin of the School of Oriental and African Studies* 25: 52–71; reprinted in his *Universals* (Chicago: Chicago University Press, 1988): 109–128.

Staal, Frits (1990). *Rules without Meaning: Ritual, Mantra and the Human Sciences* (New York: Peter Lang).

Strawson, P. F. (1959). *Individuals: An Essay on Descriptive Metaphysics* (London: Methuen).

Strawson, P. F. (1966). *The Bounds of Sense* (London: Methuen).

Strawson, P. F. (1998). 'Intellectual Autobiography', in L. Hahn ed., *The Philosophy of P. F. Strawson* (Chicago: Open Court): 16–21.

Streumer, Bart (2008). 'Are There Irreducibly Normative Properties?', *Australasian Journal of Philosophy* 86.4: 537–561.

Stuchlik, Jakob (2009). *Der Arische Ansatz: Erich Frauwallner und der Nationalsozialismus* (Vienna: Verlag der Österreichischen Akademie der Wissenschaften).

Tagore, Rabindranath (1921). 'Letter to C. F. Andrews', New York, March 13th 1921, in *The English Writings of Rabindranath Tagore* (New Delhi: Sahitya Akademi, 1996), vol. 3: 287–290.

Tambiah, S. J. (1979). 'A Performative Approach to Ritual' *Proceedings of the British Academy* 45: 113–169; reprinted in his *Culture, Thought and Social Action* (Cambridge, Mass: Harvard University Press, 1985): 123–166.

Tarafdar, Momtazur Rahman (1965). *Husain Shāhi Bengal 1494–1538 AD: A Socio-Political Study* (Dacca: Asiatic Society of Pakistan).

Thakur, Anantalal (2003). *Origin and Development of the Vaiśeṣika System*. History of Science, Philosophy and Culture in Indian Civilization, vol. 2, part 4 (Delhi: Centre for Studies in Civilizations).

Thibaut, George (1910). 'The *Bhāṣya* of Shabara Svāmin on the *Mīmāṃsā-sūtras* of Jaimini', *Indian Thought* 2.

Todeschini, Alberto (2010). 'Twenty-two Ways to Lose a Debate: a Gricean Look at the *Nyāyasūtra*'s Points of Defeat', *Journal of Indian Philosophy* 38: 49–74.

Truschke, Audrey (2012). *Cosmopolitan Encounters: Sanskrit and Persian at the Mughal Court* (Columbia University doctoral dissertation).

Tubb, Gary and Boose, Emery (2007). *Scholastic Sanskrit: A Manual for Students* (New York: American Institute of Buddhist Studies).

Tucci, G. (1949). *Tibetan Painted Scrolls* (Rome: La Libreria dello Stato), 3 vols.

Tucci, G. (1957). 'The Fifth Dalai Lama as a Sanskrit Scholar', *Sino-Indian Studies* 5: 235–240; reprinted in his *Opera Minora*, part 2 (Rome: Dott. Giovanni Bardi Editore, 1971): 589–594.

Uckelman, Sara (2009). 'Indian Logic and Medieval Western Logic: Some Comparative Remarks', http://www.illc.uva.nl/Publications/ResearchReports/X-2009-04.text.pdf

Ui, Hakuju (1917). *Vaiśeṣika Philosophy According to the Daśapadārthaśāstra* (London: Royal Asiatic Society).

Upādhyāya, Baldev (1983). *Kāśī kī pāndity-paramparā* (Varanasi: Visvavidyalaya Prakasana; 2nd edn. 1994).

Vaidya, P. L. (1948). *Ṭoḍarānandam, An Encyclopaedic Work on Dharmaśāstra Compiled under the Patronage of Rājā Ṭoḍar Mal.* vol. 1. (Bikaner: Anup Sanskrit Library).

van Fraasen, B. C. (2002). 'A History of the Name "Empiricism"', in his *The Empirical Stance* (Yale: Yale University Press).

van Melsen, Andrew G. (1952). *From Atomos to Atom: The History of the Concept Atom*; trans. Henry Koren (Pittsburgh: Duquesne University Press).

Veezhinathan, N. (2006). 'Saṅgati', in Pranab K. Sen 2006: 793–798.

Venn, J. A. ed. (1910–13). *Biographical Register of Christ's College 1505–1905, and the Earlier Foundation, God's House 1448–1505* (Cambridge: Cambridge University Press), entry on John Marshall.

Verhagen, Pieter C. (1994). *A History of Sanskrit Grammatical Literature in Tibet*; vol. 1: *Transmission of the Canonical Literature* (Leiden: E. J. Brill).

Vidyabhusana, Satischandra (1910). 'Yaśovijaya Gaṇi', *Journal of the Asiatic Society of Bengal* 6: 463–469.

Vidyabhusana, Satischandra (1971). *A History of Indian Logic* (Delhi: Motilal Banarsidass).

Vivekananda (1957a [c.1895]). 'Reply to the Madras Address', in *The Complete Works of Swami Vivekananda* (Calcutta: Advaita Ashram), vol. 4: 331–353.

Vivekananda (1957b [1902]). 'Conversations and Dialogues', in *The Complete Works of Swami Vivekananda* (Calcutta: Advaita Ashram), vol. 7: no. XXVII.

Wada, Toshihiro (1990). *Invariable Concomitance in Navya-Nyāya* (Delhi: Sri Satguru Publications).

Wada, Toshihiro (2007). *The Analytical Method of Navya-Nyāya* (Groningen: Egbert Forsten).

Ward, William (1811). *Account of the Writings, Religion and Manners of The Hindoos* (Serampore: Mission Press).

Westerståhl, D. (1988). 'Quantifiers', in the *Handbook of Philosophical Logic; vol. 4: Topics in the Philosophy of Language*, D. Gabbay & F. Guenther eds (Dordrecht: Reidel).

Williams, Bernard (1973). 'Deciding to Believe', in his *Problems of the Self* (Cambridge University Press): 136–151.

Williams, Bernard (2002). *Truth & Truthfulness* (Princeton: Princeton University Press).

Williamson, Timothy (1982). 'Intuitionism Disproved?' *Analysis* 42: 203–207.

Williamson, Timothy (1987a). 'On Knowledge and the Unknowable', *Analysis* 47: 144–148.

Williamson, Timothy (1987b). 'On the Paradox of Knowability', *Mind* 96: 256–261.

Williamson, Timothy (1996). 'Knowing and Asserting', *Philosophical Review* 105: 489–523.

Williamson, Timothy (2000). *Knowledge and its Limits* (Oxford: Clarendon Press).

Wilson, Catherine (2008). *Epicureanism and the Origins of Modernity* (Oxford: Oxford University Press).

Wilson, W. W. (1877). *A Statistical Account of Bengal*; vol. 2: Districts of Nadiyā and Jessor (London: Trubner & Co. Reprinted Delhi: D. K. Publishing House, 1973).

Wilson. W. W. (1897). *Annals of Rural Bengal*. 7th edn. (London: Smith, Elder & Co.).

Wittgenstein, Ludwig (1958). *Philosophical Investigations*, trans. G. E. M. Anscombe (Oxford: Blackwell).

Wittgenstein, Ludwig (1961). *Tractatus Logico-Philosophicus*, trans. D. F. Pears and B. F. McGuinness (New York: Humanities Press.)

Wood, Allen (2000). 'What Dead Philosophers Mean', in Dieter Schönecker and Thomas Zwenger eds *Understanding Kant*, (Würzburg: Königshausen and Neumann): 272–301.

Wright, Crispin (1992). *Truth and Objectivity* (Harvard: Harvard University Press).

Wright, Crispin (1999). 'Truth: a Traditional Debate Reviewed', in S. Blackburn and K. Simmons eds, *Truth* (Oxford: Oxford University Press, 1999): 203–238.

Wright, Crispin (2000). 'Truth as Sort of Epistemic: Putnam's Peregrinations', *Journal of Philosophy* 97: 335–364.

Index

A number in **bold** indicates the page on which a particular individual is most fully introduced.

absence, or non-being (*abhāva*) as a category 155, 166–7, 169–71, 177–8, 200–2, 210–11, 225, 227, 231, 233, 241
  generic and specific 229
Abū-l-Fażl 4, **13**, 23, 40, 52, 75, 78, 90
Agra 18, 19, 37, 77
Akbar 4, 7, 13, 19, 20, 22, 23, 25, 32, 40, 44, **51–3**, 57–9, 75–8
Annambhaṭṭa 91, **99**, 202–3, 250
Anquetil Duperron, A. H. 15, 22
Aristotle 125, 166, 239
  Aristotelian scholasticism 7, 9, 94, 151
  doctrine of form 215, 218
  progressive Aristotelians 1–3, 5, 115, 204
atomism 2, 16–18, 20, 166, 168, 171, 172, 175, 179, 201, 207, 212–19, 247
  do atoms have weight? 214, 216, 217
  molecules 212–5, 218
Aurangzeb 13, 19, 30, 37, **52–3**, 54

Bacon, Francis **1**, 2, 3, 9, 16–17, 142, 249
Basso, Sébastien 2, 3, 65, **214–6**, 218
Bayle, Pierre 15, **16**
being (*bhāva*):
  four categories in Veṇīdatta 205
  six categories 166–7, 175, 178, 200
  two grades 170–2
Bernier, François ix–x, **13–19**, 21, 74, 83, 161, 216, 247
Bhagavad-gītā 20, 22, 28, 35–6, 107
Bhartṛhari 105–6, 175, 177, 191
Bhāsarvajña 182, **188–90**, 197, 200, 205
Bhaṭṭa Vādīndra 190
Bhaṭṭoji Dīkṣita 99–100, 223
Bhavānanda Siddhāntavāgīśa 46, 52, **79**, 80, 85–6, 94–9, 106, 150, 237
Buddhist philosophical theory 4, 8, 33, 35, 67, 70, 72, 82, 93, 97–8, 105, 111, 113–14, 139, 158, 167, 170, 180, 189, 194, 213, 237–40
  see also Nāgārjuna; scepticism, Madhyamaka as; Tibet

Caitanya 39, **42–3**, 44, 58
Cārvāka ('materialism') 17, 35, 120, 158
category (*padārtha*):
  concept of 168, 171
  rejection and inclusion 49, 170, 202, 207
  seven-category ontology 52, 200–13
causal power (*śakti*) 200–2, 210, 211, 215
Chishtī, ʿAbd al-Raḥmān 25, 41
colonialism:
  and educational reform 10, 249
  India's emergence from 153, 249
  see also East India Company
commentary 89, 91–5, 102–16
  as crucible for cutting-edge research 89, 100, 152
  elliptical nature of Raghunātha's 45–6, 93, 98, 246–7
  hidden meaning 6, 66, 81, 82, 106–7, 115, 161, 250
  mediating a conversation between past and present 6, 52, 73, 91, 102–3, 246, 250
  principles-and-gloss text 112–6
  refutation-commentary 133, 147, 250
  as teaching notes 75, 86, 107, 204–5
  as weaving a text 103, 107–12
  wrongly associated with stagnation 6, 106, 249
creativity, and location in the penumbra of educational power 51, 74, 80–1, 88, 247–8

Dāniṣmand Khān **14**, 19, 30, 74, 215, 248
Dārā Shukoh 13–16, 19–21, **22–30**, 32, 36–8, 47, 71, 77, 161, 215, 244
definition, as a speech-act 66–7, 94, 128, 156, 158, 203
Delhi 40, 41, 51–4, 58–9, 76
Descartes, René **1–3**, 9, 14, 123, 152, 158, 215–6, 247, 248
  Discourse 15, 68, 244–5
  Principles of Philosophy 6, 102, 115–116, 159–61
Dharmakīrti 97, 103, 113, 194, 237–243
Dharmaśāstra ('disciplinary system of jurisprudence') 5, 58–9, 76, 90
differentiator (*viśeṣa*) 172, 187, 202, 205–9
Digby, Kenelm 2
Dinakara Bhaṭṭa 79, 203

Diṅnāga 97, 105, 113, 238
Dryden, John 16

East India Company 20, 39, 55–6, 59
education:
institutions 10, 40, 56, 65, 74, 153, 248, 249, 251; *see also* ṭol
methods 32, 84–5, 94, 100, 246; see also manual
empiricism 2, 16–17, 20, 142, 144, 173, 182, 186, 212
epistemology:
contextualist 126
of mathematics 174, 181–6
naturalism about 139, 142–4, 147, 153–7, 201, 203–5
Nyāya as non-Cartesian 126, 158–61
performativist 130, 145
primacy of, according to Gaṅgeśa 45, 132
in the ancient Indian disciplines 119–21
see also evidence; scepticism; way of gaining knowledge
evidence:
concept distinguished from that of cause 125–6, 153–7
self-evident truth 115, 124–5, 143
two grades of epistemic warrant in Gaṅgeśa 134–5, 146, 156

fictional names 5, 48, 95, 170, 175, 208
Fludd, Robert 15
Frauwallner, Erich, on the 'new reason' 100, 151, 198–9
Froimont, Libert 1–2

Gadādhara Bhaṭṭācārya 46, 52, 84, 85, **86–7**, 90, 93–9, 109, 194, 237, 248
Gaṅgeśa Upādhyāya 5, 7–9, 18, 45–6, 48, 51, 66–7, 92, 94–5, **131–9**, 142–4, 145–57, 161, 191, 223
Gassendi, Pierre 2, 3, 13–17, 92, 115, **215–8**
Gautama (*aka* Akṣapāda) 91–2, 140
Nyāya-sūtra 91, 109–110, 112, 122–7, 131–2, 135, 147, 157–61, 167, 202–3, 232
genres, philosophical 9, 66, 80, 83, 89–101, 102–3, 107, 112–5, 133, 147, 237, 250
Gokulanātha Upādhyāya 17, 57, 86, 95, 98, 133
Gosvāmi, Jīva 44, 78
Gosvāmi, Rūpa 44, 78
Gosvāmi, Sanātaṇa 44, 51
Govinda Śarman 19, 33, 38, **78**, 95, 98
Grueber, Johann 18

Halbfass, Wilhelm:
on European perception of India 245, 249
misinterprets Matilal 250
Hamel, Jean-Baptiste du 2
Harirāma Tarkavāgīśa Bhaṭṭācārya 68, 75, 80, **86**, 87, 90, 96–8, 237
history:
European history of philosophy excludes India 246, 249
methods for studying intellectual 7, 63–73, 246
of Navadvīpa 39–41, 51–6
'standard' history of philosophy 1, 214, 249
Hume, David 16
Ḥusayn Shāh **41–2**, 44, 51, 58, 248

Ibn al-'Arabī 13, 20; see also *waḥdat al-wujūd*
illocutionary intervention 7, 50, 63–73, 78, 81, 88, 102, 115–6, 127, 150, 167, 199, 203, 205, 219, 250
infallibilism 144, 147, 156, 206
inference (*anumāna*) 112, 141, 186
emphasis on, exaggerated 56, 94, 202, 248–9
inferential misfires 129–30, 145–6, 206
inquiry:
importance of examples 105, 121, 122, 160, 186, 237–9
methods of 4, 8, 84, 91, 121–3, 131, 135, 136, 138, 143, 147, 158–61, 167, 206, 247
multi-agent 158–60, 247
paradox of 120–1, 178
possibility of, *see* scepticism
target of 121, 145, 153–5, 178
two models 135
intentionality 86–7, 124, 137, 147–8, 150, 157, 168, 200–1, 223
Islam and India 7, 13, 25, 36–8, 39–41, 44, 51–3, 57–9, 74, 77–8, 84, 116
Islamic philosophical theory 22–30, 32, 33, 75, 244

Jagadīśa Tarkālaṃkāra 46, 80, 84, **85–6**, 93, 94, 97, 98, 196, 248
Jagannātha Tarkapañcānana of Triveni 54, 57, 59, 94, 97, 223
Jahāngīr 52, 53, 59
Jaina philosophical theory 20–1, 31–38, 113, 158
Jainas and the Mughal court 19
Jānakīnātha Bhaṭṭācārya Cūḍāmaṇi **81**, 84, 91, 94

Panicle of Principles about Reason 82, 83, 85, 95, 99, 250
Janārdana Vyāsa **83**, 95, 99
Jayadeva (*aka* Pakṣadhara) **45**, 90, 94, 149, 150
Jayanta Bhaṭṭa 3–4, 64, 105, 111, 232
Jayarāma Nyāyapañcānana 14, 19, 38, 53, 67, 74, **83–4**, 85, 87, 93, 94, 96, 97, 106, 150, 209
Garland of Categories 95, 101, 152, 201, 208, 211–18, 240, 247, 250
Garland of Principles 86, 91, 98, 101, 115, 126, 157–61, 246, 247
Jones, William 21, 57, 59

Kaṇāda (*aka* Ullūka) 17, 187
Vaiśeṣika-sūtra 69–70, 80, 91–2, 96, 110–11, 119–120, 182, 186, 187, 190, 212
Kaṇāda Tarkavāgīśa **81–2**, 94
Kant, Immanuel 22, 185, 250
Kathmandu 20
Kauṇḍabhaṭṭa 95, 99, 223, 250
Kavīndra Sarasvatī **14**, 15, 19, 22, 38, 77, 83
kinematics 166, 171, 200, 210, 212, 215–6, 218
impetus 212, 214, 218
Krishna, Daya, on the 'new reason' 88, 251
Kṛṣṇacandra, Rājā 7, **53–5**, 58–9, 248
Kṛṣṇadāsa Sārvabhauma **79**, 97, 212
Pearl-necklace of Principles about Reason 81, 85, 99, 113, 203, 250
Kumārila Bhaṭṭa 35, 66, 103, 109, 115, 120, **135**, 138, 146, 150

Laugākṣī Bhāskara 67, 83, 95, 98–9, 201, 211, 214, 237
Leibniz, Gottfried 2, 3, 115
'letter of judgement' (*nirṇaya-patra*) from 1657: 19, 22, 65, 78, 80, 86, 158
limitor (*avacchedaka*) 47, 90, 98, 195, 225, 229, 232–3
two types 230
linguistics:
as a method for philosophy 9, 49, 95, 100, 107, 223, 241, 250
philosophical grammar 79, 86, 87, 95, 97
Locke, John x, 16, 173–4

Mādhavadeva Bhaṭṭācārya 19, 92, 98, 151, 240
Essence of Reason 49–50, 95, 100, 133, 152, 176, **201–2**, 205–6, 209–10, 241
Madhusūdana Sarasvatī 20, 54, 75, **77–8**, 107, 223
Mahādeva Bhaṭṭa 19, 91
Mahādeva Puṇatāmakara 20, 48, 65, 77, **80**, 95, 241
Precious Jewel of Reason 80, 100–1, 133, 147–56
Examination of Selfhood as a Natural Kind 48, 80, 95, 208
Malebranche, Nicolas 15
Maṇḍanamiśra 146
Mansingh 53, **77–8**
manuals for training 79, 81, 89–91, 98–100, 113, 153, 211
rival manuals used by different schools 20, 75, 85, 250
their conservative nature 99, 100
manuscripts 14, 18, 20, 39, 42, 76, 84, 93, 152–3
Marshall, John **20–21**, 78
Mathurānātha Tarkavāgīśa **84**, 85, 93, 94, 97, 98, 104, 113, 149, 237
Matilal, Bimal Krishna:
on the 'new reason' 46, 67, 156–7, 199
as a thinker 72–3, 250
matter, material 17, 18, 80, 158, 168, 212, 214–9
mechanical philosophy 214–19
medicinal or therapeutic understanding of philosophy 8, 33, 123, 139, 167, 247
Mīmāṃsā ('disciplinary system of ritual exegesis') 5, 8, 35, 49, 66, 76, 109, 119–20, 131–44, 145, 148, 150, 153, 158, 210, 212
Mithilā 5, 8, 9, 17, 18, 42–3, 45, 48, 51–2, 57–8, 75–6, 81–4, 86, 93–5, 133, 149, 150, 180–1, 190, 240, 248
modernity:
and authorial concern with originality 4, 45, 82, 245
and the conception of one's duties towards the past 1, 6, 48–9, 91–2, 96, 102, 106, 115, 244–6
and creative adaptation 3, 48–9, 59, 73, 115, 247
global rather than exclusively European origins 3–6, 10, 14, 16, 249–51
and the individual 80; *see also* self
as a lack of deference 4, 8, 48, 90, 96, 244, 246
and new religious cultures 44
two models of 1–6
More, Henry 20
Morin, Jean-Baptiste 2, 3
Mughal court 7, 10, 13–14, 18–19, 22, 37–8, 39–40, 52–5, 58–9, 77–8, 81, 248
Murāri Miśra 35, 135

Nāgārjuna 72, 122–3, 126, **132**, 134, 147
Nāgeśa Bhaṭṭa 95, 99–100, 223
Nārāyaṇa Bhaṭṭa 75, 76
Navadvīpa (*aka* Nadia; Nuddea) 4, 9, 17–20, 39–60, 67, 74–89, 93, 95, 97, 152, 181, 248–9
negation 133, 177, 201, 223–234
 negative particle 49, 82, 97, 169–70, 197–8
Neoplatonism 15, 20, 29
neutrality as an intellectual virtue 33–7, 244
'new deniers', the 213–5, 217
'new reason', the:
 begins with Raghunātha 5, 7
 geographical locations 4, 8
 historical phases 149–50
 three central ideas 247
Nīlakaṇṭha Caturdhara 19, 106–7, 109
Nobili, Roberto 17–18
normativity:
 context-dependence of normative terms 67, 71
 normative reasons 126
 reductivism about 173, 201–4
numbers:
 counting-dependence 173–4, 182–7, 191–2
 indefinite pluralities 191–4
 Praśastapāda's 'eight moments' theory 182–6
 as properties of objects 187–91
 Raghunātha's new theory 194–8
 and the successor function 189–90
Nyāya ('disciplinary system of critical inquiry'):
 ancient 4, 8, 18, 122;
 see also Gautama
 compatibility with Vaiśeṣika 203
 Navya 17, 131–3;
 see also 'new reason'
nyāya, maxim of practical reason 4, 128, 146

Oldinburgh, Henry 16
'only' (*eva*) as a quantifier 86, 97–8, 181, 194, 202, 211, 237–43
d'Orville, Albert 18
ownership (*svatva*) 33, 65, 67, 83, 95, 200, 202, 208–9, 211, 217–8

Pāṇini 17, 79, 97, 105–6, 107, 108, 228, 238
Patañjali 105–6, 224
patronage 10, 14, 19, 30, 32, 39, 41–3, 52–4, 57–9, 65, 67, 74–7, 83–4, 153, 216, 247–8
Persian 7, 13–16, 20, 22–6, 28, 29, 30, 32, 36, 40, 55, 76, 78, 116, 216, 247
Plato 15, 65, 120, 166, 197, 215
Plotinus 29–30; *see also* Neoplatonism
political power 7, 10, 37, 51, 75, 78, 81
Pollock, Sheldon, on the 'new reason' 3, 100, 151, 153, 198–9
Prabhākara Miśra 35, **135**, 137, 138, 140, 142, 150, 210, 212
Pragalbha Miśra **52**, 133
Praśastapāda 17, 92, 96, 108, 109, 122, 146, 159, 165–80, 181–5, 189, 200, 201, 204–5, 211–12

quantifiers:
 generalised versus Aristotelian 223, 239, 243
 medieval and modern theories about, 235
 noun phrases as restricted, 224, 232–6
 numbers as, 193–4
 see also 'only'; limitor

Rāghava Pañcānana Bhaṭṭācārya **82**, 97
Raghudeva Nyāyālaṃkāra Bhaṭṭācārya 19, 32, 65, **80**, 86, 92, 93, 94, 95, 97, 106, 133, 150, 207–8
 Survey of What is Essential about Substance 80, 95, 176, 201, 212
Raghunandana 43
Raghunātha Śiromaṇi 20, 32–3, 43, **44–52**, 57, 59, 67, 74–100, 102, 113, 131, 133, 165, 203–10, 213, 223, 237, 240
 as a modern philosopher 4–9, 17, 39, 149–54, 181, 245–50
 Inquiry into the True Nature of Things 4–6, 17, 18, 45–8, 90, 95–6, 150, 194–5, 199, 200–20, 247, 250
 non-reductive realism of 46, 96, 165, 168, 180, 194–201
 Treatise on Finite Verbal Forms 45, 90, 95, 97
 see also commentary, elliptical nature of Raghunātha's; number, Raghunātha's new theory
 Treatise on Negation 45, 49, 90, 97, 199, 225,
Rāmabhadra Sārvabhauma 33, 45, 67, **82**, 83–6, 91–6, 97–9, 207, 209
Rāmakṛṣṇa (16th c., student of Raghunātha) 52, 75
Rāmakṛṣṇa, Rājā (17th c., patron of Jayarāma) 53, 67, 83
Rāmakṛṣṇa, Dharmarāja (19th c. commentator) 52, 67
Rāmānuja 87, 112, 146
Rāmarudra Tarkavāgīśa 79, 99
Rāmnāth 'the Wild' 57, 97
realism:
 ameliorated 165, 173, 174, 176

about emergent colours (*citra-rūpa*) 33, 83, 180, 217
scientific 166, 175, 179, 213–4
sophisticated 96, 165, 179–80, 204
about universals 166–72
and verification 175–9
about wholes 165–6, 171, 179–80, 213–4
religious cosmopolitanism 24–6, 36–8
Rome 17, 18, 29
Roth, Heinrich 18
Royal Society, the x, 16, 248
Rudra Nyāyavācaspati 33, 52, 76, **78**, 93, 94, 95, 97
Russell's paradox 190

Śabara 66, 103, 109, 120–1
Samarqandī, Rukn-ud-din 40
Saṃghabhadra 114
sampradāya ('transmitted tradition of teaching') 85, 88, 246, 250
Śaṅkara (Ācārya) 27
Brahma-sūtra-bhāṣya 19, 24, 28, 37, 110, 120–1, 248
Śaṅkara [Śaṃkara] Miśra 83–4, 93, 133, 150, 158, 180–3, 190–3
śāstra ('disciplinary intellectual system') 34–6, 65–6, 68–70, 107–8, 116, 246, 250
scepticism 49, 131–3
Gaṅgeśa's response 142–4
Jayarāma against radical scepticism 158–9
Madhyamaka as scepticism 122–3, 126, 132, 134, 147–9, 159
Mahādeva's response 153–7
and the paradox of inquiry 119–21
Pyrrhonic 16, 34, 132
Śrīharṣa as a sceptic 127–30
Schopenhauer, Arthur 22
self, the:
distinct from body 37, 158–9, 166, 168
as individual 8, 47–51, 69–70, 80, 95, 110–11, 166, 203, 207–8
nature when liberated 83, 86, 133
in Sufism and Neoplatonism 27–8, 30
Yaśovijaya on 32, 33, 35–6
Sennert, Daniel 3, 151, 218
Shāh Jahāṇ 14–5, 19, 22, 37, 52, 59, 77
Śivacandra, Rājā 53, 57
Skinner, Quentin 7, 9, 50, 63–73, 246, 250; *see also* illocutionary intervention
spider, as a metaphor 15, 16, 21
Spinoza, Baruch 2, 3, 6, 15, 16, 27, 92, 102, 107, 115
Śrī Rāma **84**, 93
Śrīdhara Bhaṭṭa 40, 109, 111, 171, 173, 184–185, 191–2
Śrīharṣa 40, 45, 52, 64, 80, 121, 127–30, **132–3**, 144, 146–7, 154, 157, 250
extent of influence on Gaṅgeśa 133
whether or not an Advaita Vedāntin 127

Tabrizi, Jalal-ud-din 40
Tagore, Rabindranath 13, 38, 73
Taraṇi Miśra 86
technical language of the 'new reason' 50, 148–9, 155, 169, 194
as a calculus of relations 219, 224–36
extensional or intensional 223, 226
primitive vocabulary 225, 228, 235
relation to natural language 225
testimony 48, 122, 139, 143, 205
thematic case role (*kāraka*) 79, 86, 97, 126, 250
Tibet, 17th c. contacts with India 17, 23, 32, 39, 105, 132, 237
Ṭoḍarmal **76**, 77
ṭol ('scholar-centred teaching arrangement') 58, 74–5, 87–8, 248, 249
translation 32, 36, 38, 245
from Latin into Persian 14
from Latin into Sanskrit 249
from Persian into English 20
from Persian into Latin 15, 22–3
from Sanskrit into Bengali 42
from Sanskrit into Chinese 200
from Sanskrit into English 57
from Sanskrit into Persian 13, 22–8, 32, 36, 38, 40, 78
from Sanskrit into Tibetan 17, 23
truth:
definition of 124–5, 145
epistemic constraints on 172–8
regulates inquiry 139–42

Udayana 5, 8, 46, 83, 91, 95, 107, 128, 147, 150, 165, 167, 169–71, 183, 188–9, 191–3, 213, 223
Offering of Flowers 87, 93, 112, 246, 250
Row of Lightbeams 45, 92, 205
Uddyotakara 47, 66, 105, 161, 192–3, 232
Upaniṣads 13–16, 20, 22–30, 35, 36, 38, 167, 244, 248

Vācaspati Miśra II 45, 82, 86, 133
Vaiśeṣika ('disciplinary system of metaphysics') 17, 166
diagram of the metaphysical world according to Vaiśeṣika 172

Vallabha 45, 52, 92, 93, 98, 165, 209, 237
Vārāṇasī (*aka* Benares; Kāśī) 4, 5, 9, 13–28, 32, 36, 38, 42–3, 48, 52, 57, 59, 65, 67, 74–81, 83–5, 87, 89, 95, 96, 99, 147, 152, 158, 161, 165, 170, 180, 201–2, 204, 248
Vardhamāna Upādhyāya 45, 52, 66, 83, 86, **92–3**, 133
Vasubandhu 113–4, 170
Vāsudeva Sārvabhauma **42–4**, 45, 51, 58–9, 75, 78, 82, 93–4
Vātsyāyana 47, 50, 66, 92, 105, 108, 110, 122–7, 186, 231
Vayer, François de la Mothe le 16
Vedānta ('disciplinary system of philosophical theology') 5, 8, 17, 18, 35, 43, 47, 51, 77–8, 83, 106, 167, 248–9
Veṇīdatta (author of *Pañca-tattva-prakāśa*) 18
Veṇīdatta Vāgīśa Bhaṭṭa xii, 18, **81**
Embellishment of the Categories 48–9, 95, 152, 205, 208–9, 247
via moderna vs via antiqua 8, 39, 82, 84, 88, 161, 246, 247
Vidyānivāsa Bhaṭṭācārya 4, 44, 51, 59, **75–9**, 107
Vidyāvācaspati, Viṣṇudāsa 42, **43–4**, 45, 76
Viśvanātha Nyāyasiddhānta Pañcānana 77, 78, 79
Vyākaraṇa ('disciplinary system of grammar') 5, 17, 44, 58, 97, 99, 100, 105, 107, 108, 150, 223, 224, 238, 241
Vyomaśiva 69–70, 111, 167, 170, 171

waḥdat al-wujūd ('unity of being') 13, 20, 25, 32, 37
way of gaining knowledge (*pramāṇa*) 8, 40, 45, 48, 112, 122–7, 129, 131–3, 135–6, 139, 143–4, 145–8, 153, 156–7, 186, 202–6
Weigel, Erhard 2, 3
Wittgenstein, Ludwig 22, 46, 93, 178, 199, 225

Yajñapati 45, 90
Yaśovijaya Gaṇi 19–21, **31–8**, 74, 78, 80, 82, 161, 223
and political liberalism 20, 33–5, 244
Yoga-vāsiṣṭha 22, 36

Lightning Source UK Ltd.
Milton Keynes UK
UKOW07f0245171114

241709UK00001B/2/P

9 780198 701507